Economic Analysis of Information and Contracts

Essays in Honor of John E. Butterworth

Economic Analysis of Information and Contracts

Essays in Honor of John E. Butterworth

Edited by

Gerald A. Feltham
University of British Columbia

Amin H. Amershi
University of Minnesota

and

William T. Ziemba
University of British Columbia

Kluwer Academic Publishers
Boston

Distributors

for the United States and Canada: Kluwer Academic Publishers, 101 Philip Drive, Assinippi Park, Norwell, MA 02061.
for the UK and Ireland: Kluwer Academic Publishers, Falcon House, Queen Square, Lancaster LA1 1RN, UK.
for all other countries: Kluwer Academic Publishers Group, Distribution Centre, P.O. Box 322, 3300 AH Dordrecht, The Netherlands

Library of Congress Cataloging-in-Publication Data

Economic analysis of information and contracts: essays in honor of John E. Butterworth/edited by Gerald A. Feltham, Amin H. Amershi, and William T. Ziemba.
p. cm.
Bibliography: p.
Includes index.
ISBN 0-89838-252-1: $60.00 (est.)
1. Accounting. 2. Information theory in economics.
3. Butterworth, John E. I. Butterworth, John E. II. Feltham. Gerald A., 1938– . III. Amershi, Amin H. IV. Ziemba, W. T.
HF5625.E28 1988
657--dc 19 87-22508
CIP

Kluwer Academic Publishers, 101 Philip Drive, Assinippi Park, Norwell, MA 02061

Typeset by Macmillan India Ltd., Bangalore 25.
PRINTED IN THE UNITED STATES.

JOHN E. BUTTERWORTH

JOHN E. BUTTERWORTH, BA, MA, MBA, Ph.D.
1926–1984

On August 4, 1984, at the age of 58, John E. Butterworth died of cancer. He is survived by his wife Faye, their six children, and his parents. He was greatly respected and appreciated by his colleagues at the University of British Columbia and by all others who knew him. He will be greatly missed.

John was born in Manchester, England, in 1926. He studied English at Cambridge, receiving his Bachelor's degree in 1947 and his Master's degree in 1950. From 1950 to 1961, John was successively a works manager, production manager, and company director for Fine Wool Fabrics Ltd. of Wexford, Ireland.

In 1962, John and his family moved to Berkeley, California. John sought to enter the North American management job market by obtaining an MBA at the University of California, and he completed that degree in 1963. In the course of his MBA studies, the faculty encouraged John to study for his Ph.D. and to enter the academic job market. John made that switch, studying accounting and operations research, and completed his degree in 1967. Upon graduation he joined the faculty at Johns Hopkins University in Baltimore, Maryland, where he taught both accounting and operations research. While John was at the University of California, Dean Philip White had attempted to entice him to join the Commerce faculty at the University of British Columbia, and in 1969 Dean White was successful in that endeavor.

At the time John came to UBC, the faculty was in the midst of significant changes. The undergraduate program was undergoing major modifications and many new faculties were being added in order to increase the faculty's research capability, to strengthen its Master's program, and to introduce a Ph.D. program. John played an important role in all of these areas, and was greatly respected for the contributions that he made.

John provided leadership to the faculty throughout his career at UBC, and particularly assisted the faculty by serving in some key management positions. He was the director of graduate studies from 1971 to 1973, chairman of the Accounting and Management Information Systems Division from 1974 to 1977, and director of the Ph.D. program from 1981 to 1984. In each case he provided strong, sensitive leadership. In addition, he served at various times on the Executive Committee; the Appointments, Promotion and Tenure Committee; the Dean's Selection Committee; and the Dean's Advisory Committee.

John also provided leadership through his course development activities. He was instrumental in developing a management planning and control emphasis in the undergraduate and graduate cost accounting courses, and in applying quantitative methods in these courses. Furthermore, he initiated a graduate course in information economics and continually modified its content so that our Master's and Ph.D. students were provided with a strong research foundation in this area.

John's leadership in various aspects of the graduate program in the Faculty of Commerce of the University of British Columbia was a natural extension of his strong interest in research. That interest had been kindled at the University of California. Accounting research underwent a dramatic change in the mid-sixties as two new major research areas were developed. At the University of Chicago, Ph.D. students were beginning to explore the relationship between accounting numbers and stock market prices and at the University of California, Ph.D. students were beginning to apply concepts from information economics to accounting theory. John was one of those students and his Ph.D. dissertation was among the very first to explore the link between accounting and information economics. The quality of that research is reflected in the fact that his dissertation received honorable mention in the McKinsey Foundation Doctoral Thesis Award. This competition was open to dissertations from all business schools in all areas of research, and the submitted dissertations were evaluated by a distinguished panel of business school researchers in a variety of disciplines.

John's dissertation was but the first step in his exploration of the fundamental economic factors that influence the demand for information in general and accounting information in particular. His research from 1967 to 1984 is reviewed in Part I of this volume.

Contents

List of Contributors

Amin H. Amershi	School of Management University of Minnesota Minneapolis, Minnesota 55455
Rick Antle	School of Organization and Management Yale University New Haven, Connecticut 06520
Phelim P. Boyle	Accounting Group University of Waterloo Waterloo, Ontario N2L 3G1
John E. Butterworth	Deceased
Masako N. Darrough	Graduate School of Business Columbia University New York, New York 10027
Joel S. Demski	School of Organization and Management Yale University New Haven, Connecticut 06520
Ronald A. Dye	Kellogg School of Management Northwestern University Evanston, Illinois 60201
Gerald A. Feltham	Faculty of Commerce and Business Administration University of British Columbia Vancouver, British Columbia V6T 1Y8
John S. Hughes	Faculty of Commerce and Business Administration University of British Columbia Vancouver, British Columbia V6T 1Y8

Patricia J. Hughes	Graduate School of Management University of California Los Angeles, California 90024–1481
Young K. Kwon	Department of Accountancy College of Commerce and Business Administration University of Illinois at Urbana-Champaign Champaign, Illinois 61820
Richard A. Lambert	The Wharton School University of Pennsylvania Philadelphia, Pennsylvania 19104
Ella Mae Matsumura	School of Business University of Wisconsin-Madison Madison, Wisconsin 53706
James A. Ohlson	Graduate School of Business Columbia University New York, New York 10027
D. Paul Newman	Department of Accounting Graduate School of Business University of Texas Austin, Texas 78712
Neal M. Stoughton	Graduate School of Management University of California Irvine, California 92717

Preface

The three coeditors knew John Butterworth for many years and had worked closely with him on a number of research projects. We respected him as a valuable colleague and friend. We were greatly saddened by his untimely death. This book is an attempt to remember him. We dedicate the volume to John with thanks for the contributions he made to our research, to the Faculty of Commerce and Business Administration at the University of British Columbia, and to the accounting profession.

This volume contains twelve invited papers on the general topic of the economic theory of information and contracts. We asked leading scholars who had known John to contribute papers. The response was very gratifying. The authors provided us with new strong research papers that should make a lasting contribution to the accounting and information economics research literature, and make us all proud to have put this volume together. The research papers in the volume are in three sections: information evaluation in multiperson contexts; contracting in agencies under moral hazard; and contracting in agencies with private information.

We begin part I with Jerry Feltham's review of John Butterworth's pioneering contributions to the accounting and information economics literature. This is followed by an introduction to the papers in the volume and the papers themselves.

Acknowledgments

First we would like to thank the numerous authors of the papers that appear in this book for their contributions to the economic analysis of information and contracts in honor of John E. Butterworth. Their cooperation, kind support, and efforts to produce outstanding papers made this book a reality. We especially appreciate their prompt responses to our demanding refereeing, editorial suggestions, and comments.

This book would not have been possible without the generous support and encouragement of Peter Lusztig, dean of the Faculty of Commerce and Business Administration at the University of British Columbia. Dean Lusztig was very supportive of this project from its inception to completion.

Finally we would like to thank the Social Sciences and Humanities and Natural Sciences and Engineering Research Councils for partial support of the research and editorial work involved with this book. We received outstanding assistance at UBC from Nalin Edirisinghe, Evelyn Fong, Nancy Thompson, and Barbara Weeks, for which we are very grateful.

Economic Analysis of Information and Contracts

Essays in Honor of John E. Butterworth

PART I: INTRODUCTION

JOHN E. BUTTERWORTH'S PIONEERING CONTRIBUTIONS TO THE ACCOUNTING AND INFORMATION ECONOMICS LITERATURE*

Gerald A. Feltham

Introduction

This paper reviews John Butterworth's contributions to accounting and other disciplines. The general nature of his scientific work is discussed and comments on theoretical issues are provided. John's path-breaking work in the application of information economics to the evaluation of accounting information systems is highlighted in the immediately following section and is followed by a review of his studies in the area of bounds on information value. Mathematical models in management accounting is the topic of the third part and John's studies on multiperson models are analyzed in the fourth section. Material contributions to agency theory in the accounting setting are

---

* This paper is a revised version of one with the same title published in *Contemporary Accounting Research* 1 (Fall 1984): 87–98.

I would like to express my appreciation to Amin Amershi and Bill Ziemba for their comments on earlier drafts of this paper.

discussed in the fifth and sixth parts and are followed by comments on John's research in the areas of oil and gas accounting, and accounting standards and regulations in Canada. Concluding remarks are offered in the last section of this paper.

Contribution to a Significant Change in Accounting Research

Prior to the mid-sixties accounting research had focused on income measurement and balance sheet valuation, primarily using Hicksian economic concepts of income and value as criteria for selecting from among alternative accounting methods. The relatively new work of Edwards and Bell, Sprouse and Moonitz, Chambers, and others were receiving considerable attention. However, the seeds of change had been planted by various authors who proposed that accountants should seek to determine the accounting methods that provide the information that would be most useful to decision makers. These seeds began to take root in the mid-sixties and led to significant changes in accounting research. At the University of Chicago, Ph.D. students such as Beaver and Brown, influenced by new developments in finance, began to explore the relationship between accounting numbers and stock market prices. Their work would lead to the large body of accounting research that explores the relationship between accounting reports and investor decisions as reflected in stock market prices.

Contemporaneously, Ph.D. students at the University of California were exposed to Baysian decision theory and its application by Blackwell to the evaluation of alternative information systems. The latter became known as information economics and it developed particularly from the work of Marschak and Radner. John Butterworth was one of those Ph.D. students, and in his dissertation he explored the application of information economics to the evaluation of accounting information systems. This was path-breaking work, and it provided part of the foundation for future applications of information economics to theoretical research in accounting. That research has expanded considerably over the past twenty-one years.

John's dissertation was entitled "Accounting Systems and Management Decisions" and a major paper from his dissertion: "The Accounting System as an Information Function," was published in the *Journal of Accounting Research* (Spring 1972). This research had two major components. The first was the use of graph theoretic and matrix algebra techniques to represent the accounting system. The income statement and balance sheet accounts are conceptualized as a network in which the balances and changes can be represented by formal mathematical relationships. Different accounting systems are represented by different matrix operators, and this facilitates the identification of the precise nature of the differences in accounting systems. This representation permitted the development of planning and decision models in which the accounting system is an important ingredient. John took advantage of the linear structure of accounting system operations and made extensive use of linear programming. These models served as a basis for some of John's future research and teaching in management accounting.

The second major component of John's initial research examined the evaluation of alternative accounting methods using concepts from information economics. John, and his peers at the University of California, were the first to explore the accounting implications of information economics. John's research was unique in its explicit modeling of the accounting system. Account and transaction recording structure were systematically related to the uncertain states, thereby modeling the information content of the accounting system in both single-period and multiple-period contexts. In this research John applied the coarseness/fineness concepts to the comparison of alternative accounting systems, and explored the use of "simple" calculations to compute "bounds" on the value of alternative systems.[1]

Bounds on Information Value

In his dissertation John had explored the calculation of upper and lower bounds on the value of both perfect and imperfect information. Direct calculation of the value of information is often very complex, whereas simpler calculations can be used to compute the bounds on information value.

John's first work in the area of bounds on information value appeared as a 1973 working paper entitled "The Evaluation of Information in Uncertain Decision Problems." In this paper a hierarchy of bounds are developed for a very general class of problems. John demonstrated that there are a variety of possible bounds that can be calculated and that the more precise bounds require more complex calculations. His hierarchy provided insight into the trade-off between the complexity of the calculation and the preciseness of the bound.

The initial paper also examined the computation of bounds in contexts where the return function is convex and where simple stochastic programming problems occur. Stochastic programming problems explicitly model the fact that management faces uncertainty when it selects and implements its initial plans, and then must adapt to the actual consequences of its actions as the uncertain events become known. John explored the selection of optimal plans in this context in a 1974 working paper entitled "Stochastic Linear

Programming with Intra-Period Adaptation, a Discrete Algorithm." Later, in an article entitled "Bounds on the Value of Information in Uncertain Decision Problems" published in *Stochastics* (1975), he and Bill Ziemba more fully developed the computation of bounds on information value in stochastic programming contexts. John encouraged Bill and their student Donald Hausch to work further. Later, in 1983, Bill and Don published part II of the study in *Stochastics.*

Mathematical Models in Management Accounting

In his dissertation, John also investigated management planning and decision making based on a formal model of accounting information systems. He then extended that research by developing a general multistage input–output model. This work, done with Berndt Sigloch, a Ph.D. student, was published in the *Accounting Review* (October 1971) in an article entitled "A Generalized Multi-Stage Input-Output Model and Some Derived Equivalent Systems." Prior work by other accounting researchers had resulted in a variety of input-output models. John and Berndt demonstrated that these previous models could be treated as special cases of their general model by properly interpreting its elements.

In a 1973 working paper entitled "Mathematical Decision Models in Managerial Accounting," John and I reviewed the accounting literature that had used mathematical decision models. In order to place these models in perspective we developed a metamodel whose general form was based upon the relationships of a discrete stochastic control process. This metamodel was a natural extension of some of the modeling that John had done previously, and it was sufficiently general that virtually any of the models in the literature could be interpreted as special cases. We then examined three major classes of models in the literature: planning models, control models, and information and simplification evaluation models. The metamodel provided a means of identifying the relationships among models and the simplifying assumptions they sometimes conceal.

Multiperson Models

Like most information economics researchers in accounting, John had focused on single-person decision contexts prior to 1975. Up to that time, the most widely known multiperson research was that found in Marschak and

Radner's *Economic Theory of Teams*. However, because of its goal congruence assumption, it was essentially an extension of the single-person model. In the early seventies, led by economists such as Arrow, Mirrlees, Spence, and Stiglitz, information economics research began to adopt a multiperson focus. John was among those who first recognized the importance to accounting research of such a shift in emphasis.

In his graduate research seminar on information economics, John discussed both Borch and Wilson's work on risk sharing and recent developments in game theory. These techniques served as a basis for the examination of information issues in multiperson settings in which each individual's preferences depend upon his own consumption. This approach to teaching is described in John and Bill Ziemba's article: "Teaching the Foundations for the Economic Analysis and Evaluation of Information Systems," in *Interfaces* (1978).

John and Amin Amershi (a Ph.D. student at the time) began to work in 1976 on a graduate-level text in management accounting entitled "The Analysis of Management Accounting Information." They proposed to take a radically different approach from that used in traditional management accounting texts. Five chapters were written and were used in John's graduate seminar. These chapters were to constitute the first section of the book, and dealt with "methodological foundations." The chapters included a general discussion of the role of information in decision making and control, the basic theory of decision making under uncertainty and the evaluation of information system alternatives, and the role of costs in simplified models of decision making. Also included were discussions of several theories of choice in multiperson contexts (including team theory, social choice, competitive game theory, and cooperative game theory), the nature of risk aversion and Pareto optimal risk sharing, and the basics of agency theory. These chapters clearly reflected John's belief that future developments in accounting theory would be based on theories of choice in multiperson contexts.

Multiperson decision making became a central element in John's research. His first research in this area appeared in a 1977 working paper which he coauthored with David Hayes and Ella Mae Matsumura. The paper, entitled "Negotiated Transfer Prices in an Uncertain Competitive World," used a cooperative game theory framework to analyze the setting of transfer prices in a context in which there are uncertain external markets, differing beliefs and risk attitudes on the part of division managers and head office, and minimal exchange of information between divisions. The paper provided a new dimension to the analysis of the transfer pricing problem, and produced results based on formal game theoretic analysis that yielded deeper insights into behavioral research on the operation of divisionalized organizations.

Amin Amershi's 1978 dissertation, entitled "Economic Resource Allocation Under Uncertainty and Differential Information—A Unified Game Approach with Agency and Accounting Applications," prompted John to work with him on research using game-theoretic and Pareto optimal risk sharing analyses to examine risk sharing and accounting issues. John and Bill cosupervised Amin's dissertation with my input as well. Several unpublished papers resulted from this work as well as the paper "Explorations in the Theory of Single- and Multiple-Agent Agencies" which appears in this volume. In a 1978 working paper, entitled "The Efficiency of Budgetary Planning and Control Information," they used cooperative game theory to examine the impact of a budgetary planning and control system in a multiperson decision context. In formulating the problem it was recognized that managers have their own preferences and beliefs; preferences are influenced by the incentive system and beliefs are influenced by both private and public information. Furthermore, the information that will be publicly available (either directly or indirectly), when action consequences have been realized ("posterior information"), influences the types of incentive contracts that can be implemented by negotiation. The cooperative model that is presented involves participation in the selection of both the incentive contracts and the information that is to be exchanged. Much of the analysis is quite technical and focuses on carefully formulating the "game" and confirming that the core of that "game" exists. The conditions for existence of the core suggest the need for extensive information exchange and provide economic support to the arguments for participative budgeting.

The above paper was followed by a 1979 working paper entitled "A Unified Economic Theory for Cooperatives, Partnerships, and Agencies." This paper applied multiperson analysis to two specific types of decision contexts. Cooperatives (often termed "syndicates") are decision contexts in which the decision makers jointly choose the information system, the production activity to be implemented, and the way in which the output is to be shared. It is assumed that all choices can be enforced by direct observation of what is implemented. Partnerships (agencies) differ from cooperatives in one key aspect: the production activity carried out by one partner is not directly observed by the other partners. This gives rise to a *moral hazard* problem in that a partner may not be motivated to implement the production activity that is "optimal" from the perspective of a cooperative (particularly if he has a disutility for the effort required by productive activity). Partnerships must recognize this fact in selecting their profit-sharing rules and the information (accounting) systems upon which they are to be based. The paper reviewed and extended previous syndicate and agency analyses, and explicitly explored the relationship between these two types of decision contexts: the necessary and sufficient conditions under which a cooperative can operate as a partnership without any welfare loss are also identified in this paper.

In chapter 6 of this volume, titled "Explorations in the Theory of Single- and Multiple-Agent Agencies," Amin Amershi and John extend the standard two-person principal/agent model in two directions, and the nature and form of the optimal contracts are explored to derive new insights. In one extension, characterization of an optimal incentive contract is shown to be equivalent to a risk-sharing contract in which the principal and the agent have diverse beliefs. In particular, the agent is represented as being "more optimistic." In another extension, the role of sufficient statistics in incentive contracts is explored and is used to provide a general result on the suboptimality of "tournaments" in contracting with multiple agents.

Agency Theory

As seen from the above, John's analysis of multiperson decision contexts shifted gradually from the perspective of Pareto optimal risk sharing and game theory to a consideration of what has been termed "agency" relationships. This is a game in which moral hazard problems exist, and John's work with Amin stressed that fact. While other researchers focused on two-person agencies (one principal and one agent) in which there are homogeneous beliefs, John and Amin considered *n*-person agencies in which diverse beliefs may be present.

In their lengthy and highly technical 1979 paper, "The Theory of Agency with Diverse Beliefs," John and Amin thoroughly analyzed a variety of aspects of the principal/agent problem in which there may be diverse beliefs and the agent's actions may or may not be observable. The analysis demonstrates that differences in beliefs can have a considerable impact on the nature of the "optimal" contract between a principal and an agent. However, after the optimal sharing rule is adjusted through side-betting for differences in beliefs, its basic form is the same as in the homogeneous beliefs case.

Subsequent to his work with Amin, John conducted additional research on the two-person agency problem with Phelim Boyle. Explicit solutions of the optimal compensation scheme for numerical examples of the two-person agency problem are often difficult to obtain because of what is termed the "Nash constraint" (which ensures that the sharing rule induces the agent to select the desired action). In a 1982 working paper entitled "Numerical Solution of Principal/Agent Problems" John and Phelim developed numerical procedures for solving a class of principal/agent problems. This paper has been updated by Phelim and appears in this book as chapter 5. In particular, they developed procedures for solving principal/agent problems in which the principal and agent have Hyperbolic Absolute Risk Aversion (HARA) utility functions with identical risk cautiousness and where the output probability function is an exponential, lognormal, or beta distribution. Numerical examples yielded insights into the nature of the optimal sharing rule and the impact of changing various utility function parameters.

HARA utility functions also played a central role in another 1982 working paper with Phelim: "Optimal Incentive Contracts with Costly Conditional Monitors." The first part of this paper considers the standard agency problem and identifies some conditions under which the optimal sharing rule is concave. The second explores the nature of the optimal investigation rule when the principal has the opportunity to obtain, at a cost, additional information about the agent's action after he has been informed about the output from that action. The authors demonstrate that the optimal "investigation strategy" is to acquire the additional information when output is high if the principal and agent have increasing risk aversion, but to acquire the additional information when output is low if they have decreasing risk aversion.

An Agency Theory Perspective of Accounting and Insurance

In addition to the technical agency-theory papers described above, which are contributions to basic research, John made significant contributions to the discussion of accounting research and accounting theory. In particular, John coauthored, with Mike Gibbins and Ray King, the lead paper for a 1981 conference on accounting research. This paper, entitled "The Structure of Accounting Theory: Some Basic Conceptual and Methodological Issues," was published in *Research to Support Standard Setting in Financial Accounting: A Canadian Perspective* and has recently been reprinted in *Modern Accounting Theory: A Survey and Guide.*

Agency theory began to have a significant impact on accounting research in the late seventies, and the paper with Gibbins and King picks up on that development. In a major section of the paper, entitled "Agency: A Basis for Accounting Theory," the agency theory perspective is described. It demonstrates, in a forceful way, the importance of the agency perspective in examining the role of accounting. It is particularly stressed that the predictive role of accounting information is an inadequate basis for the development of accounting theory. Instead, accounting reports, with their stress on objectivity, play a more significant role in the explicit and implicit contracting that takes place between managers and subordinates, owners and managers, creditors and equity holders, and other contracting parties. The agency-theory perspective helps to explain many of the choices that have been made by accounting regulators and the positions taken by firms in their support of or objection to proposed changes in accounting standards.

After establishing the agency-theory perspective, the authors discuss some methodological issues in, and provide a review of, recent accounting research. In their discussion of methodology they stress the distinction between positive and normative theory, and the distinction between theoretical and empirical research. The review of recent accounting research is relatively succinct, but the authors do an excellent job of classifying and describing the major types of accounting research. They classify this research in terms of the type of response to accounting reports and standards that is being investigated, including responses by individuals, groups, securities, market participants, and firms. In their concluding remarks they emphasize the importance of additional theoretical and empirical research that adopts a positive, agency-theory perspective.

Another contribution to the agency-based accounting literature is the 1983 paper by John Butterworth and Haim Falk: "The Methodological Implications of a Contractual Theory of Accounting." The paper begins with a discussion of two paradigms that provided two fundamentally different views of accounting in the early part of this century: the value paradigm espoused by Canning and the stewardship paradigm espoused by Paton. The authors state that these two paradigms "set the stage for an analysis of the methodological dichotomy which has persisted in accounting research for at least sixty years, and which is maintained currently." The value paradigm is linked to research into the predictive role of accounting information and the stewardship paradigm is linked via agency-theory research to its contractual role. The authors provide an insightful discussion of the implications of the contractual role for empirical research and some of the theoretical weaknesses of current empirical research.

John's contribution to the insurance discipline is reflected in his paper "Links Between Modern Finance and Insurance," with Phelim Boyle published in 1982 in *Geld, Banken and Versicherungen* (Money, Banking and Insurance). This paper reviewed the history of research into risk sharing in the insurance industry, and related it to research in finance that deals with optimal risk sharing. The problems of moral hazard and adverse selection in risk sharing and their implications for optimal insurance contracts are also discussed.[2]

Accounting for the Oil and Gas Industry in Canada

John and Haim Falk coauthored a monograph on "Financial Reporting—Theory and Application to the Oil and Gas Industry in Canada," which appeared in March 1986. This research was funded by the Society of Management Accountants of Canada. The monograph begins with an overview and summary followed by the following chapters:

2. Information Attitudes of the Contracting Paradigm
3. Accounting for the Oil and Gas Industry: The Basic Issues
4. The Research Methods
5. The Extent of Disclosure on Financial Statements: Scalogram Analysis
6. The Extent of Disclosure on Financial Statements: Individual Items Analysis
7. Accounting Standards and Regulations
8. Commonalities and Differences with Respect to Accounting Measures
9. Capital Structure, Management Incentives, and Accounting Income: A Proposed Model for Efficient Contracting

and several appendices.

The monograph contains both theoretical and empirical analyses. John's analytical skills and deep understanding of accounting theory are clearly reflected in chapters 2 and 9. Chapter 2 analyzes paradigms that have significantly influenced accounting thought and paved the way for our contractual theory of accounting. These included money-value, stewardship, and capital-market paradigms and related empirical research. John and Haim then focus on agency theory and its empirical tests.

The money-value paradigm was based on an available, but inappropriate, economic paradigm. In contrast, the stewardship paradigm attempted to explain and codify observed accounting phenomena without recourse to economic theory. Consequently, neither has theoretically defensible implications for the choice of accounting methods. Capital-market paradigms, concerned with the value of predictive information in a market setting, lack implications for the calculation of accounting net income. For example, they do not suggest that a firm should report anything other than cash flow components, or data that may be useful in forecasting cash flows.

The agency (contracting) paradigm is concerned with the economic effect of contractual arrangements between managers and investors but contains no easily testable hypotheses. John and Haim discuss complex but realistic systems and argue that these systems can be implemented only if contracts are based on information that can be verified and the statistical properties of the contractual information are known by the parties. Historic cost accounting principles satisfy these criteria. The contracting paradigm also provides an economic rationale for the existence of reporting standards based on accrued accounting. They analyze two important accounting issues: adequate aggregate level of disclosure and a choice of an optimal accounting measure for efficient contracting.

They selected the oil and gas industry in Canada for empirical testing of certain major aspects of the proposed contracting paradigm for four reasons:

1. Oil and gas extractive activities involve high, firm-specific risks and risk sharing is fundamental to contracting.
2. There has been much public debate on "preferred" accounting methods (e.g., successful efforts vs. full cost), and an important objective of the monograph is to explain this preference issue.
3. Oil and gas firms enjoy relatively great freedom in financial reporting and that freedom facilitates exploration of economic reasons for extended, voluntary disclosure.
4. The industry plays a vital role in Canada's as well as the world's economy.

Chapters 3 through 8 present the empirical analysis, which was primarily done by Haim Falk; and then chapter 9 concludes the book with further theoretical analysis that significantly benefits from John's analytical skills. A model is formulated which depicts key factors that determine the economic consequences of accounting information. Chapter 9 stresses the contracting role of accounting information, with particular emphasis on external reporting.[3] In particular, the model considers an entrepreneur who has access to a continuum of risky investments and who seeks to obtain capital and share risks by issuing equity securities and bonds in a two-period context. The contracts with the suppliers of capital specify the entrepreneur's compensation schedule and a restriction on first-period dividends, both of which are based on reported accounting income. In this analysis it is demonstrated that the depreciation method employed in computing accounting income has an impact on which contracts are selected (and their capital structure) and on the anticipated consequences of the optimal contracts. The relevance of this to the oil and gas study is that "full costing" and "successful efforts" are essentially two different depreciation methods.

Accounting Standards and Regulations

Two papers by John and Haim Falk examine some aspects of accounting standard setting and regulation in the Canadian context. The first paper,

"Accounting Standards: Perceived Cost/Benefit Relationships—A Survey," was presented at the 1984 Workshop on "The Relationship, Between Accounting Research and Practice" in Brussels. It examines the perceived effectiveness of Canadian accounting standards. The authors concluded that the trading status of reporting firms and the complexity of accounting standards may explain some aspects of the effectiveness or ineffectiveness of some accounting standards.

The second paper, "The Effectiveness of Canadian Oil and Gas Pipeline Price Regulation: 1976–1982" (which appeared in the June 1985 *Canadian Journal of Administrative Sciences*) examines the effectiveness of the regulatory agency in achieving its proclaimed goals in price regulation. It draws on existing theories for regulation and discusses some possible implications of the compulsory accounting system for oil and gas pipelines for the regulatory decision making process.

Concluding Remarks

I have provided a review of John Butterworth's significant contributions to accounting research. His poineering work in the application of information economics, mathematical modeling, and agency theory was emphasized. John's contribution went well beyond the technical research aspects. He developed and articulated the implications of analytical research for both accounting practice and accounting research.

Some of John's contributions are conveyed in his published research, but much of it is contained in his unpublished working papers and manuscripts. Unfortunately for the accounting fraternity, some of it is best known only by those of us who had the privilege of knowing and working with him.

John Butterworth's Papers

"Accounting Systems and Management Decisions," unpublished Doctoral Thesis, University of California, Berkeley (1967).

"A Generalized Multi-Stage Input–Output Model and Some Derived Equivalent Systems," *Accounting Review* (October 1971), with B.A. Sigloch.

"The Accounting System as an Information Function," *Journal of Accounting Research* (Spring 1972).

"Mathematical Decision Models in Managerial Accounting," unpublished paper (1973), with G.A. Feltham.

"The Evaluation of Information in Uncertain Decision Problems," unpublished paper (1973).

"Stochastic Linear Programming with Intra-Period Adaptation, a Discrete Algorithm," unpublished paper (1974).

"Bounds on the Value of Information in Uncertain Decision Problems," *Stochastics* (1975), with W.T. Ziemba.

"The Analysis of Management Accounting Information," unpublished manuscript (1976), with A.H. Amershi.

"Negotiated Transfer Prices in an Uncertain Competitive World," unpublished paper (1977), with D.C. Hayes and E.M. Matsumura.

"The Efficiency of Budgetary Planning and Control Information," unpublished paper (1978), with A.H. Amershi.

"Teaching the Foundations for the Economic Analysis and Evaluation of Information Systems," *Interfaces* (1978), with W.T. Ziemba.

"A Unified Economic Theory for Cooperatives, Partnerships, and Agencies," unpublished paper (1979), with A.H. Amershi.

"The Theory of Agency with Diverse Beliefs," unpublished paper (1979), with A.H. Amershi.

"Explorations in the Theory of Single- and Multiple-Agent Agencies," this volume, with A.H. Amershi.

"The Structure of Accounting Theory: Some Basic Conceptual and Methodological Issues," in S. Basu and J.A. Milburn (eds.) *Research to Support Standard Setting in Financial Accounting: A Canadian Perspective*, Proceedings of the 1981 Clarkson Gordon Foundation Research Symposium (Halifax, Nova Scotia, May 20–21, 1981). Reprinted in R.R. Mattessich (ed.) *Modern Accounting Research: A Survey and Guide* (Vancouver: General Accountants Research Foundation, 1984), with M. Gibbins and R.D. King.

"Links Between Modern Finance and Insurance," *Geld, Banker and Versicherungen* (1982), with P.P. Boyle.

"Numerical Solution of Principal/Agent Problems," this volume, with P.P. Boyle.

"Optimal Incentive Contracts with Costly Conditional Monitors," unpublished paper (1982), with P.P. Boyle.

"The Methodological Implications of a Contractual Theory of Accounting," unpublished paper (1983), with H. Falk.

"Capital Structure, Management Incentives, and Accounting Income," unpublished paper (1983), with H. Falk.

"Accounting Standards: Perceived Cost/Benefit Relationships—A Survey," unpublished paper (1984), with H. Falk.

"The Effectiveness of Canadian Oil and Gas Pipeline Regulation: 1976–1982," *Canadian Journal of Administrative Sciences* (June 1985), with H. Falk.

Financial Reporting—Theory and Application to the Oil and Gas Industry in Canada. Hamilton, Ontario: The Society of Management Accountants of Canada, (1986), with H. Falk.

Notes

1. The quality and significance of John's dissertation research is also evidenced by the second prize award from the McKinsey Foundation Doctoral Thesis Awards. This competition was open to dissertations from all business schools in all areas of research, and the submitted dissertations were evaluated by a distinguished panel of business school researchers in a variety of disciplines.

2. John and Phelim had received a research grant from the Huebner Foundation for a proposal entitled "Optimal Insurance Contracts: Basic Conceptual and Methodological Issues." Their joint research papers were part of that study, but they had intended to do more to relate agency theory to optimal insurance contracts.

Agency theory was also the central theme of a research proposal that had received significant funding by the Social Sciences and Humanities Research Council of Canada. This proposal, coauthored with Amin Amershi, was entitled "An Economic Analysis of Incentive Control Systems in Organizations."

Unfortunately, John's death prevented him from contributing his deep knowledge to the completion of these two major research projects.

3. A related paper, "Capital Structure, Management Incentives, and Accounting Income," was presented at a 1983 Workshop in Brussels.

INTRODUCTION TO THE RESEARCH PAPERS IN THIS VOLUME

All papers in this volume examine aspects of the two related fields generally known as information economics and agency theory. Most of the authors teach accounting and their papers have implications for accounting, but they examine general information and agency issues that are applicable to a broad range of information and contractual settings. Atkinson and Feltham (1982), Baiman (1982), Verrecchia (1982), and Feltham (1984) provide reviews of information economics and agency-theory research, with particular emphasis on accounting implications. Hirshleifer and Riley (1979) provide a general survey of information analysis in the economics literature. The interested reader is encouraged to read these review articles to obtain an overview of the two fields.

The twelve papers in this volume are categorized into three basic groupings of four papers each. Part II is concerned with information evaluation in multiperson contexts. Part III discusses contracting in agencies under moral hazard. Part IV examines contracting in agencies with private information.

The four papers in part II discuss information evaluation in multiperson contexts. Both public and private information are considered, and the contexts vary from capital markets to two-person games. A rich variety of insights into the factors that influence the value of information are provided.

Information economic analyses initially focused on single-person decision contexts and, in the fifties, Blackwell provided the key result in this area, generally known as "Blackwell's informativeness result." In the first paper, "Blackwell Informativeness and Sufficient Statistics with Applications to Financial Markets and Multiperson Agencies," Amin H. Amershi reexamines that result. He provides a general version of its Markov kernal form, proving it more directly and identifying the essence of the result. The analysis develops links between Blackwell's result and the earlier Halmos–Savage theory of sufficient statistics. The paper then utilizes the preceding analysis to derive general results on the comparative value of public information structures for contracting in agencies under moral hazard and risk sharing among investors with diverse beliefs. Probability theory is a key ingredient in information economic analysis. The first appendix to this paper provides a tutorial on probability theory that will assist the reader of this paper and those who seek to use this theory in their own information economic analyses.

The impact of public information in competitive markets became an important area of analysis in the seventies. While most papers have focused on pure exchange economies, it has become apparent that the primary value of information in markets occurs when it can influence the allocation of resources among productive opportunities and consumption. The second and third papers contribute to our understanding of the impact of public information under the latter conditions.

James A. Ohlson examines "The Social Value of Public Information in Production Economies." A neoclassical production-exchange economy is considered, with only weak restrictions on preferences, beliefs, technologies, information characterization, and markets. The analysis develops a unified approach to information and production choice, with particular focus on unanimity issues in an incomplete market setting.

The paper by Young K. Kwon and D. Paul Newman, "Costly Public Information: Optimality and Comparative Statics," examines the impact of information in an economy in which investors have negative exponential utility functions, returns are normally distributed, and investors can store goods from one period to the next. These restrictive assumptions about preferences and beliefs are widely used in the information economics literature and permit the use of comparative statics to identify the relationship between the optimal choice of information precision and attributes of preferences, beliefs, and information cost.

Joel S. Demski's paper, "Value of Information in Bimatrix Games," shifts the focus from public to private information and from competitive markets to two-person games. In single-person decision theory and in production economies with public information, more information is at least as preferred as less information (subject to redistributive effects and ignoring information costs). The value of additional information becomes more complex when the information is privately acquired. This paper considers the strategic use and inference of private information in a variety of two-person noncontractual settings. In some situations, such as teams and constant-sum games, private information has positive value, whereas in others, such as defensive and symmetric games, it has negative value. The basic analysis considers single-play games, but that is extended to repetitive play and the exploration of reputation issues.

Information asymmetries began to become an important part of the economics and accounting literature during the midseventies. One of the most important information asymmetries results in what is commonly called *moral hazard*. This problem arises when a principal contracts with an agent who is to take an action which the principal cannot observe, which is directly costly to the agent, and which influences the likelihood of outcomes that are beneficial to the principal. The basic principal/agent problem is to determine the contract that will be offered to the agent by the principal in order to induce the agent to take the action desired by the principal.

The four papers in part III discuss contracting in agencies under moral hazard. The first three papers contribute to our understanding of the nature of optimal contracts in this context. The fourth paper limits its consideration to linear contracts and uses comparative statics to provide insights into how various factors influence these contracts.

Phelim P. Boyle and John E. Butterworth obtain explicit solutions to numerical examples in their paper "The Principal/Agent Problem—Numerical Solutions." Explicit solutions are often difficult to obtain because of the "incentive compatibility" (Nash) constraint. This paper establishes numerical procedures for computing optimal incentive contracts when both the principal and the agent have HARA utility functions with identical risk cautiousness. Examples highlight some of the technical issues that arise and cover a range of distributional and risk aversion assumptions.

In "Explorations in the Theory of Single- and Multiple-Agent Agencies," Amin H. Amershi and John E. Butterworth first provide insights into the nature of the optimal contract in the standard principal/agent problem. They demonstrate that the characterization of the optimal incentive contract is equivalent to an efficient pure risk-sharing contract based on heterogeneous beliefs. In particular, the agent is depicted as if he has "more optimistic" beliefs about the outcome. This characterization is also used in demonstrating that optimal contracts are not necessarily based on sufficient statistics for the available information. The latter part of the paper extends the analysis to multiple-agent agencies. A set of general conditions are identified under which contracts based on a sufficient statistics for the available information strictly dominates the use of tournaments, or any other incentive scheme that only produces a countable number of evaluations.

Ella Mae Matsumura extends the basic principal/agent model to encompass the sequential choice of two actions in her paper "Sequential Choice Under Moral Hazard." The analysis is similar to a two-period model in that the outcome of the first action is observed prior to selecting the second. However, in this paper preferences are defined over the total compensation, which facilitates examination of the wealth and information effects the initial outcome may have on the choice of the second action. These effects are examined by varying the context from one in which the first outcome provides no information about the second outcome to one in which it provides perfect information.

In the final paper in part III, "Risk Sharing and Valuation Under Moral Hazard," Patricia J. Hughes considers the moral hazard problem in a competitive market in which an entrepreneur seeks to share risks with investors by selling them a share of her company. Assuming negative exponential utility functions and normally distributed returns facilitates identification of the optimal share of the company to be retained by the entrepreneur. The model also permits analysis of the impact of various preference and belief parameters on the optimal share to be retained.

Part IV continues to examine principal/agent contracting, but introduces information asymmetries with respect to events other than actions. In the first two papers, private information is obtained prior to contracting. In the third paper, private information is acquired after contracting but prior to the selection of an action. Finally, in the last paper the action outcome is private information. The analyses consider entrepreneurs entering capital markets, contracting in decentralized organizations, and contracting with accountants.

Gerald A. Feltham and John S. Hughes, in their paper "Communication of Private Information in Capital Markets: Contingent Contracts and Verified Reports," examine signaling by an entrepreneur with private precontracting information. The basic context is described as a game in which the informed player moves first and in which he communicates his private information by the type of contract he offers investors. The analysis characterizes the optimal signaling contract, demonstrating that it depends on the stability criterion used to identify an equilibrium. The analysis is extended to examine the demand for verified reports issued either prior or subsequent to contracting with investors, and the incentives for contracting prior to the acquisition of private information.

In the second paper, "Managerial Compensation: Linear Sharing vs. Bonus Incentive Plans Under Moral Hazard and Adverse Selection," Masako N. Darrough and Neal M. Stoughton consider moral hazard and signaling issues simultaneously. To facilitate their analysis, they too assume negative exponential utility functions and normally distributed returns and initially consider only linear contracts. In discussing linear contracts, only the mean of the manager's private information and his action are unknown to investors. Bonus contracts are then introduced and demonstrated to be useful devices in dealing with difficult signaling problems that arise when investors do not know either the mean or the variance of the manager's private information.

Ronald A. Dye, in "Intrafirm Resource Allocation and Discretionary Actions," analyzes a principal/agent context in which there are two agents, a manufacturer and a retailer. The retailer sells the output of the manufacturer and both obtain perfect information about their productivity after contracting with the principal but before selecting their actions. This special structure provides some interesting insights into the potential role of transfer pricing in incentive contracting.

The final paper by Rick Antle and Richard A. Lambert, "Accountants' Loss Functions and Induced Preferences for Conservatism," examines a principal/agent context in which a principal (user) contracts with an agent (accountant) to provide information that will be valuable to the principal. Information acquisition is a costly process that the agent will shirk unless appropriately motivated. Furthermore, the signal outcome from the agent's information activity is private information and, hence, the signal reported to the principal need not be the same as that observed. The optimal contract is determined and the agent's incentives for conservative reporting are explored.

References

Baiman, S. [1982]. "Agency Research in Managerial Accounting: A Survey," *Journal of Accounting Literature* 1, 152–213.

Atkinson, A.A., and G.A. Feltham [1982]. "Agency Theory Research and Financial Accounting Standards." *Research to Support Standard Setting in Financial Accounting: A Canadian Perspective*, S. Basu and J.A. Milburn (eds.). Toronto: Clarkson Gordon Foundation, 259–289.

Feltham, G.A. [1984]. "Financial Accounting Research: Contributions of Information Economics and Agency Theory." *Modern Accounting Research: History, Survey and Guide*, R. Mattessich (ed.). Vancouver: Canadian Certified General Accountants' Research Foundation, 179–207.

Hirshleifer, J., and J.G. Riley [1979]. "The Analytics of Uncertainty and Information: An Expository Survey." *Journal of Economic Literature* 17, 1375–1421.

Verrecchia, R.E. [1982]. "The Use of Mathematical Models in Financial Accounting." *Journal of Accounting Research Supplement* 20, 1–41.

PART II: INFORMATION EVALUATION IN MULTIPERSON CONTEXTS

1 BLACKWELL INFORMATIVENESS AND SUFFICIENT STATISTICS WITH APPLICATIONS TO FINANCIAL MARKETS AND MULTIPERSON AGENCIES

Amin H. Amershi

This paper has two purposes. The first is partly tutorial: I want to develop Blackwell's theory of information value in a way that makes the essential intuition transparent. In the process I will present a generalization of Blackwell's [1951] seminal result on *informativeness* that is related to Marschak and Miyasawa's [1968] concept of *garbling*.[1,2] More important, I want to show that garbling is intimately linked to the more useful and general theory of *sufficient statistics*, which has been at the center stage of progress in statistical theory ever since the concept was proposed by Fisher [1922] and cast into its present form by the factorization theorem of Halmos and Savage [1949]. While the garbling idea has intuitive appeal for initiation into information economics, I believe that too much mental reliance on it tends to obscure the important point that both Blackwell's concept and sufficient statistics essentially arise from properties of the conditional probability measures given the statistics. Consequently, I want to highlight this aspect and show the connections between the Blackwell theory and sufficient statistics that become apparent if we focus on the meaning and properties of these conditional measures. Later in the paper I exploit these connections when I discuss applications to financial markets and agencies. Further, the conditional probability approach is most useful in sequential decision processes—*stochastic control*—where we have to deal with conditional probabilities at each stage given the information in prior stages of the decision process.[3]

The second purpose of this paper is to apply the tools and links between Blackwell informativeness and sufficient statistics to two areas of much interest in economics:

1. the ordering of the social value of information structures (systems) in capital markets in which economic agents with diverse beliefs share risks; and
2. the value-ordering of information structures (or systems) on which Nash equilibrium compensation contracts can be based in multiagent agencies under moral hazard.

The results in capital markets generalize the pioneering work of Hakansson ([1977], [1978]) and the recent work of Amershi [1985]. I show that Blackwell sufficiency implies informativeness in the Pareto (social)-value sense for risk sharing. Further, I show that the efficient risk sharing of a complete exchange market can be achieved through trading of securities based on a *minimal* Halmos–Savage sufficient statistic that accommodates the investors' diverse beliefs. While I do not include production in the analysis here, the recent work of Feltham [1985] shows that the results also hold in a setting where production and exchange take place simultaneously.

The results on multiagent agencies generalize the work of Holmstrom ([1979], [1982]), Gjesdal [1982], Amershi and Hughes [1987], and Mookherjee [1984]. I show that Blackwell sufficiency essentially implies contract informativeness in a Nash equilibrium.

To summarize, I show here that the concepts of Blackwell sufficiency and Halmos–Savage sufficiency connect informativeness of information structures in three diverse economic settings: single-person decision making, contractual informativeness in multiagent agencies, and risk sharing in capital markets.

The following section crystallizes the essence of Blackwell informativeness in a single-person decision setting. The next section provides a general Blackwell informativeness-garbling result and connections to sufficient statistics. The final sections of this paper develop the informativeness results in capital markets and the contractual informativeness results in agencies.

Appendix A is a rather long, partly tutorial, appendix which contains some of the elementary and advanced concepts from probability theory used here.

Its purposes are amplified in the appendix's introduction. Appendix B contains proofs of the results in the body of the text.

Stochastic Control Theory and Blackwell Informativeness

Almost all treatments of Blackwell's theory on informativeness begin by explaining the meaning of the Markov kernel result, namely:

> Information system η is *more informative* (hence more useful) than information system γ if there is a Markov kernel $Q(y|x)$ from the set of signals $Y_\eta = \{x_1, \ldots, x_n\}$ to $Y_\gamma = \{y_1, \ldots, y_m\}$ such that
>
> $$P(y_i|\omega) = \sum_{j=1}^{n} Q(y_i|x_j)P(x_j|\omega)$$
>
> where $\omega \in \Omega = \{\omega_1, \ldots, \omega_k\}$ is a set of parameters

While this approach is useful if one wants to quickly get to Blackwell's result, it is too mechanical and obscures the role of Blackwell's result and information in the general theory of sequential decision choice. Further, this approach is deficient in intuition as to the connections to the theory of sufficient statistics and, from there, the connections to multiperson decision theory. Hence, I shall abandon this common mechanical approach and start from fundamental decision theory and build up to Blackwell's result.

Visualize a *single-cycle, single-person information-decision choice structure* as the general game against nature in the "time" sequence shown in figure 1–1 (here time is "notional" time, though in practice it could be *real* time).[4]

Formally, the general single-cycle decision environment consists of the following objects:

1. The spaces Ω, S, H, Y, A and X.
2. The kernels $P(s|\omega)$, $P(\eta|\omega, s)$, $P(y|\omega, s, \eta)$, $P(a|\omega, s, \eta, y)$, $P(x|\omega, s, \eta, y, a)$, $\omega \in \Omega$, $s \in S$, $\eta \in H$, $y \in Y$, $a \in A$, $x \in X$.
3. A von Neumann-Morgenstern measurable utility function u: $X \to \mathfrak{R}$.

Definition 1.1

A *single-cycle* (*stage, period*) *choice problem* consists of a set A of *acts*, a set H of *information systems* (*structures*), a *utility function* u on the set X of *outcomes* (*payoffs*), a *subset* of kernels $P(a|\omega, s, \eta, y)$ on A and a *subset* of kernels

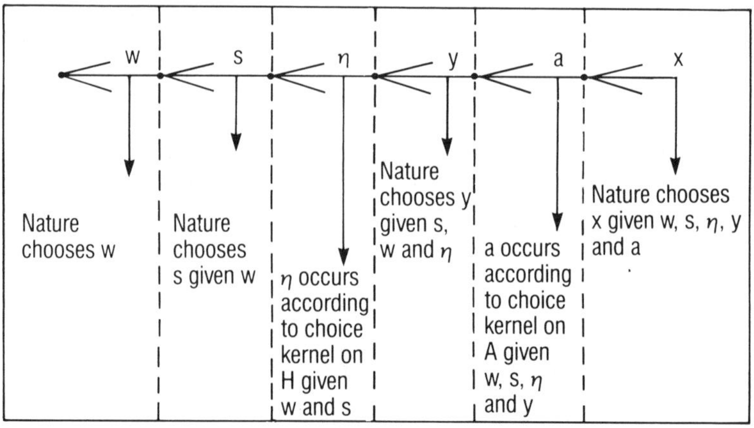

Figure 1–1. General Single-Cycle Decision Structure

$P(\eta | \omega, s)$ on H. The last two objects are called *decision kernels* (or *behavioral strategies*) in *acts and information choices* respectively.

The restriction of the available decision kernels reflects both the availability of decision information and restrictions on choices from A or H. For example, if the decision maker has no information at the time of selection of a system from H, $P(\eta | \omega, s)$ would be from the set of kernels independent of (ω, s), namely the unconditional probability measures on H. Similarly, to reflect only the knowledge (η, y) at the time of action selection from A, restrict the choice of decision kernels $P(a | \omega, s, \eta, y)$ to the subset of kernels $P(a | \eta, y)$. Also, restricting choice within H or A can be accomplished by kernels *concentrated* on subsets of H or A. For example, a pure strategy $a \in A$, knowing only (η, y), can be modeled by a 0–1 kernel $P(a | \eta, y)$ on A, concentrated on $\{a\}$. The description of the decision problem as a chain of kernels admits a certain symmetry that is useful in conceptualization of the issues.[5]

For the moment, I have not adopted a standard Bayesian description of the problem with given prior on Ω because I want to develop the Blackwell theory, which is in a *prior-free setting*. Blackwell's informativeness results are stronger than Bayesian versions with a fixed prior on $\sigma(\Omega)$. However, the Blackwell decision problem makes special assumptions about the *costs* of the information structures, which makes it a special case of the general single-cycle decision structure, as I shall now discuss.

Definition 1.2

A *Blackwell decision problem* is a single-cycle decision problem with the following restrictions on the decision structure:

1. The kernels $P(x|\omega, s, \eta, y, a)$ are independent of (s, η, y).
2. The kernels $P(y|\omega, s, \eta)$ are of the 0–1 type defined by random variables $\eta: S \to Y$.
3. The kernels $P(\eta|\omega, s)$ are independent of (ω, s) and concentrated on points $\{\eta\}$ in H.
4. There exists a kernel $P(s|\omega)$ from Ω to S.
5. No prior on Ω is given.

Restriction 1 in the Blackwell decision problem formalizes a *costless-information* choice problem in that the costs [i.e., the *effects* of (s, η, y)] do not impinge on the outcome lotteries $P(x|\omega, a)$ on X. Restriction 2 implies that the information systems η are functions from S to Y. Blackwell and Girschick [1954] term S the "sample space of observations." I shall call this *the fundamental* (*signal*) *sample space* and Ω the *space of parameters* or "*states*" *of nature* (as in Savage [1954]). Observe that we need not be given S a priori. For instance, I can start out with a Blackwell decision problem defined by a family of signal spaces and kernels indexed by η as $\{[Y_\eta, P_\eta(y|\omega), \omega \in \Omega] | \eta \in H\}$, where Y_η is the set of signals from η. If the kernels $P_\eta(y|\omega)$ for each $\omega \in \Omega$ obey the Kolmogorov consistency conditions (see Bauer [1972], p. 360) then I can define a product measure on the (possibly infinite) product set $S = \Pi_{\eta \in H} Y_\eta$ and the product σ-algebra $\sigma(\Pi_{\eta \in H} Y_\eta) = \sigma(S)$. The random variable $\eta: S \to Y_\eta$ has the distribution $P_\eta(y|\omega)$ at each $\omega \in \Omega$. I term this S the *canonical sample space*. Henceforth, I shall assume that the sample space S (either a priori or by the canonical process above) is *always* defined.

Restriction 3 implies that not only is the choice of $\eta \in H$ independent of any information about $\omega \in \Omega$ or $s \in S$, but that randomization is unnecessary. The reason is that Blackwell's development is designed to (partially) order systems $\eta \in H$ and not randomizations over H. Of course, the ordering (if complete) of systems could induce an order on $P(\eta)$ on H, but in most single-person settings, randomizations are unnecessary and so the exercise becomes academic. Restrictions 4 and 5 make the Blackwell theory prior-probability free.

The value of an *information-decision choice* $(\eta, P(a|\eta, y))$ for any fixed $\omega \in \Omega$ in the Blackwell setting is the expected utility

$$V(\eta, P(a|\eta, y)|\omega) = \int_{Y_\eta}\int_A\int_X u(x)\,dP(x|\omega, a)\,dP(a|\eta, y)\,dP_\eta(y|\omega)$$

$$= E\{E[E(u(x)|\omega, a)|\eta, y]|\eta, \omega\} \tag{1.1}$$

where Y_η denotes the image set of signals from $\eta: S \to Y$. $P_\eta(B|\omega) = P(\eta^{-1}(B)|\omega)$ for all $B \in \sigma(Y_\eta)$ is the measure on $\sigma(Y_\eta)$ induced by η from $P(s|\omega)$ on s. The conditional expectation

$$\theta(\omega, a) = E(u(x)|\omega, a) = \int_X u(x)\,dP(x|\omega, a) \tag{1.2}$$

defines a measurable function from $\Omega \times A$ to $\mathfrak{R}$. Consider the family of functions $\Lambda = \{\theta(\cdot, a)|a \in A\}$ defined by fixing the parameter $a \in A$ and varying ω in the conditional expectations in (1.2). Then the decision kernel $P(a|\eta, y)$ amounts to a randomization (lottery) over Λ such that the value $V(\eta, P(a|\eta, y)|\omega)$ in (1.1) is simply the expected value of these randomizations with respect to the (lottery) probability measure $P_\eta(y|\omega)$ for each ω. When $\Omega = \{\omega_1, \ldots, \omega_n\}$ is finite, Λ is a closed and bounded n-dimensional set in $\mathfrak{R}^n$ and if we consider the *convex hull*[6] $C(\Lambda)$ of Λ, a choice of a decision kernel $P(a|\eta, y)$ amounts to a choice of a point $\theta \in C(\Lambda)$. Consider then a function $\delta: Y_\eta \to C(\Lambda)$. Let $\delta(y, \omega)$ be the ωth component of the vector θ chosen by δ at y. Then $V(\eta, P(a|\eta, y)|\omega)$ is equivalent to the number, for some function δ,

$$V(\eta, \delta|\omega) = \int_{Y_\eta} \delta(y, \omega)\,dP_\eta(y|\omega) \tag{1.3}$$

for each ω. Consequently, the set of vectors $B(P_\eta, C(\Lambda)) = \{b(P_\eta, \delta) = [V(\eta, \delta|\omega_1), \ldots, V(\eta, \delta|\omega_n)]\}$ completely defines a Blackwell decision structure. Letting $C(\Lambda)$ vary with u and A as $C(\Lambda(u, A))$ completely specifies the class of Blackwell decision structures that can arise with information system η. Observe that the nature of the utility function u or the action set A has no impact on the description of the *totality* of all classes $C(\Lambda(u, A))$ that can arise with η. Hence, this description frees η from the immediate economic environment in considering its impact on decisions.

For precisely this reason Blackwell [1953], for a finite $\Omega = \{\omega_1, \ldots, \omega_n\}$, starts out abstractly with the sets $B(P_\eta, C(\Lambda))$ and $C(\Lambda)$ in $\mathfrak{R}^n$ as above. He calls the set $C(\Lambda)$ the space of decisions, and P_η the experiment. In the event that Y_η is finite (i.e., $Y_\eta = \{y_1, \ldots, y_N\}$), the formulation above degenerates into a set of matrixes and convex sets. Thus $P_\eta = [P_{ik}]$ is a $n \times N$ Markov matrix such that $P_\eta(y_k|\omega_i) = P_{ik}$, and a decision function $\delta: Y_\eta \to C(\Lambda)$ is representable by a matrix $D = [d_{ki}]$, where $d_{ki} = \delta(y_k, \omega_i)$, $\delta(y_k, \cdot) \in C(\Lambda)$.[7] The vector $b(P_\eta, \delta)$ is then the diagonal of the matrix product $P_\eta D$. $B(P_\eta, C(\Lambda))$ is the set of all such diagonals as D varies. Thus,

$$V(\eta, D|w_i) = \sum_{k=1}^{N} P_{ik} d_{ki} = b(P_\eta, \delta|\omega_i)$$

For the case of finite Ω, Blackwell [1953] defines η as *more informative* than γ if $B(P_\gamma, C(\Lambda)) \subseteq B(P_\eta, C(\Lambda))$ for *all choice settings* $C(\Lambda)$ in $\mathfrak{R}^n$. This means that for each expected utility vector $b(P_\gamma, \delta)$ attainable under the system γ and decision function δ, the same vector is also attainable by some α under the system η. Marschak and Miyasawa [1968] point out correctly that "*at least as informative*" would have been much more appropriate than "more informative." However, I shall retain the original Blackwell terminology of "more informative" which has become entrenched. The next theorem is the famous Blackwell result.

Theorem (Blackwell [1953])[8]

Let $\Omega = \{\omega_1, \ldots, \omega_n\}$ be a finite set. Then a system η is more informative than γ *if and only if* there exists a Markov kernel $P(z|y)$ from Y_η to Y_γ such that for each $\omega \in \Omega$, $B \in \sigma(Y_\gamma)$,

$$P_\gamma(B|\omega) = \int_{Y_\eta} P(B|y)dP(y|\omega) \tag{1.4}$$

Observe that Blackwell's result is *purely statistical*, which makes it a *strong economic* result because it is free of all economic parameters (the utilities, action sets etc.) of the problem. It is easy to see that if η is more informative than γ, then for any prior $P(\omega)$ on Ω the Bayes value of η is greater than or equal to that of γ for any utility function u and act set A.[9] Hence Blackwell's result is also *prior free*, making it a strong Bayesian decision-theoretic result.

What, then, is the key idea in Blackwell's theorem? It is the observation that the kernel $P(z|y)$ is *independent of* $\omega \in \Omega$. This observation is crucial, because from Doob's theorem, for any $\omega \in \Omega$, a kernel $P(z|y, \omega)$ that yields at each ω the marginal measure $P_\gamma(z|\omega)$ through an integral equation like (1.4) always exists (see appendix A). Hence, *Blackwell's theorem is essentially a statement about the independence from* ω *of the Doob kernel* $P(z|y, \omega)$.

This observation is the basis of Marschak and Miyasawa's ([1968], p. 149) *garbling* interpretation of Blackwell informativeness. Marschak and Miyasawa define γ to be a garbled version of η if the Doob kernels $P(z|y, w)$ equal the kernel $P(z|y)$ for *all* $\omega \in \Omega$. Then it is obvious that:

$$\gamma \text{ garbled from } \eta \Rightarrow \eta \text{ is Blackwell more informative than } \gamma$$

The converse, however is *not necessarily* true. That is, η is Blackwell more informative than $\gamma \not\Rightarrow \gamma$ garbled from η. Hence garbling is a more stringent form of informativeness. The independence of $P(z|y, \omega)$ from ω has strong links to the theory of sufficient statistics (see the following section) as expounded by Halmos and Savage [1949]. Further, as I shall show below, there is a representation by which Blackwell informativeness is equivalent to a restricted form of statistical sufficiency.

Blackwell Informativeness and Statistical Sufficiency

Blackwell [1953] proved the informativeness result for the case when Ω, the parameter set, is finite but the signal spaces Y_η and Y_γ could be infinite. To connect it with the theory of sufficient statistics and to apply to multiperson decision problems (such as the agency problem discussed at the end of this chapter), a generalization of Blackwell's result to infinite parameter sets is needed. This generalization and further extensions can be found in the work of Le Cam [1964], Strassen [1965], and Meyer [1966]. However, these works are highly abstract and contain much ancillary material of no immediate concern to us. This makes them rather inaccessible to the applied-decision theorist. I shall, therefore, spell out here a new general version of Blackwell's result such that the connections to sufficient statistics and the applications considered later are transparent. The proof provided in appendix B is new and interesting in its own right.

General Blackwell Informativeness Result and Garbling

Definition 1.3

An information system η is *Blackwell more informative* than a system γ for a *fixed* state space of parameters Ω if the maximum expected utility attained in *any* Blackwell decision problem given any parameter $\omega \in \Omega$ using the information system γ can also be attained using the information system η.

Theorem 1.1

Let η and γ be two systems on $(S, \sigma(S))$ taking values in Y_η and Y_γ respectively. Consider the following statements.

(1) η is more informative than γ.
(2) There exists a unique Markov kernel $P(z|y)$ from Y_η to Y_γ such that

$$P_\gamma(B|\omega) = \int_{Y_\eta} P(B|y)dP_\eta(y|\omega) \tag{1.5}$$

for each $\omega \in \Omega$ and $B \in \sigma(Y_\gamma)$.
(3) There exists a Markov kernel $P(z|y)$ from Y_η to Y_γ such that

$$P(B|y, \omega) = P(B|y) \tag{1.6}$$

for all $\omega \in \Omega$ and $B \in \sigma(Y_\eta)$, where $P(B|y, \omega)$ is the Doob kernel from Y_η to Y_γ for each $\omega \in \Omega$.

The following relationships hold among these statements:

a. (1) $\Leftrightarrow$ (2) (generalized Blackwell theorem)
b. (3) $\Rightarrow$ (2) (garbling $\Rightarrow$ Blackwell informativeness)
c. (2) $\not\Rightarrow$ (3) (Blackwell informativeness $\not\Rightarrow$ garbling in general)

The next two corollaries are trivial, but often used, consequences, whose proofs are left to the reader.

Corollary 1.1

For *any* prior probability measure $P(w)$ on Ω, *any* utility function u and *any* action set A, let $V(\eta, u, A, P(w))$ denote the *Bayes' value* of a system η for the *optimal choice of strategy* δ^* based on η, u, A and the prior $P(w)$. (That is, $V(\eta, u, A, P(w))$ is the expected value from η on using δ^*.) If η is more informative than γ, then $V(\eta, u, A, P(w)) \geq V(\gamma, u, A, P(w))$.

Corollary 1.2

Let η and γ be two information systems such that Y_η and Y_γ are Borel subsets of $\mathfrak{R}^n$ and $\mathfrak{R}^m$ respectively. If $\sigma(\gamma) \subseteq \sigma(\eta)$, then η is more informative than γ.

The converse to corollary 1.1 is nontrivial. It has been proved for finite ω by Blackwell [1951], and by a similar reasoning we can extend it to the general case here. The converse to corollary 1.2 is not true in general. This means that η can be more informative than γ, and yet the partition of η can be coarser than that of γ. Although this appears counterintuitive, it is true because *Blackwell's informativeness ordering is a weak partial order. It is not asymmetric.* To understand this we need the concept of sufficient statistics to which the Blackwell development is related.

Blackwell Informativeness and Sufficient Statistics

The following definition of sufficiency is standard in the mathematical statistics literature. It is originally attributed to Halmos and Savage [1949].[10]

Definition 1.4 (Sufficient Statistic/Sufficient σ-algebra)

Let $P_\Gamma = \{P_\lambda | \lambda \in \Gamma\}$ be a class of probability measures that are absolutely continuous with respect to a probability measure P (i.e., P *dominates* P_λ, $\lambda \in \Gamma$) on a measurable space $(Z, \mathscr{B})$.[11] Then a random variable $T: Z \to M$ (respectively a sub-σ-algebra $\mathscr{F} \subseteq \mathscr{B}$) into a space $(M, \mathscr{K})$ is called a *sufficient statistic* (*a sufficient σ-algebra*) for the family P_Γ if the kernels $P(\cdot | T, \lambda)$ [respectively, $P(\cdot | \mathscr{F}, \lambda)$] on $\mathscr{B}$ are *independent* of λ in the sense that there exists a kernel $P(\cdot|\cdot)$: $\mathscr{B} \times Z \to [0, 1]$ such that $P(B|z)$ is $\sigma(T)$ measurable for each $B \in \mathscr{B}$, and

$$P(B|z) = P(B|T, \lambda)(z) \qquad [\text{respectively, } P(B|\mathscr{F}, \lambda)(z)] \tag{1.7}$$

within a $P(\cdot|\lambda)$ null set $N(B, \lambda)$ for each λ.

Intuition. It is important to grasp the intuition of this. Suppose there is a measurable space $(Z, \mathscr{B})$ [like our sample space $(S, \sigma(S))$] on which is defined a class of probability measures $P_\Gamma = \{P_\lambda | \lambda \in \Gamma\}$. Several examples are now given.

Example 1.1

(a) Let $(\mathfrak{R}, \mathscr{B}(\mathfrak{R}))$ be the real Borel space on which is defined a normal density function with distribution measure $N(\mu, \sigma)$. Suppose the variance

σ is known but the mean is unknown, that is $-\infty < \mu < \infty$. Then $\Gamma = \{\mu\} = (-\infty, \infty)$, $P_\Gamma = \{N(\mu, \sigma) | -\infty < \mu < \infty\}$ and $(Z, \mathscr{B}) = (\mathfrak{R}, \mathscr{B}(\mathfrak{R}))$.

(b) This example is the same as (a) except that we now have a random sample of size n, $s = [\tilde{x}_1, \ldots, \tilde{x}_n]$, drawn from the underlying population $(\mathfrak{R}, \mathscr{B}(\mathfrak{R}))$. Then the measurable space of interest is the n-product.

$$S = \mathfrak{R} \times \ldots \times \mathfrak{R}$$

and the probability measures are

$$P_\mu = N(\mu, \sigma)^n, \quad \mu \in (-\infty, \infty)$$

(c) Let $(X, \mathscr{F})$ and $(Y, \mathscr{G})$ be a two measurable spaces. Let $Q(y|x)$: $\mathscr{G} \times X \to [0, 1]$ be a kernel from X to Y. Then, $Q(y|x)$ can also be considered as a class of probability measures on Y as follows:

$$\Gamma \equiv X, \lambda \equiv x; \quad \text{and} \quad P_\lambda \equiv Q(\cdot|x) \quad \text{on} \quad \mathscr{G}$$

Returning to the definition, it says that a statistic T: $Z \to M$ is termed sufficient (for the parameter λ) if, regardless of which *prior* P_λ prevails, the posteriors $P(\cdot | T, \lambda)$ are identical (almost everywhere) to some fixed kernel $P(\ | T)$ that depends only on T. That is, *all statistical information* about the parameter λ is captured by the statistic T; and, thus, conditioning further with respect to λ does not add to our knowledge given $P(\cdot | T)$.

It is now easy to see where I am going. Theorem 1.1 part 3, says that η is Blackwell more informative than γ if the conditional measures on $\sigma(Y_\gamma)$ given $\eta(s) = y \in Y_\eta$, $w \in \Omega$, namely $P(B|y, w)$ for $B \in \sigma(Y_\gamma)$ are *independent* of the parameter w. Thus, Blackwell's informativeness is some form of *local-sufficiency* comparison between two information systems, whereas Halmos–Savage provide a *global-sufficiency* concept. This intuition is crystallized in the next few results. But first I provide the usual decomposition of densities characterization of sufficient statistics of elementary textbooks (e.g., see DeGroot [1970]).

Theorem (Halmos–Savage [1949])

Let P_Γ be a family of probability measures dominated by a σ-finite measure μ on the space $(Z, \mathscr{B})$. A measurable function T: $Z \to M$ is sufficient for P_Γ *if and only if* there exists a nonnegative measurable map h: $Z \to \mathfrak{R}$, and for each P_λ a measurable map g_λ: $M \to \mathfrak{R}$, such that the Radon–Nikodym density of P_λ with respect to μ is given by the *decomposition* (*factorization*)[12]

$$f_\lambda(z) = h(z) \cdot g_\lambda(T(z)) \qquad \text{for each } z \in Z \tag{1.8}$$

In order to clinch the relationship between Blackwell informativeness and Halmos–Savage statistical sufficiency, I need the *Bayesian* concept of sufficient statistics. Definition 1.4 and the Halmos–Savage theorem on sufficient statistics provided above are called *non-Bayesian* concepts because they do *not* involve any *prior probability measure* on the parameter space Γ. Raiffa and Schlaiffer ([1961], p. 32) provide a Bayesian concept of statistical sufficiency.

Definition 1.5 (Bayesian Sufficient Statistic)

Let $P_\Gamma = \{P_\lambda | \lambda \in \Gamma\}$, be class of probability measures on a finite dimensional Euclidean Borel space $(\mathfrak{R}^n, \mathscr{B}(\mathfrak{R}^n))$ dominated by σ-finite measure μ. Let Γ be an open subset of $\mathfrak{R}^k$, and $(\Gamma, \mathscr{B}(\Gamma))$ the Euclidean Borel space of the parameters. Let Π be a class of *prior probability* measures on $\mathscr{B}(\Gamma)$ dominated by a σ-finite measure ψ. Denote by $f(z|\lambda)$ a version of the density of P_λ w.r.t. (with respect to) μ on $\mathfrak{R}^n$, and by $\pi(\lambda)$ a version of the density of a measure $H \in \Pi$ w.r.t. ψ. A version of the *joint density* of (z, λ) over the product space $(\mathfrak{R}^n \times \Gamma, \sigma(\mathscr{B}(\mathfrak{R}^n) \times \mathscr{B}(\Gamma)))$ is

$$g(z, \lambda) = f(z|\lambda)\pi(\lambda) \tag{1.9}$$

Let $\tilde{m}$: $\mathfrak{R}^n \to \mathfrak{R}^q$ be a *statistic* (random variable), and let $P(m|\lambda)$ be the induced probability measure on the Borel sets $\mathscr{B}(\mathfrak{R}^q)$ given a probability measure P_λ on $\mathfrak{R}^n$. Suppose each such induced measure has a density $h(m|\lambda)$ w.r.t. some σ-finite measure on $\mathscr{B}(\mathfrak{R}^q)$. A *version* of the *posterior* (*conditional*) density of λ given m is given by Bayes' theorem as

$$\pi(\lambda|m) = \frac{h(m|\lambda) \cdot \pi(\lambda)}{\int_\Gamma h(m|\lambda)\pi(\lambda)\, d\lambda}$$

Then a statistic T: $\mathfrak{R}^n \to \mathfrak{R}^q$ is called a *Bayesian sufficient statistic* for the family of prior probability measures Π on Γ if the posterior densities obey

$$\pi(\lambda| T(z) = t) = \pi(\lambda|z) \qquad \text{for all} \quad z \in \mathfrak{R}^n, \pi(\lambda) \tag{1.10}$$

Intuitively this means that the posterior beliefs about which parameter $\lambda \in \Gamma$ prevails given the summary statistic $T(z) = t$ is identical to the posterior beliefs that would obtain if *all* of the information z was known. It may seem that the non-Bayesian and Bayesian concepts of sufficient statistics are different, but that is *not* true. They are identical!

Theorem (Zacks [1971], p. 91)

Given any Bayesian model with a product probability space ($\mathfrak{R}^n \times \Gamma$, $\sigma(\mathscr{B}(\mathfrak{R}^n) \times \mathscr{B}(\Gamma))$, $f(z|\lambda)$, $\pi(\lambda)$) as in definition 1.5, a statistic T: $\mathfrak{R}^n \to \mathfrak{R}^q$ is a *Bayesian-sufficient statistic* for every family of priors Π on Γ *if and only if* it is a (*non-Bayesian*) *sufficient statistic* for the family of measures P_Γ.

I will now show the connections between Blackwell informativeness and statistical sufficiency.

Theorem 1.2

(1) Let $P(\cdot|\omega)$ be a class of measures in a Blackwell decision problem on S dominated by a probability measure (or a σ-finite measure). Then a sufficient statistic T: $S \to Y_T$ is *more informative than any* other system γ: $S \to Y_\gamma$.
(2) For each Blackwell decision problem, there exists a *minimal most informative system* η^* in that any other system γ which is also most informative cannot have a σ-algebra $\sigma(\gamma)$ that is a proper subset of $\sigma(\eta^*)$.
(3) If S is a countable set, the words "σ-algebra" in (2) can be replaced by "partition" and the words "proper subset of" by "coarser than."

In theorem 1.1 (b) and (c) I showed that garbling (in the sense that the Doob kernels $P(B|y, \omega) = P(B|y)$, $B \in \sigma(Y_\gamma)$, $y \in Y_\eta$) *implies* that η is Blackwell more informative than γ, but that the converse is not necessarily true. Given the development of sufficient statistics above, the intuition behind theorem 1.1 (b) indicates that Blackwell informativeness of η over γ implies that η is *somehow* sufficient for γ. There is a sense in which this is true, as the next result shows.

Theorem 1.3

Let $P(\cdot|\omega)$ be a class of probability measures in a Blackwell decision problem on S dominated by a σ-finite measure. Let η: $S \to Y_\eta$ and γ: $S \to Y_\gamma$ be two information systems and let $X = Y_\eta \times Y_\gamma$ be the product space of (y, z) ($y \in Y_\eta$, $z \in Y_\gamma$) with the product σ-algebra $\sigma(X) = \sigma(\sigma(Y_\eta) \times \sigma(Y_\gamma))$. Let $P(\cdot|\omega, \eta, \gamma)$ denote *some* class of probability measures on $\sigma(X)$ varying with $\omega \in \Omega$ and dependent on η and γ. Suppose all spaces are either Euclidean spaces or open sets of Euclidean spaces.

(1) Let $P(\cdot|\omega, \eta, \gamma)$ be the joint measure induced by the vector statistic $[\eta, \gamma]$: $S \to Y_\eta \times Y_\gamma$ on $\sigma(X)$ via $P(\cdot|\omega)$ on $\sigma(S)$. Let $\bar{\eta}$: $X \to Y_\eta$ be the *projection* of X onto Y_η as $\bar{\eta}(y, z) = y$. (Similarly define $\bar{\gamma}$: $X \to Y_\gamma$). *If* $\bar{\eta}$ is a *sufficient statistic* for the family $P(\cdot|\omega, \eta, \gamma)$ on $\sigma(X)$, *then* η is *Blackwell more informative* than γ.

(2) Let η be *Blackwell more informative* than γ. Let $P(C|y)$ be the *Markov kernel* such that,

$$P_\gamma(C|\omega) = \int_{Y_\eta} P(C|y)\, dP_\eta(y|\omega) \qquad \text{for } C \in \sigma(Y_\gamma)$$

where P_γ and P_η are induced measures on $\sigma(Y_\gamma)$ and $\sigma(Y_\eta)$ as defined in theorem 1.1. Define now a family of joint measures $P(\cdot|\omega, \eta, \gamma)$ on $\sigma(X)$ by the *unique Hahn extensions of measures process* (see Burrill [1972]) from

$$Q(B \times C|\omega, \eta) = \int_B P(C|y)\, dP_\eta(y|\omega), \qquad B \in \sigma(Y_\eta), C \in \sigma(Y_\gamma)$$

Let $\bar{\eta}$ and $\bar{\gamma}$ be the projections defined in (1) above. If all probability measures, conditional or otherwise, have densities, then $\bar{\eta}$ is a *sufficient statistic* for the family $Q(\cdot|\omega, \eta) \equiv P(\cdot|\omega, \eta, \gamma)$.

Theorem 1.3 may seem to contradict (c) of theorem 1.1. However, observe that the joint measures $P(\cdot|\omega, \eta, \gamma)$ in (1) of theorem 1.3 are induced from $P(\cdot|\omega)$ on $\sigma(S)$ onto $\sigma(X)$ via the vector statistic $[\eta, \gamma]$, but the joint measures $Q(\cdot|\omega, \eta)$ in (2) of theorem 1.3 are derived from the Blackwell Markov kernel $P(C|y)$. These two joint measures *may* be different and thus (c) of theorem 1.1 would be true for the induced joint measures but not for the joint measures derived from the Blackwell kernel.

The interrelationships between the Halmos–Savage concept of sufficient statistics and Blackwell's concept of informativeness motivate the following definition:

Definition 1.6 (Blackwell sufficiency)

Let η and γ be the two information systems in a Blackwell decision problem. Then η is *Blackwell sufficient* for γ if η is *Blackwell more informative* than γ.

Corollary 1.3

1. *Every* sufficient statistic T is Blackwell sufficient for *all* information systems γ defined on S.
2. If an information system η is Blackwell sufficient for the system γ, it does *not* imply η is a sufficient statistic for S.

Corollary 1.3 shows that we may *partially* order systems through the concept of Blackwell informativeness and that the partial order has a least upper bound. However, the concept of Blackwell sufficiency is a *pairwise* comparison concept (see theorem 1.3), whereas the standard sufficiency criterion is a global concept.

Partition Ordering

Corollary 1.2 shows that if the *partition* induced by information system η on S is *at least as fine* as that induced by the system γ, then η is Blackwell more informative than γ. I now give an example to show that the converse is not true.

Example 1.2

Let $S = \{s_1, s_2, s_3, s_4, s_5\}$ and let $P(s_k|\omega)$, $\omega \in \Omega = \{\omega_1, \omega_2, \omega_3\}$ be some family of measures such that the Radon–Nikodym densities

$$f(s_k|\omega_j) = \frac{P(s_k|\omega_j)}{\frac{1}{3}\sum_{j=1}^{3} P(s_k|\omega_j)}$$

for $j = 1, 2, 3$ jointly produce a partition on S that is coarser than the finest partition. Assume that this partition is $\{\{s_1, s_2\}, \{s_3, s_4\}, \{s_5\}\} = \rho_{\hat{T}}$. Then $T: S \to \mathfrak{R}$ producing $\rho_{\hat{T}}$ is clearly a minimal sufficient statistic. The identity function *id*: $S \to S$ as $id(s) = s$ produces the partition $\rho = \{\{s\}|s \in S\}$ which is finer than that of T. Yet, T is Blackwell more informative than *id* (of course, *id* is also Blackwell more informative than T). Indeed, (2) of theorem 1.2 shows that there is a least upper bound on the Blackwell order of systems which need not coincide with the identity function, whereas the least upper bound on partition orderings is the finest partition on S (i.e., the singleton partition produced by *id*: $S \to S$).

Green and Stokey [1978] provide a partition *representation*, other than partitions on S, that make a strictly fine partition order in the representation equivalent to the Blackwell informativeness order between η and γ. In my sufficient statistics development, its analog is theorem 1.3, part (2). Which approach (sufficient statistics or partition) one uses, therefore, will depend on the problem at hand. While, in general, the statistical literature demonstrates the power of the concept of sufficient statistics, in some economic situations the partition approach may produce clearer intuition. In the next two sections, however, I shall analyze two well-known multiperson economic decision situations by the sufficient statistics approach because it yields deeper insights into these situations.

Necessary and Sufficient Informational Conditions for Pareto Efficient Risk Sharing in Incomplete Markets

Suppose $(S, \sigma(S))$ is a measurable space of uncertainty in the economy; $X_M: S \rightarrow \mathfrak{R}$ is a "market" *aggregate* "wealth" in one commodity, cash;[13] and $\{1, \ldots, I] = I$ is a group of economic agents whose beliefs on the σ-algebra of events $\sigma(S)$, termed here the *fundamental σ-algebra of events*, are denoted by $P_i, i \in I$.[14] Let U_i denote the ith agent's utility for cash. It is well known (Borch [1962]) that the necessary and sufficient conditions for *unconstrained* Pareto optimal sharing of the market risk X_M by the sharing functions $Z_i: S \rightarrow \mathfrak{R}$ such that $\Sigma_i Z_i = X_M$ are given by the marginal conditions

$$\lambda_i U_i'(Z_i(s))g_i(s) = \lambda_j U_j'(Z_j(s))g_j(s) \tag{1.11}$$

for some positive weights $\lambda_i > 0$, for each i, j in I and $s \in S$.[15] (The functions $g_i(s)$ are appropriate *Radon–Nikodym* (*R–N*) densities associated with P_i on $\sigma(S)$. U_i' denotes the first-order derivative of U_i.)

Two issues arise: (1) What do the sharing functions $Z_i(s)$ look like in general, and (2) what exchange markets in securities admit such Pareto optimal allocations Z_i? Using the development in the preceding section, I provide answers to these two questions in this section.

Brief Literature Survey

The literature on risk sharing has two distinct strands, both tracing their roots to the classic paper by Arrow [1953] (and later amplified by Arrow and Debreu—see Debreu [1959]) on the exchange of risks as commodities in exchange markets. The well-known concepts of *complete markets* and *Arrow–Debreu securities* come from these works.

The first strand (issue 1 above) characterizes the efficient sharing of a *gamble* among a group I of individuals. They may already own portions of the risk (in terms of shares of production plans) and want to redistribute it, or they may be contemplating a totally new risky venture. In either case, the issue is in the form of the Pareto optimal sharing functions Z_i given an information structure on the space of uncertainties. Borch's [1962] paper, the classic in this literature, established powerful first-order necessary and sufficient conditions (equation 1.11) for Pareto optimal risk sharing under *full* information about $s \in S$ [that is, given information $\sigma(S)$]. He also showed (see also Mossin [1973]) that Z_i are linear functions of the form $a_i X_M + b_i$ (where a_i and b_i are constants) *if and only if* the beliefs P_i are *homogeneous and* the *utility functions* are of the *HARA* (hyperbolic absolute risk aversion) class. Wilson [1968] showed that if certain conditions are satisfied, the group behaves as a *syndicate* with a common utility over the gamble and beliefs over S. Amershi and Stoeckenius [1983] have corrected and extended Wilson's results to show that linearity of sharing rules implies syndication but the converse (as originally claimed in Wilson [1968]) does not hold.

The second strand of research (issue 2) examines the efficiency of exchange markets. It is more extensive and I will restrict the survey to those contributions that I find most relevant to the problem studied here.[16] The problem of interest is the structure of the securities market that facilitates the desired type of risk sharing. The classic Arrow–Debreu result showed that if the set of securities "*spans*" the *whole* range of uncertainty $\sigma(S)$—markets are *complete* w.r.t. $\sigma(S)$ [i.e., there is a contingent claims market for each $A \in \sigma(S)$)—then traders can trade through these elementary Arrow–Debreu securities from their endowed position to an unconstrained Pareto optimal risk-sharing arrangement.[17]

It was presumed in the literature that if trading is restricted to linear multiples of a set of securities representing claims to primary assets, full Pareto efficient risk sharing would be impossible unless the securities *span* the linear space of Arrow–Debreu certificates or the utilities are HARA and beliefs are homogeneous. Ross [1976] (see also John [1984]) proposed that trading in securities need not be restricted to the primitive securities, but could be carried out in an augmented market with options based on these securities. Under appropriate conditions, the primitive securities and options could span the space of Arrow–Debreu certificates.

Radner [1968] argued that trading under uncertainty is not necessarily restricted by securities, but by information.[18] He assumed that traders can exchange contingent claims based on any event $B \in \sigma(S)$ *as long as the event B will be observable* to the contracting parties at the time the claims are settled. The implication of this for Pareto efficient risk sharing is immediate. Since the Z_i are measurable with respect to some σ-algebra (besides $\sigma(S)$ of course), as long as events in that σ-algebra are observable, the Z_i can be constructed from trading in contingent claims based on that σ-algebra of events.

This profound insight more or less merged the two questions raised above. If the functional nature of the Z_i can be determined, then the minimal σ-algebra generating these is determined; and if this information structure is observable, a market structure based on that σ-algebra would yield Z_i through trade.

Radner [1968] also showed that no matter what σ-algebra $\mathscr{B}$ is observable, trading restricted to $\mathscr{B}$ will always yield allocations of X_M that are Pareto optimal with respect to $\mathscr{B}$ but not necessarily with respect to some larger σ-algebra $\mathscr{B}'$.[19] It can happen, though, that allocations Pareto optimal w.r.t. $\mathscr{B}$ may also be $\mathscr{B}'$ Pareto optimal even though $\mathscr{B} \subseteq \mathscr{B}'$. Allocations Z_i that are Pareto efficient with respect to the fundamental σ-algebra, $\sigma(S)$, are called fully Pareto efficient (FPE).

Hakansson's ([1977], theorem 4, p. 183) seminal result showed that if S is finite, FPE allocations can be obtained through trading on events revealed by an information system $\eta: S \to Y_\eta$ *if and only if* the partition of η on S is such that the aggregate risk $X_M(s)$ and the probability ratio $P_i(s)/P_j(s)$ of the investors for all i and j remains constant across states in each subset of the partition.[20]

Amershi [1985], extending the work of Hakansson, has identified a particular type of *sufficient statistic* F^* (sufficient with respect to the beliefs P_i on $\sigma(S)$), whose induced σ-algebra $\sigma(F^*)$ includes *both* the σ-algebra $\sigma(X_M)$ of X_M, and the σ-algebra $\sigma(T^*)$ of the minimal sufficient statistic T^* as the minimal information structure on which FPE risk sharing *must* be based. All the previous results on information structures leading to FPE are special cases of this general result.

The purpose here is to provide a proof of this result and other extensions using the development in the preceding section.[21] Recently Feltham [1985] has extended some of these results to include *both production and exchange*, but we shall consider only exchange here.

Necessary and Sufficient Conditions for Full Pareto Efficient Risk Sharing

The basic model consists of a measurable space $(S, \sigma(S))$ that captures the total uncertainty in the economy. There are $i = 1, \ldots, I$ traders in the economy whose respective beliefs on the fundamental σ-algebra of events $\sigma(S)$ are represented by probability measures P_i. There are two dates in the economy $t = 0, 1$ and a set of *primary assets* (or *production plans*) X_k, $k = 1, \ldots, K$, such that $X_k: S \to \mathfrak{R}$ denotes the cash flows at date 1 from the asset.[22] Traders have preferences on date-1 cash flows represented by von Neumann–Morgenstern utility functions $U_i: \mathfrak{R} \to \mathfrak{R}$. All traders are risk averse (i.e., the U_i are concave) and nonsatiable (i.e., $U_i(x_1) > U_i(x_2)$ whenever $x_1 > x_2$). Each trader i has an initial endowment $\bar{\alpha}_{ik} X_k$ of asset k such that $\Sigma_i \bar{\alpha}_{ik} = 1$ for each k. Each trader is an expected utility maximizer of date-1 cash flows.

The problem under investigation here is the nature of the full Pareto-efficient (FPE) risk-sharing *allocations* $Z_i: S \to \mathfrak{R}$, where the $\sigma(S)$ to $\sigma(\mathfrak{R})$ measurable functions Z_i share the total market portfolio X_M so that $\Sigma_i Z_i = X_M = \Sigma_k X_k$.

A set of allocations Z_i, denoted $\{Z_i\}$, will be called a *risk-sharing contract*, and individual components Z_i will be called the ith trader's *trading* (consumption) *allocation*. In this section I suppress consideration of the market mechanisms through which Z_i are constructed. (That will be considered briefly on page 47.)

It should be noted that we are in the framework of arbitrary probability spaces $(S, \sigma(S), P_i)$. For mathematical tractability, I restrict attention to contracts and assets that are elements in the Hilbert space $L^2(S, \sigma(S), P)$ of square integrable random variables w.r.t. the probability measure $P = (\Sigma_i P_i)/I$. (Thus $P(A) = \Sigma_i P_i(A)/I$ for each event $A \in \sigma(S)$.) Observe that P_i are absolutely continuous w.r.t. P (i.e., $P(B) = 0$ implies $P_i(B) = 0$). The choice of P, the *pooled measure*, will become clear as we proceed.

Definition 1.7 (Pareto Order on Risk-Sharing Contracts)

Let $\{Z_i\}$ and $\{Z'_i\}$ be two risk-sharing contracts. Then $\{Z_i\}$ is *Pareto superior* to $\{Z'_i\}$ if

$$E_i(U_i(Z_i)) \geq E_i(U_i(Z'_i)) \qquad \text{for all } i \tag{1.12}$$

with strict inequality holding for *at least one i*. If the inequalities are strict for all i, it is *strictly* Pareto superior. The order generated on the set of contracts as above is called the *Pareto order* on this set.

Definition 1.8 (Pareto Optimal Contract)

A contract $\{Z_i\}$ is Pareto optimal if there does not exist a Pareto superior allocation in the set of contracts *available* for trade.

Economies in which contracts can be traded *without* constraints (i.e., in the entire space of functions $L^2(S, \sigma(S), P)$) are termed *complete*. An economy that is *restricted* to a subset C of contracts in the full set $L^2(S, \sigma(S), P)$ is called *incomplete*. A contract is called *fully Pareto efficient* (FPE) if it is Pareto optimal in a complete economy *even though* it may be generated in an incomplete economy.

The major results in this section show that there are information structures (sub-σ-algebras) $\sigma(F) \subset \sigma(S)$ called MAS σ-algebras such that contracts restricted to choices from the incomplete economy $L^2(S, \sigma(F), P)$ yield FPE. These σ-algebras are produced by information systems $F: S \to Y_F$ whose definition is given next.

Definition 1.9

A public information system $F: S \to Y_F$ is *market aggregating* and *sufficient* (MAS) if $\sigma(X_M) \subseteq \sigma(F)$, and F is a *sufficient statistic* for the family of measures P_i, $i = 1, \ldots, n$ on $\sigma(S)$.

Theorem 1.4

Let F be a MAS public information system in the economy.

(1) For any risk-sharing contract $\{Z_i\}$, there exists another risk-sharing contract $\{Z_i^*\}$ measurable with respect to F constructed as

$$Z_i^* = E(Z_i | F) \qquad \text{almost surely (a.s.)} \tag{1.13}$$

such that $E_i(U_i(Z_i^*)) \geq E_i(U_i(Z_i))$ for every i. (Here E_i is the expectation operator w.r.t. P_i and E is the expectation w.r.t. the *pooled probability* measure P.)

(2) If U_i are *strictly concave*, the inequalities above are strict if Z_i are not $\sigma(F)$ measurable.

Theorem 1.4 shows that a contract cannot be improved with information beyond *any* MAS system. The next question is whether a fully Pareto-optimal (FPE) contract can be based on any other public information system *other than* a MAS system. The answer to this question is no, as will be seen in theorem 1.5. The proof of theorem 1.5 accesses the classic marginal rates result of Borch [1962] and a corollary that falls out directly from it that is of independent interest.

Theorem (Borch [1962])

Let U_i be differentiable. A risk-sharing contract $\{Z_i\}$ is FPE *if and only if* there exist weights $\lambda_i > 0$ such that for each i and j,

$$\lambda_i U_i'(Z_i(s))g_i(s) = \lambda_j U_j'(Z_j(s))g_j(s) \qquad \text{for all } s \in S \tag{1.14}$$

where U_i' is the derivative of U_i w.r.t. its argument and $g_i(s)$ are w.r.t. any σ-finite R–N densities μ dominating P_i.

The next result is the "no-infinite-side-bet" condition that is intuitively well known and falls out immediately from equation 1.14.

Corollary 1.4

If $\{Z_i\}$ is a Pareto optimal contract w.r.t. to any information structure $\mathscr{F}$ then *necessarily*, the $\mathscr{F} \subseteq \sigma(S)$ measures P_i are absolutely continuous w.r.t. to each other. That is, there does not exist an event $B \in \mathscr{F}$ such that $P_j(B) = 0$ and $P_i(B) > 0$ for some $i \neq j$.

Theorem 1.5

Let U_i be differentiable. A Pareto optimal contract $\{Z_i\}$ is FPE *if and only if* the public information system it is based on is a MAS system.

The next result completely characterizes a Pareto efficient contract in terms of the *minimal* and *only* information necessary to generate FPE.

Theorem 1.6 (Complete Characterization of FPE)

Let U_i be differentiable and let $\{Z_i\}$ be any FPE contract. Then:

(1) Z_i is measurable w.r.t. the σ-algebra induced by X_M and $g_1, \ldots, g_I$, namely $\sigma(X_M, g_1, \ldots, g_I)$.
(2) The information system $F^* = (X_M, g_1, \ldots, g_I)\colon S \to \mathfrak{R}^{I+1}$ is the *minimal* MAS on which Z_i can be based (i.e., there does not exist another MAS F such that $\sigma(F) \subset \sigma(F^*)$ by *proper* inclusion).

Hence there exist a measurable $Z_i^*: \mathfrak{R}^{I+1} \to \mathfrak{R}$ such that for each $i = 1, \ldots, I$,

$$Z_i(s) = Z_i^*(X_M(s), g_1(s), \ldots, g_I(s)) \qquad \text{for each } s \in S \tag{1.15}$$

We now derive the Arrow–Debreu, Hakansson [1977], Rubinstein [1975], and Milgrom–Stokey [1982] results as corollaries to the main results.

Corollary 1.5 (Arrow [1953], Debreu [1959])

Let S be finite. A Pareto optimal contract $\{Z_i\}$ based on the *complete information system* $id: S \to S$ such $id(s) = s$ is FPE.

Proof: It is obvious that $id(s)$ is a MAS system. Q.E.D.

Corollary 1.6 (Hakansson [1977], theorem 4, p. 183)

Let S be finite. Let $\{Z_i\}$ be a Pareto optimal contract based on a system $\eta: S \to \mathfrak{R}$. Let $\Pi_{(\eta)} = \{\{s \mid \eta(s) = r\} \mid r \in \mathfrak{R}\}$ be the *partition* induced by η on S. Then $\{Z_i\}$ is FPE *if and only if*

i. $X_M(s) = X_M(s') \forall s, s' \in B, B \in \Pi_{(\eta)}$ (i.e. the aggregate wealth X_M is constant across states in each B in $\Pi_{(\eta)}$).
ii. $P_i(s)/P_j(s) = P_i(s')/P_j(s') \forall s, s' \in B, B \in \Pi_{(\eta)}$ (i.e. the probability ratios are constant across states in each B in $\Pi_{(\eta)}$).

Proof: (i) implies that $\sigma(X_M) \subseteq \sigma(\eta)$; (ii) implies that η is a sufficient statistic for the beliefs P_i. Hence η is a MAS system. The result follows from theorem 1.5. Q.E.D.

The classic Borch [1962] result for homogeneous beliefs falls out as a corollary and is reproduced here for completeness.

Corollary 1.7 (Borch [1962])

If beliefs are homogeneous, an FPE contract $\{Z_i\}$ is a composite function of the market cash flows X_M.

Proof: When P_i are identical, X_M is a MAS system. Q.E.D.

Corollary 1.8 (Rubinstein [1975], Milgrom and Stokey [1982])

Let $S' = S \times Y$ be some extended state space with event σ-algebra $\sigma(S') = \sigma(S \times Y)$ on it. Let the economy be otherwise the same as before except for this modification with P_i' now defined on $\sigma(S \times Y)$. Let U_i be strictly concave. Define projection random variables $\eta_Y: S \times Y \to Y$ as $\eta_Y(s, y) = y$, and $\eta_S: S \times Y \to S$ as $\eta_S(s, y) = s$, for all $(s, y) \in S'$.

i. Suppose the "information" η_Y is *statistical* in that

$$P_i(\eta_Y \in D \mid \eta_S) = P_j(\eta_Y \in D \mid \eta_S) \qquad \text{for all } D \in \sigma(Y), i, j. \tag{1.16}$$

ii. Suppose S is *payoff relevant*; that is, all assets $X_k(\cdot)$ are 1–1 functions of s alone and they do not vary across the y components.

Then for any contract $\{Z_i\}$, there exists a contract based on η_S such that $E_i(U_i(Z_i^*)) \geq E_i(U_i(Z_i))$. Furthermore, if $\{Z_i\}$ depend nontrivially on $y \in Y$, then $\{Z_i^*\}$ is strictly Pareto superior to $\{Z_i\}$.

Proof: The proof follows from theorem 1.5 if we can show that η_S is a MAS system.

From theorem 1.1(3), we see that condition i implies that the information system η_Y is a garbling of η_S. Hence η_S is Blackwell more informative than η_Y and from theorem 1.3 (2), η_S is a sufficient statistic for P_i on S'. Condition ii implies that $\sigma(X_i) \subseteq \sigma(\eta_S)$. Hence η_S is a MAS system as required. Q.E.D.

Notice that the proof of corollary 1.8 shows that *to say η_Y is "statistical" is equivalent to saying η_S is a sufficient statistic.* Also, the assumption of payoff relevance is too strong in general because sharing contingent on $s \in S$ is not necessarily required for FPE as shown in theorem 1.6. It is conceivable that with transactions costs, we would expect trading to take place on the coarser MAS system rather than the payoff-relevant one.

Market Structures Facilitating FPE

A result that combines all the spanning results in the literature on FPE falls out from our results above.

Theorem 1.7

Let E be an economy of traders and assets. If E is an *incomplete economy with constraint C*, then the competitive trading equilibrium contract is FPE under *any* initial endowment and preferences U_i *if and only if C spans the space $L^2(S, \sigma(F^*), P)$* where $\sigma(F^*) = \sigma(X_M, g_1, \ldots, g_I)$, and F^* is the minimal MAS system generated by market portfolio X_M and the densities $g_1, \ldots g_I$ identified in 2 of theorem 1.6.

Theorem 1.7 disregards fluke constraints C which do not span $L^2(S, F^*, P)$ yet achieve FPE. This can happen if the initial endowments are such that the traders trade to a *particular* FPE Z_i^* that is a member of C. Changing the endowments would destroy the FPE nature of C. Theorem 1.7 is, however, an *endowment- and preference-free* result and provides the criterion by which we can create the various FPE-facilitating market structures that have been proposed in the literature, such as the Arrow–Debreu complete-market structures (Debreu [1959]), Hakansson *supershares* (Hakansson [1977]) market, Ross [1976] (John [1984]) *options* market structure, and others. We may also create several new ones but we do not do so here (see Amershi [1985]).[23]

A Numerical Example

Here a numerical example is provided to consolidate the intuition underlying development in the two previous sections. Another example is found in Amershi [1985].

Example 1.3

Consider $S = \{s_1, s_2, s_3, s_4, s_5, s_6\}$ and three primitive assets $X_1(s)$, $X_2(s)$ and $X_3(s)$ where X_1 is a riskless bond. Let $I = 2$. The following tableau lays out the asset and aggregate $X_M(s)$ cash flows.

	s_1	s_2	s_3	s_4	s_5	s_6
X_1	1	1	1	1	1	1
X_2	2	3	9	7	3	3
X_3	3	2	5	7	9	9
X_M	6	6	15	15	13	13

$X_M = X_1 + X_2 + X_3$

Now consider the following four sets of beliefs on $\sigma(S)$ written out in full:

		s_1	s_2	s_3	s_4	s_5	s_6
Set 1	$P_1 =$	[0.2	0.2	0.18	0.12	0.15	0.15]
	$P_2 =$	[0.2	0.2	0.06	0.04	0.25	0.25]
Set 2	$P_1 =$	[0.12	0.08	0.2	0.2	0.2	0.2]
	$P_2 =$	[0.18	0.12	0.1	0.3	0.15	0.15]
Set 3	$P_1 =$	[0.2	0.2	0.2	0.2	0.1	0.1]
	$P_2 =$	[0.1	0.15	0.2	0.25	0.15	0.15]
Set 4	$P_1 =$	[0.2	0.2	0.2	0.2	0.1	0.1]
	$P_2 =$	[0.1	0.15	0.2	0.38	0.12	0.05]

It is assumed that *only the information generated by the asset cash flows is observable by all traders.* Hence, public information systems for contracting or trading can only be constructed from X_1, X_2 and X_3.

First, consider the beliefs P_1 and P_2 in each example set. This is a family of probability measures. Now consider $P = (P_1 + P_2)/2$, the *pooled probability* measure. Thus, $P(s) = (P_1(s) + P_2(s))/2$ for each $s \in S$. This measure is crucial for our purposes and particular attention should be paid to it. Clearly, P dominates P_1 and P_2. The Radon–Nikodym densities of P_1 and P_2 w.r.t. P are the functions g_i: $S \to \mathfrak{R}$ such that $g_i(s) = P_i(s)/P(s)$.

Finally consider two information partitions that are common to all the examples. These are:

(a) $\Gamma(X_M) = \{B_1 = \{s_1, s_2\}, B_2 = \{s_3, s_4\}, B_3 = \{s_5, s_6\}\}$
(b) $\Gamma(X_1, \quad X_2) = \{A_1 = \{s_1\}, \quad A_2 = \{s_2\}, \quad A_3 = \{s_3\}, \quad A_4 = \{s_4\}, A_5 = \{s_5, s_6\}\}$

Partition (b) is termed *payoff relevant.*

Set 1: The economy in this example set is FPE with $\Gamma(X_M)$ because X_M is a MAS system. Furthermore, this is the minimal (theorem 1.6) MAS partition and any partition coarser than this will not work. Also, this example satisfies the requirement for a Hakansson (corollary 1.6) economy. The payoff-relevant partition $\Gamma(X_1, X_2)$ has redundant information for the attainment of FPE contracts. The FPE contracts Z_i will be such that they will not vary across states in the events $B_k \in \Gamma(X_M)$ (i.e., Z_i will be composite functions of X_M).

Set 2: The economy here is *not* FPE with the partition $\Gamma(X_M)$ but it is with the partition $\Gamma_2 = \{C_1 = \{s_1, s_2\}, C_2 = \{s_3\}, C_3 = \{s_4\}, C_4 = \{s_5, s_6\}\}$. Furthermore, Γ_2 is the minimal MAS partition w.r.t. which the economy is FPE. Again here, the FPE contracts will be a function of the C_k's and not the elements in the C_k's. Finally, we can see that the payoff-relevant partition $\Gamma(X_1, X_2)$ has redundant information insofar as FPE is concerned.

Set 3: Here the payoff-relevant partition $\Gamma(X_1, X_2)$ is MAS and all the remarks pertaining to the other partitions in example sets 1 and 2 apply to this partition.

Set 4: There is *no* public information system that is a MAS system because the minimal MAS partition is the finest Arrow–Debreu partition $\Gamma_4 = \{\{s\} | s \in S\}$. Hence the economy *cannot* achieve FPE unless Γ_4 becomes observable.

The Social Value of Information

The spanning result theorem 1.7 enables us to resolve one of the issues in the study of the social value of information (see Amershi [1981] for a fuller treatment). This is: When would an *information system* η: $S \rightarrow Y$ have social value at date $t = 0$? An information system η is defined to have social value if trading at $t = 1$ contingent on the signals generated by η permits the economy to generate contracts that are Pareto superior to the contracts generated without the information (see Ohlson and Buckman [1981] for a survey). This information is used in contingent contracting and, thus, such a system is called *insurance information.* An immediate consequence of theorem 1.7 follows.

Corollary 1.9

Some insurance information system η will have social value in *at least one* economy E under constraint C *if and only if* C does *not* span $L^2(S, \sigma(F^*), P)$ where F^* is the minimal MAS system $\sigma(X_M, g_1, \ldots, g_I)$ as in theorem 1.6.

There are several other issues connected with information value such as the timing of the information release (see Hirshleifer [1971]), the reduction in moral hazard, the generation of spot trading, and the like that we shall not pursue here (see Amershi [1981] for a development).

Comparative Value of Performance Information in Multiperson Agencies Under Moral Hazard

In this section we will apply the informativeness and sufficient statistics results of the section on Blackwell informativeness and statistical sufficiency to the problem of comparing the value of information from performance monitors in agencies. In the foregoing section we compared information that is used *purely* for risk sharing, but in this section we shall consider information that is used for *both* risk sharing and *incentives.*

Introductory Remarks and Brief Literature Survey

Consider the owner (the *principal*) of some productive assets, each of which is managed by a manager (an *agent*). The principal rents out these assets to the agents because they provide some skill, or time, or other productive inputs that he cannot provide. Call these productive inputs "effort." The final output of goods depends on the effort of the agent and some random event θ. Further, the principal cannot observe the effort of the agents nor θ. Everything else (preferences, beliefs, etc.) is *common knowledge* (i.e. known to everybody, and everybody knows everybody knows, etc.). Both principal and agent have *symmetric information* about the uncertainty θ, namely both know the *structure* of the probability space (Ξ, $\sigma(\Xi)$, P) of the various possible *realizations* of θ, but neither observes the realization θ (nor has private information about it). In short, no "adverse selection" problems are present in the setting under consideration here.

This economic scenario is well known in the economics literature and is called an *agency under moral hazard* because the agents may have incentives to shirk, depending on the situation and the compensation that the principal pays them. The situation with one agent has been extensively studied in the literature.[24] The case of agencies with multiple agents is just now beginning to be explored.[25]

There is a major distinction between single- and multiple-agent agencies. If each agent's output is totally independent of any other agent's output, then the situation *obviously* boils down to several single-agent agencies. However, if this is not the case, then after the principal commits himself to a contract, the agents may play the subgame (by collusion or otherwise) in a manner not desired by the principal. Hence, even though a contract is a Nash equilibrium[26] in the whole game, it may not be a Nash equilibrium in the agent's subgame,[27] or it may not be immune to collusion. In view of this, the contract mechanisms must produce stronger more durable equilibria in the agents' subgame.[28] In this paper *I shall ignore these subgame issues* and assume that if a contract is a Nash equilibrium in the whole game, it is also implementable in the agents' subgame.

What I wish to investigate here, having made this simplifying assumption, is the comparative value of different types of *performance information.* By performance information I mean the information that is available to the principal *after* the agents' have supplied their efforts, and the output has occurred. The totality of this performance information could be *just the market value of the output.*[29] Or it could be several additional signals such as revenues, costs, breakdowns of revenues and costs, etc. (see, e.g., Amershi [1984] and Amershi and Hughes [1987]). Typically, the performance information is garnered by an *accounting system.* If there are production interdependencies among the agents, the principal may find it useful to use one agent's data to motivate another agent.

Normally the accounting system does *not* report the *totality of all performance information,*[30] but reports some aggregate of that available information.[31] Both the principal and the agents *only* observe these reports. Thus, the agency contracts can be based only on these reports. Call a reporting system a *performance information system* or a *monitor.*

The problem facing the principal is to determine which performance monitor produces the best contract.[32] Recent research on this problem in the single-agent agency shows that the resolution of the problem relies heavily on the concepts of Blackwell informativeness (see, e.g., Gjesdal [1982]) and sufficient statistics (see, e.g., Holmstrom [1979], [1982]; Amershi [1984], and Amershi and Hughes [1987]). In this section I shall extend two of the main results in the literature to multiperson agencies.[33]

The Model

Let A_i denote the set of productive acts a_i available to the agent $i = 1, \dots, q$. We may assume A_i to be a subset of a *normed space.*[34] Let $A = A_1 \times A_2 \times \cdots \times A_q$, be the joint action set. Cash flow (output) designated by the random variable X taking values in $\mathfrak{R}$, has a parametrized distribution indexed by $a \in A$, denoted $F(x|a)$.[35] Correlated with output are several observables, $s = [y_1, \dots y_n]$, $s \in S$ generated by random variables $Y_1, \dots, Y_n$. I term S the *fundamental sample space of possible performance observations* (signals, realizations of $Y_1, \dots, Y_n$, etc.) *from the agency.*

Each s is a vector that either *includes x, the output, as a component* or *x can be derived from s.*[36] Let $P(s|a)$ denote the probability measure on S generated by $a \in A$. The principal has a class of performance monitors H, which are measurable functions η: $S \to M_\eta$ from S to spaces of *reports* (signals) M_η. The principal can *actually* observe *only* a report from some η he choses. Further, the compensation scheme he designs for the agents can depend *only* on the reports on s from the particular monitor η being used. Denote a compensation scheme for the ith agent by the measurable function Z^i_η: $M_\eta \to \mathfrak{R}$ where $Z^i_\eta(m)$ denotes the compensation of the agent $i = 1, \ldots, q$ given report m. The principal then receives the residual wealth $x - \Sigma_i Z^i_\eta$.

The principal has a von Neumann–Morgenstern utility g: $W \to \mathfrak{R}$ where W is the set of wealths over which it is defined. Agents have von Neumann–Morgenstern utility functions U_i: $W \times A_i \to \mathfrak{R}$, where the dependence on the actions implies the nonpecuniary components in the agent's preference order that lead to shirking.[37]

The principal's design problem is (1) to choose an information monitor η, and (2) to devise a compensation scheme Z^i_η for each agent to induce a Nash equilibrium optimal response a_i by each agent that maximizes his (the principal's) expected utility. Formally, this design (*for a given* η) problem is the optimization problem (a)–(d) below:

$$\underset{\{Z^i_\eta, a_i\}}{\text{maximize}} \quad E(g(X - \Sigma_i Z^i_\eta) | a) \tag{a}$$

$$\text{subject to:} \quad E(U_i(Z^i_\eta, a_i) | a) \geq \bar{U}_i \qquad i = 1, \ldots, q \tag{b}$$

$$a_i \in \arg\max_{\hat{a}_i} E(U_i(Z^i_\eta, \hat{a}_i) | [a/\hat{a}_i]) \qquad i = 1, \ldots, q \tag{c}$$

$$a \in A, \; Z^i_\eta \quad \text{in some function space} \tag{d}$$

$$\text{where } [a/\hat{a}_i] = [a_1, \ldots, a_{i-1}, \hat{a}_i, a_{i+1}, \ldots, a_q]$$

Here $E(\cdot | a)$ represents expectation over S with respect to the measure $P(s | a)$. It is assumed that both principal and agents have homogeneous beliefs.

Line (a) specifies the principal's rational behavior of maximizing his expected utility from the residual $X(s) - \Sigma_i Z^i_\eta(s)$ after paying the agents $Z^i_\eta(s)$. Constraint (b) specifies that the principal must pay each agent enough in Nash equilibrium to work for him rather than go elsewhere where he can earn (expected utility) at least $\bar{U}_i$. Constraint (c) shows that each agent i chooses a best response a_i (hence the "arg max") *given* that the other agents stick to $a_1, \ldots, a_{i-1}, a_{i+1}, \ldots, a_q$. Thus, no agent finds it optimal to deviate from his component of a if all other agents stick to their components, which implies that a is a Nash equilibrium. Specification of the choice spaces of the principal and agents is given in constraint (d).

Definition 1.10

A monitor η is *weakly preferred* to γ if the expected utility of the principal from an optimal contract based on η is *at least as large as* that from γ.

Assumption: Unless otherwise specified, we shall assume that each agent's utility is *separable* as

$$U_i(w, a_i) = u_i(w) - v_i(a_i)$$

where $u_i(w)$ is strictly concave and increasing and v_i is increasing and convex in a_i.[38]

Definition 1.11

A contract (Z^*, a^*), where $Z^* = [Z_1^*, \ldots, Z_q^*]$, and $a^* = [a_1^*, \ldots, a_q^*]$ is termed a *best contract* if it is the *optimal contract* based on the monitor $id(s) = s$.

Observe that a "best" contract is at least as good as *any* other contract. Thus the terminology "best" is well suited to the problem at hand.

The Results

Theorem 1.8

Suppose performance monitor $\eta: S \to M_\eta$ is *Blackwell more informative* than the monitor $\gamma: S \to M_\gamma$ with respect to the family of measures $\{P(s|a)|a \in A\}$. Suppose also *any one* of the following conditions holds:

1. The principal is risk-neutral.
2. The output variable X and the monitor γ are *conditionally independent* given η (i.e., $P(X, \gamma|a, \eta) = P(X|a, \eta) \cdot P(\gamma|a, \eta)$).
3. The output X is $\sigma(\eta)$ measurable (i.e., $X(s) = h(\eta(s))$ for some measurable function $h: M_\eta \to R$).

Then, the principal *weakly prefers* η over γ.

Corollary 1.10

In theorem 1.8, let the principal's utility be *strictly* increasing and the agent be *strictly* risk averse. If the optimal compensation scheme $Z_\gamma = [Z_\gamma^1, \ldots, Z_\gamma^q]$

based on γ is not $\sigma(\eta)$ measurable [i.e., it is not a composite function of $\eta(s)$ at all $s \in S$], then under the conditions of theorem 1.8, the principal *strictly* prefers η over γ.

Corollary 1.11

(1) If the principal is risk-neutral and the agents are strictly risk-averse and all utilities are strictly increasing in wealth, then any best contract (Z^*, a^*) is such that it can be based on any sufficient statistic $T: S \to Y_T$ for the family $\{P(s|a) | a \in A\}$. That is, $Z^*(s) = h(T(s))$ for some $h(\cdot)$ at $s \in S$.

(2) If the principal and the agents are strictly risk-averse with increasing-in-wealth utilities, then any best contract Z^* is necessarily $\sigma(X, T)$ measurable (i.e., $Z^*(s) = K(X(s), T(s))$ for all $s \in S$) where T is any sufficient statistic for the family $\{P(s|a) | a \in A\}$.

Theorem 1.8 generalizes the main weak-informativeness result in Gjesdal ([1982], theorem 3). Corollary 1.11 generalizes the "only if" part of Holmstrom ([1979], proposition 3) and Holmstrom ([1982], theorem 5).

The intuition underlying the results is significant in understanding the economics of performance evaluation information in agencies. If the principal has access to two performance *monitors* (statistics) η and γ based on S, then the *statistical inference properties of* η and γ regarding the action $a \in A$ considered as a parameter for the family of probability measures $P_A = \{f(s|a) | a \in A\}$ are *crucial* in their relative *economic comparison as monitors* in agencies. I would like to pursue this point a bit further here (and in the process explain the intuition underlying the results here and other such results found in Holmstrom ([1979], [1982]), Gjesdal [1982], Amershi [1984], Amershi and Hughes [1987], among others).[39]

Observe first that by specifying an appropriate compensation scheme based on $\gamma: S \to M_\gamma$, the principal can induce, as a Nash response from the agents, any $a \in A$. That is, once a particular statistic γ is chosen, there *always exists* an incentive compensation mechanism $Z_\gamma = [Z_\gamma^1, \ldots, Z_\gamma^q]$ *based on* γ that in equilibrium produces a desired a. Consequently, once $(\gamma, \hat{a})$ are chosen, there is nothing further to infer about $\hat{a}$ from γ *given* the mechanism Z_γ, because $\hat{a}$ is guaranteed to occur. Yet this is *not* the issue in the *comparison of statistics*. To see this, consider another statistic $\eta: S \to M_\eta$, as in theorem 1.8. "η *Blackwell more informative than* γ" is a *statistical statement* about the *statistical inferential* properties of η over γ in the class of probability measures

P_A as shown earlier. It means that η is *better able to distinguish* which $a \in A$ prevails given a data vector $s = [y_1, \ldots, y_n]$ than γ.

It follows, therefore, that since the principal wants to reduce the externalities on his residual wealth position due to shirking, if η is Blackwell more informative than γ, then to induce any $a \in A$ as a Nash equilibrium, it would be better to base the reward structure on η than γ. This is the *main* intuitive content of theorem 1.8, and it is further sharpened by corollaries 1.10 and 1.11.[40]

To summarize, if H is a class of statistics $\eta: S \rightarrow M_\eta$ on which the principal can base equilibrium compensation schemes, then the statistical inference properties possessed by each $\eta \in H$ vis-a-vis the set of probability measures P_A (i.e., w.r.t. the parameter $a \in A$) are of fundamental importance to the principal ex ante in *ordering H* according to the principal's *welfare*. Furthermore, and this again is of critical importance in positive theory (see Hart and Holmstrom [1985]), an ordering on H based *purely on statistical properties* makes it a *powerful economic* construct because the immediate economic environment (the principal's and agent's utilities and disutilities) has no bearing on the ordering.

Notes

1. Blackwell attributes the original result in finite signal spaces and finite parameter sets to Bohnenblust, Shapley and Sherman [1949]. He provides two results. One is a new proof for the Bohnenblust, Shapley and Sherman result (this new proof is presented also in Blackwell and Girschick [1954], p. 328) and the second is a generalization of this to finite parameter sets and infinite signal spaces.

2. "Informativeness" is a statistical issue and occurs in both single-period and multiperiod decision making under uncertainty. I want to clarify the probabilistic and economic content of the issue here.

3. More direct approaches (see e.g., Blackwell and Girschick [1954]) are also possible, but the linkage between a general stochastic control formulation of decision making and the Blackwell theory prove to be useful in applications that involve a sequence of decisions.

4. Multiple-cycle problems are simply chains of single-cycle problems. Other authors use the words "stage" or "period" for cycle.

5. It is well known that under appropriate compactness and continuity restrictions on the objects, there is no need for randomized choices in a Bayesian setting (i.e., when we have a prior measure $P(w)$ on Ω and we wish to make optimal decision-making choices). Standard textbooks on decision theory do this, but the above stochastic control formulation allows us more flexibility as well as easy connections with the theory of games with perfect recall (see Kuhn [1953]) where decision kernels are called behavioral strategies. Following this logic, we may call decision kernels concentrated at single points *pure strategies.*

6. The set of all convex combinations of elements in Λ (see Holmes [1976]).

7. Every Markov matrix defines a Markov kernel and every Markov kernel on finite spaces is a Markov matrix. The rows of a Markov matrix, therefore, sum to 1.

8. The formulation here is not as Blackwell [1953] stated it. His result is stronger because he proves the equivalence between the Bohnenblust–Shapley–Sherman criterion of sufficiency and his informativeness concept. However, the formulation as presented here is the more useful for applications to information economics, as I shall show in this paper.

9. The Bayes value is attained by integrating the vector $b(P_\eta, \delta^*)$ with respect to $P(w)$ on Ω for an optimal choice function δ^* based on η.

10. The usual factorization-of-densities definition for sufficient statistics is not really a definition but a theorem due to Halmos and Savage [1949], as will be shown momentarily.

11. Instead of a probability measure we can have *any* σ-finite measure μ. Both are equivalent as one implies the other (see Schmetterer [1976], p. 186).

12. This is simply the usual probability density (e.g. normal, exponential, etc.) when μ is the Lebesgue measure on $\mathfrak{R}^n$.

13. Although I shall use an economy with one commodity—cash, most of the results here would go through with appropriate modifications with multiple commodities. Second, the market aggregate wealth is the *total amount* of *net production* from productive actions (taken prior to the exchange) *plus* the *total* amount of endowments in the economy. It should be noted that for *different* productive acts, the market aggregate wealth X_M would be different. I do not allow the agents to make the productive decisions endogenously; they are exogenously specified. This avoids problems of unanimity, etc. that are not our concern here.

14. It is important to note here that I consider this to be the σ-algebra corresponding to the *most detailed description of the uncertain events in the economy*. No further description produces a σ algebra strictly larger than $\sigma(S)$. The reason why I mention this here is that there is a lot of confusion as to what is meant by "complete" markets, and all of this can be traced to a lack of understanding about completeness with respect to $\sigma(S)$ versus completeness with respect to some *sub-σ-algebra* $\mathscr{F} \subseteq \sigma(S)$ (probably induced by an information system $\eta: S \to Y_n$).

15. Unconstrained means that every event in the σ-algebra $\sigma(S)$ is observable. *Identical* Borch first-order conditions would hold if I were to take a sub-σ-algebra (information structure) $\mathscr{F} \subseteq \sigma(S)$, and restrict the P_i to $\mathscr{F}$ if X_M is $(\mathscr{F}, \mathscr{B}(\mathfrak{R}))$ measurable. In this case, the Borch first-order conditions would look identical to equation 1.11 except that Z_i, λ_i may be different, and, in particular, the Radon–Nikodym densities g_i would now be with respect to P_i over $\mathscr{F}$ and *not* P_i over $\sigma(S)$.

16. Apologies are tendered to the authors of the many excellent surveys and works in this literature not cited here.

17. In the original treatments by Arrow and Debreu, S was *finite*, or the σ-algebra $\sigma(S)$ was finite (possibly generated by a finite partition $\rho(S)$ of "payoff relevant" sets in S). In this case, it was convenient (if $\# S$ or $\# \rho(S)$ was n) to lay out the elementary Arrow-Debreu securities in the form of a security *tableau* (i.e., a matrix) with n rows and n columns, each row corresponding to some $s \in S$ (or $A \in \rho(S)$), with \$1 paid in the sth column and 0's elsewhere.

It is obvious that given these elementary Arrow-Debreu certificates, one can create any contingent claim certificate for any $B \in \sigma(S)$. This in turn implied unconstrained Pareto optimal risk sharing. It should be noted also that each trader's initial endowment, as well as X_M (and individual production plans), were assumed to be $\sigma(S)$ measurable. Hence no information asymmetries were allowed.

In current treatments (see, e.g., Radner [1968], [1972] and [1974], Kreps [1979] , Amershi [1981], [1985]) one talks about contingent claims w.r.t. σ-algebras and not partitions etc. One major reason is that in the partition approach, spanning considerations and linear algebra swamp the more fundamental informational issues. Hence, here I shall take the σ-algebra-information structure approach, and explain the spanning results from this perspective.

18. Of course, exogenous institutional restrictions may prevent trading in some securities that

are tradeable without these restrictions. This causes an *institutional* incompleteness in the securities market. Such institutional restrictions can also be placed on the Ross [1976] options market and, therefore, the effects of institutional restrictions are best resolved after understanding the nature of the restrictions, which are often political in nature.

Our interest lies in the effects of *endogenous* restrictions on the formation of markets due to a lack of information, but on which no institutional restrictions are placed. As Stiglitz ([1981], p. 236) has observed, it is somewhat schizophrenic to assume some form of institutional incompleteness in the markets and then consider the value of additional information whose effect is to augment the set of tradeable securities.

19. There is a great deal of semantic confusion regarding the phrase "complete markets." As originally coined and used by Arrow and Debreu, it meant that the security markets had enough securities to trade in contingent claims based on the *fundamental* σ-algebra, $\sigma(S)$. Radner [1968] somewhat generalized the terminology and defined completeness *with respect to a given information structure* $\mathscr{B} \subseteq \sigma(S)$. Thus, if it is known prior to trade that *at most* only $\mathscr{B}$ will be *mutually* observable to consummate exchange contracts, then there is no point in talking about completeness with respect to $\sigma(S)$. In this case, the original probability spaces $(S, \sigma(S), P_i)$ should be replaced by $(S, \mathscr{B}, P_i)$ where P_i is now the original P_i on $\sigma^i(S)$ restricted to $\mathscr{B}$.

However, this change is only cosmetic. If the traders decide before trade that $\sigma(S)$ is the most complete description of the uncertainty, yet due to some reasons, only a proper subalgebra $\mathscr{B} \subset \sigma(S)$ would be *mutually* observable, then for analyzing the trading economy, one should *at first* restrict attention to contingent claims based on $\mathscr{B}$. And in this generalized sense, if the set of securities span the contingent claims based on $\mathscr{B}$, the market could be called "complete."

Yet if $\sigma(S)$ was really the fundamental uncertainty, and suppose the information structure expanded (due to additional production or informational activities) from $\mathscr{B}$ to $\sigma(S)$, then it is possible that the original Pareto optimal allocations w.r.t. $\mathscr{B}$ could be dominated by new Pareto optimal allocations w.r.t. $\mathscr{B}$ plus additional information. This point is somewhat subtle, and it causes unnecessary confusion to call a market structure complete if it is complete w.r.t. $\mathscr{B}$ but not necessarily $\sigma(S)$.

In view of this, I shall retain the original Arrow–Debreu concept of completeness as that pertaining to $\sigma(S)$, and the latter Radner concept of completeness as *$\mathscr{B}$-completeness* to emphasize completeness w.r.t. $\mathscr{B}$ but not necessarily w.r.t. some larger $\mathscr{B}'$!

20. Special cases of this result were independently derived by Milgrom and Stokey [1982] ("statistical information") and Rubinstein [1975] ("no spot trading"). This will become clear when we unify all these results here.

21. These proofs and extensions are not provided in Amershi [1985]. The reason we provide them here is to show the power of the sufficient-statistic approach to information-structure comparisons initiated earlier.

22. All the results here extend to multiperiod economies if the utilities are *time additive* (see Amershi [1981] for details).

23. As explained in Amershi [1985], as long as unlimited short-selling is allowed, *individual endowments need not* be $\sigma(F^*)$ measurable. However, if short-selling is restricted, then it is necessary (as shown by Hakansson [1977]) for there to be a "superfund" (a mutual fund) that facilitates the trading from initial endowments to FPE allocations in C.

24. See, for example, Ross [1973], Mirrlees ([1975], [1976]). Harris and Raviv [1979], Holmstrom [1979], and Grossman and Hart [1983]. Baiman [1982] provides a nice survey.

25. See, for example, Holmstrom [1982], Myerson [1982], Mookherjee [1984], and Amershi and Cheng [1987].

26. For game theoretic terminology and concepts the reader is referred to van Damme [1983].

27. This means it may not be *subgame perfect or sequentially rational* (see Selten [1975] or van Damme [1983]).

28. Amershi and Cheng [1987] discuss the "*implementability*" of contract mechanisms in more detail. See, also, Ma [1987].

29. This is the case which has been most studied in the literature.

30. For example, the primary information of an accounting system would be the journal entries in an evaluation period, and these could be in the tens of thousands, even for a medium-sized firm.

31. Examples of these reports are the familiar "income statement," the "statement of financial position," etc.

32. The problem arises because the cost of using one monitor differs from the cost of using another. Obviously there is no problem if all monitors have identical costs, but this is clearly not the case in reality. However, in the literature and here, the cost of the monitors is not explicitly included in the model.

33. The results extend the *weak* informativeness results of Blackwell more informative monitors (Gjesdal [1982]) and sufficient statistics (Holmstrom [1979], [1982]). The issue of strict informativeness is beyond the scope of this paper and has been dealt with in detail elsewhere (Amershi and Hughes [1987]).

34. In the literature, A is usually taken to be an interval of $\mathfrak{R}$ (i.e., a is a scalar). Unfortunately, this invites a rather narrow interpretation of a as labor. However, in general, a is simply the totality of all inputs supplied by the agent, and thus the more general interpretation of "effort" a is the description of a *production plan*. Since such a description need not be a scalar, a general normed space (which could be a set of functions) is the more appropriate object for our purposes.

35. When $i = 1$, and $A = A_1 \subseteq \mathfrak{R}$, it is assumed in the literature that $F(x|a_2) \geq F(x|a_1)$ with strict inequality for some x on a set of positive measure whenever $a_1 > a_2$. That is, the distributions on X indexed by a obey *first-order stochastic dominance*. Here, since A_i is in a normed space, we may not have an order on A_i (unless we start out with an ordered space). Since we do not need stochastic dominance in the results here, we do not assume it.

36. The vector s could be infinite-dimensional. This does not cause any problems as long as S is a Polish space.

37. The action a_i represents "effort" and $U_i(w, a_i)$ captures the effect of effort a_i at wealth w for the agent.

38. This assumption is standard in the literature and relaxing it would usher in problems of randomization over a (see Gjesdal [1982]) that I want to avoid.

39. This point is important because there are essentially two main aspects in the study of agency contracts: (a) the comparative statics of different contracts *given* a performance evaluation monitor; and (b) the comparative statics of different performance evaluation monitors based on S. It is the latter area that is studied here and in the literature cited. Researchers pursuing purely line (a) *often* tend to lose sight of the critical importance of the underlying statistic on which compensation is based. On the other hand, as the literature cited shows, line (b) is *inextricably linked* to the *statistical inference properties of the monitors*, because now the issue facing the principal is the choice of the information system itself. This dichotomy corresponds well with single-person decision theory and information economics developed in earlier sections of this paper.

40. While this main intuition is now clear (and this is enough for corollaries 1.10 and 1.11), the special parts of theorem 1.8 need a bit more elaboration. Part (1) simply capitalizes on the fact that when the principal is risk-neutral, knowledge about the cash flows (output) x is unimportant in contracting, and comparisons between η and γ rely *purely* on their distinctive inferential

properties in providing incentives. Parts (2) and (3) make statements about x because now the principal is risk-averse, and the principal wants to *both* share the risks of x and provide incentives. Thus knowledge of x is valuable. Part (3) is obvious because it says that if x can be derived from knowledge of η, then η can act as both a risk-sharing and an incentive information system, and thus welfare comparison between η and γ can be based solely on the statistical Blackwell informativeness of η over γ. Part (2) essentially says that once the principal knows that η is Blackwell more informative than γ, then he can tilt in favor of η if, *given* η and a, there are no statistical dependencies between γ and x. The reason is that if there were such dependencies, then even though the statistical inferential properties of η are better than those γ regarding $a \in A$ (hence for incentive purposes η "dominates" γ), these advantages may be offset by the "*insurance*" information in γ about x used in risk sharing.

APPENDIX 1A: *Some Essential Probability and Statistical Theory*

This appendix summarizes some essential probability and statistical theory used in this chapter. Most researchers who have had a sustained training in probability theory and statistics (for example, courses that cover most of Ash [1972] or Burrill [1972] *and* Schmetterer [1976]) will be familiar with the material here. This appendix is, therefore, *primarily* intended for social scientists who do mathematical modeling but whose training in probability and statistical theory is limited.

Some Elementary Concepts and Results

Basic Set Theory

A *set* Ω is any collection of objects ω with a well-defined property. For example $\Omega = \{\omega | \omega$ is the number of dots on the face of a die$\} \equiv \{\omega | \omega = 1, 2, 3, 4, 5, 6\} \equiv \{1, 2, 3, 4, 5, 6\}$. This example shows that there are various ways one can write out the *same* set of objects. Another example: $\Omega = \{\omega | \omega$ is a real number less than 2 but greater than or equal to $1\} \equiv$

$\{\omega|\omega\in\mathfrak{R}$ and $1\leq\omega<2\}$. If ω belongs to a set Ω, it is called an *element* of the set, written $\omega\in\Omega$. The *empty set* is denoted $\varnothing$. A *subset* B of a set Ω (denoted $B\subseteq\Omega$) is a well-defined set contained in Ω. Examples: $B=\{1,2,3\}\subseteq\Omega=\{1,2,3,4,5,6\}$; $B=\{\omega|\omega\in\mathfrak{R},\ 1<\omega<2\}\subseteq\Omega=\{\omega|\omega\in\mathfrak{R},\ 1\leq\omega<2\}$. For *any* set Ω, it is always true that $\varnothing\subseteq\Omega$, and $\Omega\subseteq\Omega$. A subset B is called *proper* if $B\subseteq\Omega$ but $B\neq\Omega$ (a proper subset is often denoted $B\subset\Omega$).

A *countable* set Ω has either a *finite* number of elements or its elements can be put into a one-to-one correspondence with the positive integers $\mathcal{N}=\{1,2,3,\ldots,n,\ldots\}$. In the later case it is called *countably infinite.* An uncountable set is always infinite, and we shall encounter uncountable sets whose cardinality (i.e., "size") is equal to the *continuum* of real numbers $\{r|r\in\mathfrak{R},0\leq r\leq 1\}$. Hence, an uncountable set will be called a continuum in this paper whenever the terminology enhances intuition.

An *indexing set* (or simply *index*) I is a set whose elements are used to index the elements of another set. Example: $I=\{1,2\}$ and $\Omega=\{\omega|\omega=$ side s of a two-sided coin$\}\equiv\{\omega|\omega=s_i,\ i\in I\}\equiv\{h,t\}$. Often, one can replace Ω by I. Also, a trivial index of Ω is Ω itself.

I shall assume that the concepts of a *union* and *intersection* of two sets A and B are known. If Ω is a set, and $B\subseteq\Omega$ is a subset, then the *complement of* B *in* Ω is denoted by $B^c_\Omega=\{\omega\in\Omega|\omega\notin B]$. If the *universe of discourse* Ω is well specified and understood, I shall drop the subscript Ω in B and write $B^c=\{\omega|\notin B\}=$ *complement of* B. It is known that $(B^c)^c=B$.

A *class of subsets* $\mathscr{C}$ *of a set* Ω is a collection of subsets of Ω which obey a particular property. Examples: (i) $\Omega=\{1,2,3,4,5,6\}$, $\mathscr{C}=\{B|B\subseteq\Omega,\ B$ is made up of two even numbers$\}\equiv\{B_1=\{2,4\},\ B_2=\{2,6\},\ B_3=\{4,6\}\}$; (ii) $\Omega=\{r|r\in\mathfrak{R},\ 1\leq r\leq 2\}$, and $\mathscr{C}=\{B|B\subseteq\Omega$, it is an open interval, and its *length* is $\frac{1}{2}\}\equiv\{B|B=(r_1,r_2)$, such that $r_2-r_1=\frac{1}{2}\}$.

De Morgan's laws state: Let $\mathscr{C}$ be a class of subsets of a set Ω indexed by I. Then

(1) $\{\cup\{B_i|i\in I\}\}^c\equiv\{\cup B_i\}^c=\cap B_i^c$

(2) $\{\cap B_i|i\in I\}\}^c=\cup B_i^c.$

Cartesian Products, Relations, and Functions

Let A and B be two sets. Then the *Cartesian product* of A and B is defined as the set

$$A\times B\equiv\{(a,b)|a\in A,\ b\in B\}$$

Observe that the set $A\times B$ contains the *ordered* tuples (a,b) with $a\in A$ and

$b \in B$. Hence it cannot contain (b, a) if $b \notin A$ or $a \notin B$, because the ordering would be changed. Let $\mathscr{C}$ be a class of sets indexed by I. Then the product of sets $A_i \in \mathscr{C}$ is defined as the *I-product*

$$\underset{i \in I}{\times} A \equiv \prod_{i \in I} A_i = \{(a_i)_{i \in I} | a_i \in A_i, i \in I\}$$

where $(a_i)_{i \in I}$ denotes an *ordered vector* of elements with the *i*th *component* equal to a_i. The vector is called *finite-dimensional* if I is finite, otherwise it is called *infinite-dimensional.*

Any subset of the product set $A \times B$ is called a *binary relation.* (By analogy *ternary*, and I-nary relations can also be defined.)

A *function* (or *mapping*) from *A into B* (*or A to B*) denoted by $f: A \to B$ is a binary relation in $A \times B$ such that: (i) *every* element in A is associated with *some* element in B under the relation; and (ii) the association is *single-valued*; that is, *only one* element in B can be associated with an element in A under f. Consequently, an easier way to visualize a function is as a *rule* that *assigns* a *unique* element in B to each element in A. The set A on which f is defined (or operates) is called the *domain* and the set B is called the *codomain* of f. Any element $a \in A$ is called an *argument* (or *variable*) of f and the element $b \in B$ to which a is assigned under f (i.e., $f(a) = b$) is called the *image or value of a under f*. The set $f(A) = \{b | \text{there exists } a \in A \text{ such that } f(a) = b\}$ is called the *image* (*set*) or *range* of f (in B).

Examples

i. $A = \{1, 2, 3, 4, 5, 6\}$, $B = \{1, \ldots, n, \ldots\} = \mathscr{N}$. $f(1) = 3$, $f(2) = 1$, $f(3) = 100$, $f(4) = 100$, $f(5) = 100$, and $f(6) = 3$ is a function $f: A \to B = \mathscr{N}$ with range $f(A) = \{1, 3, 100\} \subseteq \mathscr{N}$.
ii. Same A, B as in (i), but $f(1) = 1^2$, $f(2) = 2^2 = 4$, $f(3) = 9$, $f(4) = 16$, $f(5) = 25$, $f(6) = 36$ is also a function $f: A \to B$ which can also be described by $f(a) = a^2 \; \forall \, a \in A$. The statement $f(3) = 9$ should be read as "the value of f in the argument 3 is 9."

Remarks: Often there is a lack of appreciation for the set-theoretic conceptualization of functions described above. Functions such as $f: \mathfrak{R} \to \mathfrak{R}$ with $f(x) = x^2$ are readily grasped. Typically these functions are visualized by their *graphs*; and for intuitive purposes, these graphs are very often confused with the functions f themselves. However, conceptualization of discrete-valued functions of the type in example (i) above is found to be difficult because the graph is now only a set of points.

In particular, this confusion about functions is the main reason why many social scientists with limited mathematical training fail to recognize that a random variable is merely a function defined on a probability space as a domain. This, in turn, produces a poor grasp of results and techniques in information economics. Similarly, this confusion makes it difficult to appreciate the fact that a function such as that in example (i) above can be *continuous*; that is, continuity of functions has nothing to do with whether one can "draw the graph without lifting the pencil"—it is a *topological* and not a *graphical* concept. Consequently, a weak understanding of the *implicit-function theorem*, which is the foundation of all marginal analysis in economics, obtains.

In view of this, I would like to emphasize to the reader that what I have covered here is just the rudiments of the topic, and one must "play" with several examples for a full appreciation of a function as an assignment rule between two sets. Further, it is essential to have this mathematical intuition to appreciate the material in this chapter.

Let $f\colon A \to B$ be a function. For each $b \in f(A)$, by definition there exists an $a \in A$ such that $f(a) = b$, where a is called *a preimage* of b. It is important to note that b can have several preimages in A. We are thus led to the concept of the *inverse correspondence* $f^{-1}\colon B \to A$ associated with any function. This is defined as follows: $f^{-1}(b) = \{a \in A \mid f(a) = b\}$ for each $b \in B$.

Observe that $f^{-1}(b)$ need not be a *singleton* subset of A. Hence, the correspondence f^{-1} is a mapping from B to $\mathscr{P}(A)$, the *power set* of A, namely the *set of all subsets* of A. That is, $f^{-1}\colon B \to \mathscr{P}(A)$. In particular, for any subset $D \subseteq B$, $f^{-1}(D) = \{a \in A \mid f(a) \in D\}$ is called the *inverse* (or *pre-*) *image* of D in A.

If $f\colon A \to B$ is a function from A into B, then f is called an *onto* function if $f(A) = B$; that is, the range of f is the whole of B. This is also equivalent to saying that $f^{-1}(b) \neq \varnothing$ for any $b \in B$.

A function $f\colon A \to B$ is called a *one-to-one* (1–1) function (or correspondence) if $f^{-1}(b)$ is a *singleton* set for each $b \in f(B)$. In this case, one can define a function, also denoted f^{-1}, as $f^{-1}\colon f(A) \to A$ such that $f^{-1}(b) = a$, where a is the single preimage of b assigned to b under f.

A function $f\colon A \to B$ that is *both* 1–1 and onto is called an *invertible* function, and it possesses a *unique inverse function*, denoted also by $f^{-1}\colon B \to A$, such that if $f(a) = b$ for some $a \in A$ and $b \in B$, then $f^{-1}(b) = a$. It is obvious that if $f\colon A \to B$ is 1–1, then $f\colon A \to f(A)$ is invertible.

Let $f\colon A \to B$ be a function, and $g\colon B \to C$ be another function. Then, the *composite function* (or *composition*) $h \equiv g \circ f$ such that h: $A \to C$ is defined as $h(a) = g(f(a))$ for all $a \in A$. One can define larger *chains* of composition in an identical manner.

Remarks: Composition of functions is another area where some confusion prevails. I mention this here because the concepts of minimal sufficient statistics and conditional probability found in this paper rely heavily on a proper understanding of the concept of composition.

Remark on Function Notation: As defined above, a function *f from A into* (*or to*) *B* is a rule that assigns to each $a \in A$ a *unique* image in B. In the mathematics literature, a function is written as f. In the social sciences literature, for *intuitive purposes*, one often encounters the notation $f(\cdot)$ or $f(a)$, where a is a *generic* element of A, to describe function f: $A \to B$. The notation $f(\cdot)$, is technically correct, but cumbersome. However, I shall often use it to emphasize the fact that it is the function *f as a whole* that is under discussion and not its value $f(\hat{a})$, at some $\hat{a} \in A$. The second notation $f(a)$ for f is, however, *technically incorrect* because $f(a)$ also denotes the *value* of $a \in A$ under f. Nevertheless, it is usually clear from the context that it is the function f that is under discussion and not the value $f(a)$, even though $f(a)$ is used. I shall also use this notation when it is necessary to emphasize that the domain of the function f is A.

Partitions, Algebras, and Sigma-Algebras

A class $\mathscr{C}$ of subsets of a set Ω is called a *partition* of Ω if for any $A \in \mathscr{C}$ and $B \in \mathscr{C}$, $A \cap B = \varnothing$ and $\cup\{A \mid A \in \mathscr{C}\} = \Omega$. Partition $\mathscr{C}_1$ is (*strictly*) *finer than* partition $\mathscr{C}_2$ (written $\mathscr{C}_1 > \mathscr{C}_2$) if for each $A \in \mathscr{C}_1$ there is a $B \in \mathscr{C}_2$ such that $A \subset B$ (notice that the inclusion is *proper*). $\mathscr{C}_1$ is called at *least as fine* as $\mathscr{C}_2$ (written $\mathscr{C}_1 \geq \mathscr{C}_2$) if for each $A \in \mathscr{C}$ there is a $B \in \mathscr{C}_1$ such that $A \subseteq B$. If $\mathscr{C}_1$ is finer than $\mathscr{C}_2$, then we may call $\mathscr{C}_2$ *coarser* than $\mathscr{C}_1$ (written $\mathscr{C}_2 < \mathscr{C}_1$). If $\mathscr{C}_1$ is at least as fine as $\mathscr{C}_2$, then we may call $\mathscr{C}_2$ *at least as coarse* as $\mathscr{C}_1$ (written $\mathscr{C}_2 \leq \mathscr{C}_1$).

The importance of partitions in the economics of information is primarily due to the following frequently used result.

Theorem

1. *Every* function f: $A \to B$ induces a partition $P(f)$ on A defined as $P(f) = \{f^{-1}(b) \mid b \in f(A)\} = \{f^{-1}(b) \mid b \in B\}$

2. With *every* partition $\mathscr{C}$ on A, one can associate a function $f_{\mathscr{C}}: A \to I$, where I is the index set for $\mathscr{C}$, such that $P(f_{\mathscr{C}}) = \mathscr{C}$.
3. Let $f: A \to B$ and $g: B \to C$ be two functions. Then $P(h) \equiv P(g \circ f) \leq P(f)$, where $h = g \circ f$ is the composition of f and g.
4. Let $\mathscr{C}_1$ be a partition with index I_1 on A, and $\mathscr{C}_2$ be another partition with index I_2. If $\mathscr{C}_2$ is at least as coarse as $\mathscr{C}_1$, then there exists a function $h: I_1 \to I_2$ such that $f_{\mathscr{C}_2} = h \circ f_{\mathscr{C}_1}$.

Proof: Trivial.

The above theorem shows that there is a one-to-one correspondence between partitions on a set A and functions defined on A. Hence, when one talks about partitions in information economics, one is implicitly talking about the associated function.

A class of subsets $\mathscr{C}$ of Ω forms an *algebra* (*field*) of subsets *in* (or *of*) Ω if:

i. $\mathscr{C}$ is *closed* with respect to complementation; that is, for each $A \in \mathscr{C}$, $A^c \in \mathscr{C}$.
ii. $\mathscr{C}$ is *closed* with respect *finite* unions; that is, if $A_1, \ldots, A_n$ is a finite collection of subsets of $\mathscr{C}$, then

$$\bigcup_{i=1}^{n} A_i \in \mathscr{C}$$

iii. $\Omega \in \mathscr{C}$.

Definition (σ-algebra)

A class $\mathscr{F}$ of subsets of a set Ω forms a *σ-algebra*, (*σ-field*, *Borel-algebra*, *Borel-field*) in (of) Ω if

i. $\mathscr{F}$ is an algebra.
ii. $\mathscr{F}$ is *closed* with respect to *countable* unions; that is, if $\{A_n | n = 1, 2, \ldots\}$ is a countable collection of sets in $\mathscr{C}$, then

$$\bigcup_{n=1}^{\infty} A_n \in \mathscr{F}$$

Lemma

1. If $\mathscr{F}$ is an algebra, then $\varnothing \in \mathscr{F}$.
2. If $\mathscr{F}$ is an algebra (σ-algebra) then it is closed w.r.t. finite (countable) *intersections* of elements in $\mathscr{F}$.

3. There always exist at least two algebras (σ-algebras) in every set Ω, called the *trivial* algebras (σ-algebras):
   (a) $\mathscr{F} = \{\varnothing, \Omega\}$
   (b) $\mathscr{P}(\Omega) =$ power set of Ω

Proof:

1. As $\Omega \in \mathscr{F}$, $\Omega^c = \varnothing \in \mathscr{F}$ by definition.
2. Trivial from De Morgan's laws and closure with respect to unions.
3. Trivial. Q.E.D.

Definition (Minimal σ-algebras)

Let $\mathscr{C}$ be a *nonempty* class of subsets of Ω. A σ-algebra, denoted usually by $\mathscr{F}(\mathscr{C})$, is called *the minimal σ-algebra generated by* (*or containing*) $\mathscr{C}$ (and it *always exists*) if for each σ-algebra $\mathscr{F}$ that contains $\mathscr{C}$, $\mathscr{F}(\mathscr{C}) \subseteq \mathscr{F}$.

Theorem (Minimal σ-algebras)

Let $\mathscr{C}$ be a class of subsets of Ω.

1. Let Ψ denote the class of all σ-algebras that contain $\mathscr{C}$ (this class always has at least one member, namely the power set $\mathscr{P}(\Omega)$). Then

$$\mathscr{F}(\mathscr{C}) = \cap \{\mathscr{F} \mid \mathscr{F} \in \Psi\}$$

2. Let $\mathscr{C}$ be a countable partition of Ω. Let $D \subseteq \Omega$ be such that D is a *countable union* of elements in $\mathscr{C}$. Let Λ be the set of *all* such countable unions. Then the minimal σ-algebra generated by $\mathscr{C}$ is

$$\mathscr{F}(\mathscr{C}) = \Lambda \cup \{\varnothing, \Omega\}$$

3. Let $f\colon \Omega \to V$ be a function, and let $\sigma(V)$ be a σ-algebra on V. Then f and $\sigma(V)$ induce a σ-algebra $\sigma(f, \sigma(V))$ on Ω as follows:

$$\sigma(f, \sigma(V)) = \{A \subseteq \Omega \mid A = f^{-1}(B),\ B \in p(V)\}$$

   This is called the *induced σ-algebra* in Ω of f and $\sigma(V)$. Whenever $\sigma(V)$ is understood or unimportant in a discussion, the notation $\sigma(f, \sigma(V))$ is shortened to $\sigma(f)$.
4. Let $\mathscr{C}_1$ and $\mathscr{C}_2$ be partitions of Ω.
   (a) $\mathscr{F}(\mathscr{C}_2) \subseteq \mathscr{F}(\mathscr{C}_1)$ *if* $\mathscr{C}_2 < \mathscr{C}_1$
   (b) $\mathscr{F}(\mathscr{C}_2) \subseteq \mathscr{F}(\mathscr{C}_1)$ *if and only if* $\mathscr{C}_2 \leq \mathscr{C}_1$

If Ω is a set and $\mathscr{T}$ is a *topology* defined on it (i.e., $(\Omega, \mathscr{T})$ is a *topological space*) then the minimal σ-algebra $\mathscr{F}(\mathscr{T})$ generated by $\mathscr{T}$ is called the *σ-algebra of Borel sets*, and $(\Omega, \mathscr{T}, \mathscr{F}(\mathscr{T}))$ is called a *Borel space.*

Elements of Probability Theory

Any tuple $(\Omega, \mathscr{F})$ is called a *measurable space* if Ω is a nonempty set and $\mathscr{F}$ is *any* σ-algebra defined on it. If $\mathscr{F}$ is fixed for a particular discussion and known, then we may call Ω a measurable space, with reference to $\mathscr{F}$ *implicit* rather than *explicit*.

Let $(\Omega, \mathscr{F})$ and $(\Lambda, \mathscr{B})$ be two measurable spaces. A function $f\colon \Omega \to \Lambda$ is called *measurable* (w.r.t. the *system* $(\mathscr{F}, \mathscr{B})$) if the induced σ-algebra of $\mathscr{B}$ under f is such that $\sigma(f, \mathscr{B}) \subseteq \mathscr{F}$. That is, $f^{-1}(B) \in \mathscr{F}$ for all $B \in \mathscr{B}$.

Remark: This is all there is to a measurable function. There is no mystery in it, and no measure (such as Lebesgue measure) or anything else is needed in its definition. All the definition says is that the preimage under f of a *measurable subset* $B \in \mathscr{B}$ is *also measurable* in Ω under $\mathscr{F}$. That is, a measurable function *preserves* measurability. Observe that the measurability of a function *critically* depends on the underlying σ-algebra. It is easy to show that a function measurable with respect to one system $(\mathscr{F}, \mathscr{B})$ of σ-algebras, *need not* be measurable w.r.t. another system.

Lemma

1. Let Ω and Λ be any two nonempty sets. Then *any constant* function $k\colon \Omega \to \Lambda$ [i.e., a function such that $k(\omega) = \lambda_0$ for some fixed $\lambda_0 \in \Lambda$] is *always* measurable w.r.t. to *any* system of σ-algebras $(\mathscr{F}, \mathscr{B})$ of Ω and Λ such that $\{\lambda_0\} \in \mathscr{B}$.
2. Let $(\Omega, \mathscr{F})$ and $(\Lambda, \mathscr{B})$ be any two measurable spaces. A function $f\colon \Omega \to \Lambda$ is a *measurable constant function if and only if* $\sigma(f) = \{\Omega, \varnothing\}$.
3. Let $(\Omega, \mathscr{F})$ be a measurable space. Then the *identity* function $id\colon \Omega \to \Omega$ [i.e. $id(\omega) = \omega$] is always measurable w.r.t to *any* σ-algebra $\mathscr{F}$ on Ω.

Proof: Exercise.

Let $(\Omega_1, \mathscr{F}_1), \ldots, (\Omega_n, \mathscr{F}_n)$ be n measurable spaces. Let $\Omega = \Omega_1 \times \cdots \times \Omega_n$ be the product set. The *product σ-algebra* defined on Ω, denoted by

$\sigma(\mathscr{F}_1 \times \cdots \times \mathscr{F}_n)$, is the *minimal σ-algebra* in Ω that contains the class of product sets $\mathscr{F}_1 \times \cdots \times \mathscr{F}_n = \{A_1 \times \cdots \times A_n | A_i \in \mathscr{F}_i, \ i = 1, \ldots, n\}$. Each $A_1 \times \cdots \times A_n$ is called a *measurable cylinder* w.r.t to the product σ-algebra $\sigma(\mathscr{F}_1 \times \cdots \times \mathscr{F}_n)$. Whenever Ω is the product of spaces as above, and is called a *product* (measurable) *space*, then it is understood that reference about measurability issues will be with respect to the product σ-algebra.

> *Remark*: Product spaces can also be defined for infinite collections of measurable spaces, but I shall not do so here. Interested readers may look up Neveu [1965]. The basic idea is more or less the same as above.

A *measure* μ on a measurable space $(\Omega, \mathscr{F})$ is a *non-negative* mapping $\mu: \mathscr{F} \to \mathfrak{R}^+$ such that:

(a) $\mu(A) \geq 0$ for all $A \in \mathscr{F}$.
(b) $\mu(\hat{A}) < \infty$ for at least one $\hat{A} \in \mathscr{F}$.
(c) If $\{A_n | n = 1, 2, \ldots\}$ is a *countable* collection of *disjoint* sets then

$$\mu\left(\bigcup_{n=1}^{\infty} A_n\right) = \sum_{n=1}^{\infty} \mu(A_n) \qquad \textit{(countable additivity)}$$

The triple $(\Omega, \mathscr{F}, \mu)$ is called a *measure space.* If $\mu(\Omega) < \infty$, then the measure is called a *finite measure.* If there exists a *countable* collection of measurable subsets $\{A_n | n = 1, 2, \ldots\}$ such that $\mu(A_n) < \infty$ for all $n = 1, 2, \ldots$, and

$$\mu\left(\bigcup_{n=1}^{\infty} A_n\right) = \mu(\Omega)$$

then μ is called a *σ-finite* measure. It is obvious that a finite measure is a σ-finite measure. It is also obvious that $\mu(\varnothing) = 0$ (prove it from the definition).

A *signed measure* γ on a measurable space $(\Omega, \mathscr{F})$ is a *real-valued* mapping $\gamma: \mathscr{F} \to \mathfrak{R}$ for which there exist two measures $\gamma^+: \mathscr{F} \to \mathfrak{R}$ and $\gamma^-: \mathscr{F} \to \mathfrak{R}$ such that $\gamma(A) = \gamma^+(A) - \gamma^-(A)$ for all $A \in \mathscr{F}$.

A *probability space* $(\Omega, \mathscr{F}, P)$ is a measure space with measure $P: \mathscr{F} \to [0, 1] \subseteq \mathfrak{R}$ such that $P(\Omega) = 1$. The elements of $\mathscr{F}$ are then called *events* and $P(A)$ is called the *probability (likelihood) of the event* $A \in \mathscr{F}$. Ω is called the set of *uncertainty* (*uncertainties*), and each $\omega \in \Omega$ is called an *elementary event* even though $\{\omega\}$ need not belong to $\mathscr{F}$ (i.e., it need not be an event). Ω is called the *sure event* (it always "occurs") and ∅ is called the *impossible event*. An event $A \in \mathscr{F}$ such that $P(A) = 0$ is called a *null* event.

Remarks: (a) For technical reasons (see Ash [1972]), it is often the case (especially when Ω is uncountably infinite as in the case $\Omega = \mathfrak{R}$) that there may be subsets of Ω which are *not* events (i.e., they need not belong to $\mathscr{F}$ on which the probability measure P is defined). One must, therefore, be careful when talking about the probability of a "*subset*" $A \subseteq \Omega$, because without verifying that $A \in \mathscr{F}$, the statement is vacuous. It should also be clear that if $\mathscr{F}_1$ and $\mathscr{F}_2$ are two σ-algebras on Ω, and $\mathscr{F}_2 \nsubseteq \mathscr{F}_1$, then a probability measure defined on $\mathscr{F}_1$ *need not* be a probability measure defined on $\mathscr{F}_2$. Thus members of $\mathscr{F}_2$ need not be events w.r.t P. On the other hand, if $\mathscr{F}_2 \subseteq \mathscr{F}_1$, and if P is a probability measure defined on $\mathscr{F}_1$, then P *restricted to* $\mathscr{F}_2$ is also a probability measure, and $(\Omega, \mathscr{F}_2, P)$ is *also* a probability space.

(b) Statisticians often call $(\Omega, \mathscr{F}, P)$ a *sample space.*

(c) A probability space is the essential object required to model random phenomena of any kind. Models of random phenomena in which the probability spaces are not properly defined are either nonsensical models, or open to misinterpretation.

Let $(\Omega, \mathscr{F}, P)$ be a probability space, and $(\Lambda, \mathscr{B})$ be a measurable space. An $(\mathscr{F}, \mathscr{B})$ measurable function $X: \Omega \to \Lambda$ is called a *random variable.*

Remarks: *Note carefully* that a random variable is *first and foremost* a function from Ω to Λ. It, therefore, *retains* any functional properties it has. The "randomness" in the random variable X comes from the fact that a probability measure exists on $\mathscr{F}$, and by measurability of X, one can define the likelihood of particular values of X as the next result shows.

Proposition

Every random variable $X: \Omega \to \Lambda$ *induces* a probability measure on $\mathscr{B}$ as $P_x(B) = P(X^{-1}(B))$ for all $B \in \mathscr{B}$.

As a consequence, one can talk about the "probability of occurrence" of an event $B \in \mathscr{B}$. Put another way we can determine the likelihood of the event that X takes values in a particular $B \in \mathscr{B}$.

Remarks: (a) Many models of random phenomena in the social science literature contain phrases like "let $\tilde{x}$ be a random variable." Such phrases may hide errors in modeling, or they create confusion because there is no clear idea as to what the underlying probability space is on which $\tilde{x}$ is a random variable. To be sure, the underlying probability space is sometimes obvious. Yet my experience shows that often these spaces are not obvious, and the reader must spend time disentangling what random variable is acting on which probability space.

(b) Many mathematical authors reserve the terminology "random variable" to the case when $\Lambda = \mathfrak{R}$. Here, I shall not do so, though it is often useful to distinguish real-valued random variables from other kinds (Ash [1972] calls the latter *random objects*).

Let $(\Omega, \mathscr{F}, P)$ be a probability space and let $(\Lambda, \mathscr{B})$ be a measurable space. If $\Lambda = \Lambda_1 \times \cdots \times \Lambda_n$, and $\mathscr{B} = \sigma(\mathscr{B}_1 \times \cdots \times \mathscr{B}_n)$ where $(\Lambda_i, \mathscr{B}_i)$ are measurable spaces, then it is often convenient (and necessary) to call a random variable $X: \Omega \to \Lambda$ a *random vector* and denote it by the *column vector* notation $X = [X_1, \ldots, X_n]^T$, where $X_i(\omega)$ is the ith component of $X(\omega)$, $i = 1, \ldots, n$, for each $\omega \in \Omega$. (The superscript T denotes *transpose*, meaning the transposition of a row vector into a column vector.) The next result shows that this terminology is justified.

Proposition

Let $(\Omega, \mathscr{F}, P)$, $(\Lambda, \mathscr{B})$, $(\Lambda_i, \mathscr{B}_i)$, $i = 1, \ldots, n$, be as above. A function $X: \Omega \to \Lambda$ is a *random vector* $X = [X_1, \ldots, X_n]^T$ *if and only if* each $X_i: \Omega \to \Lambda_i$ is a random variable.

Proof: Exercise.

Let $X: \Omega \to \mathfrak{R}$ be a random variable from some probability space $(\Omega, \mathscr{F}, P)$ to the real Borel space $(\mathfrak{R}, \mathscr{B}(\mathfrak{R}))$. Since X induces a probability measure $P_x(\mathscr{B})$ on $\mathscr{B}(\mathfrak{R})$ via P, it also induces a *probability distribution* function defined by $F_x: \mathfrak{R} \to \mathfrak{R}$ as

$$F_x(r) = P_x(X \in (-\infty, r])$$

for all $r \in \mathfrak{R}$. ($P_x(X \in (-\infty, r])$ is also conveniently written as $P(X \leq r)$).

Observe that F_x is a real-valued function, continuous from the right (as the measure P is "continuous from the right" (see Burrill [1972]) in a measure-theoretic sense). Several well-known properties of probability distributions are extensively discussed in all elementary probability texts, and I shall not do so here.

In an analogous manner, we may define a distribution of a vector $X: \Omega \to \mathfrak{R}^n$ as the function: $F_x: \mathfrak{R}^n \to \mathfrak{R}$:

$$F_x(r) = P_x(X \in (-\infty, r])$$

where $r = [r_1, \ldots, r_n]^T \in \mathfrak{R}^n$ is any arbitrary point vector, and,

$$(-\infty, r] = (-\infty, r_1] \times (-\infty, r_2] \times \cdots \times (-\infty, r_n]$$

Remark: The main advantage of distribution is that it translates working with probability measures to working with real-valued functions F_x. Neveu [1965] claims there is no advantage to this and it causes conceptual confusion. Other probabilists disagree (see Feller [1966]). For our purposes, this debate is irrelevant.

It is well known (see Ash [1972], Burrill [1972]) that if one can define a function

$$F: \mathfrak{R} \to \mathfrak{R} \qquad (\text{or} \quad F: \mathfrak{R}^n \to \mathfrak{R})$$

that has the properties of a probability distribution, then one can derive a probability measure P_F associated with it on the Borel sets $\mathscr{B}(\mathfrak{R})$.

The interesting property of P_F is that if we take $(\mathfrak{R}, \mathscr{B}(\mathfrak{R}), P_F)$ as the probability space and define the *identity* random variable

$$id: \mathfrak{R} \to \mathfrak{R} \qquad (\text{or} \quad id: \mathfrak{R}^n \to \mathfrak{R}^n)$$

as $id(r) = r$, then the distribution of id on $\mathfrak{R}$ (or $\mathfrak{R}^n$)

$$F_{id(r)} \equiv F$$

It is for this reason that in several models one encounters statements like "let F be a distribution on $\mathfrak{R}$." Implicit in all these statements is the canonical probability structure explained above.

The expectation of an integrable real-valued function $h(x)$ of a random variable X with respect to a probability measure P on a probability space $(\Omega, \mathscr{F}, P)$, namely

$$E(h(X)) = \int_{\Omega} h(X)\,dP$$

can be replaced by

$$\sum_i h(x_i)P(x_i)$$

if X is a discrete-valued (finite or countably infinite) variable taking values $\{x_1, x_2, \ldots\}$ or by

$$\int_{\mathfrak{R}^m} h(x)f(x)dx = \int_{x_m} \int_{x_{m-1}} \cdots \int_{x_1} h(x)f(x)dx_1 \ldots dx_m$$

if X is a "continuous" (technically "absolutely continuous") random vector whose probability distribution $F(x) = P(X \leq x)$ has a density $f(x)$ with respect to Lebesgue measure on $\mathfrak{R}^m$ (see the following section for the meaning of "density").

Some Necessary Advanced Concepts

For technical reasons (see Ash [1972]) I shall assume all spaces to be complete, separable metric spaces (i.e., Polish spaces) with some σ-algebra defined on them (i.e., they are *measurable*). The minimal σ-algebra that includes the metric topology in such spaces may be called the *σ-algebra of Borel sets.*

Most measure-theoretic results and concepts in probability have elementary counterparts in finite probability spaces $\Omega = \{\omega_1, \ldots, \omega_n\}$ with the set of *all subsets* as the σ-algebra $\mathscr{F}$, and a probability measure P on $\mathscr{F}$ generated by the *mass function* $p(\omega) = P(\{\omega\})$, $\omega \in \Omega$. There is one concept and a result depending on it that is absolutely crucial to the development of the theory of conditional probability expectation in arbitrary probability spaces. These are the concept of *absolute continuity* of measures and the *Radon–Nikodym theorem* (see Ash [1972] or Burrill [1972]). I shall state these here and provide intuitive interpretations.

Absolute Continuity of Measures

Let μ and ν be two measures (one or both could also be probability measures or ν could be a measure and μ a signed measure) on the σ-algebra $\mathscr{F}$ of a measurable space $(\Omega, \mathscr{F})$. If $\nu(A) = 0 \Rightarrow \mu(A) = 0$ for any such $A \in \mathscr{F}$, then μ is said to be *absolutely continuous w.r.t.* ν on $\mathscr{F}$ (or ν is said to *dominate* μ on $\mathscr{F}$).

Example 1

Let $\Omega = \{\omega_1, \omega_2, \omega_3, \omega_4\}$ and $\mathscr{F}$ = set of all subsets of Ω. Let $\mu = P$ be a probability measure such that $P(\omega_1) = 0.75$, $P(\omega_2) = 0.25$, $P(\omega_3) = 0$, and $P(\omega_4) = 0$. Let ν be a measure on F such that $\nu(\omega_1) = 1$, $\nu(\omega_2) = 2$, $\nu(\omega_3) = 3$, and $\nu(\omega_4) = 0$. (Observe that ν is not a probability measure). Then μ is absolutely continuous w.r.t. ν.

The Radon–Nikodym Theorem

Let $(\Omega, \mathscr{F})$ be a measurable space. Then a signed measure μ is absolutely continuous w.r.t. a measure v *if and only if* there is a real-valued $\mathscr{F}$-measurable function $g: \Omega \to \mathfrak{R}$ such that

$$\mu(A) = \int_A g(\omega) dv \qquad \text{for all} \quad A \in \mathscr{F}$$

The function g is termed a (*Radon–Nikodym*) *density* (or *derivative*) of μ w.r.t. v. Further, if another function $h: \Omega \to \mathfrak{R}$ is such that $h(w) = g(w)$ except on a set $A \in \mathscr{F}$ with $v(A) = 0$, then h is also a *version* of the Radon–Nikodym density g.

Example 2

The well-known standard probability densities such as the exponential, normal, gamma, etc. are the Radon–Nikodym densities of their respective probability measures w.r.t. the Lebesgue measure on the Borel sets in $\mathfrak{R}$ (or $\mathfrak{R}^n$).

Example 3

Consider the situation of example 1. This is a discrete space case. For any subset $A \subseteq \Omega$,

$$P(A) = \sum_{\substack{\omega \in A \\ v(\omega) \neq 0}} \frac{P(\omega)}{v(\omega)} v(\omega)$$

Then

$$g(\omega) = \begin{cases} P(\omega)/v(\omega) & v(\omega) \neq 0 \\ 0 & \text{elsewhere} \end{cases}$$

is a Radon–Nikodym density of μ w.r.t. v.

Often, in continuous cases, the phrase "probability density" is used, but technically it means the "Radon–Nikodym" density.

Conditional Probability Measures and Expectations

Let $(\Omega, \mathscr{F}, P)$ be a probability space. Let $A \in \mathscr{F}$ be an event with probability $P(A) > 0$. Suppose $(\Omega, \mathscr{F}, P)$ is the model of some random phenomenon. Then if we are told that A has occurred, it means that the random phenomenon has transpired in such a way that it is possible to state categorically that event A prevails. For example, let $\Omega = \{1, 2, 3, 4, 5, 6\}$ be the model of a roll of one die with 6 faces. Then, $\mathscr{F}$ = set of all subsets of Ω, and P on $\mathscr{F}$ is derived from a probability mass function $p(\omega) = P(\{\omega\}) = \frac{1}{6}$ for all $\omega \in \Omega$.

Consider the event $A = \{1, 2, 3\}$. The random phenomenon occurs in such a way that it is possible to answer yes or no to the question" has A occurred?" Thus, when the die is rolled and an observer observes 2, he announces "A has occurred."

Now, if there is a decision maker who relies on the announcements of the observer, then he knows for sure only that $A = \{1, 2, 3\}$ has occurred, but he is not sure whether it was a 1 or 2 or 3. However, given the *information* that A has occurred, the *sure event* is now not only Ω, but also A. That is, there is a *reduction* in his uncertainty on Ω which can be reflected in a *posterior* (or *conditional*) *probability measure* on Ω that is *concentrated* on A (i.e., $P(A^c) = 0$). Hence it is possible to define the conditional probability measure on $\mathscr{F}$

$$P(\cdot|A): \mathscr{F} \to [0, 1]$$

such that

$$P(B|A) = \frac{P(B \cap A)}{P(A)} \qquad \forall B \in \mathscr{F}$$

The probability space $(\Omega, \mathscr{F}, P(\cdot|A))$ is called the *probability space given the event A*. Now consider the σ-algebra of events $\mathscr{F}_A = \{B \cap A | B \in \mathscr{F})$. This is just the σ-algebra $\mathscr{F}$ *restricted* to A. Then clearly $(A, \mathscr{F}_A, P(\cdot|A))$ is also a probability space, and it is *isomorphic* to $(\Omega, \mathscr{F}, P(\cdot|A))$ up to a null set. Hence, we may consider either probability space as representing the information that A has occurred. The choice is determined by convenience.

The elementary concept of conditional probability measures runs into trouble when $P(A) = 0$, because then $P(\cdot|A)$ as defined above is vacuous. For example, if $\tilde{x}$ is a normally distributed random variable, and $\tilde{y}$ is another variable correlated with $\tilde{x}$, we cannot compute the conditional probability measure of the event $B = \{\omega | \tilde{y} \in [1, 2]\}$ given the event $\tilde{x} = 3$. That is, $P(\cdot|\tilde{x} = 3)$ cannot be defined using the elementary approach above.

Since these situations are more the rule than the exception, another, more sophisticated, method is needed to generate conditional probability measures given some information. It is in the construction of such measures that the Radon–Nikodym theorem is indispensable.

I shall not go through the details of this construction here (see Ash [1972] for an excellent exposition). However, briefly, the procedure is as follows. Instead of defining conditioning given an event A, a more general conditioning *σ-algebra* approach is adopted. That is, *information* is defined in terms of *σ-algebra*. For example, if $(\Omega, \mathscr{F}, P)$ is the basic probability space, *any* sub-σ-algebra $\mathscr{D} \subseteq \mathscr{F}$ is called an *information structure* on Ω. (The terminology arises primarily due to the fact that often such information structures are the induced σ-algebras of random variables—which can be considered as *information* or *signalling* devices—defined on Ω.)

Step 1: Let $(\Omega, \mathscr{F}, P)$ be the basic probability space. Let $\mathscr{D} \subseteq \mathscr{F}$ be an information structure. For each $B \in \mathscr{F}$ let χ_B be the indicator random variable of B. Let $\tilde{X} : \Omega \to \mathfrak{R}$ be a real-valued random variable (with respect to $\mathscr{F}$ and $\mathscr{B}(\mathfrak{R})$, the σ-algebra of Borel sets on $\mathfrak{R}$) with a finite expectation (i.e., $E(\tilde{X}) < \infty$). For each $B \in \mathscr{D}$, the expectation of $\tilde{X}$ over B is also defined and is equal to

$$E(\tilde{X} \mid B) \equiv E[\chi_B \cdot \tilde{X}] \equiv \int \chi_B \cdot \tilde{X}\, dP \equiv \int_B \tilde{X}\, dP$$

Then $E(\tilde{X} \mid \cdot): \mathscr{D} \to \mathfrak{R}$ defines a signed measure on $\mathscr{D}$ which is absolutely continuous w.r.t. the probability measure P on $\mathscr{D}$. Hence by the Radon–Nikodym theorem, there exists a real valued $(\mathscr{D}, \mathscr{B}(\mathfrak{R}))$ measurable function $g: \Omega \to \mathfrak{R}$ such that

$$E(\tilde{X} \mid B) = \int_B \tilde{X}\, dP = \int_B g\, dP \quad \forall\, B \in \mathscr{D}$$

This function g is denoted by $E(\tilde{X} \mid \mathscr{D})$ and is called the *conditional expectation of* $\tilde{X}$ *given the information* $\mathscr{D}$. This function is *not* unique, but is unique *almost everywhere*. That is, there is an *equivalence class* $[E(\tilde{X} \mid \mathscr{D})]$ which *represents* the conditional expectation, but whose members differ from each other only on events $B_0 \in \mathscr{D}$ where $P(B_0) = 0$. Each representation is called a *version* of $E(X \mid \mathscr{D})$. That is, if $E^1(X \mid \mathscr{D})$ and $E^2(X \mid \mathscr{D})$ are both representations of $E(X \mid \mathscr{D})$, then $E^1(x \mid \mathscr{D})(\omega) = E^2(x \mid \mathscr{D})(\omega)$, for all $\omega \in \Omega$ except for $\omega \in B_0$ such that $P(B_0) = 0$.

Step 2: The *conditional probability function* on $\mathscr{F}$ given information structure $\mathscr{D} \subseteq \mathscr{F}$ is defined as follows:

For each $A \in \mathscr{F}$, let χ_A be the indicator random variable of A. Then the *conditional probability of A given $\mathscr{D}$* is defined as

$$P(A|\mathscr{D}) \equiv E(\chi_A|\mathscr{D})$$

Recall again that this is not unique and there is a whole class of functions which are versions of $P(A|\mathscr{D})$, but which differ from each other as random variables on $(\Omega, \mathscr{D}, P)$ to $[0, 1] \subseteq \mathfrak{R}$ only on events B_0 in $\mathscr{D}$ of *measure zero* [i.e., $P(B_0) = 0$].

Consider now a class of conditional probability functions $\{P(A|\mathscr{D})|A \in \mathscr{F}\}$. Each such class can be represented by a function

$$P(\cdot|\mathscr{D}): \mathscr{F} \times \Omega \to [0, 1]$$

such that for each fixed $\omega \in \Omega$,

$$P(\cdot|\mathscr{D})(\omega): \mathscr{F} \to [0, 1]$$

is a function from $\mathscr{F}$ to [0, 1] giving the "conditional probabilities" of events $A \in \mathscr{F}$ given ω. For each fixed $A \in \mathscr{F}$,

$$P(A|\mathscr{D}): \Omega \to [0, 1]$$

is a $(\mathscr{D}, \mathscr{B}(\mathfrak{R}))$ measurable function from $(\Omega, \mathscr{D})$ (note $\mathscr{D}$ *NOT* $\mathscr{F}$) to $(\mathfrak{R}, \mathscr{B}(\mathfrak{R}))$.

In general, for any arbitrary probability space, for any fixed $\omega \in \Omega$, the function $P(\cdot|\mathscr{D}): \mathscr{F} \to [0, 1]$ defined above *need not* be a probability measure *almost everywhere* w.r.t. $\mathscr{D}$ in Ω. There could exist a non-null event $\underline{B} \in \mathscr{D}$ such that $P(\cdot|\mathscr{D})(\omega): \mathscr{F} \to [0, 1]$ are *not* probability measures on $\mathscr{F}$ for each $\omega \in \underline{B}$. However, whenever $P(\cdot|\mathscr{D}): \mathscr{F} \times \Omega \to [0, 1]$ is a probability measure on $\mathscr{F}$ for *every* fixed $\omega \in \Omega$, then it is called a *kernel* (*or regular conditional probability meausre*) on $\mathscr{F}$ *given the information* $\mathscr{D}$. (Other terminology employed in the mathematics literature is *transition function* (Neveu [1965]) and *stochastic transformation* (Blackwell [1953]).)

If a kernel exists given the information $\mathscr{D}$, then the conditional expectation $E(\tilde{X}|\mathscr{D})$ of any random variable $\tilde{X}$ is an expectation in the usual sense w.r.t. the kernel. That is,

$$E(\tilde{X}|\mathscr{D}) = \int_{\Omega} \tilde{X}\, dP(\cdot|\mathscr{D})$$

Remarks: (a) The conditional expectation function $E(\tilde{X}|\mathscr{D})$ is a *random variable* defined *on* Ω, measurable w.r.t. $\mathscr{D}$ (i.e., $\sigma(E(\tilde{X}|\mathscr{D})) \subseteq \mathscr{D}$). This is the most general definition of conditional expectation. It makes the intuitive notion of conditional expectation technically correct, but the intuition remains.

(b) When $\mathscr{D}$ is the induced σ-algebra of some other random object $\tilde{Y}: \Omega \to \Lambda$, where $(\Lambda, \mathscr{B})$ is another measurable space (i.e., $\mathscr{D} = \sigma(\tilde{Y})$), then it is customary to write $E(\tilde{X} \mid \tilde{Y})$ instead of $E(\tilde{X} \mid \sigma(\tilde{Y}))$. For this case we have two possibilities for defining conditional expectation (see Ash [1972]):

i. the *general definition* $E(\tilde{X} \mid \tilde{Y})$ as above; or
ii. the *point definition* $E(\tilde{X} \mid \tilde{Y} = y)$ [or $E(\tilde{X} \mid y)$, $y \in \Lambda$].

I shall not dwell on this; details can be found in Ash [1972]. Intuitively, we may interpret $E(\tilde{X} \mid \tilde{Y} = y)$ as the "*conditional expectation of $\tilde{X}$ given $\tilde{Y} = y$.*" In this case $E(\tilde{X} \mid y)$ is a random variable defined on $(\Lambda, \mathscr{B})$ to $(\mathfrak{R}, \mathscr{B}(\mathfrak{R}))$ as

$$E(\tilde{X} \mid \cdot): \Lambda \to \mathfrak{R}$$

The relationship between $E(\tilde{X} \mid \tilde{Y})$ and $E(\tilde{X} \mid y)$ is one of *composition*, as

$$E(\tilde{X} \mid \tilde{Y}) = E(\tilde{X} \mid \cdot) \circ \tilde{Y}$$

(c) $P(\tilde{X} \mid \tilde{Y} = y)$, $(P(\tilde{X} \mid y))$ are defined by indicator functions as before.

(d) Most of the properties of $E(\tilde{X} \mid \mathscr{D})$ or $(E(\tilde{X} \mid y)$ etc.) are identical to those of the standard expectation. For example, $E(\tilde{X} + \tilde{Z} \mid \tilde{Y}) = E(\tilde{X} \mid \tilde{Y}) + E(\tilde{Z} \mid \tilde{Y})$ (*almost everywhere*). I shall not list these properties here. However, there is one powerful property (see Loeve [1971]), called the *smoothing property* that I will now explain.

Consider the *sub σ-algebras* $\mathscr{D}_1$ and $\mathscr{D}_2$ of $\mathscr{F}$. Suppose $\mathscr{D}_1 \subseteq \mathscr{D}_2$. Then

$$E(E(\tilde{X} \mid \mathscr{D}_1) \mid \mathscr{D}_2) = E(E(\tilde{X} \mid \mathscr{D}_2) \mid \mathscr{D}_1) = E(\tilde{X} \mid \mathscr{D}_1)$$

That is, *under repeated conditioning* the *smaller* σ-algebra prevails.

(e) Kernels may not exist in general. However, whenever the probability spaces are also Polish spaces, a fundamentally important result by Doob [1953] shows that kernels *always* exist. These are called the (*Doob*) *kernels*.

Return now to the general development of conditioning.

Definition

Let $(X, \mathscr{F})$ and $(Y, \mathscr{B})$ be arbitrary measurable spaces. Then a function

$$Q(\cdot \mid \cdot): \mathscr{B} \times X \to [0, 1]$$

is called a (*probability*) *kernel* from X to Y if, for *each* $B \in \mathscr{B}$, $Q(B \mid \cdot)$ is a measurable function from X to $[0, 1]$ and for *each* $x \in X$, $Q(\cdot \mid x)$ is a probability measure on $\mathscr{B}$.

Interpret $Q(B|x)$ intuitively as the probability of entering the set B at stage 2 given that $x \in X$ obtains at stage 1. Also, in order to emphasize the conditioning and conditioned variables, I shall abuse notation and write $Q(y|x)$ for the kernel rather than $Q(\cdot|\cdot)$. It is well known from Tulcea's theorem (see Neveu [1965]) that if P is a probability measure on X, then P combined with a kernel Q produces a unique product probability measure on $\sigma(X \times Y)$. I denote this by PQ which is defined by (Hahn extension—see Burrill [1972])

$$PQ(B_1 \times B_2) = \int_{B_1} Q(B_2|x)\,dP$$

for all $B_1 \times B_2$ in $\sigma(X \times Y)$. If $Q(z|x, y)$ is a kernel from $X \times Y$ to Z and $P(y|x)$ is a kernel from X to Y, then for each $x \in X$, $P(\cdot|x)Q(\cdot|x, y)$ defines a kernel from X to $Y \times Z$. For any measure μ on X, μPQ defines a product measure on $\sigma(X \times Y \times Z)$. Extensions to countable number of spaces also hold. *Note* also that we may *interpret* (and I do so in this chapter) the kernel $P(s|\omega)$ as a *family of measures* $\{P(\cdot|\omega)|\omega \in \Omega\}$ on a measurable space S.

The next result is fundamentally important.

Theorem (Doob [1953])

Let $(X, \mathscr{F}, P)$ be a probability space, and let $(Y, \mathscr{B})$ and $(Z, \mathscr{D})$ be measurable spaces such that Z is a Polish space. Let $h: X \to Y$, $g: X \to Z$ be random variables. Then there exists a kernel $Q(z|y)$ from Y to Z such that $Q(\cdot|\cdot)$ is a version of the conditional probability function $P(g = z|h = y)$.

Finally we have the definition of a Markov kernel.

Definition

A kernel $Q(x_{n+1}|x_1, \ldots, x_n)$ from $X_1 \times \cdots \times X_n$ to X_{n+1} is called a *Markov kernel* if for a fixed x_n, $B \in \mathscr{F}_{n+1}$ (the σ-algebra on X_{n+1}), the function is independent functionally of the variables $[x_1, \ldots, x_{n-1}]$. That is,

$$Q(x_{n+1}|x_1, \ldots, x_n) = Q(x_{n+1}|x_n) \qquad \text{for all} \quad x_1, \ldots, x_{n+1}$$

Remarks: The Markov kernel defined above is called a *one-stage* (one-level-*memory*) Markov kernel. By obvious modification, we can define a k-level-memory Markov kernel for $k \leq n$.

APPENDIX 1B: *PROOFS OF RESULTS*

Proof of the General Blackwell Informativeness Result (Theorem 1.1)

Definition

$B(\Omega, \mathfrak{R})$ denotes the (Banach) space of *bounded real functions* $\theta: \Omega \to \mathfrak{R}$ with the *sup norm* $\|\theta\| = \sup\{|\theta(\omega)| \,|\, \omega \in \Omega\} < \infty$ where $|\ |$ is the modulus (absolute value) of a real number.

Every number $r \in \mathfrak{R}$ is embedded in $B(\Omega, \mathfrak{R})$ through the constant functions $\theta_r(w) = r$ for all $\omega \in \Omega$.

Definition (Blackwell Decision Structure)

A Blackwell decision problem given a fixed Ω is specified by a set $\Lambda - \{\theta(\cdot, a) | a \in A\}$ of elements in $B(\Omega, \mathfrak{R})$ indexed by a Borel set $A \subseteq \mathfrak{R}^n$ called the actions, and the convex hull $C(\Lambda)$ of Λ.

The above definition provides a generalization to arbitrary parameter spaces of the Blackwell development (see the sufficient statistics section). The next lemma is essential to the proof of the general theorem and is of independent interest. It formalizes the intuition that expectation is essentially a convex combination, and, thus, it should lie in the convex hull of objects being "expected" out. We need "vector" integration in the proof (see Lang [1969]).

Lemma

Let Y_η be a signal space associated with a system η. Let Q be a probability measure on $\sigma(Y_\eta)$. Then for any Borel measurable function

$$f\colon Y_\eta \to C(\Lambda)$$

into a closed convex set $C(\Lambda)$, the vector expectation $E(f|Q) = \int_{Y_\eta} f\,dQ$ (if it exists) is an element of $C(\Lambda)$.

Proof: Let $L = B(\Omega, \mathfrak{R})$. By integrability, $E(f|Q) \in L$. If (a) or (b) below are true, then the result is true.

(a) f is almost surely (a.s.) constant with respect to (w.r.t.) Q.
(b) f is not *a.s.* constant w.r.t. Q, and $E(f|Q) \in C(\Lambda)$.

Suppose now neither (a) nor (b) holds. We will show that this leads to a contradiction. Since $x_0 = E(f|Q) \notin C(\Lambda)$ and since $\{x_0\}$ is compact and $C(\Lambda)$ is closed, by a consequence the Hahn–Banach theorem (see Holmes [1976]), there exists a strictly separating linear functional $\lambda\colon L \to \mathfrak{R}$ such that $\lambda(x_0) < \alpha$ and $\lambda(f(y)) > \alpha$ for some number α. But this implies that $E[\lambda(f(y))|Q] > \alpha$ (otherwise it would imply that $\lambda(f(y)) = \alpha$ almost surely, which is false) and $\lambda(x_0) < \alpha$. Since λ is a linear functional, $E[\lambda(f(y))|Q] = \lambda[E(f(y)|Q)]$ (see Lang [1969] p. 245) which is a contradiction, and so (a) or (b) must be true. Q.E.D.

For any measurable function $\delta\colon Y_\eta \to C(\Lambda)$, let $\delta(y|\omega)$ denote the value of the ωth component of the function (considered as a vector) $\delta(y)$ in $C(\Lambda)$. Now define the function $b(P_\eta, \delta)\colon \Omega \to \mathfrak{R}$ by the expectation (if it exists)

$$b(P_\eta, \delta|\omega) = \int_{Y_\eta} \delta(y|\omega)\,dP_\eta(y|\omega)$$

at each ω of the pure decision strategy $\delta\colon Y_\eta \to C(\Lambda)$. Let $B(P_\eta, C(\Lambda))$ denote the set of all such $b(P_\eta, \delta)$ as δ varies.

Definition

A system η is (Blackwell) *more informative* than γ if for each closed convex set $C(\Lambda)$,

$$B(P_\gamma, C(\Lambda)) \subseteq B(P_\eta, C(\Lambda))$$

Proof of theorem 1.1

(a) For (1)⇔(2), let (2) hold. Consider any pure decision function $g\colon Y_\gamma \to C(\Lambda)$ with expectation

$$\int_{Y_\gamma} g(\cdot, \omega)\, dP_\gamma(z|\omega) \tag{1B.1}$$

where $g(z, \omega)$ is the ωth component of $g(z)$ for each $z \in Y_\gamma$. From equation (1.5), (1B.1) becomes

$$\int_{Y_\eta}\int_{Y_\gamma} g(\cdot, \omega)\, dP(z|y)\, dP_\eta(y|\omega)$$

Consider the function $h(y) = \int_{Y^\gamma} g(z)\, dP(z|y)$. From the above lemma, it follows that $h(y) \in C(\Lambda)$. Hence $h\colon Y_\eta \to C(\Lambda)$ is a legitimate decision function h based on η which yields at each $\omega \in \Omega$ the same expectation as g based on γ. Thus η is more informative than γ.

Conversely, let (1) hold. Consider the closed convex set $C(\Lambda)$ of non-negative constant functions in $B(\Omega, \mathfrak{R})$

$$C(\Lambda) = \{\theta(\omega) | \theta(\omega) = r,\ r \geq 0,\ r \in \mathfrak{R}\}$$

Hence, each decision function $\hat{g}\colon Y_\gamma \to C(\Lambda)$ is essentially a real-valued, non-negative measurable function $g\colon Y_\gamma \to \mathfrak{R}$ such that $\hat{g}(z|\omega) = g(z)$ for all $\omega \in \Omega$. (This also holds for decision functions $h\colon Y_\eta \to C(\Lambda)$.) Consider any real-valued non-negative measurable function $g\colon Y_\gamma \to \mathfrak{R}$. By more informativeness of η over γ, there exists a non-negative measurable function $h\colon Y_\eta \to \mathfrak{R}$ such that

$$\int_{Y_\gamma} g(z)\,dP_\gamma(z\,|\,\omega) = \int_{Y_\eta} h(y)\,dP_\eta(y\,|\,\omega) \tag{1B.2}$$

for each $\omega \in \Omega$. Since any general measurable function $g\colon Y \to \mathfrak{R}$ is the sum $g = g^+ - g^-$ of two non-negative measurable functions g^+ and g^-, (1B.2) implies that for each measurable function g for which the sum of integrals of g^+ and g^- on the left side of (1B.2) exist for each ω, there is a measurable function h for which the sum of the integrals on the right side exist for each ω and the equality in (1B.2) holds.

Consider then the map $H\colon M_\gamma \to M_\eta$ of the space of all real-valued measurable (w.r.t. Y_γ) functions M_γ for which the integrals on the left side of (1B.2) exist for each ω to a similar space for Y_η, namely M_η, as follows:

$$g(z) \overset{H}{\to} h(y) \tag{1B.3}$$

Clearly H is linear, positive-homogeneous and for any sequence of monotone increasing non-negative functions $\langle g_n \rangle$ in M_γ,

$$\sup H(g_n) = H(\sup g_n) \tag{1B.4}$$

We claim that there is a unique kernel $P(z\,|\,y)$ from Y_η to Y_γ such that

$$\int_{Y_\gamma} g(z)\,dP(z\,|\,y) = h(y) \tag{1B.5}$$

for all non-negative $g(z) \geq 0$ in M_γ.

To this end, define a kernel in the following manner: For each $B \in \sigma(Y_\gamma)$, and for the indicator function $\chi_B\colon Y_\gamma \to \mathfrak{R}$ such that $\chi_B(z) = 1$, $z \in B$, $\chi_B(z) = 0$, $z \notin B$, let $\chi_B(z) \overset{H}{\to} h_B(\cdot)$. $P(B\,|\,y) = h_B(y)$ defines a kernel from Y_η to Y_γ. Since every non-negative measurable function is the limit of a sequence of simple functions (i.e., sums of real-valued multiples of indicator functions) it follows that any other kernel $Q(z\,|\,y)$ from Y_η satisfying (1B.5) must coincide with $P(z\,|\,y)$ on the indicators and thus on the entire space M_γ. Hence for H as defined above, $P(z\,|\,y)$ as defined above is unique. The result then follows from (1B.2).

(b) To show (3) ⇒ (2), we have from Doob's theorem

$$P_\gamma(B\,|\,\omega) = \int_{Y_\gamma} \chi_B\,dP_\gamma(z\,|\,\omega) = \int_{Y_\eta} P(B\,|\,y, \omega)\,dP_\eta(y\,|\,\omega)$$

Since $P(B\,|\,y, \omega) = P(B\,|\,y)$ for all ω, the result follows.

(c) It is trivial to construct a counter example with $\Omega = \{\omega_1, \omega_2\}$. $Y_\eta = \{y_1, y_2\}$ and $Y_\gamma = \{z_1, z_2\}$ to show (2) $\not\Rightarrow$ (3) in general. Q.E.D.

Proof of Theorem 1.2

(1) Consider any system $\gamma: S \to Y_\gamma$. By definition 1.4, the conditional probability function of $\gamma^{-1}(B) \in \sigma(\gamma)$ given T is independent of ω. This implies that the Doob kernel of γ given T is independent of $\omega \in \Omega$ and the result follows from theorem 1.1(b).

(2) It is known (see Schmetterer [1976], p. 214) that for any family of probability measures $\{P(s|\omega)|\omega \in \Omega\}$ dominated by a σ-finite measure, there is a *minimal sufficient statistic* $\eta^*: S \to Y_{\eta^*}$. The minimality arises from the fact any other sufficient statistic T is such that there exists a function $m: Y_T \to Y_{\eta^*}$ such that η^* is equal to the composition $m \circ T$. The result follows from paragraph 1 (above) and this minimality of η^*.

(3) This is obvious. Q.E.D.

Proof of Theorem 1.3

(1) This follows directly from theorem 1.2, part (1).

(2) Consider *any* class Π of prior probability measures on the set of parameters Ω with densities (with respect to some σ-finite measure) $\pi(\omega)$. Then we can define joint measures on $\Omega \times X$ by the concatenation of the kernel and the measures $H(\omega)$ of the densities $\pi(\omega)$ (see page 79). For simplicity denote these by

$$G(y, \omega) = H \cdot Q(x|\omega, \eta)$$

By definition of $Q(x|\omega, \eta)$, it is straightforward to show from Bayes' theorem that the posteriors are related by

$$\pi(\omega|\bar{\eta}(x) = y) = \pi(\omega|x)$$

for each density $\pi(\omega)$ in the class Π. It follows from definition 1.5 that $\bar{\eta}: X \to Y_\eta$ is a Bayesian sufficient statistic for Π. From Zacks theorem, $\bar{\eta}$ is therefore also a *sufficient statistic* for the family $Q(x|\omega, \eta) \equiv P(x|\omega, \eta, \gamma)$. Q.E.D.

Proof of Theorem 1.4

(1) First we show that Z_i^* as defined in equation (1.13) is a legitimate risk-sharing contract. Observe that $\{Z_i^*\}$ is a contract because

$$\Sigma_i E(Z_i|F) = E(\Sigma_i Z_i|F) = E(\boldsymbol{X}_M|F) \qquad \text{a.s.} \tag{1B.6}$$

(we will not continue to use the "a.s." henceforth, it being understood that all conditional expectation statements are always a.s.) and $E(\boldsymbol{X}_M|F) = \boldsymbol{X}_M$ since F is MAS. Now $E_i[U_i(Z_i^*)] = E_i[U_i(E(Z_i|F))]$ by construction of Z_i^*. By Jensen's inequality for conditional expectations $E_i[U_i(E(Z_i|F))] \geq E_i[E(U_i(Z_i)|F)]$. Since P_i is absolutely continuous w.r.t. the pooled measure P, P_i has a R–N density g_i w.r.t. P. By the Radon–Nikodym theorem, the expectation w.r.t. P_i can be replaced by one w.r.t. P in the right-hand side of the inequality above to get

$$E_i[U_i(E(Z_i|F))] \geq E[g_i(E(U_i(Z_i)|F))] \tag{1B.7}$$

But as F is sufficient w.r.t. P_i, $\sigma(g_i) \subseteq \sigma(F)$. By the smoothing property of conditional expectations (see page 78) the right-hand side of (1B.7) becomes

$$E[g_i(E(U_i(Z_i)|F))] = E[E(g_i U_i(Z_i)|F)] \tag{1B.8}$$

But the right-hand side of (1B.8) is the expectation of a conditional expectation w.r.t. F under the measure P. From this and the Radon–Nikodym theorem, the right-hand side of (1B.8) becomes

$$E[E(g_i U_i(Z_i)|F)] = E[g_i U_i(Z_i)] = E_i(U_i(Z_i)) \tag{1B.9}$$

The result follows from (1B.7), (1B.8), and (1B.9).

(2) If Z_i are not $\sigma(F)$ measurable, then $E(Z_i|F) \neq Z_i$ and if U_i are strictly concave, Jensen's inequality holds strictly and the result follows. Q.E.D.

Proof of Corollary 1.4

This follows from equation (1.14), (now restricted to $\mathscr{F}$ as explained in note 15) because $g_i(s) = \lambda_j U_j'(Z_j(s))g_j(s)/\lambda_i U_i'(Z_i(s))$ implies that if $P_j(B) = 0$ then $\int_B g_i(s)dP = 0$. Q.E.D.

Proof of Theorem 1.5

Let F be MAS. If any U_i (say, U_1 without loss of generality) is risk-neutral, then it is well known from Borch's theorem that all other traders will receive shares $Z_i = C_i$, a constant for each $i = 2, \ldots, I$ and $Z_1 = \boldsymbol{X}_M - \Sigma_{i=2}^I C_i$. But constants are always measurable w.r.t. may σ-algebra and hence Z_i are $\sigma(F)$ measurable for $i = 2, \ldots, I$. Z_1 is a function of $\boldsymbol{X}_M$ and constants and thus is $\sigma(\boldsymbol{X}_M)$ measurable and since F is MAS, it is also F measurable.

Now suppose all U_i are strictly risk-averse. If Z_i are not $\sigma(F)$ measurable, then by theorem 1.4 we can generate a strictly Pareto-superior contract. Hence, Z_i must be FPE.

Conversely suppose Z_i are $\sigma(F)$ measurable for some F. From corollary 1.4 we know that since P_i are absolutely continuous w.r.t. each other, we can take μ to be P_1 in the Borch first-order conditions (1.14). Hence the conditions (1.14), since $g_1(s) = 1$, now become

$$\lambda_i U_i'(Z_i(s))g_i(s) = \lambda_1 U_1'(Z_1(s)) \qquad \text{for each } s \in S, \quad \text{and } i \qquad (1B.10)$$

From this we get, omitting the arguments s, $g_i = \lambda_i U_i'(Z_i)/\lambda_1 U_1'(Z_1)$ which implies that g_i are $\sigma(F)$ measurable since Z_i and Z_1 are. Consequently, F is a sufficient statistic. Since $\Sigma_{i=1}^{I} Z_i = X_M$, X_M is also $\sigma(F)$ measurable and so F is MAS. Q.E.D.

Proof of Theorem 1.6

We prove (1) and (2) together: The system $F^*(s) = [X_M(s), g_1(s), \ldots, g_I(s)]$ is MAS by definition 1.9. It is obviously minimal, because for any MAS F, $\sigma(F^*) \subseteq \sigma(F)$. By a property of measurable functions (see appendix 1A), a function measurable w.r.t. a σ-algebra generated by another function is a composite function of the latter and thus (1.15) follows. Q.E.D.

Proof of Theorem 1.7

If C spans $L^2(S, \sigma(F^*), P)$, it follows from theorem 1.4 that if $\{Z_i^*\}$ is an equilibrium contract, Z_i^* is $\sigma(F^*)$ measurable since F^* is a MAS system. From theorem 1.5 it follows that $\{Z_i^*\}$ is FPE. *Conversely*, suppose the contract $\{Z_i^*\}$ is FPE. Then from theorem 1.5 it must be that Z_i^* is $\sigma(F^*)$ measurable as F^* is a MAS system. It follows that F^* must be costlessly and publicly observable for Z_i^* to obtain. $L^2(S, \sigma(F^*), P)$ contracts would then be enforceable and so C spans $L^2(S, \sigma F(^*), P)$. Q.E.D.

Proof of Theorem 1.8

Let (Z_γ, a_γ) be the optimal contract under γ where $Z_\gamma = [Z_\gamma^1, \ldots, Z_\gamma^2]$, and $a_\gamma = [a_\gamma^1, \ldots, a_\gamma^2]$. Since η is more informative than γ, there is a Markov kernel $P(t|m)$ from M_η to M_γ. Now consider the conditional expectations for $m \in M_\eta$.

$$E(u_i(Z^i_\gamma(t))|m) = \int_{M_\gamma} u_i(Z^i_\gamma(t))\, dP(t|m) \tag{1B.11}$$

By concavity of $u_i(w)$ in w, it follows that for each m there is a certainty equivalent $\delta_i(m)$ such that $u_i(\delta_i(m)) = E(u_i(Z^i_\gamma(t)|m))$. Under the compensation scheme δ_i: $M_\eta \to \mathfrak{R}$ based on η as just defined, the agents' expected utilities at each $a \in A$ are given by

$$\int_{M_\eta} u_i(\delta_i(m))\, dP_\eta\,(m|a) - v_i(a_i) = \int_{M_\eta}\int_{M_\gamma} u_i(Z^i_\gamma(t)) dP(t|m) dP_\eta(m|a) - v_i(a_i)$$

$$= \int_{M_\gamma} u_i(Z^i_\gamma(t))\, dP_\gamma(t|a) - v_i(a_i) \tag{1B.12}$$

The last equality in (1B.12) follows from theorem 1.1, part (2).

It follows that both $\delta_i(m)$ and $Z^i_\gamma(t)$ generate the same utility for each agent at each a and hence each agent's optimal choice given $\delta_i(m)$ is still a^i_γ if the other agents stick to their components of a_γ. Thus (δ, a_γ) is a feasible η-contract for the principal, where $\delta = [\delta_1(\cdot), \ldots, \delta_q(\cdot)]$.

Since u_i is concave and nondecreasing,

$$\delta_i(m) \le \int_{M_\gamma} Z^i_\gamma(t)\, dP(t|m) = E(Z^i_\gamma(t)|m) \tag{1B.13}$$

Since g is also nondecreasing, (1B.13) implies that $g(x - \Sigma_i \delta_i(m)) \ge g(x - \Sigma_i E(Z^i_\gamma(t)|m))$. For each fixed x and m by Jensen's inequality, then,

$$g(x - \Sigma_i \delta_i(m)) \ge \int_{M_\gamma} g(x - \Sigma_i Z^i_\gamma(t))\, dP(t|m) \tag{1B.14}$$

Thus, integrating both sides of (1B.14) with respect to the product measure of X and η on $\mathfrak{R} \times M_\eta$ at any a, we get

$$\int_{M_\eta}\int_{\mathfrak{R}} g(x - \Sigma_i \delta_i(m))\, dP(x|m, a)\, dP_\eta(m|a)$$

$$\ge \int_{M_\eta}\int_{\mathfrak{R}}\int_{M_\gamma} g(x - \Sigma_i Z^i_\gamma(t))\, dP(t|m)\, dP(x|m, a)\, dP_\eta(m|a) \tag{1B.15}$$

We shall show that the right-hand side of (1B.15), under any of the conditions (1), (2), or (3) of the theorem, is equal to

$$\int_{M_\gamma}\int_{\mathfrak{R}} g(x-\Sigma_i Z^i_\gamma(t))\,dP(x|t, a)\,dP_\gamma(t|a) \tag{1B.16}$$

(1) When g is risk-neutral, the conclusion is obvious once the expectation over x is separated out and theorem 1.1, part (2), is applied.

(2) Under conditional independence between t and x, and by Fubini's theorem (Ash, [1972]), the right-hand side of (1B.15)

$$\int_{\mathfrak{R}}\int_{M_\eta}\int_{M_\gamma} g(x-\Sigma_i Z^i_\gamma(t))dP(t|m)dP_\eta(m|x, a)dP(x|a) \tag{1B.17}$$

But from Blackwell informativeness of η over γ and part (2) of theorem 1.3, (1B.17) becomes

$$\int_{\mathfrak{R}}\int_{M_\eta}\int_{M_\gamma} g(\ldots)dP_\gamma(t|m, a)dP_\eta(m|x, a)dP(x|a). \tag{1B.18}$$

(1B.18), by Fubini's theorem, becomes

$$\int_{M_\eta}\int_{M_\gamma}\int_{\mathfrak{R}} g(\ldots)dP(x|m, a)dP_\gamma(t|m, a)dP_\eta(m|a) \tag{1B.19}$$

which is conditioning and unconditioning of (1B.16) by η and thus equal to (1B.16).

(3) If $\boldsymbol{X}$ is $\sigma(\eta)$ measurable, it follows from corollary 1.2 that η is Blackwell more informative than $\boldsymbol{X}$. Hence η is Blackwell more informative than $[X, \gamma]$. Hence, there exists a Markov kernel from M_η to $\mathfrak{R} \times M_\gamma$, denoted by $P(x, t|m)$.

In (1B.11) replace $P(t|m)$ by $P(x, t|m)$, so that the right-hand side of (1B.15) becomes

$$\int_{M_\gamma}\int_{\mathfrak{R}\times M_\gamma} g(x-\Sigma_i Z^i_\gamma(t))dP(x, t|m)dP_\eta(m|a) \tag{1B.20}$$

From part (2) of theorem 1.3, this is equal to

$$\int_{M_\eta}\int_{\mathfrak{R}\times M_\gamma} g(\ldots)dP_{[x,\gamma]}(x, t|m, a)dP_\eta(m|a) \tag{1B.21}$$

which is simply conditioning and unconditioning by η, so that this is equal to (1B.16) (using Fubini's theorem) as was required. Q.E.D.

Proof of Corollary 1.10

When the agents are strictly risk-averse in wealth and have increasing utility, and if some $Z_y^i(s)$ is not a function of $\eta(s)$ for $s \in S$, then there is a set $B_a^i \in M_\eta$ of positive probability measure $P_\eta(B_a^i|a) > 0$ for each a such that for $m \in B_a$, and by Jensen's inequality, the inequality (1B.13) is strict. Since g is strictly increasing, from Jensen's inequality, (1B.14) is also strict for all x, for $m \in B_a^i$. This implies that inequality (1B.15) is also strict and the rest of the proof mimicks the proof of theorem 1.8. Q.E.D.

Proof of Corollary 1.11

(1) From theorem 1.3, a sufficient statistic is Blackwell more informative than any other system. From Corollary 1.10, if Z^* is not based on T, then there is a strict improvement based on T, which contradicts the best nature of Z^*. The result then follows.

(2) Again from theorem 1.3 and Corollary 1.10, Z^* has to be a composite function of (X, T). Q.E.D.

References

Amershi, A.H. [1981]. "Social Value of Information, Spot Trading and Rational Expectations Equilibria in Incomplete Exchange Markets." Working paper, Graduate School of Business, Stanford University.

Amershi, A.H. [1984]. "Informativeness in Agencies: Contractual Sufficiency versus Statistical Sufficiency." Working paper, University of British Columbia.

Amershi, A.H. [1985]. "Complete Analysis of Full Pareto Efficiency in Financial Markets for Arbitrary Preferences." *Journal of Finance* 40, 1235–1243.

Amershi, A.H., and Cheng, P. [1987]. "Implementable Equilibria in Accounting Contexts: An Exploratory Study." *Contemporary Accounting Research* (forthcoming).

Amershi, A.H., and Hughes, J.S. [1987]. "Multiple Signals, Statistical Sufficiency and Pareto-Orderings of Best Agency Contracts." Working paper, University of British Columbia.

Amershi, A.H., and Stoeckenius, J.H.W. [1983]. "The Theory of Syndicates and Linear Sharing Rules." *Econometrica* 51, 1407–1416.

Arrow, K.J. [1953]. "The Role of Securities in the Optimal Allocation of Risk

Bearing." *Colloques Internationaux du Centre National de la Recherche Scientifique* 40, 41–49.

Ash, R.B. [1972]. *Real Analysis and Probability*. New York, Academic Press.

Baiman, S. [1982]. "Agency Research in Managerial Accounting: A Survey." *Journal of Accounting Literature* 1, 154–213.

Bauer, H. [1972]. *Probability and Elements of Measure Theory*. New York: Holt, Rinehart and Winston.

Blackwell, D. [1951]. "Comparison of Experiments." *Proceedings of the Second Berkeley Symposium on Mathematical Statistics and Probability*. Berkeley: University of California Press, 93–102.

Blackwell, D. [1953]. "Equivalent Comparisons of Experiments." *Annals of Mathematical Statistics* 24, 267–272.

Blackwell, D. and Girschick, M.A. [1954]. *Theory of Games and Statistical Decisions*. John Wiley. New York.

Bohnenblust, H.F., Shapley, L.S., and Sherman, S. [1949]. "Reconnaissance in Game Theory." Unpublished RAND RM–208.

Borch, K. [1962]. "Equilibrium in a Reinsurance Market." *Econometrica* 30, 424–444.

Burrill, C. [1972]. *Measure, Integration and Probability*. New York: McGraw-Hill.

van Damme, E. [1983]. *Refinements of the Nash Equilibrium Concept*. New York: Springer-Verlag

Debreu, G. [1959]. *Theory of Value*. New Haven: Cowles Foundation.

DeGroot, M. [1970]. *Optimal Statistical Decisions*. New York: McGraw-Hill.

Doob, J. [1953]. *Stochastic Processes*. New York: John Wiley.

Feller, W. [1966]. *An Introduction to Probability Theory and Its Applications*, vol. II. New York: John Wiley.

Feltham, G.A. [1985]. "The Impact of Public Information in Efficient Sequential Markets." Working paper, University of British Columbia.

Fisher, R.A. [1922]. "On the Mathematical Foundations of Theoretical Statistics." *Philosophical Transactions of the Royal Society, London, Section A* 222, 309–388.

Gjesdal, F. [1982]. "Information and Incentives: The Agency Information Problem." *Review of Economic Studies* 49, 373–390.

Green, J., and Stokey, N. [1978]. "Two Representations of Information Structures and Their Comparisons." Technical Report 271, IMSSS, Stanford University.

Green, J., and Stockey, N. [1983]. "A Comparison of Tournaments and Contracts." *Journal of Political Economy* 91, 349–364.

Grossman, S., and Hart, O. [1983]. "An Analysis of the Principal-Agent Problem." *Econometrica* 51, 7–45.

Hakansson, N. [1977]. "The Superfund. Efficient Paths Toward Efficient Capital Markets in Large and Small Countries." In *Financial Decision Making Under Uncertainty*, H. Levy and M. Sarnat, eds. New York: Academic Press.

Hakansson, N. [1978]. "Welfare Aspects of Options and Supershares." *Journal of Finance* 33, 759–776.

Halmos, P.R., and Savage, L.J. [1949]. "Application of the Radon-Nikodym Theorem to the Theory of Sufficient Statistics." *Annals of Mathematical Statistics* 20, 225–241.

Harris, M., and Raviv, A. [1979]. "Optimal Incentive Contracts with Imperfect Information." *Journal of Economic Theory* 20, 231–259.

Hart, O. and Holmstrom, B. [1985]. "The Theory of Contracts." Mimeo, MIT.

Hirschleifer, J. [1971]. "Private and Social Value of Information and the Reward to Inventive Activity." *American Economic Review* 61, 561–574.

Holmes, R.B. [1976]. *Geometric Functional Analysis and Its Applications* New York: Springer-Verlag.

Holmstrom, B. [1979]. "Moral Hazard and Observability." *Bell Journal of Economics* 10, 74–91.

Holmstrom, B. [1982]. Moral Hazard in Teams." *Bell Journal of Economics* 13, 324–340.

John, K. [1984]. "Market Resolution and Valuation in Incomplete Markets." *Journal of Financial and Quantitative Analysis* 19, 29–44.

Kreps, K. [1979]. "Three Essays on Capital Markets." Working paper, Stanford University.

Kuhn, H. [1953]. "Extensive Games and the Problem of Information." In *Contributions to the Theory of Games*, vol. 2, H. Kuhn and A. Tucker (eds.) Princeton: Princeton University Press.

Lang, S. [1969]. *Analysis II*. Reading, MA, Addison-Wesley.

Le Cam, L. [1964]. "Sufficiency and Approximate Sufficiency." *Annals of Mathematical Statistics* 35, 1419–1455.

Lehman, E.L. [1983]. *Theory of Point Estimation*. New York: John Wiley.

Loeve, M.M. [1977]. *Probability Theory*, 4th ed. New York: Springer-Verlag.

Ma, C. [1987]. "Unique Implementation of Incentive Contracts with Many Agents." Working paper, London School of Economics.

Marschak, J. and Miyasawa, K. [1968]. "Economic Comparability of Information Systems." *International Economic Review* 9, 137–174.

Meyer, P.A. [1966]. *Probability and Potentials*, Waltham, MA: Blaisdell Publishing Company.

Milgrom, P. and Stokey, N. [1982]. "Information, Trade and Common Knowledge." *Journal of Economic Theory* 27, 17–27.

Mirrlees, J. [1975]. "The Theory of Moral Hazard for Optimal Insurance." Unpublished,, Nuffield College, Oxford.

Mirrlees, J. [1976]. "The Optimal Structure of Incentives and Authority within an Organization." *Bell Journal of Economics* 7, 105–131.

Mookherjee, D. [1984]. "Optimal Incentive Scheme with Many Agents." *Review of Economic Studies* 51, 433–446.

Mossin, J. [1973]. *Theory of Financial Markets*. Englewood Cliffs, NJ: Prentice-Hall.

Myerson, R. [1982]. "Optimal Coordination Mechanisms in Generalized Principal-Agent Problems." *Journal of Mathematical Economics* 10, 67–81.

Neveu, J. [1965]. *Mathematical Foundations of the Calculus of Probability* San Francisco: Holden Day.

Ohlson, J.A., and Buckman, A.G. [1981]. "Toward a Theory of Financial Accounting: Welfare and Public Information." *Journal of Accounting Research* 19, 399–433.

Radner, R. [1968]. "Competitive Equilibrium under Uncertainty." *Econometrica* 36, 31–58.
Radner, R. [1972]. "Existence of Equilibrium of Plans, Prices, and Price Expectations in a Sequence of Markets." *Econometrica* 40, 289–303.
Radner, R. [1974]. "Market Equilibrium and Uncertainty: Concepts and Problems." In *Frontiers of Quantitative Economics*, M.D. Intrilligator and D.A. Kendric (eds.). Amsterdam: North-Holland.
Raiffa, H., and Schlaiffer, R. [1961]. *Applied Statistical Decision Theory*. Boston: Harvard University Press.
Ross, S.A. [1973]. "The Economic Theory of Agency: The Principal's Problem." *American Economic Review* 63, 134–139.
Ross, S. [1976]. "Options and Efficiency." *Quarterly Journal of Economics* 90, 75–89.
Rubinstein, M. [1975]. "Securities Market Efficiency in an Arrow–Debreu Economy." *American Economic Review* 65, 812–824.
Savage, L. [1954]. *The Foundations of Statistical Analysis*. New York: John Wiley.
Schmetterer, L. [1976]. *Introduction to Mathematical Statistics*. New York: Springer-Verlag.
Selten, R. [1975]. "Reexamination of the Perfectness Concept for Equilibrium Points." *International Journal of Game Theory* 4, 25–55.
Stiglitz, J.E. [1981]. "The Allocation Role of the Stock Market: Pareto Optimality and Competition." *Journal of Finance* 36, 235–251.
Strassen, V. [1965]. "The Existence of Probability Measures with Given Marginals." *Annals of Mathematical Statistics* 36, 423–439.
Wilson, R. [1968]. "The Theory of Syndicates." *Econometrica* 36, 119–132.
Zacks, S. [1971]. *The Theory of Statistical Inference*. New York: John Wiley.

2 THE SOCIAL VALUE OF PUBLIC INFORMATION IN PRODUCTION ECONOMIES*

James A. Ohlson

This paper analyzes the welfare effects of public information in decentralized production and exchange economies. Following Hirshleifer's [1971] well-known paper, the pure exchange case has been subject to detailed investigation, and conditions for the welfare unanimity of (more) information are well understood. (Ohlson and Buckman [1981] summarize these results). On the other hand, attempts to deal with production and exchange simultaneously have been sparse. Arrow [1979] and Hakansson [1977] discuss some of the difficulties involved. The only formal and explicit unanimity results appear to be due to Kunkel [1982] and Trueman [1983]. These authors derive results within relatively confined settings, and, accordingly, conclusions have been limited. With only weak restrictions on individuals' preferences/beliefs, firms' opportunities, characterization of information, and markets, the analysis here provides a comprehensive treatment of public information's welfare role in neoclassical production and exchange economies.

* The author wishes to thank Jerry Feltham and Brett Trueman for valuable comments on an earlier draft of this paper.

The study of information and decentralized production leads to a number of questions which must be dealt with. First, how does information analysis relate to problems generally subsumed by the heading "theory of the firm under uncertainty"? As the reviews by Baron [1979], Kreps [1979], Leland [1973], and Nielsen [1978] indicate, issues of stockholder unanimity and the appropriateness of value-maximization are intricate. No reasons suggest that these problems become any easier when the information varies. Nevertheless, stockholder unanimity about changes in information, changes in production, or simultaneous changes in information and production should follow from a unified theoretical framework. Second, the literature usually considers public information as an externality. While presumably a reasonable contention, the question remains: in what sense does information induce an externality in a production setting? Third, information analysis suggests that no-cost information performs a more constructive welfare function in production and exchange as compared to pure exchange—at least if the production plans and allocations are efficient given the available information. (The theme is present in Hirshliefer's [1971] article.) Thus, in economies with efficient allocations, does additional costless information lead to increased efficiency?

The key insights can be summarized as follows:

1. Information introduces no substantively new twists to stockholder unanimity theory and the induced optimality of value-maximization. Conditions for unanimity (or its absence) when both production and information vary, link directly to, and are identified from, the conditions that imply production unanimity (or its absence) in the "standard theory." This unified perspective covers both perfectly competitive markets (i.e., there is ex ante unanimity), and noncompetitive markets in which endowments are appropriately restricted.

2. Information affects the ensemble of goods supplied—or feasible *mixes* of consumption across dates and states—thereby causing an externality. While this feature applies no less in pure exchange, a key insight notes that the information externality is conceptually identical to the production externality associated with the market-making of firms. In a stock-market economy the market-value rule works at the most for *quantities* produced, but not for *what* goods are produced (see Kreps [1979]). Thus, information and production externalities are equivalent because they jointly determine the available markets, or the types of contracts that can be entered into. Although the two externality sources—information and markets available—generally interact with each other, a unified framework merges them into only one externality source: the span of the commodity space. This effect of information must be distinguished from the externality that arises because *all* firms can exploit public information to choose "better" production plans.

3. The idea of incremental information improving on the set of efficient allocations is much more applicable in pure exchange than in production and exchange. This counterintuitive result does not relate to the potential sub-optimality of value-maximization or to the production or information externalities associated with market making. The matter emanates from a more basic observation: incremental information moves the (expected) utility-locus of efficient allocations *uniformly* to the northeast if and only if production plans are held constant.

The outline of the paper is as follows. First, notation and other preliminaries are introduced. The next two sections develop information/production unanimity results assuming constrained Pareto efficient equilibria within settings of perfectly competitive markets and imperfectly competitive markets, respectively. The following section disregards issues of unanimity and considers instead the relative efficiency of alternative information and production specifications. Finally, the last section derives unanimity results when allocations are fundamentally flawed, that is, not constrained Pareto efficient.

Basic Notation and Preliminaries

The economies of concern consist of $i = 1, \ldots, I$ consumers/individuals, and $j = 1, \ldots, J$ firms. Consumption occurs at two dates, labeled date-0 and date-1, respectively. There are $s = 1, \ldots, S$ mutually exclusive states, the true state being fully revealed at date-1. Without risk of confusion, the conventions $s \in S$, $i \in I$, $j \in J$ are also used. Firms plan signal contingent production decisions and individuals plan signal contingent trading/consumption decisions prior to date-0; at date-0 public information (possibly null) is made available to firms and individuals. The information affects firms' and individuals' feasible and actual plans. Individuals and firms have identical information about the environment.

The notation that relates to information, firms, and individuals follows.

Information

The information at date-0 is characterized by a function defined on S, $y = \eta(s)$, where y is the signal, $y = 1, \ldots, Y$, or alternatively, $y \in Y$. The information function η induces a partition on the state space S. Let $S_y \equiv \{s | \eta(s) = y\}$; then $S_1, S_2, \ldots, S_Y$ constitute subsets of S such that $\cup_y S_y = S$ and $S_y \cap S_{y'} = \varnothing$ if $y \neq y'$. (No information, or the null partition, is defined by $S_1 = S$). A partition η'' is at least as fine as, or weakly more informative than, η' if and only if for each $y'' \in Y''$ some $y' \in Y'$ exists such that $S''_{y''} \subseteq S'_{y'}$.

Firms' Plans and Opportunities

A production plan of firm j is characterized by an output row vector $a_{1j} \equiv (a_{1j1}, \ldots, a_{1js}, \ldots, a_{1jS})$, and input row vector $a_{0j} \equiv (a_{0j1}, \ldots, a_{0js}, \ldots, a_{0jS})$. The first vector is non-negative, the second non-positive, and both are S-dimensional. The dimensionality means that there is only one good ("cash") indexed across dates and states; a_{1js} is the (terminal) dividend distributed and $-a_{0js}$ is the capital invested by firm j in state s. The date-1 output vectors can be summarized by the $J \times S$ matrix $A_1 \equiv [a_{1js}]$; similarly, define $A_0 \equiv [a_{0js}]$. No additional characteristics—such as complete markets—restrict the output matrix A_1. However, the input matrix A_0 satisfies *measurability* relative to the prevailing information function η. That is, $a_{0js} = a_{0jt}$, whenever $s, t \in S_y$, all $j \in J$. In words, the planned input decisions can be contingent only on the available information. The extreme case of null information requires a_{0js} to be the same for all s. The production opportunity set of the jth firm, denoted by $\Omega_j(\eta)$, thus depends on η; and these sets incorporate the measurability constraints on the input vectors a_{0j}. It further follows that *costless* information (from the jth firm's point of view) expands production opportunities (i.e., $\Omega_j(\eta'') \supseteq \Omega_j(\eta')$ when η'' is no less informative than η').

Firms' Values

The column vector $P \equiv (P_1, \ldots, P_J)$ denotes the net values of firms' input/output patterns prior to the release of any signal from η. Given the absence of arbitrage, it follows that there exists non-negative implicit price vectors $v_1 \equiv (v_{11}, \ldots, v_{1S})$, $v_0 \equiv (v_{01}, \ldots, v_{0S})$ such that

$$P_j = \sum_s (a_{1js} v_{1s} + a_{0js} v_{0s}) \qquad \text{all } j$$

or, more compactly,

$$P = A_0 v_0 + A_1 v_1 = Av$$

where $A \equiv (A_0, A_1)$ and $v \equiv (v_0, v_1)$. It will be convenient to normalize v_0 (and P) such that $\Sigma_s v_{0s} = 1$: the unconditional acquisition of one unit of date-

0 input costs \$1. Neither v_0 nor v_1 is necessarily unique, but, as is well known, this causes no concern. A necessary but insufficient condition for the date-0 vector v_0 to be unique is perfect information. The date-1 vector v_1 is unique if and only if A_1 is of rank S (complete markets).

Individuals

Individuals consume at dates zero and one across states. Denote the two consumption row vectors by $c_{0i} \equiv (c_{0i1}, \ldots, c_{0iS})$ and $c_{1i} \equiv (c_{1i1}, \ldots, c_{1iS})$; let $c_i \equiv (c_{0i}, c_{1i})$. Similar to production plans, the measurability constraint restricts c_{0i}: $c_{0is} = c_{0it}$ whenever $s, t \in S_y$, each y. Other constraints on c_i depend on the individual's wealth and the exchange opportunities (see below). Preferences are given by $V_i(c_i)$; and, in general, the only restriction on V_i requires that more is preferred to less: $c_i'' \geq c_i'$ implies $V_i'' > V_i'$. Assumptions such that V_i derives from Savage's axioms and thus represents an individual's "expected utility" are generally unnecessary. Each individual has endowments in the date-0 consumption good, denoted by the row vector $\bar{c}_{0i}$. To allow for the null-partition, $\bar{c}_{0is}$ is independent of s. Individuals are also endowed with shares in the different firms, $\bar{\vartheta}_i \equiv (\bar{\vartheta}_{i1}, \ldots, \bar{\vartheta}_{iJ})$, for which total supplies add up to one ($\Sigma_i \bar{\vartheta}_{ij} = 1$).

The next issue relates to conditions for an equilibrium.

First, the equilibrium allocation $(c_i)_i$ satisfies the conservation equations:

$$\sum_i c_{0i} \leq \sum_i \bar{c}_{0i} + \sum_j a_{0j} \tag{2.1a}$$

$$\sum_i c_{1i} \leq \sum_j a_{1j} \tag{2.1b}$$

Second, the analysis must consider assumptions about firms' behavior. The approach developed here generally takes the (alternative) production plans as exogenous. Under certain narrow conditions one may introduce endogenous production by assuming that firms maximize their (net) market values P_j.

Third, there is the issue of how information affects individuals' trading opportunities. The literature suggests a number of models. This paper considers most of these, and subsequent analysis provides appropriate formalizations.

Initially it suffices to model the trading/consumption opportunities given no information. No information serves as a natural starting point for purposes of analyzing the welfare consequences of alternative production plans alone. As will be demonstrated, extending the analysis when production plans and information functions vary simultaneously is not all that different, once the more basic problem has been developed properly.

Given the null partition, express an individual's budget constraint as

$$c_{0i}v_0 + \vartheta_i(P - A_0 v_0) \leq \bar{c}_0 v_0 + \bar{\vartheta}_i P \tag{2.2}$$

where c_{0i} satisfies the extreme measurability constraint $c_{0is} = c_{0it}$, all $s, t \in S^1$. Thus, individuals trade the (single) date-0 consumption good in a spot market. Markets for state-contingent future delivery of the date-1 consumption good do not exist. Instead, as is usual in a stock-market economy, an individual acquires a date-1 consumption pattern via shareholdings:

$$c_{1i} = \vartheta_i A_1 \tag{2.3}$$

Each individual maximizes V_i subject to (i) the budget constraint (2.2) and (ii) the measurability constraint on c_{0i}. Given the production plans (A_0, A_1), and the conservation equations (2.1a) and (2.1b), mild regularity conditions on preferences $(V_i)_i$ ensure the existence of an exchange equilibrium with consumption plans $(c_i)_i$ and implicit prices v. An equilibrium stated in terms of security holdings and security prices can be derived via the matrixes of plans: $c_{1i} = \vartheta_i A_1$ and $P = A_1 v_1 + A_0 v_0$. Conversely, $(c_{1i})_i$ and v_1 derive from any equilibrium stated in terms of $(\vartheta_i)_i$ and P.

Perfectly Competitive Markets and Stockholder Unanimity

This section evaluates the impact of a change in the production/information specification on stockholders' welfare. The focus is on conditions sufficient for stockholders to be unanimous about the desirability of a production or information change. Markets are assumed to be perfectly competitive. (This assumption is relaxed in the next section.)

The analysis commences with a welfare comparison of two alternative production plans within the null information setting. Conditions for production unanimity are well understood in that context. Nevertheless, by carefully dissecting the problem, the reasons for unanimity become unusually transparent. The incremental complication of varying information in addition to production plans then resolves as a direct extension of the more basic null-information unanimity problem.

Let CO_i denote the ith individual's consumption opportunity set, $c_i \in CO_i$. This set depends on the budget constraint, the available information, and the markets. Given null information and equation (2.2), restate CO_i in terms of three separate conditions:

(a) Affordability:

$$c_{0i}v_0 + c_{1i}v_1 \leq \bar{c}_{0i}v_0 + \bar{\vartheta}_i P \tag{2.4a}$$

(b) Measurability of date-0 consumption:

$$c_{0is} = c_{0it} \qquad \text{all } s, t \in S \tag{2.4b}$$

(c) Date-1 consumption vector is in the span of A_1:

$$c_{1i} \in C(A_1) \equiv \{c_{1i} | c_{1i} = \vartheta_i A_1 \qquad \text{all } \vartheta_i\} \tag{2.4c}$$

Restrictions (2.4a) and (2.4c) derive directly from $\vartheta_i(P - A_0 v_0) = \vartheta_i A_1 v_1$ and $c_{1i} = \vartheta_i A_1$. Thus, $c_i \in CO_i$ if and only if c_i satisfies constraints (2.4a), (2.4b), and (2.4c).

The measurability condition (2.4b) seems awkward and more like excess baggage than something of analytical convenience. This claim makes sense, but only under the null partition. The analytical usefulness of (2.4a)–(2.4c) becomes more evident when information varies and is non-null.

It is important to appreciate the role of condition (2.4c). Firms make markets in date-1 consumption vectors via the securities-states tableau A_1. This matrix determines the set of available date-1 consumption *mixes*. The model assigns no similar role to A_0 because a spot market exists for the date 0 good. Accordingly, the exchange equilibrium allocation is said to be *constrained Pareto efficient* (*CPE*) *relative to* A_1. That is, there exists no allocation of consumption goods satisfying (2.1a), (2.1b), (2.4b), and (2.4c) that Pareto dominates the equilibrium allocation implied by utility maximization subject to (2.4a), (2.4b), and (2.4c), and market clearing (2.1a) and (2.1b).

Consider next two economies with identical endowments $(\bar{c}_{0i}, \bar{\vartheta}_i)_i$, but differing in production plans. Let (A_0'', A_1'') and (A_0', A_1') denote the two sets of plans, and let P'' and P' be the associated vectors of firms' values. These two economies display *perfectly competitive markets, PCM, relative to each other if there exists a common implicit price-vector.* The terminology is appropriate since any consumption plan available in both economies costs the same. Firms therefore have not affected the prices of consumption and input/output goods although their plans have changed. (However, the change in plans may well have had an impact on security prices and the ensemble of goods available.) Formally, if $K(P, A_0, A_1)$ denotes the set of possible implicit price systems given (P, A_0, A_1),

$$K(P, A_0, A_1) \equiv \left\{(v_0, v_1) | P = A_1 v_1 + A_0 v_0, \qquad (v_0, v_1) > 0, \sum_s v_{0s} = 1\right\} \tag{2.5}$$

then PCM obtains if and only if $K(P'', A_0'', A_1'') \cap K(P', A_0', A_1') \neq \varnothing$. Although v'' and v' are not generally unique, PCM is conveniently stated simply as $v' = v''$. Note that for any $c_{1i} \in C(A_1)$, the quantity $c_{1i}v_1$ is unique for all $v \in K(P, A_0, A_1)$].

The structure of individuals' consumption opportunity sets, and the definition of PCM, imply the following straightforward result.

Lemma 2.1

Let A'' and A' be two production specifications, with information being null in both cases. Suppose further that

i. $\bar{\vartheta}_i \geq 0$ all $i \in I$ (non-negative endowments)
ii. $v'' = v'$ (perfectly competitive markets)
iii. $P'' \geqq P'$ (relative values conditions);
iv. $C(A_1'') \supseteq C(A_1')$ (spanning condition).

Then all individuals are at least as well off in the double-primed economy.

Proof: Conditions i, ii, and iii imply a less-tight constraint (2.4a) in the double-primed economy. A similar relative relaxation applies for (2.4c) because of condition iv. Constraint (2.4b) is unaffected by a production change. Hence, $CO_i \subseteq CO_i''$ for all i, and no individual is worse off in the double-primed economy.

The unanimity proposition is referred to as ex ante stockholder unanimity. The literature generally imposes the additional but redundant restriction of exact spanning, that is, $C(A_1'') = C(A_1')$. The exact-spanning restriction, however, is relevant in Fisher's separation theorem: all stockholders agree that firms should maximize their (net) market values.

Corollary 2.1

Let endowments be non-negative and markets PCM. If, additionally, the space $C(A_1')$ remains unperturbed by changes in feasible production plans, then all individuals are unanimous about the optimality of firms' maximizing their net market values.

One easily identifies the critical role of PCM in the lemma and corollary above. PCM eliminates redistributive effects due to price changes in consumption goods (i.e., changes in implicit prices, and not stock prices!) in response to production changes. Therefore, in inequality (2.4a) production changes impact only on the right-hand side.

It should be emphasized that Fisher's separation theorem does not require complete markets. The only appealing feature of market completeness in this context is a fixed commodity space—i.e., $C(A_1)$ equals $C(I)$ across *all* production plans. Any other scheme fixing the commodity space (and this is indeed necessary) works as well. The problem of fixing the commodity space is therefore also present in a certainty stock-market economy where goods are indexed by kind—e.g., bread, fish, wheat, . . . , rather than by basis vectors of date-1 consumption patterns (plus date-0 consumption). Classical value-maximization theory generally applies only if the kinds of commodities produced and traded are exogenously given; the model allows only variations in quantities produced. Conversely, given a fixed commodity space and perfectly competitive markets, the induced optimality is value-maximization. The concept of "spanning," which originally attracted much attention in the theory of the firm under uncertainty, is not peculiar to uncertainty since it simply states that the menu (mix) of goods supplied cannot change arbitrarily with plans. Hence, the possibility of uncertainty does not by itself lead to complications in the theory of stockholder unanimity.

The noncomplexity of uncertainty per se suggests a straightforward analysis of information because (the absence of) information merely puts simple linear restrictions on the contracts available. Hence, information partially delineates the commodity space, further allowing the identification of unanimity conditions from "basic principles."

The lemma and corollary above establish the basics. The analysis now shifts to welfare comparisons when production plans *and* information vary simultaneously. This analysis requires an exchange model that determines the equilibrium allocation of consumption vectors when information is non-null. In a stock-market economy individuals trade shares and the date-0 good contingent on, or in anticipation of, the information available. To model this one can choose from a number of rational-expectations models. However, the key attribute of any economic regime is its economic efficiency characteristic, not the particulars spelling out the opening and closing of markets. A natural extension of the previous no-information analysis assumes that the equilibrium allocation of consumption is *constrained Pareto efficient* (*CPE*) *relative to* A_1 *and* η. Given the restrictions on consumption plans implicit by the market-matrix A_1 and the measurability requirement on $(c_{i0}, \vartheta_i)_i$, these allocations do not permit Pareto improvement. (A formal definition of CPE relative to (A_1, η) is provided below.)

The assumption that the equilibrium allocation attains CPE relative to (A_1, η) implies that in an equilibrium setting each individual's budget constraint reduces to

$$c_{i0}v_0 + \sum_j \sum_y \vartheta_{ijy}\left(P_{jy} - \sum_{s \in S_y} a_{0js}v_{0s}\right) \leq \bar{c}_{0i}v_0 + \sum_j \sum_y \bar{\vartheta}_{ij}P_{jy} \tag{2.6}$$

where P_{jy} denotes the price of security j given signal y. The absence of arbitrage ensures the existence of positive vectors v_0 and v_1 such that

$$P_{jy} = \sum_{s \in S_y} (a_{1js} v_{1s} + a_{0js} v_{0s}) \qquad \text{all } j \in J,\ y \in Y \tag{2.7}$$

The fraction of firm j's shares held by individual i given signal y is ϑ_{ijy}. The measurability requirement on c_{0i} is now given by $c_{0is} = c_{0it}$ if $s, t \in S_y$ for some $y \in Y$. (And, of course, $(a_{0j}, a_{1j}) \in \Omega_j(\eta)$, $j \in J$.)

Although the consumption-opportunity set implied by the budget constraint (2.6) is slightly more complicated as compared to the null partition, a restatement similar to (2.4a)–(2.4c) is feasible. First, note that $\Sigma_y P_{jy} = (a_{0j},\ a_{1j})(v_0, v_1) = P_j$, which means that the right-hand sides of the budget equations (2.2) and (2.6) are the same. Second, let $\delta(A_1, \eta)$ denote the block-diagonalization of A_1 as induced by η. Formally, express A_1 as

$$A_1 \equiv [A_{11} \quad \ldots \quad A_{1y} \quad \ldots \quad A_{1Y}]$$

where $A_{1y} \equiv [a_{1js}]$, $s \in S_y$ only. Thus, η partitions A_1 into Y adjacent matrixes of size $J \times S_Y$. The operation $\delta(A_1, \eta)$ block-diagonalizes A_1:

$$\delta(A_1, \eta) \equiv \begin{bmatrix} A_{11} & & \\ & A_{1y} & \\ & & A_{1Y} \end{bmatrix}$$

where all entries off the block-diagonal are zero. The procedure results in a matrix $\delta(A_1, \eta)$ with $J \times Y$ rows and S columns.

The following three constraints now fully specify the consumption opportunity set CO_i.

Affordability:

$$c_{0i} v_0 + c_{1i} v_1 \leq \bar{c}_{0i} v_0 + \bar{\vartheta}_i P. \tag{2.8a}$$

Measurability of date-0 consumption:

$$c_{0is} = c_{0it} \qquad \text{if } s, t \in S_y \text{ for each } y \in Y \tag{2.8b}$$

Date-1 consumption is in the span of $\delta(A_1, \eta)$:

$$c_{1i} \in C(\delta(A_1, \eta)) \tag{2.8c}$$

Restrictions (2.8a), (2.8b), and (2.8c) generalize (2.4a), (2.4b) and (2.4c). The affordability constraints (2.8a) and (2.4a) are identical for every η, and (2.8b) and (2.8c) are identical to (2.4b) and (2.4c) if η is null since $\delta(A_1, \eta = \text{null}) = A_1$. The relaxation of either or both of these two constraints potentially improves the risk sharing. The constraint (2.8c) emanates from the measurability requirement on share holdings—i.e., for any states $s, t \in S$, $\vartheta_{ijs} = \vartheta_{ijt}$ if $s, t \in S_y$. The most restrictive case occurs when the partition is null and ϑ_{ijs} does not vary with s.

The exchange equilibrium resulting from individuals' maximizing V_i subject to (2.8a)–(2.8c) and market clearing is CPE relative to (A_1, η) in the following sense: there exists no allocation satisfying the conservation equations (2.1a) and (2.1b) and the information/market constraints (2.8b) and (2.8c) that strictly Pareto dominates the equilibrium allocation.

Budget equation (2.6) appears somewhat peculiar in that the summation runs over not only securities but also signals. Individuals are therefore given the opportunity to optimally coordinate their holdings and contracts across different signals. For this reason the equilibrium allocation achieves CPE relative to (A_1, η).

The contrived nature of (2.8b) introduces no limitations per se, since all CPE allocations can be generated using (2.6) or equivalently, (2.8a), (2.8b), and (2.8c). In particular, note that models of sequence equilibria with budget constraints

$$\hat{c}_{i0} + \sum_j \hat{\vartheta}_{ij} P_j \leq \bar{c}_{i0} + \sum_j \bar{\vartheta}_{ij} P_j \tag{2.9a}$$

$$c_{i0y} P_{0y} + \sum_j \vartheta_{ijy} \left(P_{iy} - \sum_{s \in S_y} a_{0js} v_{0s} \right) \leq \hat{c}_{i0} P_{0y} + \sum_j \hat{\vartheta}_{ij} P_{jy}, \tag{2.9b}$$

imply (2.6) and support a CPE equilibrium relative to (A_1, η) provided that the $(J+1) \times Y$ matrix $[P_{jy}]$ has rank Y. In this dynamic model $\hat{c}_{i0}, c_{i0y}$, are scalars, $P_{0y} \equiv \sum_{s \in S_y} v_{0s}$, and the preliminary holdings, $(\hat{c}_{i0}, \{\hat{\vartheta}_{ij}\}_j)$, result from a prior trading round. The CPE conclusion can be inferred from Kreps [1979]. However, since not all sequence equilibria achieve CPE relative to (A_1, η), a subsequent section relaxes this requirement.

Assuming exogenous production/information specifications, the welfare analysis under varying information compares (A_0'', A_1'', η'') to (A_0', A_1', η'), where $\eta'' \neq \eta'$ and $A_0'' \neq A_0'$ or $A_1'' \neq A_1'$ or both, and how the two settings affect $(V_i'')_i$ relative to $(V_i')_i$. An alternative more sophisticated approach views (A_0'', A_1'') and (A_0', A_1') as endogenously determined matrixes. The latter case is analyzed naturally subsequent to the more basic binary comparison problem. As an obvious generalization of lemma 2.1 one obtains the following proposition.

Proposition 2.1

Let (A'', η'') and (A', η') be two economies differing in their production/information, where η'' is non-null and η' is the null partition. Suppose that the two economies generate CPE allocations relative to their respective securities-states tableaus and partitions. Further suppose the following:

i. $\bar{\vartheta}_i \geq 0$ all $i \in I$ (non-negative endowments)
ii. $v'' = v'$ (perfectly competitive markets)
iii. $P'' \geqq P'$ or, equivalently, $\sum_{y \in Y''} P''_{jy} \geq P'_j$ for all j (relative-value condition)
iv. $C(\delta(A''_1, \eta'')) \supseteq C(A'_1)$ (spanning condition)

Then all individuals are at least as well off in the double-primed economy.

Proof: The double-primed setting relaxes the three constraints (2.8a), (2.8b), and (2.8c); thus, $CO_i \subseteq CO''_i$ for all $i \in I$.

The proof shows that proposition 2.1 directly extends lemma 2.1. The only new feature relates to the relaxation of (2.8b) due to incremental information. Thus, given the CPE and PCM conditions, information introduces no fundamentally distinct contortions to the theory of stockholder unanimity.

It is suggestive that one should be able to eliminate assumption iii, $P'' \geqq P'$, since firms can select better plans when more information is available. This view makes sense if a firm's market value measures "better" plans and, additionally, information is free and there are no production externalities. *The latter two conditions imply that* $\Omega_j(\eta'') \supseteq \Omega_j(\eta')$, *and the relative value condition* (*iii*) *is automatically satisfied provided that firms maximize their* (*net*) *market values.*

The impact of information on constraints (2.8a)–(2.8c) identifies its welfare effects. Constraints (2.8b) and (2.8c) jointly determine the menu of available consumption patterns. The measurability constraint (2.8b) is relaxed if, and only if, the information function η'' is at least as informative as η'. Making η'' more informative than η' does not, however, necessarily enlarge the spanning set (2.8c). Although pure exchange (i.e., when $A''_1 = A'_1$) assures that (2.8c) holds, it is not generally true that $C(\delta(A''_1, \eta'')) \supseteq C(\delta(A'_1, \eta'))$ when $A''_1 \neq A'_1$ and η'' is finer than η'. The only exception to this negative observation occurs when η'' is perfectly informative (i.e., $\eta''(s) = s$): the rank of $\delta(A_1$, perfect information) equals S regardless of A_1.[2] It follows that individuals agree on the global optimality of perfect (costless) information and value-maximization. Any movement away from perfect information or any other firm objective leads to, at least weakly, a welfare loss for every individual. Thus, given PCM and CPE, with less than perfect information, or non-value-maximizing firms, each of the constraints (2.8a), (2.8b), and (2.8c) tighten and reduce every individual's consumption opportunities.

The perfect information requirement is obviously rather extreme, and it must therefore be emphasized that one cannot infer that more information is generally better than less since the space $C(\delta(A_1'', \eta''))$ may not include $C(\delta(A_1', \eta'))$ as a subspace when $\eta''(s) \neq s$. It also follows that the relationship $P'' \geqq P'$, implied by costless information and value-maximization, may not be desirable from at least some stockholders point of view since a firm j that moves from P_j' to P_j'' can affect the space (2.8c) adversely. This externality associated with value-maximization is, of course, also present in the null-information case: the corollary of lemma 2.1 relies on the arbitrary assumption of a fixed market span across feasible production plans. The same arbitrary assumption in the context of proposition 2.1 suffices for condition iv. If $C(A_1'') = C(A_1')$ and η'' is at least as informative as η', then one easily shows that $C(\delta(A_1'', \eta'')) \supseteq C(\delta(A_1', \eta'))$. Hence, the following provides the appropriate generalization of corollary 2.1

Corollary 2.2

Assume that (i) endowments are non-negative and that (ii) PCM holds. Further assume that $C(A_1')$ is unperturbed by changes in production plans. Then all individuals are unanimous about the optimality of firms' maximizing their net market values, and more no-cost information is preferred to less.

The relaxation of constraint (2.8a) represents a positive wealth effect. Given cost-free information, and conditions i and ii in proposition 2.1 (see also corollary 2.2), firms can exploit incremental information to maximize the wealth effect. Corollary 2.2 follows since the maximization of the wealth effect is optimal provided that the choice of production plan does not affect the span of the matrix A_1'. As in corollary 2.1, a fixed production span eliminates the interactive effects between endowed wealth and the available consumption mixes due to choice of production plan.

What happens if the jth firm must bear the cost of incremental information production? The production opportunity set $\Omega_j(\eta'')$ no longer subsumes $\Omega_j(\eta')$, and one cannot conclude that value-maximization over production plans and information implies $P_j'' \geq P_j'$. But even if η'' is acquired at a negative present value—i.e., $P'_j > P''_j$, shareholders' interests may be better served than with η'. Information affects constraints (2.8b) and (2.8c) as well, so their potential relaxation might exceed the disadvantage of a decrease in shareholders' endowed wealth.

The above discussion shows that a firm's choice of information introduces the same problem as choice of production, and why—even with PCM and CPE—value-maximization typically does not work. Both a_{j1} and η impact broadly on the economy's exchange opportunities. In other words, *firms' plans, as well as information, are "public goods" to the extent they determine the commodity space.* Costly information magnifies this externality problem and one cannot expect decentralized information choice to perform efficiently. Similarly, even in a simple no information stock-market economy, the production of an optimal menu of goods is unlikely since firms go unrewarded for their market-making activity.[3]

The measurability constraint (2.8b) seemingly prevents any general unanimity conclusions for information functions that are noncomparable on the fineness dimension. This claim is obviously true unless for some reason the date-0 optimal consumption plans are signal-independent (i.e., the constraints $c_{0is} = c_{0it}$ do not bind the equilibrium). Conditions sufficient for this independence are known (Ohlson [1984]): (i) signal-probabilities are homogeneous across individuals, and utilities are time-additive; and (ii) aggregate supply of date-0 consumption is constant over states. These two assumptions have an additional interesting implication. The relative value condition reduces to a comparison of expected market values.

Proposition 2.2

Let (A'', η'') and (A', η') be two production/information specifications where η'' is not necessarily finer (coarser) than η'. Suppose that the two allocations satisfy CPE relative to their securities states-tableaus and information functions. Further suppose the following:

i. $\bar{\vartheta}_i \geq 0$ all $i \in I$ (non-negative endowments)
ii. $v'' = v'$ (perfectly competitive markets)
iii. $P'' \geqq P'$ (relative value condition)
iv. $C(\delta(A''_1, \eta'')) \supseteq C(\delta(A'_1, \eta'))$ (spanning condition)
v. (a) $p_i(y) = p_j(y)$, any $i, j \in I$ and $y \in Y'$ or $y \in Y''$ (homogeneous signal beliefs)

(b) $V_i = \sum_s p_i(s)\, U_i(c_{0is}) + V_{1i}(c_{1i})$ (time-additive utilities)

vi. $\sum_j a'_{0js}$ and $\sum_j a''_{0js}$ are s-independent (date-0 aggregate net supplies are state independent).

Then all individuals are at least as well off in the double-primed economy. Moreover, condition iii can be stated equivalently as

iii*. $E[P''_{j\tilde{y}}/P''_{0\tilde{y}}] \geq E[P'_{j\tilde{y}}/P'_{0\tilde{y}}]$, all $j \in J$

where $P''_{0y''}(P'_{0y'})$ defines the unit cost of date-0 consumption in event $y'' \in Y''$ $(y' \in Y')$:

$$P''_{0y''} \equiv \sum_{s \in S_{y''}} v''_{0s},\ y'' \in Y''$$

Proof: Given conditions v, a, b and vi, CPE-allocations of the date-0 good are easily shown to be signal-independent. (See Ohlson [1984].) Constraint (2.8b) is therefore irrelevant in equilibrium, and (2.8a), (2.8c) relax because of assumptions i–iv. Thus, nobody is worse off in the double-primed economy. One further readily derives that in equilibrium

$$\sum_{s \in S_y} v_{0s} = p(y)$$

where y is a signal from either Y' or Y''. The expectational pricing structure iii* therefore follows by definition since $p(y) = P_{0y}$.

Pure exchange simplifies the conditions necessary for proposition 2.2. The spanning condition (iv) is now satisfied if and only if η'' is at least as fine as η'. Assumption vi becomes unnecessary since it must hold for the null partition. Further, one need not worry about the valuation relationship iii since $A' = A''$ and $v' = v''$ imply that $P'' = P'$. In fact, without too much difficulty, one deduces that the expectational valuation relationship iii* and pure exchange imply PCM, thereby rendering assumptions ii and i superfluous. (Clearly, i has no role if $P'' = P'$). In sum, assumption iii* with equality, combined with those on preferences/beliefs, implies that all individuals are at least as well off in a more informative pure-exchange economy. The production setting permits no similar strengthening of results. On the other hand, production may improve individuals' welfare even though η'' and η' do not compare on the fineness dimension since production potentially relaxes both (2.8a) and (2.8c).

Just as the constraints (2.8b) need not bind the equilibrium, the same may apply to (2.8c). The obvious case assumes HARA-class utilities with identical risk cautiousness.[4] The effects of information and production on the span of $\delta(A_1, \eta)$ become irrelevant, again underscoring the similarities between markets and information as externalities.

The PCM assumption is strong, and one cannot expect its occurrence without considerable structure on the economy. If the equilibrium allocations $(c_i')_i$ and $(c_i'')_i$ are identical, then, trivially, the two economies have a common implicit price system. This case, however, precludes a strictly positive welfare improvement and accordingly is of no real interest. Specific cases of strict welfare improvement and PCM can be concocted, but these are generally singular and not applicable for arbitrary (non-negative) endowments. With arbitrary endowments the only PCM economies I know of are those in which at least one individual has preferences that are linear in c_{i0} and c_{i1} (i.e., basically a risk-neutral individual).[5] The deeper theoretical issue deals with the existence of approximations when the economy consists of a large number of individuals and firms. To discuss this complex matter is beyond the confines of the paper. Suffice to mention, no clear-cut and easily interpretable results appear to be available (see Rubinstein [1978] for a negative result, and Hart [1979] for a positive one). In view of this limitation associated with PCM, a comprehensive analysis of information in production economies must consider non-PCM economies as well.

Stockholder Unanimity without Perfectly Competitive Markets

In response to the restrictiveness of the PCM assumption, part of the literature analyzes shareholder production unanimity without such markets. Implicit prices now depend on the production plans, and two economies may not have a common implicit price system. The seminal work is due to Ekern and Wilson [1974]. They show that unanimity is possible by replacing the assumption about markets with one about individuals' endowments. Specifically, the endowments are assumed to be equilibrium holdings relative to an existing set of plans. For this reason the theory is often referred to as *ex post stockholder unanimity theory*, in contrast to the *ex ante* theory which relies on PCM. This section reviews the *ex post* theory, and thereafter extends the analysis to economies with non-null information. The assumption of CPE-allocations is retained throughout. (A subsequent section relaxes this assumption.) Thus, the outline and content of the current section closely parallels the previous one, except that one assumption (on endowments) has been substituted for another (on the implicit prices). To facilitate interpretations, let $\Delta v_1 \equiv v_1'' - v_1'$ (and $\Delta v_0 \equiv v_0'' - v_0'$) denote changes in implicit prices due to a change in the production and/or information specification.

Ekern and Wilson [1974] derive their unanimity conclusion assuming that (1) the production changes are local (small) and (2) that the span of the securities-states tableau remains unchanged. Both conditions mitigate against extending the analysis to settings in which information varies. Although changes in production plans can be small, partition changes are inherently discrete. Similarly, the date-0 and date-1 commodity spaces must generally change with η. However, recent work by Ohlson [1985] relaxes the Ekern-Wilson assumptions by allowing for discrete changes in production plans as well as changes in the span of A_1.

Lemma 2.2

Let A'' and A' be two production specifications, with information being null in both cases. Suppose further that:

i. $\bar{\vartheta}_i \geq 0$ all $i \in I$ (non-negative endowments)
ii. $\vartheta'_i = \bar{\vartheta}_i$, $c'_{0i} = \bar{c}_{0i} + \bar{\vartheta}_i A'_0$, $i \in I$ (endowments are equilibrium holdings in the single-primed setting)
iii. $A''_1 v''_1 + A''_0 v''_0 \geqq A'_1 v''_1 + A'_0 v''_0$ or, equivalently, $P'' \geqq P' + A'_1 \Delta v_1$ (relative value condition)
iv. $C(A''_1) \supseteq C(A'_1)$ (spanning condition)

Then all individuals are at least as well off in the double-primed economy.

Proof: The optimal policy (c'_{0i}, c'_{1i}) is affordable also in the double-primed economy:

$$\begin{aligned}\bar{c}_{0i} v''_0 + \bar{\vartheta}_i P'' &\geq \bar{c}_{0i} v''_0 + \bar{\vartheta}_i (A'_1 v''_1 + A'_0 v''_0) \\ &= c'_{0i} v''_0 + \bar{\vartheta}_i A'_1 v''_1 = c'_{0i} v''_0 + \vartheta'_i A'_1 v''_1 \\ &= c'_{0i} v''_0 + c'_{1i} v''_1.\end{aligned}$$

The inequality derives from conditions i and iii. The three equalities derive from condition ii, and because $A'_0 v''_0 = A'_0 v'_0$ and $c'_{1i} = \vartheta'_i A'_1$. Given assumption iv, it follows further that $c'_i \in CO''_i$. The conclusion is immediate.

The result obtains simply because for every individual the optimal consumption plan in the single-primed economy is also available in the double-primed economy. The relationship is weaker than the one exploited for ex ante unanimity: it is no longer generally true that $CO'_i \subseteq CO''_i$. As a further implication, and this point is not always appreciated, ex post unanimity theory does not allow for a "corollary" about the unanimity of value-maximization (even if the span of A_1 is fixed across plans). Contemplated plans rank at the most relative to existing (single-primed) plans. There might be several contemplated plans all of which are preferred to the current one (i.e., they all meet the conditions of the lemma), yet the individuals' rankings of the preferred plans may not be unanimous. This limitation affects the ex post analysis, with or without information.

The lemma 2.2 extends to economies with information.

Proposition 2.3

Let (A'', η'') and (A', η') be two economies differing in their production and information, where η'' is non-null and η' is the null partition. Suppose that the equilibrium allocations of the two economies satisfy CPE relative to their respective securities-states tableaus and partitions. Further assume that

i. $\bar{\vartheta}_i \geq 0$ all $i \in I$ (non-negative endowments)

ii. $\vartheta'_i = \bar{\vartheta}_i$, $c'_{i0} = \bar{c}_{i0} + \bar{\vartheta}_i A'_0$ all $i \in I$ (endowments are equilibrium holdings in the single-primed setting)

iii. $A''_1 v''_1 + A''_0 v''_0 \geqq A'_1 v''_1 + A'_0 v''_0$ or, equivalently,

$$\sum_{y \in Y''} P''_y \geqq P' + A'_1 \Delta v_1 \qquad \text{(relative-values condition)};$$

iv. $C(\delta(A''_1, \eta'')) \supseteq C(A'_1)$ (spanning condition).

Then all individuals are at least as well off in the double-primed economy.

A formal proof is omitted since it follows along the same lines as the lemma. That is, c'_i is not only affordable in the double-primed economy, but also feasible because this economy relaxes constraints (2.8b) and (2.8c). Therefore $c'_i \in CO''_i$, and no individual is worse off with CO''_i rather than CO'_i.

As usual, pure exchange with a change in information simplifies the conditions. Condition iii holds automatically, further making i irrelevant. Likewise, as was also observed in the previous section, pure exchange implies condition iv. It follows that ii suffices for more information to weakly improve individuals' welfare. (Ohlson and Buckman [1981], proposition 10, p. 428, state necessary and sufficient conditions for a strict improvement.)

The preceding section notes that for costless information $\Omega_j(\eta'') \supseteq \Omega_j(\eta')$, so that value-maximizing firms satisfy the relative-value condition iii in proposition 2.1. In the context of proposition 2.3, value-maximization *combined* with an assumption that firms view the (equilibrium) implicit price vector as fixed implies condition iii: $A''v'' \geqq A'v''$ (although $P'' \geqq P'$ does not follow). Nevertheless, such firm behavior has no solid economic foundation. First, as noted, in the non-PCM ex post theory of the firm there is no unanimity about the desirability of value-maximization unless the *only* economies compared are (A'', η'') and (A', η'). Second, firms must take the implicit price vectors as fixed—i.e., firms perceive markets as being PCM—although they are not. Kreps [1979] notes that this perceived competition/without competition modeling has an element of irrationality built into it. Moreover, *no* theory suggests that the quantities $P_j'' - P_j'$ can be of interest in the theory of optimal production choice unless $\Delta v = 0$ (or at least approximately so). The reason is simple: if $\Delta v \neq 0$ then production changes impact not only on the right-hand side of the budget constraint (2.8a) but also on its left-hand side. Under the circumstance one cannot expect a unanimous ranking of production plans. The possibility of varying information does not affect this negative observation.

The conclusions about information in the non-PCM, ex post, analysis are basically similar to the PCM, ex ante, analysis. In either case, a welfare improvement due to incremental information requires stringent conditions, and the conditions relevant derive directly from the standard stockholder unanimity theory. The ex ante theory assumes PCM and proves $CO_i' \subseteq CO_i''$; the ex post non-PCM theory assumes equilibrium endowments and proves $c_i' \in CO_i''$ without $CO_i' \subseteq CO_i''$. Both cases therefore focus on consumption opportunities, which affordability determines but partially. Additionally one must consider the broad opportunity effects of production and information. These effects reduce to linear constraints on available consumption mixes, and in that regard information and production are similar. Thus, information changes in conjunction with production changes introduces few new complexities. The relevant conditions are fundamentally equivalent to those required in the standard theory of the firm, and it makes no difference whether the question deals with unanimity or the optimality of value-maximization.

Efficiency and Alternative Production and Information Specifications

One common justification for value-maximization is that this criterion leads to (constrained) Pareto efficiency. To some extent the theory of the firm is salvaged, the "cost" being the abandonment of shareholder unanimity. Focusing on firms' contributions to overall economic performance, rather than particular individuals' (shareholders) well being, entails an important switch in philosophy. No consideration is given to distribution issues. Conditions for preferred plans typically can be weakened since $(V_i'')_i$ and $(V_i')_i$ need not be compared for each i. Instead, the interest pertains to the $(V_1, \ldots, V_I)$-loci for two sets of CPE allocations. A particularization of endowments is unnecessary since one contrives the set of all CPE consumption plans by varying endowments, given any production and information specification.

The following lemma—pertaining to null information—modifies the classical result by allowing variation in the commodity spaces (i.e., the securities-states tableaus).

Lemma 2.3

Let A'' and A' be two production specifications, with information being null in both cases, and where $C(A_1'') \supseteq C(A_1')$. Let $(c_i'')_i$ be any CPE equilibrium relative to A_1'' with implicit prices v''. Assume further that

$$1A''v'' - 1A'v'' > 0$$

Then no consumption allocation available in the single-primed setting Pareto dominates $(c_i'')_i$.

A proof is easily concocted via a simple modification of the standard case with $C(A_1'') = C(A_1')$. (For a proof, see Nielsen [1978].)

Lemma 2.3 generalizes directly to include variations in information.

Proposition 2.4

Assume the production and information specifications are such that η'' is finer than η' and $C(\delta(A_1'', \eta'')) \supseteq C(\delta(A_1', \eta'))$. Let $(c_i'')_i$ be any CPE equilibrium relative to (A_1'', η'') with implicit prices v''. Assume further that

$$1A''v'' - 1A'v'' > 0$$

Then no consumption allocation in the single-primed economy Pareto dominates $(c_i'')_i$.

A few observations are appropriate. First, the interpretation of the inequality is that the value of aggregate (net) output (or GNP) is greater in the double-primed economy than in the single-primed economy. The measurement of GNP relies on the v'' implicit price system, because the allocation characterized is $(c_i'')_i$. Second, all of the conditions are necessary and, without restrictions or preferences/beliefs, the result is the sharpest possible. (Restrictions on preferences/beliefs or production/information might lead to relaxations similar to proposition 2.3). Third, the relative aggregate value condition is, as usual, implied if all firms are assumed to maximize their (net) market values and the information is costless [i.e., $\Omega_j(\eta') \subseteq \Omega_j(\eta'')$ for all j]. However, the caveats associated with value-maximization mentioned in the previous section apply with equal force here. Fourth, proposition 2.4, unfortunately, does *not* imply that the double-primed CPE allocations dominate the single-primed allocations in the sense that for every single-primed CPE allocation there exists a Pareto-preferable double-primed allocation. The two $(V_i)_i$-loci can intersect each other, and proposition 2.4 yields only a local result. In a classical certainty setting, this possibility has long been known, and Samuelson [1950] provides a particularly lucid analysis. His argument generalizes directly to an information/production setting in which (2.8b) is nonbinding (e.g., assume conditions v and vi in proposition 2.2), and $C(\delta(A_1'', \eta'')) = C(\delta(A_1', \eta'))$. The commodity spaces for efficient allocations are identical, and the utility-loci intersect if $1A''v' < 1A'v'$ for some $(c_i')_i$ allocation since $1A''v'' > 1A'v''$. Such an example is easily constructed.

The possibility of intersecting efficient utility-loci has an important implication. The fact that one individual might be worse off in a more informative economy with both efficient production and consumption plans is *not* necessarily a redistributive issue. More precisely, fix the endowments and consider two economies in which firms value-maximize taking the implicit prices as given. Suppose further that for some reason $C(\delta(A_1'', \eta'')) = C(\delta(A_1', \eta'))$, and that the equilibrium results in $V_i(c_i'') < V_i(c_i')$ for some i. Even though η'' is finer than η', and $1A''v'' > 1A'v''$ because of value-maximization, one cannot conclude that there exists a suitable redistribution of $(c_i'')_i$ that Pareto dominates $(c_i')_i$. This outcome is the more surprising since pure exchange does not imply a similar negative conclusion: if one individual is worse off in pure exchange due to incremental information, then this is *necessarily* a redistributive effect. The two efficient utility-loci never intersect in pure exchange (although they may be identical).

The ambiguous impact of more information in a decentralized production economy does not contradict the basic fineness theorem. Nor does it depend on, or illustrate, the intrinsic limitation of value-maximization.

In a centralized economy, incremental (costless) information is always better than less. Specifically, consider the following planner's problem:

$$g(\eta) \equiv \max_{(c_i)_i,\,(a_j)_j} V_1 \tag{2.10}$$

subject to:

1. $V_i = k_i$, $i = 2, \ldots, I$; the k_i are predetermined constants;
2. conservation constraints (2.1a) and (2.1b);
3. $a_j \in \Omega_j(\eta), j \in J$;
4. $c_{1i} \in C(\delta(A_1, \eta))$, $i \in I$; and
5. measurability of c_{0i}, $i \in I$.

It is obvious that incremental information is no worse than less: $g(\eta'') \geq g(\eta')$.

Due to the externality associated with the span of $\delta(A_1, \eta)$, the optimizing production plans in (2.10) do not necessarily replicate in a decentralized economy in which firms maximize their values (with perceived competition). For this reason, value-maximization implies only the GNP-inequality in proposition 2.4; in contrast, the condition $C(\delta(A_1'', \eta'')) \supseteq C(A_1', \eta')$ is imposed. If for some reason there is exact spanning across production plans, then the optimal plans replicate in a decentralized economy. As usual, the role of uncertainty and information is easily dealt with following an identification of the commodity space.

The variability of the space $C(\cdot)$ does not, however, explain why the two efficient utility-loci associated with η'' and η' may intersect each other. The reason is more basic. The optimal production plans that solve (2.10) depend on the predetermined constants $k_2, \ldots, k_I$, and the plans chosen therefore dovetail with the desired distribution of individuals' well-being. Given some η, as $k_2, \ldots, k_I$ vary so do the optimal production plans. The analysis of efficient utility-loci presents no such harmony, since each utility-locus derives from a fixed set of plans. The plans chosen, and aggregate supplies, may not be particularly efficient for *hypothetical* distributions of welfare. This conclusion is valid even if one fixes $C(\delta(A, \eta))$. In a curious and surprising fashion, the positive social-value aspect of information is more robust and direct under pure exchange compared to production economies.

The major conclusion of this section is much the same as in previous ones: the analysis of information's welfare implications are identifiable from basic principles. The difficulty of inferring relative efficiency from measures of planned GNP is identical in settings with certainty, no information but uncertainty, and varying information.

Unanimity When Allocations Are Not CPE

This section considers the implications of removing the CPE requirement. The equilibrium allocations no longer coordinate across signals in contrast to those of the perfectly competitive markets. To develop such a model, assume that the individual faces a budget constraint for each signal, and the endowed wealth depends on the signal. In this setting there are $y = 1, \ldots, Y$ budget constraints. Each can be stated as

$$\sum_{s \in S_y} c_{0is} v_{0s} + \sum_j \vartheta_{ijy} (P_{jy} - \sum_{s \in S_y} a_{0js} v_{1s}) \leq \sum_{s \in S_y} \bar{c}_{0is} v_{0s} + \sum_j \bar{\vartheta}_{ij} P_{jy}$$

Also, as usual, c_{0i} and a_{0j} must be measurable relative to the underlying information function.

The following constraints determine an individual's consumption opportunity set:

$$\sum_{s \in S_y} (c_{0is} v_{0s} + c_{1is} v_{1s}) \leq \sum_{s \in S_y} \bar{c}_{0is} v_{0s} + \bar{\vartheta}_i P_y \qquad y = 1, \ldots, Y \tag{2.11a}$$

$$c_{0is} = c_{0it} \text{ when } s, t \in S_y, \text{ some } y \tag{2.11b}$$

$$c_{1i} \in C(\delta(A_1, \eta)) \tag{2.11c}$$

While constraints (2.11a)–(2.11c) are similar to (2.8a)–(2.8c), they are more stringent because (2.11a) is more stringent than (2.8a). Specifically, given any implicit price system and endowments, the above consumption opportunity set constitutes a strict subset of the one implied by (2.8a)–(2.8c) when $\eta \neq \eta^0$. [Adding the Y constraints in (2.11a) results in (2.8a).] Accordingly, individuals generally attain less welfare in this setting compared to the CPE economy. Indeed, the equilibrium implied by (2.9) is only *signal-efficient* (SE) relative to (A_1, η), and SE is necessary but not sufficient for CPE.

At least one reason suggests why the above economies are interesting. Individuals cannot hedge against the uncertainty associated with random endowed wealth and opportunities. No "signal-insurance" opportunities exist, and exchanges of shares occur subsequent to the release of the (uncertain) signal. One can argue that this second-best scenario is more realistic than the unlimited coordination of holdings across signals required for CPE-allocations.

Modifications of proposition 2.1, where markets are PCM, and proposition 2.3, where markets are non-PCM, pose no difficulties.

Proposition 2.5

In propositions 2.1 and 2.3, the CPE requirement can be removed if condition iii is replaced by

$$P''_{jy} \geq \sum_{s \in S_y} (a'_{1js} v''_{1s} + a'_{0js} v''_{0s}) \qquad \text{all } y \in Y'' \quad \text{and} \quad j \in J$$

Kunkel [1982] proves a special non-PCM case of proposition 2.5. He assumes conditionally complete (A_1'', η'') [i.e., $C(\delta(A_1'', \eta'')) = C(I)$] and this condition satisfies iv in proposition 2.3.

Corollary 2.3 (Kunkel)

Assume that individuals' endowments are non-negative and currently in equilibrium. Then all individuals are at least as well off in a more informative economy provided that (1) markets are conditionally complete, and (2) firms value-maximize and perceive perfect competition for each signal.[6]

Hakansson, Kunkel and Ohlson ([1982] in parts of their lemma II) identify the pure-exchange non-PCM case of proposition 2.5: with endowments being in equilibrium, no individual is worse off in a more informative economy. Further, to the extent additional trading occurs it follows that the allocation is Pareto superior. Lemma II of their paper provides necessary and sufficient conditions for a strict improvement. These conditions are much more demanding than those of a production setting because the only source of improvement is due to superior risk sharing. Production also permits superior plans. A sufficient condition for strict welfare improvement in propositions 2.1, 2.2, 2.3, and 2.5 is that the valuation inequalities are strict for at least one security (and signal in 2.5).

Notes

1. Note that $P_j - a_{0j}v_0$ equals the value of firm j subsequent to the shareholders's capital contribution.
2. The statement presumes some output in each state, i.e., $1A_1 > 0$.
3. The statement needs a qualification. If Hart's [1979] much sharper notion of competitive markets (i.e., demands for shares are perfectly elastic) is used, then spanning becomes irrelevant and value-maximization is optimal. (This also requires final shareholdings to be non-negative.) The analysis of the present paper easily extends to accommodate this sharper notion of competitivity.
4. Of course, HARA-class utilities require that $C(\delta(A_1, \eta))$ includes the unit vector.
5. This means that constraints (2.8b) and (2.8c) are nonbinding for *all* individuals, *and* markets are PCM, if and only if all individuals have (identical) linear preferences. Only the wealth constraint (2.8c) becomes relevant, and value-maximization is optimal. Thus, with no particular restrictions on endowments, there is agreement about the optimal amount of costly information production if and only if all individuals are identically risk-neutral. Trueman [1983] proves this result.
6. Strictly speaking, the value-maximization condition requires an additional assumption about $\Omega_j(\eta)$:

$$\max_{a_j} P_j = \sum_y \max_{(a_{js};\, s\in S_y)} P_{jy} \qquad (v \text{ fixed})$$

That is, there are no cross-signal effects on production choice.

References

Arrow, K.J. [1979]. "Risk Allocation and Information: Some Recent Theoretical Developments." *The Geneva Papers on Risk and Insurance* 12, 23–25.

Baron, D. [1979]. "Investment Policy, Optimality, and the Mean-Variance Model." *Journal of Finance* 34, 206–232.

Ekern, S., and Wilson, R. [1974]. "On the Theory of the Firm in an Economy with Incomplete Markets." *Bell Journal of Economics* 5, 171–180.

Hakansson, N.H. [1977]. "Interim Disclosure and Public Forecasts: An Economic Analysis and a Framework for Choice." *Accounting Review* 52, 396–416.

Hakansson, N.H., Kunkel, J.G., and Ohlson, J.A. [1982]. "Sufficient and Necessary Conditions for Information to Have Social Value in Pure Exchange." *Journal of Finance* 37, 1169–1181.

Hart, O.D. [1979]. "On Shareholder Unanimity in Large Stock Market Economies." *Econometrica* 47, 1057–1083.

Hirshleifer, J. [1971]. "The Private Value and Social Value of Information and the Reward to Inventive Activity." *American Economic Review* 61, 561–574.

Kreps, D. [1979]. "Three Essays on Capital Markets." Working Paper, Stanford University.

Kunkel, J.G. [1982]. "Sufficient Conditions for Public Information to Have Social Value in a Production and Exchange Economy." *Journal of Finance* 37, 1005–1013.

Leland, H.E. [1973]. "A Capital Asset Markets, Production, and Optimality: A Synthesis." Technical Report No. 115, IMSSS, Standford University.

Nielsen, N.C. [1976]. "The Investment Decision of the Firm under Uncertainty and the Allocative Efficiency of Capital Markets." *Journal of Finance* 31, 587–602.

Nielsen, N.C. [1978]. "On the Financing and Investment Decision of the Firm." *Journal of Banking and Finance* 2, 79–101.

Ohlson, J.A. [1984]. "The Structure of Asset-Prices and Socially Useless/Useful Information." *Journal of Finance* 39, 1417–1435.

Ohlson, J.A. [1985]. "Ex Post Stockholder Unanimity: A Complete and Simplified Treatment." *Journal of Banking and Finance* 9, 387–399.

Ohlson, J.A., and Buckman, A.G. [1981]. "Toward a Theory of Financial Accounting: Welfare and Public Information," *Journal of Accounting Research* 19, 399–433.

Rubinstein, M. [1978]. "Competition and Approximation." *Bell Journal of Economics* 9, 280–286.

Samuelson, P.A. [1950]. "Evaluation of Real National Income." *Oxford Economic Papers* (new series) 2, 1–29.

Trueman, B. [1983]. "Necessary and Sufficient Conditions for Achieving Stockholder Unanimity over the Production of Information." Working Paper, University of California at Los Angeles.

3 COSTLY PUBLIC INFORMATION: OPTIMALITY AND COMPARATIVE STATICS*

Young K. Kwon
and
D. Paul Newman

The value of public information in markets has been analyzed in a variety of settings. Ohlson and Buckman [1981] provide an overview and synthesis, demonstrating that the efficiency criterion satisfied by an information structure is crucially dependent on the market regime, available securities, and endowments. For example, if securities span the state space, (public) information is redundant. Similarly, the Pareto dominance of information structures (over, for instance, null information) is inextricably related to endowments, the number of trading points, homogeneity of market participants, and other variables.

We continue investigation of the implications of publicly available information in the spirit of Ohlson and Buckman.

> . . . the purpose of information is to facilitate and improve upon the consumption investment plans of individuals transacting in a market setting. This must

* Helpful comments were provided by participants of workshops at University of California at Berkeley and University of Wisconsin at Madison. In addition, the suggestions by the editors were quite valuable.

> be viewed as a very weak requirement since it simply means that somewhere along the line (accounting) information has to be related to individuals' well-being. Naturally, a major research implication will then be one of investigating the effects of information, and changes in information, on the welfare induced by the resulting allocation(s) of goods. (Ohlson and Buckman [1981], p. 543)

However, we expand the usual analysis in a number of ways. First, a stylized economy is considered in which public information is shown to have *social value*. Then, by positing a reasonable production function for information (i.e., allowing for costly information), the optimal *quantity* of information is determined. Next, we conduct a comparative statics analysis on our results, the predictions of which are empirically testable in principle. Thus, rather than restricting our attention exclusively to social value (which may be viewed by some as a foregone conclusion given our assumptions), we enlarge the analysis to include a variety of additional issues.

A number of caveats are in order. First, we consider what is similar to Ohlson and Buckman's [1981] *iterated market regime*. Investors are allowed to trade to equilibrium in available securities prior to the introduction of information. (Here, we simply endow traders with null-information equilibrium holdings, but the effect is the same.) Thus, the distributional effect of information is minimized. Second, we assume that firms' decisions are exogenous.[1] Third, investors are allowed to borrow or lend at an exogenous risk-free rate. Immediately, we have some hope of demonstrating social value of information using Pareto dominance as the criterion of social value, since the ability to shift consumption streams across periods creates demand for information. Fourth, we consider only the predictive value of information. The post decision value (stewardship or contracting role) is ignored.[2] Fifth, specific utility functions and beliefs are posited. The advantage is, of course, tractability. On the other hand, our results may be sensitive to the assumptions made. In defense, however, the assumptions are consistent with the traditional capital asset pricing model (CAPM) for risky assets. This list of restrictions is designed to place the analysis conducted here in an appropriate setting, since such assumptions have been demonstrated to be crucial to conclusions in similar papers.

In the next section, the underlying economic structure is described. Following this, the Pareto optimal amount of (costly) information in the economy is derived. The next section contains comparative statics and testable implications. A conclusion follows in the final section.

The Economic Structure

We characterize periodic earnings of firms as random realizations from a fixed population. As a result, measurements of firms' earnings play a role similar to statistical sampling and can therefore be useful for predicting firms' future earnings. Accounting measurements, in particular, may be subsumed in this characterization. From this perspective, financial accounting is viewed as a systematic process of measuring the underlying economic events of a firm within the "allowed" precision requirements of generally accepted accounting principles (GAAP). The predictive value of accounting information, then, will be shown to be directly related to the precision requirements of GAAP.

Throughout this paper, we consider a competitive and perfect capital market. There are I investors (indexed by $i = 1, 2, \ldots, I$) and J risky firms (indexed by $j, k = 1, 2, \ldots, J$). Every investor i is characterized by: (1) an endowment of income or savings $\bar{x}_i > 0$; (2) an endowment of firm ownership fractions $(\bar{\theta}_{ij})_j$ where $\Sigma_i \bar{\theta}_{ij} = 1$ for all j; and (3) a utility function $u_i(c_{i1}, c_{i2})$ over current and future consumption vectors (c_{i1}, c_{i2}). For analytic tractibility, we assume that all investors' preferences exhibit constant absolute risk aversion (i.e., constant risk tolerance, cf. Pratt [1964]).

Assumption 3.1

The utility function of investor i has the form

$$u_i(c_{i1}, c_{i2}) = -e^{-c_{i1}/r_i} - e^{-c_{i2}/r_i} \tag{2.1}$$

where $r_i > 0$ is the constant risk-tolerance index (i.e., the inverse of the absolute risk-aversion index). All investors are expected utility maximizers and are allowed to borrow or lend at the same per period risk-free yield $\rho = 1$.[3]

We have assumed time additivity with no discounting for convenience. Similarly, we have posited negative exponential utility functions to obtain closed-form solutions. Such utility functions have been used (for similar reasons) to evaluate information effects by Grossman and Stiglitz [1976], Huber [1978], and Verrecchia [1982]. The risk-free yield ρ is set equal to one to simplify subsequent analysis. However, all results follow for $\rho > 0$.

Denote by $\tilde{y}_j$ the total return of firm j that accrues to equity holders.[4] The random vector $\tilde{\mathbf{y}} = (\tilde{y}_1, \tilde{y}_2, \ldots, \tilde{y}_J)$ then describes total equity returns of all risky firms. For analytical tractibility, we also assume:

Assumption 3.2

The equity return vector $\tilde{\mathbf{y}} = (\tilde{y}_1, \tilde{y}_2, \ldots, \tilde{y}_J)$ is jointly normally distributed with mean $\boldsymbol{\mu} = (\mu_1, \mu_2, \ldots, \mu_J)$ and nonsingular variance-covariance matrix $\Sigma = (\sigma_{jk})$. (Thus, investors' beliefs are homogeneous with respect to firms' returns.)

As a result, the market portfolio of all risky firms,

$$\tilde{y}_M = \sum_{j=1}^{J} \tilde{y}_j \tag{3.2}$$

is normally distributed with mean and variance:

$$\begin{aligned} \mu_M &= \sum_{j=1}^{J} \mu_j \\ \sigma_M^2 &= \sum_{j,k=1}^{J} \sigma_{jk} \end{aligned} \tag{3.3}$$

The systematic risk of firm j is then defined by

$$b_j = \frac{\operatorname{cov}(\tilde{y}_j, \tilde{y}_M)}{\operatorname{var}(y_M)} = \frac{1}{\sigma_M^2} \sum_{k=1}^{J} \sigma_{jk} \tag{3.4}$$

for all j.[5]

We now introduce an information system η_λ where $\lambda > 0$ is a parameter which indicates the *precision* (or accuracy) of the system. Before making their consumption-investment decisions, all investors observe realizations z_j of random *signals* $\tilde{z}_j$ that are correlated with equity returns of firms:

$$\tilde{z}_j = \tilde{y}_j + \tilde{\varepsilon}_j \tag{3.5}$$

where $E(\tilde{\varepsilon}_j) = E(\tilde{y}_j\tilde{\varepsilon}_j) = 0$ and

$$\operatorname{var}(\tilde{\varepsilon}_j) = \frac{1}{\lambda}\sigma_j^2 \tag{3.6}$$

In other words, system η_λ allows investors to obtain unbiased predictions $E[\tilde{y}_j|\tilde{z}_j = z_j]$ of equity returns y_j: $E(\varepsilon_j) = 0$. However, system η_λ is noisy: $\operatorname{var}(\tilde{\varepsilon}_j) > 0$. The quantity λ describes the precision of system η_λ: the prediction errors $\operatorname{var}(\tilde{\varepsilon}_j)$ decrease if and only if the parameter λ increases. We shall call λ the *amount of information* for the system η_λ. This representation is relatively general. For example, including bias ($E(\tilde{\varepsilon}_j) \neq 0$) would have no impact, since investors can correct for known bias (thus, changes in the information system to correct for bias should have no impact on our results). In addition, $\operatorname{var}(\tilde{\varepsilon}_j)$

is allowed to vary across firms. Thus, for fixed λ, the information system may have different predictive ability across firms.

Denote by $\tilde{\mathbf{z}} = (\tilde{z}_1, \tilde{z}_2, \ldots, \tilde{z}_J)$ the information about $\tilde{\mathbf{y}} = (\tilde{y}_1, \tilde{y}_2, \ldots, \tilde{y}_J)$ that is provided by a given accounting information system η_λ, and let $\tilde{\boldsymbol{\varepsilon}} = (\tilde{\varepsilon}_1, \tilde{\varepsilon}_2, \ldots, \tilde{\varepsilon}_J)$ denote the corresponding error vector.

Assumption 3.3

An accounting information system η_λ is characterized by

$$\tilde{\mathbf{z}} = \tilde{\mathbf{y}} + \tilde{\boldsymbol{\varepsilon}} \tag{3.7}$$

where the random vectors $\tilde{\mathbf{y}}$ and $\boldsymbol{\varepsilon}$ are uncorrelated and the error vector $\tilde{\boldsymbol{\varepsilon}}$ is normally distributed with mean $\mathbf{0} = (0, 0, \ldots, 0)$ and variance-covariance matrix

$$E = \frac{1}{\lambda}\Sigma \tag{3.8}$$

The (societal) cost $f(\lambda)$ of the system η_λ is increasing and convex:

$$f'(\lambda) > 0 \qquad \text{and} \qquad f''(\lambda) \geq 0 \tag{3.9}$$

for all $\lambda > 0$, where the cost is measured in units of income.

Let p_j represent the total equity price of firm j at the capital market equilibrium. The initial wealth of investor i then has the form

$$\bar{w}_i = \bar{x}_i + \sum_{j=1}^{J} \bar{\theta}_{ij} p_j \tag{3.10}$$

for all i. If investors are not allowed to trade prior to the introduction of η_λ, distributional effects may occur due to changes in equilibrium prices (the *no iterated market* in Ohlson and Buckman [1981]). To reduce such distributional effects, it will be convenient to assume that all investors are endowed with equilibrium positions in all risky firms (or allow trading prior to signal release).

Assumption 3.4

The initial endowed positions of all investors in risky firms are consistent with the capital market equilibrium:[6]

$$\bar{\theta}_{ij} = \frac{r_i}{r} \tag{3.11}$$

for all i and j, where $r > 0$ is the sum of the constant risk-tolerance indexes across investors:

$$r = \sum_{i=1}^{I} r_i \tag{3.12}$$

These assumptions represent the stylized economic environment. Of course, the theory to be developed is contingent on this characterization and should be interpreted accordingly. The most severe (and convenient) assumption is that of negative exponential utility, which allows a number of simplifications. More general assumptions have been made by others (see Ohlson and Buckman [1981]), but generality is achieved at the expense of specific results and predictions. We view this as a necessary, if undesirable, trade-off.

The distinction between our model and that of Hakansson et al. [1982] merits clarification. In Hakansson et al., assumptions of (1) time additive preferences (our assumption 3.1); (2) HARA utility functions with identical risk cautiousness (our assumption 3.1); (3) homogeneous beliefs (our assumption 3.2); and (4) equilibrium endowments (our assumption 3.4) are shown to preclude social value of public information. Our model differs from that of Hakansson et al., in that an exogenously fixed risk-free yield ρ is assumed, which permits aggregate consumption shifts between the current and future periods. Allowing the shift (at a *fixed* price ρ) creates the demand for and social value of public information. The ability to shift consumption between periods at a fixed price can be viewed as analogous to a limited form of production (i.e., transformation of current consumption into future consumption at a constant return to scale). The positive value of public information is demonstrated in the next section.

The Value of Public Information

Ultimately in this section, we wish to determine a Pareto-optimal amount of public information given its cost structure. We first consider expected utilities under the null-information system η_0. We then compare these utilities to those that can be attained with a system η_λ, first considering η_λ as costless and then introducing cost. Thus, we can identify whether the system η_λ has positive social value, defined, as usual, by

$$E[u_i|\eta_\lambda] \geq E[u_i|\eta_0] \qquad \text{for all } i$$

$$E[u_i|\eta_\lambda] > E[u_i|\eta_0] \qquad \text{for at least one } i$$

First, consider the case where the null system η_0 is adopted. By assumptions 3.1 and 3.2, we can describe the consumption-investment decision of investor i as follows:

$$\underset{\{c_{i1},\, x_i,\, (\theta_{ij})_j\}}{\text{maximize}} \left[u_i(c_{i1}) + Eu_i\left(x_i + \sum_{j=1}^{J} \theta_{ij} \tilde{y}_j \right) \right] \tag{3.13}$$

subject to

$$c_{i1} + x_i + \sum_{j=1}^{J} \theta_{ij} p_j = \bar{w}_i$$

where c_{i1} = the amount of current consumption, x_i = the amount of savings or borrowing, and θ_{ij} = the equity share fraction of firm j. The total equity share prices p_j are to be determined by the market equilibrium condition: $\Sigma_i \theta_{ij} = 1$ for all j.

Theorem 3.1

Under assumptions 3.1, 3.2, and 3.4, the following hold at the capital market equilibrium:

i. The expected utilities of investors have the form

$$E[u_i^* | \eta_0] = -2\exp\left[-\frac{1}{2r}\left(\frac{r\bar{x}_i}{r_i} + \mu_M - \frac{1}{2r}\sigma_M^2 \right) \right] \tag{3.14}$$

ii. The aggregate level of savings x is

$$x = \frac{1}{2}\left[\bar{x} - \mu_M + \frac{1}{2r}\sigma_M^2 \right] \tag{3.15}$$

where $\bar{x} = \Sigma_i \bar{x}_i$.

iii. The prices of individual firm equities are

$$p_j = \mu_j - \frac{1}{r} b_j \sigma_M^2 \tag{3.16}$$

Proof: (For a proof, see appendix.)

We observe from expression (3.15) that the aggregate savings level x critically depends on the return characteristics μ_M and σ_M^2 of the market portfolio. When expected future consumption provided by the investor's risky investment portfolio increases (i.e., μ_M increases), the marginal expected utility of future consumption decreases, and therefore, the investor shifts to increased current consumption. For the same reason, a decrease in dispersion (i.e., σ_M^2) of future consumption increases current consumption. The desire to balance current and future consumption is the source of information demand in our model.

Expression (3.16) is the well-known capital asset pricing model (CAPM) of Sharpe [1964], Lintner [1965], and Mossin [1966]:

$$\mu_j - \rho p_j = b_j(\mu_M - \rho p_M) \tag{3.16}$$

for all j (note that $\rho = 1$ by assumption 3.1). For later reference, we define the residual risk component of firm j as

$$\tilde{\xi}_j = (\tilde{y}_j - \mu_j) - b_j(\tilde{y}_M - \mu_M) \tag{3.17}$$

for all j, where b_j represents the systematic risk of firm j [cf. equation (3.4)]. As a result, we have

$$E(\tilde{\xi}_j) = 0 \qquad \text{and} \qquad \operatorname{cov}(\tilde{\xi}_j, \tilde{y}_M) = 0 \tag{3.18}$$

for all j. In particular, variables $\tilde{\xi}_j$ and $\tilde{y}_M$ are independently distributed since they are jointly normal.

Next, consider the case where an accounting information system η_λ is adopted (cf. assumption 3.3). If a signal $\tilde{\mathbf{z}} = \mathbf{z}$ is released to the capital market through the system η_λ, then, all investors revise their expectations:

$$\begin{aligned} E(\tilde{\mathbf{y}}|\tilde{\mathbf{z}} = \mathbf{z}) &= \boldsymbol{\mu} + \Sigma(\Sigma + E)^{-1}(\mathbf{z} - \boldsymbol{\mu}) \\ \operatorname{var}(\tilde{\mathbf{y}}|\tilde{\mathbf{z}} = \mathbf{z}) &= \Sigma - \Sigma(\Sigma + E)^{-1}\Sigma \end{aligned} \tag{3.19a}$$

(cf., e.g., Taylor [1974, theorem 12.6]). It then follows from (3.8) that

$$\begin{aligned} E(\tilde{\mathbf{y}}|\tilde{\mathbf{z}} = \mathbf{z}) &= \boldsymbol{\mu} + \frac{\lambda}{\lambda + 1}(\mathbf{z} - \boldsymbol{\mu}) \\ \operatorname{var}(\tilde{\mathbf{y}}|\tilde{\mathbf{z}} = \mathbf{z}) &= \frac{1}{\lambda + 1}\Sigma \end{aligned} \tag{3.19b}$$

for all realizations $\mathbf{z}$ of the random signal $\tilde{\mathbf{z}}$ for the system η_λ. In particular, the distribution $\tilde{y}_M$ of the market portfolio conditional upon the signal $\tilde{\mathbf{z}} = \mathbf{z}$ is normal with mean and variance:

$$\begin{aligned} E(\tilde{y}_M|\tilde{\mathbf{z}} = \mathbf{z}) &= \mu_M + \frac{1}{\lambda + 1}(z_M - \mu_M) \\ \operatorname{var}(\tilde{y}_M|\tilde{\mathbf{z}} = \mathbf{z}) &= \frac{1}{\lambda + 1}\sigma_M^2 \end{aligned} \tag{3.20}$$

where $\mathbf{z} = (z_1, z_2, \ldots, z_J)$ and $z_M = \Sigma_j z_j$. As a result, expected utilities, aggregate savings, and firm equity prices all depend upon the realization z_M. Since $\tilde{z}_M$ is normal with mean and variance

$$E(\tilde{z}_M) = \mu_M$$

$$\operatorname{var}(\tilde{z}_M) = \frac{\lambda + 1}{\lambda}\sigma_M^2$$

we obtain the results.

Theorem 3.2

Assume that assumptions 3.1–3.4 are satisfied, and that an accounting information system η_λ is adopted. Ignoring the costs of the system η_λ, the following hold:

i. The expected utilities of investors are

$$E[u_i^* | \eta_\lambda] = -2\exp\left\{-\frac{1}{2r}\left[\frac{r\bar{x}_i}{r_i} + \mu_M - \frac{2+\lambda}{4r(\lambda+1)}\sigma_M^2\right]\right\} \tag{3.21}$$

ii. The expected aggregate savings level is

$$Ex = E[\Sigma_i x_i] = \frac{1}{2}\left[\bar{x} - \mu_M + \frac{1}{2r(\lambda+1)}\sigma_M^2\right] \tag{3.22}$$

iii. The expected prices of firm equities are

$$Ep_j = \mu_j - \frac{1}{r(1+\lambda)} b_j \sigma_M^2$$

Proof: (For a proof, see appendix.)

Comparing (3.14) and (3.21), observe that costless information production is socially valuable unless it is exclusively noise ($\lambda = 0$). It also follows from (3.15) and (3.22) that investors as a group increase their current consumption on average as equity returns become more certain with information.

Next, we consider the optimal level of costly information production. As a first step for such an investigation, it will be convenient to express expected utilities (3.21) explicitly considering any required contribution to finance information:

$$U_i^*(w_i, \lambda) = -2\exp\left\{-\frac{1}{2r}\left[\frac{rw_i}{r_i} + \mu_M - \frac{2+\lambda}{4r(\lambda+1)}\sigma_M^2\right]\right\} \tag{3.23}$$

for all i, where w_i is the income after contribution $(\bar{x}_i - w_i)$ for information production has been deducted and λ denotes the amount of information. Since the societal cost of the system η_λ is $f(\lambda)$, information production can fully be financed if and only if

$$f(\lambda) = \sum_{i=1}^{I} (\bar{x}_i - w_i)$$

In order to determine an optimal amount λ^* of information, we must then solve:

$$\underset{\{(w_i),\lambda\}}{\text{maximize}} \sum_{i=1}^{I} v_i U_i^*(w_i, \lambda) \tag{3.24}$$

subject to

$$\sum_{i=1}^{I} w_i + f(\lambda) = \sum_{i=1}^{I} \bar{x}_i$$

where the constants v_i are positive weights. Assuming an interior solution $[w_i^* > 0$ and $\lambda^* > 0]$ of (3.24), we obtain

$$f'(\lambda) = \frac{\sigma_M^2}{4r(1+\lambda)^2} \tag{3.25}$$

Thus, (3.25) is the condition specifying the optimal level of information production, assuming information is produced (i.e., the cost is not too high). The optimization problem (3.24) is treated from the perspective of a benevolent agency that knows all relevant preferences, beliefs, and costs. Thus, no prices appear in the program. As equation (3.25) shows, the optimal λ^* (if positive) depends on both the aggregate risk-tolerance index r of investors and the information production technology $f(\lambda)$. These are strong informational requirements. This is a typical analysis in welfare theory and focuses on the *feasibility* of allocations (see Ohlson [1979]). Walker [1981] and Kwon [1982] demonstrate that a mechanism exists which, without complete knowledge, can facilitate an optimal production level for a public good, such as information.

Comparative Statics

In this section we consider the implications of varying certain parameters and assumptions in our original formulation. Certain of these variations are designed to identify the sensitivity of the theory with respect to assumptions. Others have (in principle) empirically testable implications using historical equity returns.

First, note the following theorem regarding our original optimization problem.

Theorem 3.3

Assume that assumptions 3.1–3.4 are satisfied, and that the optimization problem (3.24) has an interior solution. The following then hold:

i. The Pareto optimal amount λ^* of information is independent of individual weights $v_i > 0$.
ii. If firm equity returns are more uncertain (σ_M^2 is larger), then the optimal λ^* must be larger.
iii. If information production is more costly, [$f(\lambda)$ is shifted upward by an increasing function]; then the optimal λ^* decreases.
iv. If investors as a group are more risk averse (r is smaller), then the optimal λ^* increases.

Proof: (For a proof, see appendix.)

Part i of the theorem is the direct result of the assumption that λ^* is an interior point. The remaining results seem rather intuitive, which serves as partial confirmation that our formulation is not unreasonable.

Next, consider the effects of exogenous changes in λ, the precision of the information system. Continuing our analogy with GAAP, one of the espoused objectives of the Securities and Exchange Commission (SEC) and various accounting boards (APB, FASB) has been to narrow the range of reporting alternatives available to firms. If successful, presumably such actions would be analogous to increasing λ. (Note that certain standards promulgated by the SEC and the FASB may have the objective of reducing bias. In our model, such efforts have no impact, since investors are fully aware of any bias inherent in the information system and can correct for that bias.) The impact of such changes on firm equity values and market variability are identified in theorem 3.4.

Theorem 3.4

In addition to assumptions 3.1–3.4, suppose that η_λ changes in such a way that the precision parameter λ increases. The following hypotheses must then hold:

i. The average signal-contingent market values of firm equities increase.
ii. The average signal-contingent variance of the market portfolio decreases.

Proof: (For a proof, see appendix.)

Both conclusions i and ii are not only plausible on intuitive grounds but also empirically testable in principle (assuming that, for example, the tightening of standards represented by GAAP has been effective). Of course, one may encounter various statistical difficulties, such as instability of the underlying parameters [such as r, μ_M, σ_M^2, and $f(\lambda)$] over the required time period.

We now examine the impact of individual firm incentives to maintain the required precision λ. To do so, we consider a *fixed* accounting information system η_λ and assume that information is released to investors that the signal $\tilde{z}_1 = z_1$ of firm 1 is "inconsistent" with η_λ.

Continuing the analogy with GAAP, such information might be implied by an auditor switch (or a delayed financial report). Market participants, given such information, would then posit a larger prediction error for firm 1:

$$\begin{aligned} \tilde{z}_1 &= \tilde{y}_1 + \tilde{\varepsilon}_1 + \tilde{\delta} \\ \tilde{z}_j &= \tilde{y}_j + \tilde{\varepsilon}_j \qquad 2 \le j \le J \end{aligned} \tag{3.26}$$

where $E(\tilde{\delta}) = E(\tilde{\delta}\tilde{\varepsilon}_k) = E(\tilde{\delta}\tilde{y}_k) = 0$ for all $1 \le k \le J$ and

$$\operatorname{var}(\tilde{\delta}) = d > 0 \tag{3.27}$$

(cf. assumption 3.3). Assume the market reaction (3.26) and (3.27), we can then show that the error matrix E of (3.8) is changed to the new error matrix:

$$E_d = \frac{1}{\lambda}\Sigma + dI_1 \tag{3.28}$$

where I_1 is the $J \times J$ matrix whose (1, 1)-entry is one and all other entries are zeros.

Theorem 3.5

Assume that assumptions 3.1–3.4 are satisfied. If information is released to the capital market that firm 1 may have violated the required precision λ, and investors react to this information according to (3.26) and (3.27), the following then hold for all small $d > 0$:

i. $E\{E[u_i^* \mid \eta_\lambda, \tilde{\delta}]\} \cong E[u_i^* \mid \eta_\lambda] \cdot e^{3\lambda^2 d/[r(\lambda+1)]^2}$

ii. $b_1(d) - b_1 \cong \dfrac{\lambda^2 d}{(\lambda + 1)\sigma_M^2}(1 - b_1)$

iii. $b_j(d) - b_j \cong \dfrac{-\lambda^2 d}{(\lambda + 1)\sigma_M^2} b_j \qquad 2 \leq j \leq J$

where $b_k(d)$ represents the revised systematic risk of firm k.

Proof: (For a proof, see appendix.)

As result i shows, all investors become worse-off when firm 1 violates the required precision. If its systematic risk is larger than one, however, firm 1 may have an incentive to do so since its systematic risk decreases, and thus its equity value increases [cf. result ii and (3.16)]. The adverse information on firm 1 may have differing effects on other firms: the systematic risk of firm $j \geq 2$ decreases (increases) if and only if its systematic risk is positive (negative).

Conclusion

Costly public information has been analyzed here with respect to optimality (social value) and predictive effects. Since efficiency properties and social value of costless public information have been shown to be functions of the triple (available securities, market regime, endowments), we have attempted to carefully specify the assumptions we have made along each dimension. One desirable characteristic of the assumptions is their compatibility with the CAPM.

We assess the theoretical feasibility of achieving Pareto optimality with costly information production and consider a number of the implications of our model through comparative static analysis. In principle, then, the representation of information effects contained herein is empirically testable. Of course, as usual, we have omitted many considerations which are relevant to information production. Any empirical propositions should be evaluated in light of those omissions.

Notes

1. See Kunkel [1982] for an analysis of the social value of information where production is allowed.

2. Holmstrom [1979], Gjesdal [1981], and Kwon et al. [1979] consider the contracting role of information.

3. Following Sandmo [1974], for instance, we assume that firms obtain their production inputs by borrowing from investors (or issuing bonds) at the same risk-free rate ρ. In a general equilibrium model, ρ would depend on total savings by investors and total borrowings by firms; correspondingly, these economic decisions are affected by information production. However, we assume in this paper that ρ is fixed exogeneously. This is consistent with the existence of a constant returns to scale "production" alternative that permits storage of the current consumption good until the next period. With $\rho = 1$, that storage activity is assumed to be costless.

4. In view of note 3, the variable $\tilde{y}_j$ represents total output minus ρ times borrowings for firm j.

5. In the literature, the systematic risks of firms are measured in terms of either total equity returns or equity rates of returns. In this paper, we use total equity returns.

6. As we show later, in the proof of theorem 3.1, investor i holds r_i/r (cf. equation (3A.4)) fraction of every risky firm at equilibrium for all i.

APPENDIX 3

The purpose of this appendix is to sketch formal proofs of our assertions in the text. For this purpose, it will be convenient to first establish the following technical results.

Lemma 3A.1

Assume that A and B are square matrixes of the same order such that A, B, and $A^{-1} + B^{-1}$ are nonsingular. The identity then holds:

$$(A + B)^{-1} = A^{-1} - A^{-1}(A^{-1} + B^{-1})^{-1}A^{-1} \tag{3A.1}$$

Proof: See, for instance, Noble [1969, theorem 5.22].

Lemma 3A.2

Assume that A and B are square matrixes of the same order and that A is nonsingular. The matrix $(A + xB)$ is then nonsingular for all real x with sufficiently small $|x|$. Furthermore, the inverse of $(A + xB)$ can be approximated as follows:

$$(A + xB)^{-1} \cong A^{-1} - xA^{-1}BA^{-1} \tag{3A.2}$$

Proof: Note that a square matrix is nonsingular if and only if its determinant is nonzero. Denote by $\det(A + xB)$ the determinant of $(A + xB)$. Since $\det(A + xB)$ is continuous in x and A is nonsingular, it is obvious that the matrix $(A + xB)$ is nonsingular for all small $|x|$.

For the approximate equality (3A.2), consider the matrix-valued function

$$f(x) = (A + xB)^{-1}$$

for all small $|x|$. Since

$$(A + xB)f(x) = I = Af(0)$$

where I is the identity matrix, we deduce

$$A\frac{f(x) - f(0)}{x} = -Bf(x)$$

Letting $x \to 0$, we then obtain

$$f'(0) = -A^{-1}BA^{-1}$$

Using the first-order approximation

$$f(x) \cong f(0) + xf'(0)$$

for all small $|x|$, we can conclude (3A.2).

Proof of Theorem 3.1

Assuming an interior solution for (3.13), we obtain

$$\begin{aligned} u_i'(c_{i1}) &= Eu_i'\left(x_i + \sum_{j=1}^{J} \theta_{ij}\tilde{y}_j\right) \\ u_i'(c_{i1})p_j &= E\left[u_i'\left(x_i + \sum_{j=1}^{J} \theta_{ij}\tilde{y}_j\right)\tilde{y}_j\right] \end{aligned} \tag{3A.3}$$

for all i and j. Due to the separation property of negative exponential utility functions (cf. Mossin [1966]), we have

$$\theta_{ij} = \frac{r_i}{r} \tag{3A.4}$$

for all i and j, where $r > 0$ describes the aggregate risk-tolerance index [cf. equation (3.12)].

Dividing the second equation by the first in (3A.3) and then using (3A.4), we derive

$$E[e^{-\tilde{y}_M/r}\cdot(\tilde{y}_j - p_j)] = 0$$

for all j, or equivalently

$$E(e^{-\tilde{y}_M/r})\cdot(\mu_j - p_j) + \operatorname{cov}(e^{-\tilde{y}_M/r}, \tilde{y}_j) = 0 \tag{3A.5}$$

Since $\tilde{y}_j = \mu_j + b_j(\tilde{y}_M - \mu_M) + \tilde{\xi}_j$ by (3.17), and the variables $\tilde{\xi}_j$ and $\tilde{y}_M$ are independently distributed, we can rewrite (3A.5) in the form:

$$\begin{aligned} \mu_j - p_j &= -\frac{\operatorname{cov}(e^{-\tilde{y}_M/r}, \tilde{y}_j)}{E(e^{-\tilde{y}_M/r})} \\ &= -b_j\frac{\operatorname{cov}(e^{-\tilde{y}_M/r}, \tilde{y}_M)}{E(e^{-\tilde{y}_M/r})} \\ &= \frac{1}{r}b_j\sigma_M^2 \end{aligned}$$

for all j. The remaining assertions (3.14) and (3.15) of theorem 3.1 are rather routinely derived.

Proof of Theorem 3.2

Assume that a signal $\tilde{\mathbf{z}} = \mathbf{z}$ has been emitted to the capital market through the accounting information system η_λ. Since the posterior expectations of investors are then described by (3.20), it follows from theorem 3.1 that the optimal expected utilities (3.14), the aggregate savings (3.15), and equity prices (3.16) all depend upon the realized signal $\tilde{\mathbf{z}} = \mathbf{z}$. Taking expectations of these three expressions with respect to the signal $\mathbf{z}$, we can obtain the assertions in theorem 3.2.

Proof of Theorem 3.3

Assertion i is obvious from (3.25). For assertion ii, observe that the left-side expression of (3.25) increases in λ but the right-side expression of (3.25) decreases in λ. Since the right-side expression is shifted upward as σ_M^2 increases, assertion ii must then hold. The proofs of assertions iii and iv are similar.

Proof of Theorem 3.4

Assertion i is a restatement of result iii in theorem 3.2. Taking the expectation of the second expression in (3.20), we can show assertion ii.

Proof of Theorem 3.5

Using lemma 3A.2, we compute the first-order approximation of the error matrix:

$$E_d^{-1} \cong \lambda\Sigma^{-1} - \lambda^2 d\Sigma^{-1} I_1 \Sigma^{-1} \tag{3A.6}$$

for all small $d > 0$ [cf. equation (3.28)]. Therefore, the variance-covariance matrix for investors' posterior expectations can be approximated by

$$\begin{aligned} &\operatorname{var}(\tilde{\mathbf{y}} \mid \tilde{\mathbf{z}} = \mathbf{z}) = \Sigma - \Sigma(\Sigma + E_d)^{-1}\Sigma && \text{(3A.7)} \\ &= [\Sigma^{-1} + E_d^{-1}]^{-1} \qquad \text{(see lemma 3A.1)} \\ &\cong [(\lambda+1)\Sigma^{-1} - \lambda^2 d\Sigma^{-1} I_1 \Sigma^{-1}]^{-1} \qquad \text{[see equation (3A.6)]} \\ &\cong \frac{1}{\lambda+1}\Sigma + \frac{\lambda^2 d}{(\lambda+1)^2} I_1 \qquad \text{(see lemma 3A.2).} \end{aligned}$$

Similarly, the investors' conditional mean has the approximation:

$$E(\tilde{\mathbf{y}} \mid \tilde{\mathbf{z}} = \mathbf{z}) \cong \boldsymbol{\mu} + \frac{\lambda}{\lambda+1}(\mathbf{z} - \boldsymbol{\mu}) - \frac{\lambda^2 d}{(\lambda+1)^2} I_1 \Sigma^{-1}(\mathbf{z} - \boldsymbol{\mu}). \tag{3A.8}$$

Using (3.14), (3A.7), and (3A.8), we can then show result i as in i of Theorem 3.2. Denote by $\sigma_{jM}(d)$ the covariance of $\tilde{y}_j$ and $\tilde{y}_M$ conditional upon the signal $\tilde{\mathbf{z}} = \mathbf{z}$ and the information that firm 1 may have misrepresented its financial report. Using the above approximation (3A.7), it is seen that

$$\begin{aligned} \sigma_{1M}(d) &\cong \frac{1}{\lambda+1}\sigma_{1M} + \frac{\lambda^2}{(\lambda+1)^2} d \\ \sigma_{jM}(d) &\cong \frac{1}{\lambda+1}\sigma_{jM} \qquad 2 \le j \le J \\ \sigma_M^2(d) &\cong \frac{1}{\lambda+1}\sigma_M^2 + \frac{\lambda^2}{(\lambda+1)^2} d \end{aligned} \tag{3A.9}$$

Combining (3.4) and (3A.9), we can then obtain assertions ii and iii in theorem 3.5.

References

Gjesdal, F. [1981]. "Accounting for Stewardship." *Journal of Accounting Research* 19, 208–231.

Grossman, S., and Stiglitz, J. [1976]. "Information and Competitive Price Systems." *American Economic Review* 66, 246–253.

Hakansson, N., Kunkel, J., and Ohlson, J. [1982]. "Sufficient and Necessary Conditions for Information to Have Social Value in Pure Exchange." *Journal of Finance* 37, 1169–1181.

Holmstrom, B. [1979]. "Moral Hazard and Observability." *Bell Journal of Economics* 10, 74–91.

Huber, C. [1978]. "The Private Value of Information in Exchange Markets." Ph.D. Dissertation, Stanford University.

Kunkel, J. [1982]. "Sufficient Conditions for Information to Have Social Value in a Production and Exchange Economy." *Journal of Finance* 37, 1005–1013.

Kwon, Y. [1982]. "Private Versus Public Production of Information." *Journal of Economic Behaviour and Organization* 3, 345–356.

Kwon, Y., Fellingham, J., and Newman, D. [1979]. "Stochastic Dominance and Information Value." *Journal of Economic Theory* 20, 213–230.

Lintner, J. [1965]. "The Valuation of Risk Assets and the Selection of Risky Investments in Stock Portfolios and Capital Budgets." *Review of Economics and Statistics* 47, 13–37.

Mossin, J. [1966]. "Equilibrium in a Capital Asset Market." *Econometrica* 34, 768–783.

Noble, B. [1969]. *Applied Linear Algebra.* Englewood Cliffs, NJ: Prentice-Hall.

Ohlson, J. [1979]. "Efficiency and the Social Value of Information in Exchange Economies." Working Paper, University of California at Berkeley.

Ohlson, J., and Buckman, A. [1980]. "Towards a Theory of Financial Accounting." *Journal of Finance* 35, 537–547.

Ohlson, J., and Buckman, A. [1981]. "Towards a Theory of Financial Accounting: Welfare and Public Information." *Journal of Accounting Research* 19, 399–433.

Pratt, J. [1964]. "Risk Aversion in the Small and in the Large." *Econometrica* 32, 122–136.

Sandmo, A. [1974]. "Discount Rates for Public Investments under Uncertainty." *Allocation under Uncertainty: Equilibrium and Optimality.* J. Dreze (ed.). New York: John Wiley, 192–210.

Sharpe, W. [1964]. "Capital Asset Prices: A Theory of Market Equilibrium under Conditions of Risk." *Journal of Finance* 19, 425–442.

Taylor, L. [1974]. *Probability and Mathematical Statistics.* New York: Harper & Row.

Verrecchia, R. [1982]. "The Use of Mathematical Models in Financial Accounting." *Journal of Accounting Research* 20, 1–42.

Walker, M. [1981]. "A Simple Incentive Compatible Scheme for Attaining Lindahl Allocations." *Econometrica* 49, 65–71.

4 VALUE OF INFORMATION IN BIMATRIX GAMES*

Joel S. Demski

Economic analysis of accounting debates focuses on the information provided by the accounting system. "Value of information" is a central theme in this approach. In a decision making context, this is illustrated by the aggregation analyses of Butterworth [1972] and Feltham [1977]. In an implementation or control context, it is illustrated by Baiman–Demski's [1980] analysis of variance investigation strategies and responsibility accounting.

The decision-making context focuses on a single individual who faces a risky choice. Information is valuable in this setting to the extent its use improves the quality of the decision at hand. This is why we refer to such information as *decision facilitating*. Similarly, in a control context an individual faces a risky choice that affects, in part, someone else's well being—as when your lawyer acts on your behalf. Here information is valuable to the

* Amin Amershi, Rick Antle, Stan Baiman, Drew Fudenberg, Jerry Feltham, and Mark Wolfson provided helpful comments. Financial support from the National Science Foundation grant IST84-10907 is gratefully acknowledged.

extent it improves the quality of the decision *or* the efficiency with which it can be implemented (including the efficiency with which the decision's outcomes can be shared). For example, an incentive structure may be used to motivate the decision maker, thereby substituting inefficient risk sharing for better monitoring. In turn, monitoring may support a motivation scheme in which less risk is imposed on the decision maker. Information used in the control process is called *decision influencing* information.

In the decision influencing sphere we have long recognized that supplying information is, in fact, a delicate matter. For example, taxation authorities jealously guard their audit strategies, just as the bank guards the combination of its safe. Separation of duties in an internal control design provides another illustration. In each case, additional information in the hands of the individual whose decision is being influenced *may* make the control problem worse. (Christensen [1982] explores this in a formalized principal/agent setting.)

This contrasts with the decision facilitating setting where, cost aside, more information is always at least as desirable as less information. At worst the additional information will prove useless, in which case it can be safely and costlessly discarded. Thus, more is better than less in this world, holding cost constant. Of course, cost does matter, and in practice we do not seriously entertain production of the maximally feasible "amount" of information.

In this paper we reexamine this "more is better than less" dictum in a decision facilitating setting, but with the addition of a strategic competitor. We find that information value is far from straightforward in a strategic setting. Depending on the nature of the competitive interaction, more may be better than less for both parties, one party, or neither party. Baiman [1975] introduced the logical possibility of such conclusions into the accounting literature. We thus follow his earlier analysis, but with explicit attention to classes of games that exhibit particular value conclusions and to the importance of repeated play in the strategic setting.

We begin with a brief review of bimatrix games. The second section presents a series of stylized games that illustrates the plethora of logical possibilities. In the third section we examine repeated play settings, where "punishment" and "reputation" factors intermix with short-run strategic considerations.

Basic Setting

Our basic setting is one is which two individuals simultaneously act in a noncooperative fashion. Each faces a finite menu of feasible choices. The payoff to each player depends on the two choices as well as nature's supply of state $s \in S$. If the first player (called Row) selects his option i and the second (called Column) selects her option j, we denote Row's payoff a_{ij}^s and Column's payoff b_{ij}^s, given that state s obtains. Also, the probability state s obtains is denoted $\pi(s)$. Each player's tastes are represented by the expectation of their respective payoffs. In other words, $\Sigma_s \pi(s) a_{ij}^s$ is the expected utility to Row if he plays choice i while Column plays choice j. As such, the payoff is simply the individual's von Neumann–Morgenstern measure of his/her outcome from the strategic encounter.

In general terms, Row has $m > 1$ options and Column has $n > 1$ options, while $|S| = p \geq 1$. We assume $\pi(s)$ and the p payoff matrixes $[a_{ij}^s, b_{ij}^s]$ are common knowledge (Aumann [1976] and Milgrom [1981]). We further assume, throughout the paper, $m = n = p = 2$. In this binary setting it is convenient to label mnemonically Row's choices Up (U) and Down (D) and Column's Left (L) and Right (R).

Now suppose Row plays $i \in \{U, D\}$ and Column plays $j \in \{L, R\}$. This (i, j) pair of choices is a (Nash) *equilibrium* if

1. $\sum_s \pi(s) a_{ij}^s \geq \sum_s \pi(s) a_{kj}^s$ for $k \in \{U, D\}$ and $k \neq i$

2. $\sum_s \pi(s) b_{ij}^s \geq \sum_s \pi(s) b_{ik}^s$ for $k \in \{L, R\}$ and $k \neq j$.[1]

To illustrate, suppose $\pi(s_1) = \pi(s_2) = \frac{1}{2}$. The payoff tables are as follows:

game s_1

	L	R
U	5.0, 6.0	4.0, 9.0
D	2.0, 1.0	4.0, 3.0

game s_2

	L	R
U	7.0, 2.0	2.0, 1.0
D	8.0, 1.0	4.0, 13.0

Thus if Row plays U and Column plays R, their respective payoffs under s_1 are 4.0 and 9.0.

The game structure when neither player has any information is the expectation of the two matrixes. This provides the following expected payoff table:

	L	R
U	6.0, 4.0	3.0, 5.0
D	5.0, 1.0	4.0, 8.0

(D, R) is an equilibrium, with respective (expected) payoffs of 4.0 and 8.0.

Now consider a setting where Row privately observes $s \in \{s_1, s_2\}$ before acting. It is common knowledge that Row has access to such an information structure, while Column does not. Thus, Column knows Row has such access, Row knows that Column knows of such access, ad infinitum. Similarly, Row knows that Column does not have such access, Column knows that Row knows this, etc. Moreover, no communication is allowed. Column's choices remain as before, that is L and R. But Row's options expand. Let gh denote a strategy of using $g \in \{U, D\}$ if s_1 obtains and $h \in \{U, D\}$ if s_2 obtains. Row now has four options: UU, UD, DU, and DD. The bimatrix structure for our illustration is now:

	L	R
UU	6.0, 4.0	3.0, 5.0
UD	6.5, 3.5	4.0, 11.0
DU	4.5, 1.5	3.0, 2.0
DD	5.0, 1.0	4.0, 8.0

Extending our earlier definition of equilibrium in obvious fashion, we see that (UD, R) is an equilibrium.

Comparing this equilibrium with that in the original game we see that Row, the informed player, is indifferent while Column is strictly improved, with $11 > 8$. The information, then, is valueless to Row and valuable to Column.

To be somewhat formal, let η^0 denote the case where neither player receives information and η^R denote the case where Row privately acquires advance state revelation. Also let $E(a|\eta)$ denote Row's and $E(b|\eta)$ Column's expected equilibrium payoff under the game with information regime η. We then say η has positive, zero, or negative value to Row depending on whether $V_R(\eta) = E(a|\eta) - E(a|\eta^0)$ is positive, zero, or negative. A parallel statement holds for Column, $V_C(\eta)$. In this particular instance, $V_R(\eta^R) = 4 - 4 = 0$, while $V_C(\eta^R) = 11 - 8 = 3$. The value of η^R is zero to Row and positive to Column.

This definitional convention is sufficient for our purpose, but two caveats should be noted. First, a rigorous specification of "value" would rest on selling prices or certain equivalents.[2] Second, we should also recognize the possibility of multiple equilibria. For instance, in the above numerical example, (DD, R) is also an equilibrium. And here the information is valueless to both players. Thus, the conclusion of whether positive value is present depends on which equilibrium we focus on. Further observe, however, that the (DD, R) equilibrium is dominated by (UD, R)—both players are at least as well off in the second, and one (Column) is strictly improved. It seems natural to focus on undominated equilibria. Throughout the analysis we assume that when faced with multiple equilibria the players will always focus on an undominated equilibrium. This convention resolves the difficulty in the example, though not in general.[3]

We now turn to an examination of particular classes of game structures that exhibit the various value possibilities.

Some Particular Game Structures

In addition to our binary restrictions ($m = n = p = 2$) we now further assume equal odds: $\pi(s_1) = \pi(s_2) = \frac{1}{2}$. Within this heavily restricted world, we vary the payoff structure to exhibit settings where introduction of information may be of positive, zero, or negative value, depending on strategic considerations called for by the payoff structure at hand. In each case the information considered is perfect-state revelation to either or both of the players. It is important to emphasize, however, that we always presume information acquisition (though not content) is common knowledge. Thus we do not consider the case where, say, Row acquires information, Column is completely oblivious to this, and Row knows this. We insist that each player knows the structure of the game being played. In a subsequent section we examine a setting where Row will, with probability δ, acquire information, where δ is common knowledge.

Team Game

We begin with a *team game* in which the players' payoffs differ by a positive affine transformation:

$$b_{ij}^{s} = \theta + \varphi a_{ij}^{s}$$

for $i \in \{U, D\}, j \in \{L, R\}, s \in \{s_1, s_2\}$ and for some constants θ and φ, $\varphi > 0$.[4]

Consider the following numerical illustration, in which $b_{ij}^{s} = -10 + 2a_{ij}^{s}$:

game s_1

	L	R
U	10.0, 10.0	12.0, 14.0
D	14.0, 18.0	16.0, 22.0

game s_2

	L	R
U	22.0, 34.0	13.0, 16.0
D	6.0, 2.0	18.0, 26.0

Without any information, the "average" game is played:

	L	R
U	16.0, 22.0	12.5, 15.0
D	10.0, 10.0	17.0, 24.0

Notice that (U, L) and (D, R) are both equilibria (a third entails randomization). (D, R), however, is distinguished by the fact it is not only undominated but delivers the maximal expected payoff in the entire matrix. Intuitively, the team game is devoid of strategic considerations. What is best for one player is best for the other.

Now suppose Row acquires perfect information. The structure of the game becomes

	L	R
UU	16.0, 22.0	12.5, 15.0
UD	8.0, 6.0	15.0, 20.0
DU	18.0, 26.0	14.5, 19.0
DD	10.0, 10.0	17.0, 24.0

The equilibrium of interest is (DU, L) in which Column plays L while R plays D in game s_1 and U in game s_2.

$$V_R(\eta^R) = 1 = E(a|\eta^R) - E(a|\eta^0) = 18 - 17$$

$$V_C(\eta^R) = 2 = E(b|\eta^R) - E(b|\eta^0) = 26 - 24$$

Both players are improved by the introduction of information to a specific player. This is no accident. To repeat, we have no strategic considerations here; what is best for one player is best for the other; thus Row would use the information if and only if doing so were best for both players.

It is routine to verify that the players respective expected payoffs are 19 and 28 if both acquire the information. [This is achieved by playing (D, R) in game s_1 and (U, L) in game s_2.] And they are 17 and 24 under η^C.

The point here is that information is never harmful in the team game.[5] Thus we encounter a multiperson variation on the Blackwell Theorem and its implication that "more" costless information is always as good as "less" costless information in a single-person setting.[6]

Proposition 4.1

The value of perfect state revelation to either or both players in the team game is nonnegative.

Proof: We develop the proof for the case where Row acquires the information. The other cases are analogous.

First observe that an undominated equilibrium in the team game has the property that the expected payoffs are maximized for each player. In the no information (η^0) case this entails

$$E(a|\eta^0) = \max_{i,j} \tfrac{1}{2}[a_{ij}^1 + a_{ij}^2] \tag{4.1}$$

and

$$E(b|\eta^0) = \max_{i,j} \tfrac{1}{2}[b_{ij}^1 + b_{ij}^2] \tag{4.2}$$

With $b_{ij}^s = \theta + \varphi a_{ij}^s$, $\varphi > 0$, the optimal choices in (4.1) and (4.2) are identical, say i^* and j^*. Suppose (i^*, j^*) is not an equilibrium. This implies $a_{ki^*}^1 + a_{kj^*}^2 > a_{i^*j^*}^1 + a_{i^*j^*}^2$ for $k \neq i^*$ or $b_{i^*k}^1 + b_{i^*k}^2 > b_{i^*j^*}^1 + b_{i^*j^*}^2$ for $k \neq j^*$. But this contradicts the maximization assumption in (4.1). Further observe that no other equilibrium could dominate (i^*, j^*), because this too would contradict the maximization assumption. De facto, this reduces the equilibrium specification to a maximization exercise.

Now consider the expected equilibrium payoffs for the case when Row is informed (η^R). A parallel argument identifies the following maximization

$$E(a|\eta^R) = \max_j \tfrac{1}{2}\left[\max_i a_{ij}^1 + \max_k a_{kj}^2\right] \tag{4.3}$$

Clearly, $E(a|\eta^R) \geq E(a|\eta^0)$, since any choice in the latter construction is feasible in the former. In turn this implies Column's equilibrium payoffs under η^R are

$$E(b|\eta^R) = \theta + \varphi E(a|\eta^R) \geq \theta + \varphi E(a|\eta^0) = E(b|\eta^0)$$

In sum, the team game displays the familiar notion that costless additional information is never harmful.

Adversary Game

Now consider the opposite setting, one in which the players' interests are perfectly opposed:

$$a_{ij}^s + b_{ij}^s = \tau^s$$

In state s, whatever one player gains is at the expense of the other, because the sum of their payoffs is a constant amount, τ^s. Call this the *adversary game*. Without loss of generality we assume the payoffs are normalized so that $\tau^1 + \tau^2 = 0$.

We begin with a numerical illustration based on the following payoff structure:

game s_1

	L	R
U	1.0, 3.0	−4.0, 8.0
D	2.0, 2.0	3.0, 1.0

game s_2

	L	R
U	2.0, −6.0	1.0, −5.0
D	0.0, −4.0	−8.0, 4.0

In the no-information case (η^0), the matrix of expected payoffs is

	L	R
U	1.5, −1.5	−1.5, 1.5
D	1.0, −1.0	−2.5, 2.5

(U, R) is an equilibrium. Conversely, when Row is informed (η^R), the game structure is represented by the following matrix:

	L	R
UU	1.5, −1.5	−1.5, 1.5
UD	0.5, −0.5	−6.0, 6.0
DU	2.0, −2.0	2.0, −2.0
DD	1.0, −1.0	−2.5, 2.5

An equilibrium is (DU, L) in which Column plays L while R plays D in game s_1 and U in game s_2.

$$V_R(\eta^R) = 2.0 + 1.5 = 3.5$$

while

$$V_C(\eta^R) = -2.0 - 1.5 = -3.5$$

The informed player gains in the example, and since the players' interests precisely offset each other this gain is at the uninformed player's expense. Intuitively, when the players are adversaries the worst that can happen to a player who becomes informed while the other does not is to play the game as it would be played absent the information. The uninformed player is at the informed player's mercy. Any advantage to the informed is at the expense of the uninformed. This is formalized in the following proposition, which clearly holds in symmetric fashion for the case where only Column is informed.[7]

Proposition 4.2

The value of perfect state revelation to Row is nonnegative for Row and nonpositive for Column in the adversary game.

Proof: This follows from the adversarial structure, in which for any pair of strategies the sum of the expected payoffs is constant. In such a setting, we invoke the minimax theorem (Luce–Raiffa [1957], Vorobev [1977]) to characterize the equilibrium expected payoffs.

If, in the η^R game, Column plays L with probability β and Row plays UU with probability α_1, UD with probability α_2, DU with probability α_3, and DD with probability α_4, the expected payoff to Row is

$$\begin{aligned}E(a|\alpha, \beta) = {} & (\alpha_1/2)\{\beta a^1_{11} + (1-\beta)a^1_{12} + \beta a^2_{11} + (1-\beta)a^2_{12}\} + \\ & (\alpha_2/2)\{\beta a^1_{11} + (1-\beta)a^1_{12} + \beta a^2_{21} + (1-\beta)a^2_{22}\} + \\ & (\alpha_3/2)\{\beta a^1_{21} + (1-\beta)a^1_{22} + \beta a^2_{11} + (1-\beta)a^2_{12}\} + \\ & (\alpha_4/2)\{\beta a^1_{21} + (1-\beta)a^1_{22} + \beta a^2_{21} + (1-\beta)a^2_{22}\}\end{aligned}$$

In turn, the minimax theorem provides that the equilibrium payoff is such that

$$E(a|\eta^R) = \max_{\alpha} \min_{\beta} E(a|\alpha, \beta) \qquad \text{subject to} \quad \begin{aligned} & 0 \le \alpha_i \le 1 \\ & 0 \le \beta \le 1 \\ & \Sigma_i \alpha_i = 1 \end{aligned} \tag{4.4}$$

Conversely, in the no-information case we have

$$E(a|\eta^0) = \max_{\alpha} \min_{\beta} E(a|\alpha, \beta) \qquad \text{subject to} \quad \begin{aligned} & 0 \le \alpha_i \le 1 \\ & 0 \le \beta \le 1 \\ & \Sigma_i \alpha_i = 1 \\ & \alpha_2 = \alpha_3 = 0 \end{aligned} \tag{4.5}$$

Any solution in (4.5) is, of course, feasible in (4.4). Hence we have $E(a|\eta^R) \geq E(a|\eta^0)$. And with $E(a|\cdot) = -E(b|\cdot)$ we also have $E(b|\eta^R) \leq E(b|\eta^0)$.

We therefore have a class of games in which the acquirer of information gains while the uninformed loses. Notice, however, that contrary to the claim for the team game we do not claim that *joint* acquisition of information has nonnegative value here. Gain to either player comes at the other's expense in the adversary game. Thus value is zero for both or positive for one and negative for the other. Our earlier numerical example illustrates this phenomenon, where Row's expected payoff is 1.5 and Column's is -1.5 under a regime of public information (compared with respective expected payoffs of -1.5 and 1.5 in the no-information regime).

Defensive Game

Our next class of games exhibits the opposite property of the team and adversary games: private information to Row has negative value to Row.

Consider the following payoff structure:

game s_1

	L	R
U	10.0, 4.0	8.0, 0.0
D	8.0, 6.0	4.0, 5.0

game s_2

	L	R
U	10.0, 4.0	5.0, 6.0
D	11.0, −100.0	6.0, 15.0

Notice that each player has dominant strategies in each matrix. If s_1 is publicly known to obtain, Row is best off playing U regardless of Column's choice and Column is best off playing L regardless of Row's choice. Exactly the opposite holds in the s_2 game. There D dominates U and R dominates L.

In the absence of any information (the η^0 case), the matrix of expected payoffs is:

	L	R
U	10.0, 4.0	6.5, 3.0
D	9.5, −47.0	5.0, 10.0

(U, L) is the unique equilibrium, since Row strictly prefers U and Column strictly prefers L given that Row will play U.

Conversely, when Row privately acquires perfect-state revelation, the game structure becomes

	L	R
UU	10.0, 4.0	6.5, 3.0
UD	10.5, −48.0	7.0, 7.5
DU	9.0, 5.0	4.5, 5.5
DD	9.5, −47.0	5.0, 10.0

Row now will surely play UD, since U is strictly dominating in the s_1 game and D is strictly dominating in the s_2 game. And the relatively poor payoff entry b^2_{DL} ensures Column will play R. So the equilibrium is (UD, R), with implied information value measures of

$$V_{\mathrm{R}}(\eta^{\mathrm{R}}) = E(a|\eta^{\mathrm{R}}) - E(a|\eta^0) = 7 - 10 = -3$$

$$V_{\mathrm{C}}(\eta^{\mathrm{R}}) = E(b|\eta^{\mathrm{R}}) - E(b|\eta^0) = 7.5 - 4 = 3.5.$$

The key to the illustration is Column's relatively poor payoff under s_2 and the (D, L) choices. If Column knows Row has access to the information, her best option is to switch to R. The net result is to "punish" Row for acquiring information, but the motive is far from punishment; it is to avoid the b^2_{DL} payoff. That is, if Row is known to access the information, Column knows it is facing Row's dominant strategy choice of U in game s_1 and D in game s_2; and b^2_{DL} makes choice of L unattractive. Column's best response is to employ choice R.

We formalize these observations in the following manner. Define a *defensive game* as one in which the following conditions hold:

(1) $a^1_{UL} > a^1_{DL}$ and $a^1_{UR} > a^1_{DR}$
(2) $a^2_{UL} < a^2_{DL}$ and $a^2_{UR} < a^2_{DR}$
(3) $a^1_{UL} + a^2_{UL} > a^1_{DL} + a^2_{DL}$ and $a^1_{UR} + a^2_{UR} > a^1_{DR} + a^2_{DR}$
(4) $b^1_{UR} + b^2_{DR} > b^1_{UL} + b^2_{DL}$
(5) $b^1_{UL} + b^2_{UL} > b^1_{UR} + b^2_{UR}$
(6) $a^1_{UL} + a^2_{UL} > a^1_{UR} + a^2_{DR}$

These algebraic conditions merely mirror the essential structure of the above numerical example. Conditions (1) and (2) ensure Row has dominant choices in each game; he strictly prefers U in game s_1 and D in game s_2. Similarly, condition (3) ensures Row strictly prefers U over D in the no-information game. (Recall $\pi(s_1)=\frac{1}{2}$.) Conditions (4) and (5) ensure Column's best response to Row's dominant strategies is to play L in the no-information game and R in the Row-informed game.[8]

Proposition 4.3

The value of perfect state revelation to Row is negative in the defensive game. The value to Column is positive if and only if $b^1_{UR} + b^2_{DR} > b^1_{UL} + b^2_{UL}$.

Proof: Conditions (3) and (5) imply (U, L) is the unique equilibrium in the no-information game. Similarly, conditions (1), (2), and (4) imply (UD, R)

is the unique equilibrium in the Row-informed game. Hence,

$$E(a|\eta^0) = \tfrac{1}{2}a^1_{UL} + \tfrac{1}{2}a^2_{UL} > \tfrac{1}{2}a^1_{UR} + \tfrac{1}{2}a^2_{DR} = E(a|\eta^R)$$

where the inequality is assumed in Condition (6). Conversely,

$$E(b|\eta^0) = \tfrac{1}{2}b^1_{UL} + \tfrac{1}{2}b^2_{UL}, \quad \text{and} \quad E(b|\eta^R) = \tfrac{1}{2}b^1_{UR} + \tfrac{1}{2}b^2_{DR}$$

Or, $E(b|\eta^R) > E(b|\eta^0)$ if and only if $b^1_{UR} + b^2_{DR} > b^1_{UL} + b^2_{UL}$.

Finally, we can show that Row cannot be "trusted" to not acquire the harmful information in the first place. Consider an expanded game where Row has the option of acquiring η^R (at zero cost) as well as selecting between U and D after observing whatever the chosen information structure (η^0 or η^R) has to offer. Row's choice of information structure as well as subsequent choice of act remain private. And Column's strategies remain as before. Regardless of Column's behavior, Row's best response is always to acquire η^R and then play UD. The only equilibrium in this expanded game is for Row to acquire the harmful information! Of course, Row would gladly pay to acquire a commitment technology that guarantees he will not acquire (conversely will ignore) harmful information. But this technology is assumed not to be available here. We will return to this phenomenon in a subsequent section.

Symmetric Game

We thus have a class of games where the value of private-state revelation to one player is weakly positive to both players (the *team game*), a second class where it is weakly positive to the informed player and weakly negative to the uninformed player (the *adversary game*), and a third where it is strictly negative to the informed player (the *defensive game*). Each of these games has an intuitive structure, one that is designed to produce the particular value of information conclusion. The following *symmetric game*, due to Levine and Ponssard [1977], provides a setting in which no uniform conclusion is possible: information may have positive, negative, or zero value. The structure lacks the intuitive appeal of that in the earlier games, but it is expressly designed to exhibit a spectrum of value conclusions.

Following Levine–Ponssard [1977], let the payoffs, denoted c, d, e, and f, have the following structure:

game s_1

	L	R
U	2c, 2c	2f, 2e
D	2e, 2f	2d, 2d

game s_2

	L	R
U	2e, 2e	2d, 2c
D	2c, 2d	2f, 2f

Yet additional structure is provided by the following conditions: (1) $c > e$ and $f > d$; (2) $c + e > d + f$; and (3) $e + f > c + d$. (Thus, $c > e > d$.) We also continue to assume $\pi(s_1) = \frac{1}{2}$.

These assumptions imply that if s_1 were publicly known to obtain, the unique equilibrium would be (U, L), with U dominating D and L dominating R. Conversely, if s_2 were publicly known to obtain, the unique equilibrium would be (D, R), with D dominating U and R dominating L.

The no-information game has the following structure:

	L	R
U	c + e, c + e	d + f, c + e
D	c + e, d + f	d + f, d + f

(U, L) is the obvious equilibrium, with (expected) payoffs of $E(a|\eta^0) = E(b|\eta^0) = c + e$.

The game in which Row privately acquires perfect-state information is

	L	R
UU	c + e, c + e	d + f, c + e
UD	c + c, c + d	f + f, e + f
DU	e + e, e + f	d + d, c + d
DD	c + e, d + f	d + f, d + f

Condition (1) makes UD a dominant strategy for Row; and, given this condition, (3) provides a unique equilibrium of (UD, R). Hence, $E(a|\eta^R) = 2f$

and $E(b|\eta^{R}) = e + f$. Row's value of information measure is then $V_{R}(\eta^{R}) = 2f - (c + e)$ while Column's is $V_{C}(\eta^{R}) = e + f - (c + e) = f - c$.

Conditions (2) and (3) require $c + d - e < f < c + e - d$ [along with $c > e > d$ when condition (1) is invoked]. Let $c = 100$, $e = 1$, and $d = 0$. This provides $V_{R}(\eta^{R}) = 2f - 101$ and $V_{C}(\eta^{R}) = f - 100$ and $99 < f < 101$. $V_{R}(\eta^{R})$ is positive while $V_{C}(\eta^{R})$ ranges from negative to positive. Conversely, let $c = 12$, $e = 11$, and $d = 10$. This implies $11 < f < 13$ along with $V_{R}(\eta^{R}) = 2f - 23$ and $V_{C}(\eta^{R}) = f - 12$. Thus $V_{R}(\eta^{R})$ and $V_{C}(\eta^{R})$ range from negative to positive, with $V_{R}(\eta^{R})$ positive over a strictly wider range of f values.[9]

Indeed, it is also possible to demonstrate conflicting conclusions concerning the value of public information in this setting. Let $c = 100$, $e = 99$, and $d = 0$. If $f = 2$, both players are harmed by the production of public information. But if $f = 150$, both strictly benefit from public information.

Thus, it is logically possible to exhibit positive, nil, or negative value of information in this setting of single-shot bimatrix games. The team game agrees with single-person decision analysis intuition (as it should, being a de facto single-person setting). The adversary game is similarly intuitive in that the informed party is never harmed and produces all of his gains at his opponent's expense. The defensive game, on the other hand, displays negative value for the informed player. And similar conclusions arise in a single class of games, depending on the particular parameter values in the payoff structure.

Repetition

Now return to the defensive game where the privately informed Row player experiences $V_{R}(\eta^{R}) < 0$. Instead of a single-shot game, we now examine the case where this game is repeated a number of times. The question is whether repetition affects the privately informed Row player's ability to exploit his information. Our focus, then, is on whether repetition improves the informed player's lot in the defensive game, where $V_{R}(\eta^{R}) < 0$. Keep in mind, however, that we could also explore a setting where repetition works to the disadvantage of the informed player. This will become clear as we proceed.

Finite Repetition

Initially we consider the case where the game is played a known finite number of times, say $T > 1$. Each period the payoff structure is as in the numerical illustration of the defensive game:

game s_1

	L	R
U	10.0, 4.0	8.0, 0.0
D	8.0, 6.0	4.0, 5.0

game s_2

	L	R
U	10.0, 4.0	5.0, 6.0
D	11.0, −100.0	6.0, 15.0

Nature selects one of the matrixes each period, in an independent, identically distributed fashion with $\pi(s_1)=\frac{1}{2}$ in each and every period. Row then privately observes nature's choice, and the players simultaneously implement their action choices and then observe their payoffs and opponent's action choice.

Each player's preferences are represented by the expected discounted sum of their respective payoffs. For payoff sequence (a_t, b_t), $t = 1, \ldots, T$. Row's payoff measure is $\Sigma_t\, a_t(1+r)^{-t}$ and Column's is $\Sigma_t\, b_t(1+r)^{-t}$ for some common discount factor $r > 0$.

Recall that in the single-shot game the equilibrium is for Row to play *UD* and Column to play *R* [with $V_R(\eta^R) < 0$ and, in this instance, $V_C(\eta^R) > 0$]. Mere repetition of this play is also an equilibrium in the finitely repeated setting. Somewhat casually, Row's (short-run) dominant choice in each period is to play *UD*. Against any such play, Column's best response is to play *R* each and every period. Conversely, Column merely "threatens" to play *R* in this setting and Row's best response is to play *UD* in each and every period. But can Row do better by *not* playing *UD*. Surely if he could make a binding commitment to always play *UU*, Column's best response would be to play *L*; and Row's (though not Column's) lot would be improved. The question is whether repetition will allow Row to accomplish something like this, without access to any formal commitment technology. Stated differently, could Row "claim" to play *UU* and ever be trusted to never use his information? If so, Column's best response would be to play *L*.

Consider this suggestion more closely. Row could play *UU* each period, and Column would trust him (by playing *L*). Any renege on Row's part collapses Column's trust, and she would then switch to *R* for the remainder of the game. Unfortunately for Row, there is no such equilibrium in this finitely repeated setting. In the final period, each player knows it is the last period and Row will surely use his information. So trust will not be encountered in the last period. At that point the game has evolved to a single-shot play scenario. In the penultimate period, however, the same conclusion surfaces. No trust will be at work in the final play of the game, so there is no point in Row giving up short-run returns to avoid Column's defensive maneuvre in the last period. Knowing this, Column plays R in the penultimate period and Row uses his information by playing UD. Continuing in parallel fashion, the scheme unravels and we are left with period-by-period repetition of the single shot (UD, R) equilibrium as the unique equilibrium in our finitely repeated defensive game setting.[10]

The difficulty here is that the one-shot game has a unique equilibrium and the end of play is always in sight. Trust is absent at the end, hence at one stage from the end, at two stages from the end, and so on. At no point does Column have an opportunity to punish Row for his play of UD. Conversely, Row is also powerless to threaten Column into playing L; no such threat is believable. The players have no "degrees of freedom" to exploit.[11]

Unbounded Repetition

Suppose instead the game is played an unbounded number of times. With unbounded repetition of the game, at any point $t = \tau$ the remaining game is identical to the game at $t = 1$. This means the end of play is never in sight. Numerous equilibria are present in this supergame. And a policy of trusting Column to never use his information can be associated with equilibrium behavior.

To see this, suppose Column plays L until she witnesses Row playing D; after that she plays R forever. Row in turn ignores his information and plays UU forever. To verify that this is an equilibrium, take an arbitrary period τ and suppose Row has been informed game s_2 obtains in the immediate period. If Row finks at this point by playing D, he will receive an immediate payoff of 11 followed by an expected per period payoff of 7 in perpetuity. His expected future discounted payoff is therefore $(1+r)^{-1}$ $(11 + 7/r)$. Conversely, he has the option of playing trustworthy now and forever after. This yields an expected future discounted payoff of $(1+r)^{-1}$ $(10 + 10/r) = 10/r$, which exceeds that of the fink option as long as $r < 3$. So, for sufficiently small r, Row will always play UU. Trust is a best response to Column's threat to play defensive. And Column's play of L is a best response to UU, just as R is a best response to UD (if trust is violated). Thus, in equilibrium, the respective payoffs are 10 and 4 in each and every period.

Of course, other equilibria are also present. Repetition of the single-shot equilibrium is one, implying respective payoffs of 7 and 7.5 in each and every period. One might argue that this is a logical equilibrium because Column can force it by always playing R. But one might also argue that Row can force the earlier equilibrium by always playing UU. The point is that numerous equilibria are present here. Another equilibrium, for example, would have the players alternate playing, in equilibrium, (UD, R) in odd-numbered periods and (UU, L) in even-numbered periods.

This reflects the fact that, for moderate discount factor r, the capitalized value of any cooperative, Pareto efficient outcome of the single-shot game can be achieved in equilibrium play of an infinitely repeated version of the game.[12] The point is that it does not follow that $V_R(\eta^R)$ is negative in an infinitely repeated version of the defensive game. Of course, it also does not follow that $V_R(\eta^R)$ is nonnegative. We have an equilibrium associated with each possibility.

Reputation

Another avenue for imbedding the defensive game in a larger game is to allow for limited repetition but also some ambiguity concerning the game structure at hand. This is readily illustrated by introducing some ambiguity as to whether Row is, in fact, informed.

Suppose the defensive game will be played twice ($T = 2$), against a succession of two separate Column players, denoted Column(1) and Column(2). Row and Column(1) will play the defensive game in period $t = 1$. Then in period 2 Row and Column(2) will play, with full knowledge of the first-stage actions taken and payoffs achieved, the identical defensive game. As usual, nature selects between the two matrixes with $\pi(s_1) = \frac{1}{2}$ in each period. Also, for convenience, let $r = 0$. This should be interpreted as a specific version of the finite repetition story, though played with a sequence of Column players. The reason for using separate Column players is to make the analysis more transparent. Column now has no interperiod strategic concerns. For example, Column(1) has no second-period concerns.

We now add the promised element of ambiguity. Let Row be privately informed with probability δ. If informed, he is informed for both periods and only he knows whether he is informed. The entire structure, including δ, is common knowledge. We call this the *defensive game with reputation*. For numerical purposes we use the same payoff data as in the earlier illustration:

game s_1

	L	R
U	10.0, 4.0	8.0, 0.0
D	8.0, 6.0	4.0, 5.0

game s_2

	L	R
U	10.0, 4.0	5.0, 6.0
D	11.0, – 100.0	6.0, 15.0

To build intuition, consider a one-shot version of such a game. If Row is informed, his dominant strategy is *UD*, while if he is not it is *U*. This implies Column's expected payoff from playing L is

$$\delta(-48) + (1 - \delta)(4)$$

while from *R* it is

$$\delta(7.5) + (1 - \delta)(3).$$

Thus, Column strictly prefers *R* for $\delta > \delta^* = 2/113$.

With this in mind, consider the $T = 2$ case. When the last stage is played, the above calculation implies Column(2) will play *R* if her assessed probability that Row is informed exceeds 2/113. This *assessed probability* (denoted $\hat{\delta}$) is, in fact, part of what must be determined by (equilibrium) play in the first stage.

Suppose, in the first stage, an uninformed Row plays *U* while an informed Row plays *UU* with probability α and *UD* with probability $(1 - \alpha)$. This implies Row plays *U* for certain if uninformed or with probability $\alpha + \frac{1}{2}(1 - \alpha)$ if informed. In turn, Column(2) observes *U* with probability $(1 - \delta) + \delta[\alpha + \frac{1}{2}(1 - \alpha)]$. If, then, Column(2) observes initial period play of *U* she will infer, via Bayes' rule, $\hat{\delta} = \delta[\alpha + \frac{1}{2}(1 - \alpha)]/\{(1 - \delta) + \delta[\alpha + \frac{1}{2}(1 - \alpha)]\}$. Conversely, observation of *D* will lead to $\hat{\delta} = 1$. (Notice that Row's playing *D* when not informed will also lead Column(2) to infer $\hat{\delta} = 1$; more will be said about this later.)

Let $\delta = 0.03$. It turns out an equilibrium is for (1) informed Row to play *UU* with probability $\alpha = 0.16517$ in the first stage and UD in the second stage; (2) uninformed Row to play *U* in both stages; (3) Column(1) to play *R*; and (4) Column(2) to play *L* if $\hat{\delta} < 2/113$, *R* if $\hat{\delta} > 2/113$, and *L* with probability $\beta = 2/7$ (and *R* with probability 5/7) if $\hat{\delta} = 2/113$.[13]

To verify this, first recall, with informed Row playing *UD* and uninformed Row playing *U* in the second period, Column(2) strictly prefers *L* if $\hat{\delta} < 2/113$ and *R* if $\hat{\delta} > 2/113$. And with $\hat{\delta} = 2/113$ she is indifferent, and the indicated randomization is acceptable.

Column(1), on the other hand, faces the following expected payoff from choice of *L*, when Row plays as indicated:

$$0.97(4) + 0.03[0.16517(4) + 0.83483(-48)] = 2.70$$

Choice of *R* yields

$$0.97(3) + 0.03[0.16517(3) + 0.83483(7.5)] = 3.11 > 2.70$$

Uninformed Row, in light of the play of Columns(1) and (2), envisions an expected payoff from initial-period choice of *U* of

$$6.5 + 10(2/7) + 6.5(5/7) = 14$$

His expected payoff from initial choice of D is

$$5 + 6.5 = 11.5$$

This reflects the fact U strictly dominates D for uninformed Row.

Finally, informed Row has UD strictly dominating in the second stage. Initial-period play of UU provides an expected payoff of

$$6.5 + 10.5(2/7) + 7(5/7) = 14.5$$

Initial play of UD yields

$$7 + (1/2)[10.5(2/7) + 7(5/7)] + (1/2)(7) = 14.5$$

DU provides

$$4.5 + (1/2)[10.5(2/7) + 7(5/7)] + (1/2)(7) = 12$$

and DD provides

$$5 + 7 = 12$$

Notice how informed Row uses his information in this equilibrium. With $\delta = 0.03 > 2/113$, a single-shot game confines him to an expected payoff of 7. But with repetition he mixes between using and not using his information in the first stage, in order to gain higher rents from his information in the second stage. This produces an advantageous tradeoff, as $14.5 > 2(7) = 14$. The key to producing this result is the ambiguity concerning whether Row is informed. This allows Row to manage his returns and his reputation (as measured by $\hat{\delta}$) for being informed. In equilibrium, Column(2) rationally believes this reputation.

It is interesting to see how informed Row's prospects fare as a function of the initial probability that he is informed. For $0 < \delta \leq 2/113$, informed Row plays UU in the first stage and UD in the second. Column(1) plays L, as does Column(2) absent any use of D in the first stage. Here, the Column players are not sufficiently threatened and it is to Row's advantage to completely withhold use of his information until the second period. Informed Row's expected payoff is, therefore, $10 + 10.5 = 20.5$. The opposite occurs when $\delta > 4/115$. Here the Column players always play R, so informed Row uses his information and plays UD in each period. His expected payoff is $7 + 7 = 14$, as would obtain in mere repetition of the single-shot game.

For $2/113 = 0.0177 \leq \delta \leq 0.02639$, informed Row plays UU in the first stage with probability $\alpha = (4 - 115\delta)/111\delta$ and UD with probability $(1 - \alpha)$, Column(1) plays L, and the remainder of the equilibrium is as described in the $\delta = 0.03$ illustration. Informed Row's expected payoff is 18. And for $0.02639 < \delta \leq 4/115 = 0.03478$ the equilibrium is identical except Column(1) plays R. Informed Row's expected payoff is 14.5.

Contrast this with a single-shot version of the game in which Row is informed with probability δ. If $\delta \leq 2/113$, Column will play R and informed Row's expected payoff is 10.5. Under the same circumstances but with repetition, informed Row's expected payoff *per period* is $(20.5)/2 = 10.25 < 10.5$. In this sense, repetition harms the informed player. This *harm* comes from the fact informed Row must underutilize his information in the reputation game. Conversely, for $2/113 < \delta \leq 4/115$ repetition is useful to the informed player. In the single-shot case, Column will play R and informed Row's expected payoff is 7. But under repetition, his per period expected payoff is $18/2 = 9$ (for $2/113 < \delta \leq 0.02639$) or $14.5/2 = 7.25$ (for $0.02639 < \delta \leq 4/115$).

Indeed, it is straightforward to demonstrate that this effect of repetition (with $T = 2$ and $r = 0$) extends to all defensive games with $a^2_{DL} - a^2_{UL} < \frac{1}{2}\{a^1_{UL} + a^2_{DL} - a^1_{UR} - a^2_{DR}\}$. In these cases there always exists a range of assessed probability δ such that repetition provides informed Row with an expected per period payoff that exceeds his single-shot payoff; and there also exists a second range of assessed probability δ such that repetition is harmful in this sense.

Proposition 4.4

There exist δ such that Row's per period expected equilibrium payoff in the defensive game with reputation is below that in the corresponding single-shot game. In addition, if $a^2_{DL} - a^2_{UL} < \frac{1}{2}\{a^1_{UL} + a^2_{DL} - a^1_{UR} - a^2_{DR}\}$ there also exist δ such that Row's per period expected equilibrium payoff exceeds that in the corresponding single-shot game.

Proof: The proof is tedious and will only be sketched. First, consider the one-shot defensive game where Row is informed with probability δ. Column will play L in this setting for all $0 \leq \delta \leq \delta^*$, where

$$\delta^* = \frac{b^1_{UR} + b^2_{UR} - b^1_{UL} - b^2_{UL}}{b^2_{DL} - b^2_{DR} + b^2_{UR} - b^2_{UL}}$$

It is readily verified that $0 < \delta < 1$.

To establish the second half of the claim, we consider the defensive game with reputation with $\delta = \delta^* + \varepsilon$, where ε is small but strictly positive. In this setting our equilibrium is: (1) uninformed Row always plays U; (2) informed Row always plays UD in the second stage, along with UU with probability α and UD with probability $1 - \alpha$ in the first stage; (3) Column(1) plays L; and (4)

Column(2) plays R if Row played D in the first stage or L with probability β and R with probability $1-\beta$ otherwise.

To specify α and β as well as verify that this is an equilibrium, initially observe that Column(2)'s posterior probability that Row is informed, conditional upon observing play of U in the first stage, must be exactly δ^*. In this case, Column(2) is indifferent between L and R and we set the β randomization so informed Row is indifferent between UU and UD at this first stage. This requires

$$\beta = \frac{\{a_{DL}^2 - a_{UL}^2\}}{\frac{1}{2}\{a_{UL}^1 + a_{DL}^2 - a_{UR}^1 - a_{DR}^2\}}$$

And by assumption we have $0 < \beta < 1$. With this indifference, we set Row's α randomization so Column(2)'s posterior is exactly δ^* when U is played in the first stage:

$$\alpha = \frac{\delta^*(2-\delta) - \delta}{\delta(1-\delta^*)}$$

For ε small but strictly positive, we have $0 < \alpha < 1$. The remainder of the equilibrium conditions are readily verified.

In equilibrium, then, informed Row's expected payoff is half of the following quantity:

$$a_{UL}^1 + a_{DL}^2 + \tfrac{1}{2}[(a_{UR}^1 + a_{DR}^2) + \beta(a_{UL}^1 + a_{DL}^2) + (1-\beta)(a_{UR}^1 + a_{DR}^2)].$$

This exceeds $(a_{UR}^1 + a_{DR}^2)$, or twice the equilibrium payoff in the one-shot game. (Uninformed Row is also strictly improved here.)

To establish the first half of the claim, consider the case where $\delta = \delta^* - \varepsilon$, with ε again small but strictly positive. The one-shot game provides an expected payoff to informed Row of $\frac{1}{2}[a_{UL}^1 + a_{DL}^2]$. But informed Row cannot match this in the two-stage game since Column(2) will play R if Row plays D at the first stage. (Uninformed Row is neither helped nor harmed in this case.)

In these instances, informed Row manages his reputation, interpreted as Column(2)'s assessed probability that he is informed, to advantage. This assessment follows from Bayesian revision, whenever possible—as when U is observed in the first period in the $\delta = 0.03$ case. Conversely, when something is observed that should not be, that is when something off the equilibrium path is observed, we assume Column(2) assesses $\hat{\delta} = 1$. Thus, in the case $\delta = 0.01$, Column(2) should only observe first-period play of U and, using Bayes' rule, conclude that $\hat{\delta} = \delta = 0.01$. But if Row plays D in the initial period, Bayes' rule is not applicable (since we are now trying to infer on the basis of a zero probability event). So we assume $\hat{\delta} = 1$ in this case. In other words, the equilibrium notion here embraces (1) beliefs and (2) strategies such that the strategies are best responses to the prevailing beliefs and anticipated strategies for each and every eventuality. Kreps–Wilson [1982b], the authors of this equilibrium notion, term this a *sequential equilibrium.*[14]

Summary

The main conclusion from this odyssey is that extrapolation of intuition about the demand for information from a single person to a competitive setting calls for a heavy dose of trepidation. It is logically possible that private information in the hands of one player benefits both players, only the informed player, only the uninformed player, or neither player. It is also logically possible that repeated play of the competitive game will alter these conclusions in a qualitatively significant way.

Armed with this warning, the next step is to rationalize the assumed payoff structures. The games analyzed here are entirely exogenous. Can we construct them from primitive market settings? Recent work by Milgrom–Weber [1982], Clarke [1983], Kirby [1985], Maksimovic [1984], and Gal-Or [1985] suggest this is possible. This is an indirect way of saying that, in the limit, a decision facilitating problem arises from a larger economic structure. We have focused on what might happen in such a larger structure, but have only scratched the surface. For example, in examining the importance of repeated play, we focused on settings where the identical single-shot game is played a number of times. Surely the stage game will change through time, due to learning, random arrival of opportunities, and fate. Similarly, we should expect the stage game to have more than two active players in most settings. The question, of course, is where to draw the line in a partial equilibrium setting. Admitting a nominal amount of strategic consideration qualitatively alters our conclusions concerning the value of information. Beyond that, the topography is unexplored.

Notes

1. This definition focuses on so-called pure strategies. This provides expositional convenience, but we should also remember that a pure strategy equilibrium need not exist. But in the mixed extension, where Row plays U with probability α and Column plays L with probability β (and an equilibrium is defined in obvious fashion) an equilibrium exists for any finite noncooperative game. (This result, due to John Nash, is discussed in Luce–Raiffa [1957] and Vorobev [1977].)

2. See Demski [1980], for example.

3. That is we may have multiple equilibria, two or more of which are undominated. The equilibrium focused on will be clear in what follows, and the use of an undominated equilibrium is sufficient for our purpose. Further observe that any randomization between *UD* and *DD* provides another equilibrium in the example, again dominated by (*UD*, *R*).

4. Von Neumann–Morgenstern representation is unique to positive affine transformation. Thus, an equivalent definition of a team game is one in which, under admissible transformation (or rescaling), the players' payoffs are identical.

5. This is clear from Marschak–Radner's [1972] study of team organizations. Indeed, equilibrium behavior in the team game is what they term person-by-person satisfactory decision rules.

6. Specialized to noiseless information structures defined as partitions of some set of states S, the Blackwell Theorem can be paraphrased as follows: Consider two costless partitions of S, η and η'. Then η is as valuable as η' for every single person decision problem defined on S if and only if η subpartitions η'. Indeed, proposition 4.1 could be strengthened to an if and only if statement concerning all information structures and team games defined on S.

7. Proposition 4.2 demonstrates a well-known implication of the structure of constant-sum or adversary games. In various forms this is studied in Ponssard–Zamir [1973], Ho–Sun [1974], Ponssard [1976], and Sorin [1980], for example.

8. Baiman's [1975] original example is somewhat related to the class of defensive games. Here, however, we impose equally likely states as well as additional structure for the uninformed player's payoffs.

9. It is not possible to have $V_R(\eta^R)$ negative for all admissible f.

10. Contrast this with the case where Row is able to exploit the ex post observability to make a binding commitment to not use his information.

11. Luce–Raiffa [1957], Kreps–Wilson [1982a], and Kreps et al. [1982] discuss this unraveling of a finite repetition game. Benoit–Krishna [1985] examine settings where the single-shot game has multiple equilibria and it is possible to achieve more interesting equilibria in the repeated game (when preferences are measured by average payoff per period).

12. Levine–Ponssard [1977] make the same point in their analysis of the symmetric game, though in a setting where preferences are measured by the average expected payoff per period. There is some delicacy in making the argument in the discounting case, as exemplified by our use of $r < 3$. See Abreu [1984] and Fudenberg–Maskin [1986].

13. In particular, we depart from pure strategies here and employ mixed strategies. The notion of equilibrium remains one of mutual best response, but with some important refinements to reflect what happens if Column(2) observes an event that should only happen with probability zero. (Kreps–Wilson [1982b])

14. More formally, a sequential equilibrium consists of beliefs and strategies that are both sequentially rational (in the sense the strategies are rational in the presence of the assessed beliefs) and consistent. Consistency is a limit condition that is readily verified in our solution to the defensive game with reputation. (See Kreps–Wilson [1982a] and [1982b].) Additional equilibrium refinements are discussed in, say, Kohlberg–Mertens [1986] and Grossman–Perry [1986].

References

Abreu, D. [1984]. "Infinitely Repeated Games with Discounting: A General Theory." Working Paper, Harvard University.

Aumann, R. [1976]. "Agreeing to Disagree." *Annals of Statistics* 4, 1236–1239.

Baiman, S. [1975]. "The Evaluation and Choice of Internal Information Systems Within a Multiperson World." *Journal of Accounting Research* 13, 1–15.

Baiman, S. and Demski, J. [1980]. "Economically Optimal Performance Evaluation and Control Systems." *Journal of Accounting Research Supplement*, 184–220.

Benoit, J., and Krishna, V. [1985]. "Finitely Repeated Games." *Econometrica* 53, 905–922.

Butterworth, J. [1972]. "The Accounting Systems as an Information Function." *Journal of Accounting Research* 10, 1–27.

Christensen, J. [1982]. "The Determination of Performance Standards and Participation." *Journal of Accounting Research* 20, 589–603.

Clarke, R. [1983]. "Collusion and the Incentives for Information Sharing." *Bell Journal of Economics* 14, 383–394.

Demski, J. [1980]. *Information Analysis.* Reading, MA.: Addison-Wesley.

Feltham, G. [1977]. "Cost Aggregation: An Information Economic Analysis." *Journal of Accounting Research* 15, 42–70.

Fudenberg, D., and Maskin, E. [1986]. "The Folk Theorem in Repeated Games with Discounting or with Incomplete Information." *Econometrica* 54, 533–554.

Gal-Or, E. [1985]. "Information Sharing in Oligopoly." *Econometrica* 53, 329–343.

Grossman, S., and Perry, M. [1986]. "A Perfect Sequential Equilibrium." *Journal of Economic Theory* 39, 97–119.

Ho, Y., and Blau, I. [1973]. "A Simple Example on Informativeness and Performance." *Journal of Optimization Theory and Applications* 11, 437–440.

Ho, Y., and Sun, F. [1974]. "Value of Information in Two-Team Zero-Sum Problems." *Journal of Optimization Theory and Applications* 14, 557–571.

Kirby, A. [1985]. *Trade Associations as Information Exchange Mechanisms.* (Ph.D. Dissertation, Stanford University.

Kohlberg, E., and Mertens, J. [1986]. "On the Strategic Stability of Equilibria." *Econometrica* 54, 1003–1037.

Kreps, D., and Wilson, R. [1982a]. "Reputation and Imperfect Information." *Journal of Economic Theory* 27, 253–279.

Kreps, D., and Wilson, R. [1982b]. "Sequential Equilibria." *Econometrica* 50, 863–894.

Kreps, D., Milgrom, P., Roberts, J., and Wilson, R. [1982]. "Rational Cooperation in the Finitely Repeated Prisoners' Dilemma." *Journal of Economic Theory* 27, 245–252.

Levine, P., and Ponssard, J. [1977]. "The Value of Information in Some Nonzero Sum Games." *International Journal of Game Theory* 6, 221–229.

Luce, D., and Raiffa, H. [1957]. *Games and Decisions* New York: John Wiley.

Maksimovic, V. [1984]. "Capital Structure and Value Creation in a Stochastic Oligopoly." Working Paper, Harvard University.

Marschak, J., and Radner, R. [1972]. *Economic Theory of Teams.* New Haven: Yale University Press.

Milgrom, P. [1981]. "An Axiomatic Characterization of Common Knowledge." *Econometrica* 49, 219–222.

Milgrom, P., and Weber, R. [1982]. "A Theory of Auctions and Competitive Bidding." *Econometrica* 50, 1089–1122.

Ponssard, J. [1976]. "On the Concept of the Value of Information in Competitive Situations." *Management Science* 22, 739–747.

Ponssard, J. [1979]. "The Strategic Role of Information on the Demand Function in an Oligopolistic Market." *Management Science* 25, 243–250.

Ponssard, J., and Zamir, S. [1973]. "Zero Sum Sequential Games with Incomplete Information." *International Journal of Game Theory* 2, 99–107.

Sorin, S. [1980]. "An Introduction to Two-Person Zero Sum Repeated Games with Incomplete Information." IMSSS Report, Stanford University.

Vorobev, N. [1977]. *Game Theory* New York: Springer-Verlag.

PART III: CONTRACTING IN AGENCIES UNDER MORAL HAZARD

5 THE PRINCIPAL/AGENT PROBLEM—NUMERICAL SOLUTIONS*

Phelim P. Boyle
and
John E. Butterworth

The principal/agent paradigm provides a useful vehicle for examining a wide range of contractual relationships. Recent theoretical advances in the modeling of this relationship have enriched our understanding of the interplay between risk sharing and incentives in the design of optimal contracts.

In the most basic model of this genre there are two economic agents—the principal and the agent—who operate in an uncertain environment. The principal engages the agent to perform a certain task where the output is both a function of the effort exerted by the agent and the random state of nature

---

* This paper represents part of a research project, sponsored by the Huebner Foundation for Insurance Education, that John Butterworth was working on before his death. I feel very privileged to have worked with John on this project. John's gifted scholarship and gracious personality made it an enriching academic and human experience.

Ruth Freedman supplied diligent research assistance for an earlier version. Financial support for the current revision from the Natural Science and Engineering Research Council of Canada is also acknowledged. Khoa Tran's assistance with computer programming for this latest version is appreciated. Jerry Feltham provided extensive and helpful comments on an earlier draft. George Blazenko and Melissa Van Kessel provided helpful assistance.

that ensues. Both the principal and agent strive to maximize their own welfare. The principal's problem is to design a contract that is efficient from a risk-sharing viewpoint and provides appropriate incentives for the agent. If the agent is work averse—an assumption normally made in these models—then he has an incentive to shirk if his actions are unobservable to the principal, giving rise to moral hazard.

The paper by Holmstrom [1979] provides a good analysis of the basic model and discusses a number of extensions and applications. There have been a number of extensions to the basic model since. Good reviews of the applications of agency theory to problems in accounting are contained in the papers by Baiman [1982] and Demski and Kreps [1982].

In many applications it is very desirable to have a complete characterization of the optimal contract but unfortunately this is a difficult task. As Clarke and Darrough [1980] have shown, the solution of the principal/agent model for the optimal sharing rule in a general setting involves technical issues which are both subtle and profound. Analytical solutions are very rare and can only be obtained by imposing restrictive assumptions on the form of the utility functions and on the probability distribution of the outcome. The purpose of the present paper is to illustrate how numerical approaches can be used in principal/agent problems to obtain the optimal sharing rule. While the approach developed here could be extended to handle more complex situations, the paper deals just with the basic single-agent, single-period model.

Even when a numerical approach is used, it is very convenient to restrict the form of the utility functions of the principal and agent to make the analysis tractable. It is assumed in the present paper that both the principal and agent have hyperbolic absolute risk aversion (HARA) utility functions with identical cautiousness. The HARA assumption leads to an explicit form for the optimal sharing rule. In the context of pure risk sharing, the assumption of HARA utility with identical cautiousness induces considerable simplifications and so it is not too surprising to see its usefulness reemerge in the context of the principal/agent problem when there is moral hazard present.

The outline of the present paper is as follows. We first set out the structure of the problem and analyze the situation when both the principal and the agent have HARA utility with identical cautiousness. We analyze both the first-best and second-best sharing rules for three different utility functions and output distribution assumptions. The utility functions selected illustrate decreasing, constant, and increasing absolute risk aversion. The corresponding distributional assumptions are the lognormal, exponential, and beta. We also summarize here the characteristics of the first-best and the second-best sharing rules in the case of the three utility-output density combinations selected. In some situations, it is necessary to impose bounds on the sharing rule (in the second-best case) and the next section, on Sharing Rule Bounds for Second-Best Solutions, discusses this point. After which, we describe the procedure we developed to obtain numerical solutions. A range of numerical illustrations is presented in the fifth section. The paper ends with a brief summary and discussion of possible extensions.

The Principal/Agent Model

Basic Elements of the Model

In this section we illustrate that the optimal sharing rule has a simple explicit form when both the principal and the agent have HARA utility functions with identical cautiousness. The model and the notation are similar to those of Holmstrom [1979]. We define:

$U_1(\cdot)$ = principal's utility function (for wealth)
$U_2(\cdot)$ = agent's utility function (for wealth)
$V(\cdot)$ = agent's disutility function (for effort)
a = action (effort) of agent
x = output depending on agent's effort and random state of nature
$s(x)$ = agent's share of output
$f(x,a)$ = probability density of output for a given action a.

The agent's utility function has two arguments: one representing wealth and one representing effort. This function is assumed separable into two components: U_2, which depends only on the agent's wealth, and V, which depends only on his effort.

It is assumed that U_1 and U_2 are strictly increasing concave and twice differentiable. Later on we impose further restrictions on these functions. The function V is assumed to be increasing convex and twice differentiable. Both parties have the same probability beliefs and jointly observe x. The density $f(x, a)$ is assumed to satisfy the monotone likelihood-ratio property which implies that an increase in a shifts the distribution of x to the right. It is assumed that the function $f(x, a)$ is twice differentiable in both of its arguments and that it has fixed support. Each individual knows the structure of the decision problem and preferences.

We consider two situations: (i) where the principal observes a, the action taken by the agent; and (ii) where the principal does not observe a. Case (i) is known as the first-best case and the principal's problem is considerably simplified by the fact that he can directly enforce the agent's action. In case (ii) the agent will select an action that optimizes his own expected utility and this adds considerable complexity.

The First-Best Case

For the first-best case, the optimal sharing rule s is obtained by solving the following problem:

$$\underset{s(x),a}{\text{maximize}} \quad G(s,a) \tag{5.1}$$

$$\text{such that} \quad H(s,a) \geq \bar{H} \tag{5.2}$$

where $G(s, a)$ is the principal's expected utility

$$G(s,a) = \int U_1[x - s(x)]f(x,a)dx \tag{5.3}$$

$H(s, a)$ is the agent's expected utility

$$H(s,a) = \int U_2[s(x)]f(x,a)dx - V(a) \tag{5.4}$$

and $\bar{H}$ is the agent's exogenously specified level of expected utility from his alternative opportunities.

Whenever both the principal and the agent have HARA utilities (for wealth) with identical cautiousness, the first-best sharing rule has a simple linear form. In the HARA case, the U_i functions can be classified into three forms. First, the power utility functions of the form

$$U_i(\cdot) = \frac{1}{(\alpha - 1)}[\alpha(\cdot) + \beta_i]^{[1-\alpha^{-1}]} \qquad \alpha \neq 0, \alpha \neq 1 \tag{5.5}$$

For $\alpha = 0$, we have the exponential utility function given by

$$U_i(\cdot) = \frac{1 - \exp[-\gamma_i((\cdot) + W_i)]}{\gamma_i} \tag{5.6}$$

and for $\alpha = 1$, we have the log utility function given by

$$U_i(\cdot) = \log_e[(\cdot) + \beta_i] \tag{5.7}$$

By convention, $i = 1$ for the principal and $i = 2$ for the agent.

It is convenient to record the first-best (linear) sharing rules corresponding to these three types of HARA utility functions. This will facilitate comparison with the second-best sharing rules which we will discuss shortly. These first-best sharing rules are obtained by solving equation (5.1) subject to constraint (5.2). If we denote by λ, the Lagrange multiplier for the constraint, then the sharing rules take the form given in table 5–1.

Table 5–1. First-Best Sharing Rules When Both Principal and Agent have HARA Utility Functions for Wealth with Identical Cautiousness

α	*Utility Function*	*First-best Sharing Rule*
$\alpha \neq 0$	Power ($\alpha \neq 1$) Logarithmic ($\alpha = 1$)	$\dfrac{\lambda^{\alpha}[\alpha x + \beta_1] - \beta_2}{\alpha(1 + \lambda^{\alpha})}$
$\alpha = 0$	Exponential	$\dfrac{\gamma_1 x + (\gamma_1 W_1 - \gamma_2 W_2) + \log_e(\lambda)}{\gamma_1 + \gamma_2}$

The Second-Best Case

If it is assumed that the agent's action is unobservable to the principal, then the agent acts to maximize his own expected utility and, thus, another constraint is added to the problem. The agent selects an action a so that

$$a \in \underset{a' \in \Omega}{\operatorname{argmax}} \{H(s, a')\} \tag{5.8}$$

where Ω is the set of all possible actions and the notation "argmax" denotes the set of arguments that maximize the function that follows. The optimal sharing rule $s(x)$ in the second-best situation is given by the solution to equation (5.1) subject to the constraints (5.2) and (5.8). For the class of problems dealt with in this paper, we assume that the optimal sharing rule can be derived using the first-order conditions (cf. Rogerson [1985] and Grossman and Hart [1983] for an analysis of the first-order approach in this connection). Given this assumption, we replace constraint (5.8) with the first-order condition for the maximization of the agent's expected utility, which is given by

$$\int U_2[s(x)] f_a(x, a)\, dx - V_a(a) = 0 \tag{5.9}$$

Following Holmstrom [1979] the maximization problem for the second-best situation leads to the following equation for the optimal sharing rule:

$$\frac{U_1'[x - s(x)]}{U_2'[s(x)]} = \lambda + \mu \frac{f_a(x, a)}{f(x, a)} \qquad \text{for all } x \tag{5.10}$$

where λ is the Lagrange multiplier for constraint (5.2) and μ is the Lagrange multiplier for constraint (5.9). Let $P(x)$ denote the left-hand side and $Q(x)$ the right-hand side of equation (5.10). From our assumptions, $Q(x)$ is an increasing function of x. For those ranges of x for which $Q(x)$ is negative, it will be necessary to place appropriate bounds on the sharing rule since $P(x)$ is always positive.

Holmstrom [1977] shows that in general, it is necessary to place bounds on the sharing rule to ensure the existence of a solution. For some of the utility functions and distributional assumptions used in this paper, it will be necessary to impose bounds on the sharing rule to obtain a meaningful solution. We will illustrate explicitly the derivation of these bounds in the context of particular examples.

Since the Lagrangian is maximized at the selected level of a, the solution to the principal's decision problem is also characterized by

$$\int U_1[x - s(x)] f_a(x, a)dx + \mu\{\int U_2[s(x)] f_{aa}(x, a)dx - V_{aa}(a)\} = 0 \qquad (5.11)$$

To obtain a solution we set the agent's expected utility equal to his reservation level $\bar{H}$, that is, we treat (5.2) as an equality and substitute in (5.4) to obtain:

$$\int U_2[s(x)] f(x, a)dx - V(a) - \bar{H} = 0 \qquad (5.12)$$

Assuming that equation (5.10) leads to a tractable expression for $s(x)$, one can solve the three equations (5.9), (5.11), and (5.12) for the optimizing triplet λ, μ, and a.

For all members of the HARA subclass (identical cautiousness), equation (5.10) can be solved to give an explicit value for $s(x)$. The functional relation for $s(x)$ at an interior point can be derived using equations (5.5), (5.6), and (5.7). For power utility, $s(x)$ satisfies

$$s(x) = \frac{Q(x)^\alpha[\alpha x + \beta_1] - \beta_2}{\alpha[1 + Q(x)^\alpha]} \qquad (5.13)$$

For exponential utility, $s(x)$ satisfies

$$s(x) = \frac{\gamma_1 x + (\gamma_1 W_1 - \gamma_1 W_2) + \log Q(x)}{\gamma_1 + \gamma_2} \qquad (5.14)$$

For log utility, $s(x)$ satisfies

$$s(x) = \frac{Q(x)(x + \beta_1) - \beta_2}{(1 + Q(x))} \qquad (5.15)$$

It should be emphasized that these three functional forms for the sharing rule are valid for values of x lying inside the appropriate bounds for each sharing rule. The bounds will depend on the nature of the output density $f(x, a)$.

Note that if $\mu = 0$, then $Q(x) = \lambda$ and we are back to the first-best solution. In the second-best case, $Q(x)$ will be a function of x involving both the output density $f(x, a)$ and its derivative $f_a(x, a)$ through equation (5.10).

Details of Output Densities Used

One of the attractions of the numerical approach suggested in this paper is that one can accomodate a wide variety of output densities. In order to illustrate our procedures, we focus on three particular functional forms for $f(x, a)$. These correspond to three well-known distributions and serve to illustrate particular features of our method. They are the exponential distribution, the lognormal distribution, and the beta distribution. The exponential distribution is often used in this literature to exhibit numerical solutions since under some preference assumptions (cf. Holmstrom [1979]) it simplifies the analysis. The lognormal distribution has often been used in the financial economics literature and permits an easy generalization to the multivariate case. The beta distribution has bounded support and this may be a useful property in some applications.

Table 5–2 gives some characteristics of these three distributions. In particular, we give the ratio $f_a(x, a)/f(x, a)$ since this plays a key role in the definitions of the sharing rule $s(x)$ in the second-best case. [cf. equations (5.13), (5.14), and (5.15).] Note that for the beta output density, the expected value of $\log(x)$ in the bottom right-hand panel of table 5–2 is defined by

$$E_B[\log(x)] = C_2 \int_0^1 \log(x) x^{a-1}(1-x)^{b-1}\,dx$$

Note that the ratio $f_a(x, a)/f(x, a)$ is bounded below by $-1/a$ for the exponential distribution but that it tends to minus infinity for both the lognormal and beta distributions as x becomes small. From equation (5.10) we note that, as λ and μ are positive, this implies that there are values of the variable x for which the right-hand side of equation (5.10) is negative in the case of the lognormal and beta distributions. This is related to the question of bounds on the second-best sharing rule as we will see in the next section.

Second-Best Sharing Rules for Different Utility—Probability Combinations

There are several different possible combinations of utility functions and probability density functions $f(x, a)$ that could be used to generate numerical

Table 5–2. Properties of the Output Density Function $f(x, a)$ for Three Selected Distributional Assumptions

Distribution *Attribute*	*Exponential*	*Lognormal*	*Beta*
$f(x, a)$	$\frac{1}{a}\exp\left[-\frac{x}{a}\right]$	$\frac{C_1}{x}\exp\left[-\frac{(\log(x)-\log(a))^2}{2\sigma^2}\right]$	$C_2 x^{a-1}(1-x)^{b-1}$
Normalizing constant		$C_1 = \frac{1}{\sigma\sqrt{2\pi}}$	$C_2^{-1} = \int_0^1 x^{a-1}(1-x)^{b-1}\,dx$
Expected value of x, given a, $E(x, a)$	a	$\exp\left[\log(a)+\frac{\sigma^2}{2}\right]$	$\frac{a}{(a+b)}$
Variance of x, given a	$2a^2$	$E(x, a)^2\{\exp(\sigma^2)-1\}$	$\frac{ab}{(a+b)^2(a+b+1)}$
$\frac{f_a(x, a)}{f(x, a)}$	$\frac{x-a}{a^2}$	$\frac{1}{a\sigma^2}\log\left[\frac{x}{a}\right]$	$\log(x) - E_B[\log(x)]$
Support	$[0, \infty)$	$[0, \infty)$	$[0, 1]$

examples. We divide the HARA utility function into three categories depending on the value of α. These correspond to

$\alpha > 0$	decreasing absolute risk aversion
$\alpha = 0$	constant absolute risk aversion
$\alpha < 0$	increasing absolute risk aversion

As indicated in table 5–3 we use these three preference assumptions in conjunction with the lognormal distribution, the exponential distribution and the beta distribution.

While there is no compelling reason for selecting the three combinations shown, it may be instructive to indicate our rationale. The exponential-

Table 5–3. Second-Best Sharing Rules for Three Different Utility Function—Probability Density Combinations

Utility Assumption	*Probability Density*	*Functional Form of Second Best Sharing Rule in Interior Region*	*Bounds Required for Sharing Rule*
Power, increasing absolute risk aversion, $\alpha > 0$	Lognormal	$\dfrac{Q(x)^{\alpha}[\alpha x + \beta_1] - \beta_2}{\alpha(1 + Q(x)^{\alpha})}$ where $Q(x) = \lambda + \dfrac{\mu}{a\sigma^2}\log\left[\dfrac{x}{a}\right]$	Yes
Exponential, constant absolute risk aversion, $\alpha = 0$	Exponential	$\dfrac{\gamma_1 x + (\gamma_1 W_1 - \gamma_2 W_2) + \log_e Q(x)}{\gamma_1 + \gamma_2}$ where $Q(x) = \lambda + \dfrac{\mu(x-a)}{a^2}$	No
Power, decreasing absolute risk aversion, $\alpha < 0$	Beta	$\dfrac{Q(x)^{\alpha}[\alpha x + \beta_1] - \beta_2}{\alpha(1 + Q(x)^{\alpha})}$ where $Q(x) = \lambda + \mu\{\log(x) - E_B[\log(x)]\}$, $E_B(\cdot)$ is defined as in table 5–2	Yes

utility–exponential-density combination leads to considerable mathematical simplicity: numerical integration is not required. The lognormal density is often associated with power utility in the financial economics literature. The beta density has bounded support and provides a natural distribution for the case of increasing absolute risk aversion since, under our assumptions, the utility function is only meaningful over a certain range of the individual's wealth.

Table 5–3 displays the functional form of the second-best sharing rule in the interior region for the three selected combinations. For the second combination, no bounds need to be imposed in the sharing rule. However, for the other two cases, bounds need to be imposed on the sharing rule. In the following section, we indicate how these bounds can be obtained.

Sharing Rule Bounds for Second Best Solutions

The characterization of the optimal sharing rule in its interior domain is given implicitly by equation (5.10). In order to determine the bounds on the sharing rule, we use the fact that the marginal utilities of both the principal and the agent have to be non-negative. In some situations, there is a range of x for which the right-hand side of equation (5.10) [i.e., $Q(x)$] is negative. For such values of x, equation (5.10) cannot be used to characterize $s(x)$ and we use instead a procedure suggested by Mirrlees [1976] to impose bounds on the sharing rule. It is convenient to deal separately with the three HARA utility functions corresponding to $\alpha > 0$, $\alpha = 0$, and $\alpha < 0$.

Sharing Rule Bounds for $\alpha > 0$

It is convenient to assume that the principal has initial wealth W_1 and that the agent has initial wealth W_2. Since the marginal utilities of both parties must be non-negative this implies that

$$-\frac{\beta_2}{\alpha} - W_2 \leq s(x) \leq x + W_1 + \frac{\beta_1}{\alpha} \tag{5.16}$$

We assume that W_1, W_2, β_1, and β_2 are all non-negative. The lower bound arises from the non-negativity of the agent's marginal utility and the upper bound arises from that of the principal. In the interior region the sharing rule is given by

$$s(x) = \frac{Q(x)^{\alpha}[\alpha(x + W_1) + \beta_1] - [\alpha W_2 + \beta_2]}{\alpha(1 + Q(x)^{\alpha})} \tag{5.17}$$

Equation (5.17) is simply a modification of the sharing rule in table 5–3 to include the initial wealth of both parties. Note that as long as $Q(x)$ is positive, $Q(x)^{\alpha}$ is positive and the $s(x)$ given by (5.17) lies within the upper bound given by equation (5.16). Note also that $Q(x)$ is an increasing function of x. When $Q(x)$ tends to zero, then $s(x)$ given by equation (5.17) tends to its lower bound given by equation (5.16). Hence, as long as the right-hand side of equation (5.10) is non-negative, we use the interior functional form of the sharing rule given by equation (5.17); otherwise, the sharing rule is set equal to its lower bound in equation (5.16).

Sharing Rule Bounds for $\alpha < 0$

In this case, we set $\alpha = -\rho$ where ρ is positive. Once again, we use the condition that the marginal utilities of both the principal and the agent have to be positive. These conditions produce the following bounds for the second-best sharing rule:

$$x + W_1 - \frac{\beta_1}{\rho} \le s(x) \le \frac{\beta_2}{\rho} - W_2 \tag{5.18}$$

In order for a meaningful interior region to exist, it is necessary that the upper bound exceed the lower bound, so we assume that

$$x + W_1 + W_2 < \frac{\beta_1 + \beta_2}{\rho}$$

The functional form of the optimal sharing rule in its interior domain is given by

$$s(x) = \frac{\rho(x + W_1) - \beta_1 + Q(x)^{\rho}(\beta_2 - \rho W_2)}{\rho(1 + Q(x)^{\rho})} \tag{5.19}$$

This last equation is obtained by solving equation (5.10) and using $-\rho$ instead of α for $\rho > 0$. As long as $Q(x)$ is positive, then $s(x)$ given by equation (5.19) lies within the bounds given by equation (5.18). When $Q(x)$ tends to zero, then from equation (5.19), $s(x)$ tends toward its lower bound

$$\frac{\rho(x + W_1) - \beta_1}{\rho}$$

Hence, in this case, we use equation (5.19) for $s(x)$ as long as $Q(x)$ is positive; otherwise we set $s(x)$ equal to its lower bound.

Sharing Rule Bounds for $\alpha = 0$

This corresponds to the case of exponential utility. The optimal second-best sharing rule is given by

$$s(x) = \frac{\gamma_1 x + (\gamma_1 W_1 - \gamma_2 W_2) + \log_e Q(x)}{\gamma_1 + \gamma_2} \tag{5.20}$$

The marginal utilities of both the principal and the agent are positive for all finite values of x and so, in this case, the only restriction on $s(x)$ arises from the possibility that the output density is such that there is a range of x for which $Q(x)$ is negative. If this is the case then the lower bound of $s(x)$ as $Q(x)$ tends to zero is minus infinity.

Note that in all three cases the critical value of x determining the interval over which $s(x)$ is bounded is the value of x which makes $Q(x)$ zero. If there are no values of x for which $Q(x)$ is zero, then no bounds are required on the sharing rule. In our situation, this is the case for the exponential output density (cf. Holmstrom [1977]). However, for both the lognormal density and the beta density there is a range of x over which $Q(x)$ is negative so that bounds on the sharing rule are needed in both these cases.

Solution Procedure

It is instructive to first describe the procedure used to obtain numerical solutions for the three utility–probability combinations in table 5–3. The form of the first-best sharing rule in each case is given in table 5–1. The necessary conditions obtained from the maximization problem in equations (5.1) to (5.4) are

$$\int U_1[x - s(x)] f_a(x, a)\, dx + \lambda\{\int U_2[s(x)] f_a(x, a) dx - V_a(a)\} = 0 \tag{5.21}$$

To obtain a solution, we replace the inequality in equation (5.2) by an equality and this together with equation (5.21) provides two equations for the two unknowns λ and a. In general, these are two nonlinear integral equations; and solving them numerically involves the use of a numerical integration algorithm as well as an algorithm for the solution of nonlinear equations. For one of our examples, the exponential-utility–exponential-density combination, it was possible to obtain analytical solutions for the integrals involved, but for the other two it was necessary to use numerical integration.

To compute the integrals numerically, the IMSL routine DCADRE was used. To ensure that the numerical integration procedure gave sufficiently accurate results, we found it convenient to compute the first four moments of the probability density functions involved and to compare them with the exact theoretical results.

The issue of accuracy is of particular importance in the case of the lognormal density where the limits of integration run from zero to infinity. There are computational problems if we set the lower limit of integration at exactly zero, and so the range of integration employed depends on the parameters of the problem. For the numerical values employed in this paper, we found that sufficiently accurate results (10 significant figures) were obtained by using the interval [0.007, 1000].

The beta density function has a range of integration from zero to one. For some of the integrals involving the beta density encountered in the second-best sharing rule problem, it was necessary to set the lower end point of integration at a very small positive number.

In order to obtain the optimal parameters λ and a, we used the IMSL routine known as ZSCNT. The user supplies initial estimates of the parameters and specifies the level of accuracy and the maximum number of iterations permitted. For the three utility–probability density combinations used in this paper, we obtained estimates of the optimal first-best values of the parameters λ and a. Specific numerical details are given in the next section.

The procedure adopted to obtain the optimal solution for the second-best case is similar. When the first-order approach is valid, equations (5.9), (5.11), and (5.12) are solved to obtain the optimal values of the parameters λ, μ, and a. For our three utility–probability density combinations, the interior form of the sharing rule is given in table 5–3. In general, numerical procedures are required to evaluate the various integrals. However, the integrals involved in the exponential-utility–exponential-output density can be evaluated in terms of known functions (as demonstrated in the appendix) and the analysis is considerably simplified. As has been noted earlier (Holmstrom [1977]), the exponential output density does not require any bounds to be placed on the sharing rule and this fact also simplifies the integrations.

For our two other combinations, bounds are required on the sharing rules. In both cases, the function $Q(x)$ becomes negative. Denote by x_M the largest value of x that makes $Q(x)$ equal to zero. For the beta distribution, we have

$$x_M = \exp\left[E_B(\log(x)) - \frac{\lambda}{\mu}\right] \tag{5.22}$$

and for the lognormal distribution,

$$x_M = a\exp\left[-\frac{\lambda a\sigma^2}{\mu}\right] \tag{5.23}$$

Note that the sharing rule is constant in the region $[0, x_M]$ and it is continuous at $x = x_M$ with the interior solution. Thus, for example, in the lognormal case with increasing absolute risk aversion ($\alpha > 0$), the agent's share in the region $[0, x_M]$ is

$$-\frac{\beta_2}{\alpha} - W_2$$

These bounds on the sharing rules add technical complexity to the solution procedure. The different functional forms of the sharing rule $s(x)$ have to be recognized in the different regions of the integration. This means that it is very unlikely that one can obtain exact analytical solutions when bounds are required for the sharing rules.

The solution for the three parameters λ, μ, and a is obtained using the IMSL routine ZSCNT as in the first-best case. As a practical matter, it is helpful to solve the first-best problem first and use the first-best estimates of λ and a as starting values for the algorithm in the second-best case. For μ, an arbitrary value of 0.5 may be used as a starting point, but some experimentation is often useful to obtain a feel for the particular problem at hand.

To present a useful comparison between the properties of the first-best solution and the properties of the second-best solution, we assumed that the agent's reservation utility level $\bar{H}$ was the same in both cases. There are, however, difficulties with this standard of comparison as we explore the comparative statics of the problem. For example, if $\bar{H}$ is viewed as the market price of the agent's services expressed in expected utility terms, it is not entirely reasonable to treat this price as being independent of the parameters describing the agent's utility function. One approach is to compute the amount the principal would pay for a perfect monitor in the second-best case in order to implement the first-best solution. The procedural details are illustrated in the next section.

Numerical Examples

In this section we present numerical examples to illustrate the solution procedure in the case of the three utility-probability density combinations described in table 5–3.

Numerical Examples for Power Utility ($\alpha > 0$) and Lognormal Output Density

The standard assumptions used for our computations in this case are summarized in table 5–4.

Table 5–4. Standard Assumptions for Power Utility and Lognormal Output Density

Parameter		*Value*
W_1	(principal's initial wealth)	3.0
W_2	(agent's initial wealth)	0.0
β_1		0.0
β_2		0.0
$\bar{H}$	(agent's reservation utility)	2.0
σ^2	(variance of lognormal density)	0.25
α	(HARA parameter)	1.5
$V(a)$	(agent's disutility function)	$0.01a^2$

We now compute the parameters of the optimal sharing rule for the first-best and the second-best case based on the assumptions of table 5–4. The results are displayed in table 5–5. Comparing the first-best solution with the second-best solution, we see that the existence of moral hazard induces a welfare loss. This is reflected in the drop of the principal's expected utility from 5.33236 to 5.14986.

The first-best sharing rule in this case is obtained using the parameter values from table 5–5.

$$s(x) = 0.28068x + 0.84204 \tag{5.24}$$

The second-best sharing rule is obtained from substituting the parameter values from table 5–5 in equation (5.17) and is

$$s(x) = \frac{Q(x)^{1.5}(x+3)}{1 + Q(x)^{1.5}} \tag{5.25}$$

where

$$Q(x) = \begin{cases} 0.44483 + 0.50909 \log\left[\dfrac{x}{11.54499}\right] & \text{for } x > 4.81857 \\ 0 & \text{for } x \leq 4.81857 \end{cases}$$

Note that in the second-best case, $s(x) = 0$ if x lies below 4.81857.

Figure 5–1 displays the first-best and the second-best optimal sharing rules for the assumptions corresponding to table 5–5. For low values of x, the agent gets less under the second-best rule. For high values of x, he fares better under the second-best rule. Note the clear impact of the lower bound on the second-best sharing rule.

Table 5–5. Optimal Solution Details for Power Utility and Lognormal Output Density

Parameter	*First-Best Situation*	*Second-Best Situation*	*Perfect Monitor Situation*
α	1.5	1.5	1.5
W_1	3.0	3.0	1.81781
W_2	0.0	0.0	0.0
β_1	0.0	0.0	0.0
β_2	0.0	0.0	0.0
σ^2	0.25	0.25	0.25
$V(a)$	$0.01a^2$	$0.01a^2$	$0.01a^2$
$\bar{H}$	2.00	2.00	2.00
Output			
λ	0.53398	0.44483	0.57191
a	13.77162	11.54499	13.76429
μ	n.a.	1.46936	n.a.
x_M	n.a.	4.81857	n.a.
Expected utility			
Principal	5.33236	5.14986	5.14986
Agent	2.00000	2.00000	2.00000
Maximum fee for perfect monitor	n.a.	n.a.	1.18219

In order to facilitate comparisons between the first-best and the second-best situations it is useful to introduce the concept of a (costly) perfect monitor. Assume that the principal can, by paying a fixed fee up front, ensure that the agent's action is observable. This means that a first-best solution can be implemented. We can compute the maximum fee that the principal would pay in this situation by requiring that the principal's expected utility be equal to his expected utility under the second-best situation; in our example, 5.14986. The final column of table 5–5 presents the results for this situation. In other words, if the principal's initial wealth were 3 he would pay a maximum flat fee of 1.18219 to acquire a perfect monitor that would provide him with the same expected utility as in the second-best case.

Table 5–6 illustrates the sensitivity of the second-best solution to variations in selected parameters. For convenience, only a few of the output parameters are presented. These include: the optimal action, the principal's expected utility, and the maximum fee the principal would be willing to pay

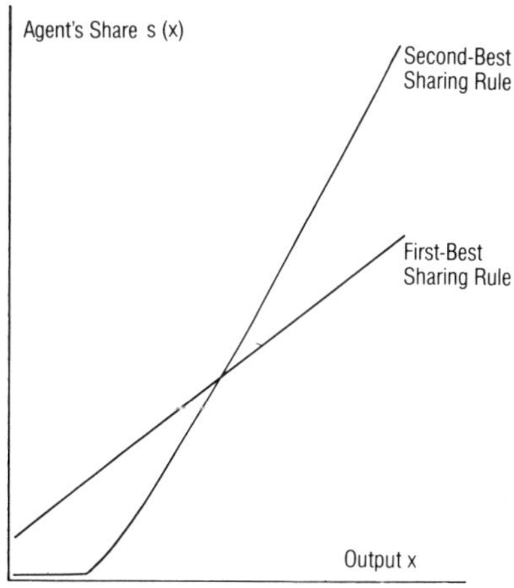

Figure 5–1. Sharing Rules for Lognormal Density and Power ($\alpha > 0$) Utility

Table 5–6. Sensitivity of Optimal Second Best Solution to Variations in the Underlying Parameters

Parameter	*Standard Case*	*Variation in* W_1	σ^2	α	$V(a)$
α	1.5	1.5	1.5	1.6	1.5
β_1	0.0	0.0	0.0	0.0	0.0
β_2	0.0	0.0	0.0	0.0	0.0
W_1	3.0	4.0	3.0	3.0	3.0
W_2	0.0	0.0	0.0	0.0	0.0
σ^2	0.25	0.25	0.26	0.25	0.25
$V(a)$	$0.01a^2$	$0.01a^2$	$0.01a^2$	$0.01a^2$	$0.0125a^2$
$\bar{H}$	2.00	2.00	2.00	2.00	2.00
Optimal action	11.54499	11.52548	11.50248	11.36647	9.96653
Principal's expected utility	5.14986	5.29854	5.14972	4.82092	4.94846
Maximum fee for perfect monitor	1.18219	1.22613	1.21071	0.95710	0.98878

to acquire a perfect monitor. This last item provides a linkage between the second-best solution and a related first-best solution for the same set of parameter values.

In table 5–6, the second column gives the assumptions and parameter values for the standard case. The third column summarizes the impact of an increase in the principal's wealth by one unit. In this case the principal's wealth W_1 always appears as a component of the term

$$[\alpha[x + W_1 + W_2] + \beta_1 + \beta_2] \tag{5.26}$$

in all the relevant equations. Hence, an increase in the principal's wealth of one unit has the same consequences as an increase in the agent's wealth of one unit or an increase in either β_1 or β_2 of α units. Expression (5.26) represents the combined risk tolerance. An increase in this quantity leads to a reduced level of effort.

Numerical Solutions for Case of Negative Exponential Utility and Exponential Output Density

This section contains specimen numerical solutions for the exponential-utility–exponential-output combination. The relevant equations can be transformed so that numerical integration is not needed and the details are given in the appendix. This situation corresponds to $\alpha = 0$ HARA utility for both the principal and the agent. The standard assumptions employed for this combination are given in table 5–7.

The first-best solution, second-best solution and maximum price of a perfect monitor for this set of assumptions are given in table 5–8.

Figure 5–2 depicts the first-best and the second-best sharing rules for the parameter values given in table 5–8. For low values of the output, the agent

Table 5–7. Standard Assumptions for Exponential Utility and Exponential Output Density

Parameter		*Value*
W_1	(principal's initial wealth)	0.25
W_2	(agent's initial wealth)	0.0
γ_1	(principal's risk aversion)	1.0
γ_2	(agent's risk aversion)	1.0
$\bar{H}$	(agent's reservation utility)	0.30748
V	(agent's disutility function)	$0.01a^2$

Table 5–8. Optimal Solution Details for Exponential Utility and Exponential Output Density

Parameter	*First-Best Situation*	*Second-Best Situation*	*Perfect Monitor Situation*
W_1	0.25	0.25	0.25
W_2	0.0	0.0	0.0
γ_1	1.0	1.0	1.0
γ_2	1.0	1.0	1.0
$V(a)$	$0.01a^2$	$0.01a^2$	$0.01a^2$
$\bar{H}$	0.30748	0.30748	0.30748
Output parameters			
λ	0.40650	0.38940	0.40583
μ	n.a.	0.51076	n.a.
a	5.81705	4.22933	5.53281
Expected utility			
Principal	0.85004	0.84319	0.84139
Agent	0.30748	0.30748	0.30748
Maximum fee for perfect monitor	n.a.	n.a.	0.09864

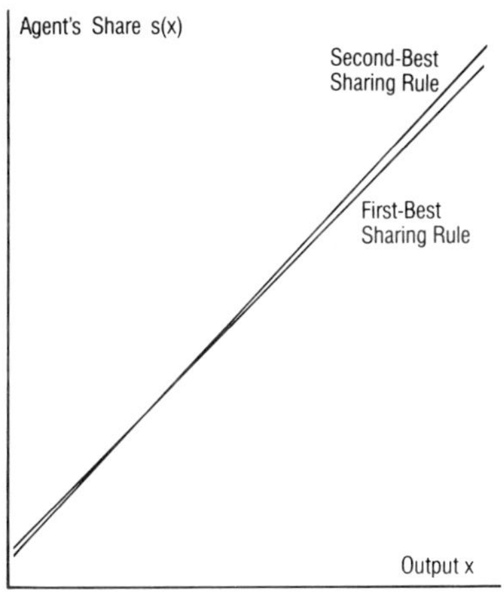

Figure 5–2. Sharing Rules for Exponential Density and Exponential Utility

does worse under the second-best rule whereas for high values of output, the reverse is true.

Table 5–9 illustrates the impact of variations in the underlying parameters on the optimal solution and on the value of the maximum fee for the perfect monitor.

Numerical Solutions for Power Utility ($\alpha < 0$) *and Beta Output Density*

The standard assumptions in this case are given in table 5–10. In order to remove negative signs, we have added a constant amount of 3 units to the utility of both the principal and the agent. This has no impact on the optimal solution parameters.

The optimal solution parameters for the first-best, second-best, and perfect monitor cases are displayed in table 5–11. Note that there is a welfare loss in moving to the second-best case and that this loss is reflected in a drop in the principal's expected utility from 2.3199 to 2.3177. Further comparative statics results could be produced as in the earlier cases.

Figure 5–3 illustrates the profile of the first-best and second-best sharing rules for the parameter values in Table 5–11. The second-best sharing rule

Table 5–9. Sensitivity of Optimal Second-Best Solution to Variations in the Underlying Parameters

Parameter	Standard Case	Variation in			
		W_1	γ_1	$V(a)$	$\bar{H}$
W_1	0.25	0.30	0.25	0.25	0.25
W_2	0.0	0.0	0.0	0.0	0.0
γ_1	1.0	1.0	1.1	1.0	1.0
γ_2	1.0	1.0	1.0	1.0	1.0
$V(a)$	$0.01a^2$	$0.01a^2$	$0.01a^2$	$0.0125a^2$	$0.01a^2$
$\bar{H}$	0.30748	0.30748	0.30748	0.30748	0.4000
Optimal action	4.22933	4.22933	4.23840	3.73219	3.90327
Principal's expected utility	0.84319	0.85084	0.81333	0.81640	0.79957
Maximum fee for perfect monitor	0.09864	0.09760	0.09086	0.09618	0.09710

Table 5–10. Standard Assumptions for Power Utility and Beta Output Density

Parameter		*Value*
W_1	(principal's initial wealth)	0.25
W_2	(agent's initial wealth)	0.0
β_1		2.0
β_2		2.0
$\bar{H}$	(agent's reservation utility)	1.0
α	(HARA parameter)	-1.0
b	(parameter of beta density)	2.0
$V(a)$	(agent's disutility function)	$0.01a^2$

Table 5–11. Optimal Solution Details for Power Utility and Beta Output Density

Parameter	*First-Best Situation*	*Second-Best Situation*	*Perfect Monitor Situation*
α	-1.0	-1.0	-1.0
W_1	0.25	0.25	0.25
W_2	0.0	0.0	0.0
β_1	2.0	2.0	2.0
β_2	2.0	2.0	2.0
b	2.0	2.0	2.0
$V(a)$	$0.01a^2$	$0.01a^2$	$0.01a^2$
$\bar{H}$	1.00	1.00	1.00
Output parameters			
λ	0.61558	0.61836	0.61656
a	4.53074	4.35176	4.53071
μ	n.a.	0.11904	n.a.
x_M	n.a.	0.00366	n.a.
Expected utility			
Principal	2.31990	2.31774	2.31774
Agent	1.00000	1.00000	1.00000
Maximum fee for perfect monitor	n.a.	n.a.	0.00185

crosses over the first-best rule as in the previous two cases. Observe that in this case, unlike the previous cases, the second-best sharing rule drops dramatically as x goes to zero.

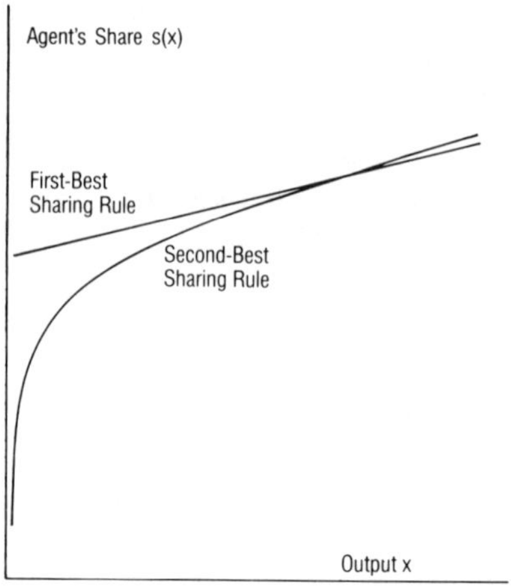

Figure 5–3. Sharing Rules for Beta Density and Power ($\alpha < 0$) Utility

Summary

This paper has illustrated how the assumption of HARA utility can simplify the principal/agent problem. In particular, when both the principal and the agent have identical risk cautiousness, the optimal sharing rule has a simple explicit form. This, in turn, facilitates the application of numerical techniques to arrive at the optimal sharing rule. Because of the usefulness of the principal/agent paradigm and the lack of exact analytical solutions, it is suggested that such techniques may prove useful in a number of applications. To illustrate the operation of the procedure, three specific examples were analyzed. These correspond to different types of HARA utility functions and different assumptions regarding the form of the output density. The algorithm can readily accommodate bounded sharing rules which arise in a number of situations.

The solution procedures developed can be applied to extensions of the basic principal/agent model. For example, both Holmstrom [1979] and Baiman and Demski [1980] have developed models illustrating how additional information can be incorporated into the sharing rule. One form of this extension involves double integration over the joint density of the output x and the signal y. Conceptually the problem can be handled using the procedures developed in this paper, but since the nonlinear solution algorithm involves many iterations and each iteration involves several double integrals, the computations quickly become very costly. Currently work is underway to reduce the cost of the algorithm by using approximate integration techniques. The methods developed here can be applied to problems involving several agents and more than one period. The development of numerical procedures to solve extensions to the basic principal model involves no new conceptual issues. In practice there may be technical issues that need to be dealt with before a workable algorithm is obtained. It is hoped that the discussion presented here stimulates other researchers to use this approach. It is suggested that the numerical algorithms presented in this paper are useful both for specific applications and extensions and for probing the structure of the optimal solution in more general situations.

APPENDIX 5
Derivation of The Three Equations for λ, μ, and a in The Case of Exponential Utility and Exponential Output

In the case of the exponential-output density, it has been already shown by Holmstrom [1977] that no bounds need be imposed on the sharing rule. The utility functions for both parties in this case are

$$\text{Principal:} \qquad \frac{1-\exp[-\gamma_1(W_1+x-s(x))]}{\gamma_1} \tag{5A.1}$$

$$\text{Agent:} \qquad \frac{1-\exp[-\gamma_2(W_2+s(x))]}{\gamma_2}-0.01a^2 \tag{5A.2}$$

The output density function in this case is

$$f(x, a)=\frac{1}{a}\exp\left[-\frac{x}{a}\right] \tag{5A.3}$$

The second-best sharing rule is given by equation (5.20) in this case.

The following definitions will be used:

$$\gamma_{11} = \frac{\gamma_1}{\gamma_1 + \gamma_2}$$

$$\gamma_{22} = \frac{\gamma_2}{\gamma_1 + \gamma_2}$$

$$\gamma_3 = \frac{\gamma_1 \gamma_2}{\gamma_1 + \gamma_2}$$

Some of the expressions that follow are in terms of the incomplete gamma function. This function $\Gamma(y, \Theta)$ is defined by

$$\Gamma(y, \Theta) = \int_{\Theta}^{\infty} e^{-t} t^{y-1} \, dt$$

This integral is only defined for $\Theta > 0$. The properties of the incomplete gamma function are summarized by Abramowitz and Stegun [1975]. Numerical algorithms are available to compute this function.

With these assumptions, we can now transform the three equations that are used to solve for the parameters of the optimal second-best sharing rule into expressions involving the incomplete gamma function. We deal first with the equation for the agent's reservation utility. Recall that this is also given by equation (5.12):

$$\int U_2[W_2 + s(x)] f(x, a) - 0.01a^2 - \bar{H} = 0 \tag{5A.4}$$

Substituting the specific functional forms for U_2, $s(x)$, and $f(x, a)$, the first term of this last equation becomes

$$\frac{1}{\gamma_2}\left[\left[1 - \int \exp\left\{-\gamma_2\left[W_2 + \frac{\gamma_1 x + (\gamma_1 W_1 - \gamma_2 W_2) + \log Q(x)}{\gamma_1 + \gamma_2}\right]\right\} \exp\left[-\frac{x}{a}\right] \frac{dx}{a}\right]\right]$$

and the integral can be expressed as

$$K \int [Q(x)]^{-\gamma_{22}} \exp\left[-\frac{x}{k}\right] \frac{dx}{a}$$

where

$$K = \exp[-\gamma_3(W_1 + W_2)]$$

$$\frac{1}{k} = \gamma_3 + \frac{1}{a}$$

$$Q(x) = \lambda + \mu\left(\frac{x - a}{a^2}\right)$$

It is now convenient to change the variable to y where

$$y = \lambda + \mu\left(\frac{x-a}{a^2}\right)$$

When $x = 0$, $y = \lambda - (\mu/a)$. Since the sharing rule does not require a bound the function $Q(x)$ is positive for all x and so the term $\lambda - (\mu/a)$ is positive. With this substitution, the integral becomes

$$K \int_{\lambda-(\mu/a)}^{\infty} [y]^{-\gamma_{22}} \exp\left\{-\frac{a^2 y + a\mu - a^2\lambda}{\mu k}\right\} a \frac{dy}{\mu}$$

Now let $t = a^2 y/\mu k$ be the new variable of integration. With this substitution, the lower limit of integration is

$$\Theta = \frac{a}{k}\left[\frac{a\lambda}{\mu} - 1\right]$$

and the integral becomes

$$K \exp(\Theta)\left[\frac{\mu k}{a^2}\right]^{-\gamma_{22}} \frac{k}{a} \int_{\Theta}^{\infty} t^{-\gamma_{22}} \exp(-t)\, dt$$

Let $Z = \mu k/a^2$, $B = \exp(\Theta)$, and note that $\gamma_{11} + \gamma_{22} = 1$. The integral can be written as

$$\frac{a}{\mu} KBZ^{\gamma_{11}} \Gamma(\gamma_{11}, \Theta)$$

since

$$Z^{-\gamma_{22}} \frac{k}{a} = Z^{\gamma_{11}} \frac{a}{\mu}$$

Thus, the complete expression for the equation setting the agent's expected utility equal to $\bar{H}$ is

$$\frac{1}{\gamma_2}\left[1 - \frac{a}{\mu} KBZ^{\gamma_{11}} \Gamma(\gamma_{11}, \Theta)\right] - 0.01a^2 - \bar{H} = 0 \tag{5A.5}$$

The transformation of the other two equations proceeds in the same way. First, we substitute the functional forms for the relevant exponential utility functions, the second-best sharing rule, and the (exponential) probability density function. To conserve space, we simply give the results. Thus, equation (5.9) can be written in the form

$$\frac{1}{\gamma_2}\left\{\frac{kBK}{a\mu}\left[Z^{\gamma_{11}} \Gamma(1 + \gamma_{11}, \Theta) - \lambda Z^{-\gamma_{22}} \Gamma(\gamma_{11}, \Theta)\right]\right\} + 0.02a = 0 \tag{5A.6}$$

Finally, equation (5.11) becomes:

$$\frac{kBK}{\gamma_1 \mu a}\{Z(\gamma_{11}+1)\Gamma(\gamma_{11}+2,\Theta)-\lambda Z^{\gamma_{11}}\Gamma(\gamma_{11}+1,\Theta)\}$$
$$+\frac{kBK}{\gamma_2 \mu a}Z^{-\gamma_{22}}\left\{Z^2\Gamma(\gamma_{11}+2,\Theta)-2\lambda Z\Gamma(\gamma_{11}+1,\Theta)+\lambda^2\Gamma(\gamma_{11},\Theta)\right.$$
$$\left.-\frac{2\mu}{a}[Z\Gamma(\gamma_{11}+1,\Theta)-\lambda\Gamma(\gamma_{11},\Theta)]-\frac{\mu^2 k}{a^2}\Gamma(\gamma_{11},\Theta)\right\}+0.02\mu=0 \tag{5A.7}$$

Equations (5A.5), (5A.6), and (5A.7) represent three nonlinear equations for the three unknowns μ, a, and λ and can be solved numerically to find the optimal triplet.

References

Abramovitz, M., and Stegun, I.A. eds. [1975]. *Handbook of Mathematical Functions with Formulas, Graphs and Mathematical Tables.* New York: Dover.

Baiman, S. [1982]. "Agency Research in Managerial Accounting: A Survey." *Journal of Accounting Literature* 1, 154–213.

Baiman, S., and Demski, J.S. [1980]. "Economically Optimal Performance Evaluation and Control Systems." *Journal of Accounting Research* 18, 184–220.

Clarke, F., and Darrough, M. [1980]. "Optimal Incentive Schemes, Existence and Characterization." *Economic Letters* 5, 305–310.

Demski, J.S., and Kreps, D.M. [1982]. "Models in Managerial Accounting." *Journal of Accounting Research* 20, 117–148.

Grossman, S.J., and Hart, O.D. [1983]. "An analysis of the Principal-Agent Model." *Econometrica* 51, 7–46.

Holmstrom, B. [1977]. "On Incentives and Control in Organizations." Ph.D. dissertation, Stanford University.

Holmstrom, B. [1979]. "Moral Hazard and Observability." *Bell Journal of Economics* 10, 74–91.

Mirrlees, J. [1976]. "The Optimal Structure of Incentives and Authority within an Organization." *Bell Journal of Economics* 7, 105–131.

Rogerson, William P. [1985]. "The First-Order Approach to Principal-Agent Problems." *Econometrica* 53, 1357–1367.

6 EXPLORATIONS IN THE THEORY OF SINGLE- AND MULTIPLE-AGENT AGENCIES*

Amin H. Amershi
and
John E. Butterworth

The purpose of this paper is to explore the theory of agencies (both for single and multiple agents) to derive additional insights into the nature of optimal contracts and the demand for information in contracting.

First we show that the standard Mirrlees [1976]–Holmstrom [1979] single-principal single-agent agency contract has an interesting interpretation as a partnership contract between two individuals with heterogeneous beliefs. Specifically, assuming that the usual local first-order conditions obtain, we may rewrite the likelihood ratio and Lagrange multipliers as simply the ratio of two heterogeneous beliefs. The numerator belief, which is the agent's belief *after* contracting at the given effort level, is shown to stochastically dominate the denominator belief, which is the principal's belief. In this form, the first-order conditions are indistinguishable from the first-order conditions of a partnership under heterogeneous beliefs. Interestingly, the agent behaves *as if*

* Professor Butterworth expired in August 1984 when the paper was more or less complete. I have taken some liberty in completing this work using some current developments. (A.H. Amershi)

he is more optimistic than the principal about higher cash flows. An example using exponential densities explores this further.

We use this characterization of the first-order conditions to show (as in Amershi [1984a] and Amershi and Hughes [1987]) why the principal need not use all the information in a minimal sufficient statistic (see Amershi [1987a]) for densities with multiple performance signals. The reason is that at optimality, the contract is pure risk sharing between *two* heterogeneous beliefs, of which the agent's implied beliefs may not even belong to the original class of output densities indexed by effort levels. This provides a new insight as to why the principal need not use all the information in a minimal sufficient statistic for the original class of output densities.

Next we change our approach to the case of finite action (or "effort") set for the agent(s). Here we rely on the global optimization formulation in Amershi ([1984b], [1987b]) to yield the Kuhn–Tucker conditions at optimality of a contract. This approach enables us to bypass the stringent conditions that must be invoked to justify the usual local-optimizaton first-order conditions approach of Mirrlees–Holmstrom. Further, the minimal sufficient statistic is now merely a vector of density ratios for each effort level a and the desired effort level a^*. This form of the minimal sufficient statistic lends itself to interpretation as *risk substitution* in optimal contracting, analogous to commodity substitution in consumption. Here we use this concept of risk substitution to show that in multiple-agent agencies, if the joint density function of the agents' performance signals is continuous, then *all relative performance evaluation* measures with a countable range of evaluations are strictly inferior in contracting to a minimal sufficient statistic. This result generalizes the result in Holmstrom [1982] who proves it for the case when the agents' outputs are independent and relative performance measure is a rank-order tournament. The result also seems to have empirical support (see Antle and Smith [1986]).

The paper first develops the connections between moral-hazard contracting and heterogeneous-belief risk sharing. It then develops the global optimization approach and the tournament result. The appendix discusses the set of actions where the Lagrange multiplier μ in the Mirrlees–Holmstrom first-order conditions is strictly positive.

The Principal/Agent Model: Insights from Risk Sharing with Heterogeneous Beliefs

The standard principal/agent model (see, e.g., Mirrlees [1976], Holmstrom [1979]) consists of a principal with utility for cash $g(w)$ *with* $g'(w) > 0$

(nonsatiation), $g''(w) \leq 0$ (concavity) for all cash (wealth) levels w, and an agent with utility for cash $u(w)$ and a separable disutility for effort $V(a)$, where $u'(w) > 0$, $u''(w) < 0$ (strictly concave or risk averse), $V'(a) > 0$, $V''(a) > 0$ (strictly convex and effort averse). The set A of effort levels is an interval of the real line $\mathfrak{R}$. Each $a \in A$ results in a lottery over the set of cash flows x.

First-Best Risk Sharing under Heterogeneous Beliefs

Consider first the case of a pure risk-sharing partnership between principal and agent. There are no information asymmetries—both principal and agent have the same prior information about which x is going to occur given a particular a, and the effort levels $a \in A$ are observable. Suppose principal and agent have heterogeneous beliefs regarding x given $a \in A$ described by two classes of density functions $\{f(x|a) \mid a \in A\}$ and $\{h(x|a) \mid a \in A\}$, respectively.[1]

It is well known from Borch [1962] that if $Z(x)$ is a Pareto optimal compensation scheme for the agent for some choice of action $a \in A$, then it satisfies the first-order conditions

$$\frac{g'(x - Z(x))}{u'(Z(x))} = \lambda \frac{h(x|a)}{f(x|a)} \tag{6.1}$$

where $\lambda > 0$ is a multiplier that depends on the agent's security level $\bar{u}$ (i.e., the minimum expected utility he can obtain from other employment), as well as the a chosen—i.e., $\lambda \equiv \lambda(a, \bar{u})$.

Suppose x is not directly observable, but, instead, two signals (t, y) are observable, with densities $f(t, y|a)$, $h(t, y|a)$, $a \in A$.[2] Then it is also easy to show (see Amershi and Stoeckenius [1983]) that the first order conditions (6.1) can be written, if the principal is risk neutral, as

$$\frac{1}{u'(Z(t, y))} = \lambda \frac{h(t, y|a)}{f(t, y|a)} \tag{6.2}$$

If the principal is risk averse (i.e., $g''(w) < 0$), and (see Amershi [1987a]) if either x is observable or derivable from knowledge of (t, y), then we have

$$\frac{g'(x - Z(x, t, y))}{u'(Z(x, t, y))} = \lambda \frac{h(x, t, y|a)}{f(x, t, y|a)} \tag{6.3}$$

In both cases (6.2) and (6.3), the dependence of Z on (t, y) is only through the ratio h/f which is a sufficient statistic for the heterogeneous beliefs for *each a*.[3]

Second-Best Contracts under Moral Hazard

Now suppose that principal and agent have homogeneous beliefs about x characterized by the density class $\{f(x|a)\,|\,a \in A\}$. If the principal cannot observe the agent's effort, he contracts on a *given level of effort* $a^* \in A$ by offering a contract $Z^*(x)$ to the agent that solves the following problem:

$$\underset{Z}{\text{maximize:}} \quad E[g(x - Z(x))|a^*] \tag{6.4}$$

$$\text{subject to:} \quad E[u(Z(x))|a^*] - V(a^*) \geq \bar{u} \tag{6.5}$$

$$a^* \in \arg\max_{a \in A} \; E[U(Z(x))|a] - V(a) \tag{6.6}$$

It is important to note here that problem (6.4)–(6.6) is different from the *simultaneous choice* of (Z^*, a^*) as found in Mirrlees [1976] and Holmstrom [1979]. We call that problem the *total choice* problem.

Here the principal first determines an optimal compensation scheme $Z^*(\cdot|a)$ that implements a desired a as a best response. If the principal wants to solve the total problem, then he optimizes the expected utility of his residual $(x - Z^*(x|a))$ over all A. It is then convenient to interpret $Z^*(x|a)$ as the (wage) *cost* of implementing a, as in Grossman and Hart [1983]. Observe also that the total problem amounts to just adding another maximization, "Maximize over a," to problem (6.4)–(6.6).

Under appropriate regularity conditions (the most appropriate for our purposes are those of Clarke and Darrough [1980], though one may appeal to Rogerson [1985] in certain cases), a solution to the problem (6.4)–(6.6) exists and satisfies the first-order

$$\frac{g'(x - Z^*(x))}{u'(Z^*(x))} = \lambda + \mu \frac{f_a(x|a^*)}{f(x|a^*)} \qquad \text{for all } x \tag{6.7}$$

where f_a denotes the derivative of $f(x|a)$ w.r.t. a. Let $\{F(x|a)\,|\,a \in A\}$ satisfy first-order stochastic dominance, namely $F(x|a_1) \leq F(x|a_2)$ for all x, with strict inequality on a set of positive probability, whenever $a_1 > a_2$. We need $\mu > 0$ to proceed further. This may or may not be true for all $a \in A$. Define $A^* = \{a \in A|\mu(a^*) > 0\}$. A^* is not empty (see appendix).

Rewrite (6.7) as (observe that $\lambda > 0$)

$$\frac{g'(x - Z^*(x))}{u'(Z^*(x))} = \lambda \left[\frac{f(x|a^*) + \frac{\mu}{\lambda} f_a(x|a^*)}{f(x|a^*)} \right] \tag{6.8}$$

Proposition 6.1

The function

$$h(x|a^*) = f(x|a^*) + \frac{\mu}{\lambda} f_a(x|a^*)$$

is a probability density function on x given $a^* \in A^*$.

Proof: Since the left hand side of (6.8) is positive and $\lambda > 0$, then $h(x|a^*) > 0$ for all x. But

$$\int h(x|a^*)\,dx = \int f(x|a^*)\,dx = 1$$

since

$$\int f_a(x|a^*)\,dx = 0$$

Q.E.D.

Therefore, we can rewrite (6.8) as

$$\frac{g'(x - Z^*(x))}{u'(Z^*(x))} = \lambda \frac{h(x|a^*)}{f(x|a^*)} \tag{6.9}$$

which is identical to (6.1). This observation leads to several interesting economic insights which we now explore.

First, (6.9) shows that optimal risk sharing under moral hazard between principal and agent at any desired a^* is equivalent to first-best optimal risk sharing between principal and agent under differential beliefs, with the agent holding the beliefs $h(x|a^*)$ and the principal holding the beliefs $f(x|a^*)$. The intuition for this is that since the agent "knows more" about a^*, the principal in effect forms a risk-sharing partnership with the agent "*having agreed*" that the agent's beliefs will be $h(x|a^*)$ and his own $f(x|a^*)$.[4] The next result throws further light on this point.

Proposition 6.2

For each desired $a^* \in A^*$, $H(x|a^*)$ first-order stochastically dominates $F(x|a^*)$. [Here $H(x|a^*)$ is the distribution of $h(x|a^*)$ and $F(x|a^*)$ is the distribution of $f(x|a^*)$.]

Proof: $f_a(x|a^*)$ changes sign as x increases, going from negative to positive because the distributions $F(x|a)$ satisfy first-order stochastic dominance. Since $\mu/\lambda > 0$ for all a (observe μ varies with a but is still > 0) it follows that for any x,

$$F(x|a^*) = \int_{-\infty}^{x} f(t|a)\,dt \geq H(x|a^*) = \int_{-\infty}^{x} h(t|a)\,dt$$

with strict inequality for some x on a set of positive measure. Q.E.D.

Proposition 6.2 shows that at any contracted a^*, the agent *behaves as if* he is more *optimistic* about high cash flows than the principal. This means that the principal can propose higher levels of compensation for high levels of x and low levels of compensation for low levels of x than would be the case if the partnership had postcontract homogeneous beliefs. From the principal's perspective, he stands to gain from this arrangement, and from *implied* beliefs $h(x|a)$, the agent also stands to gain. Observe, therefore, that the incentive structure that the principal has devised has "made" the agent more optimistic, which in turn results in the Pareto-optimal risk-sharing arrangement under the optimistic beliefs. Of course, it is well known that $Z^*(x)$ will depart from the pure risk-sharing compensation under homogeneous beliefs if it is incentive-compatible with the desired a^*. What is new here is that the correct incentive structure effectively creates a Pareto-optimal risk-sharing partnership between principal and agent by making the agent *effectively* more optimistic, and thereby willing to depart from the optimal risk-sharing arrangement under homogeneous beliefs in the manner shown.

The empirical implication of the above findings is important. To an outside observer of a partnership compensation contract, the risk-sharing contract between the partners does not reveal whether the contract is a pure risk-sharing arrangement under heterogenous beliefs, or an incentive-compatible risk-sharing arrangement under moral hazard. That is, observing the form of $Z^*(x)$ *alone*, without any additional information, would not enable the observer to distinguish the economic environment that led to the contract. Thus, incentive-compatibility of a contract is not testable unless the observer knows for sure that moral hazard obtains *and* that both partners' original beliefs were homogeneous. This raises important issues about experimental design. It is rare for an observer to be able to observe the entire bargaining process that determines $Z^*(x)$. Laboratory experiments (see Berge et al. [1986]) may be one method of testing the *entire* model.

Next, we delve a bit deeper into the nature of the beliefs $h(x|a)$. For example is $h(x|a)$ of the same *type* (or *family*) as $f(x|a)$? We consider the special case of the standard exponential density.[5]

Example

Let $A = [0, \infty)$.

$$f(x|a) = \frac{1}{a}\exp\left(-\frac{x}{a}\right) \qquad x > 0$$

Then,

$$f_a(x|a) = \frac{-1}{a^2}\exp\left(-\frac{x}{a}\right) + \frac{x}{a^3}\exp\left(-\frac{x}{a}\right)$$

Hence, for a contract on $a \in A$,

$$h(x|a) = \left(1 + \frac{\mu x}{\lambda a^2} - \frac{\mu}{\lambda a}\right)\left[\frac{1}{a}\exp\left(-\frac{x}{a}\right)\right]$$

That is,

$$h(x|a) = (Kx + B)f(x|a) \tag{6.10}$$

where

$$K = \frac{\mu}{\lambda a^2}, \quad B = 1 - \frac{\mu}{\lambda a}$$

Expression (6.10) shows that $h(x|a)$ does *not* belong to the exponential family (see Lehmann [1983]). Indeed, it is not any commonly known density. This implies that the implied beliefs $h(x|a)$ of the agent not only do not belong to the class $\{f(x|a) | a \in A\}$ (i.e., it is not a mere shift in parameter), but it also is not a member of the general exponential family!

Since $h(x|a) > 0$ for all $x > 0$, we have that this implies that for all $a \in A$

$$1 - \frac{\mu}{\lambda a} > 0 \Leftrightarrow \lambda > \frac{\mu}{a} \Leftrightarrow a > \frac{\mu(a, \bar{u})}{\lambda(a, \bar{u})} \tag{6.11}$$

Expression (6.11) is an interesting relationship between $\mu(a, \bar{u})$ and $\lambda(a, \bar{u})$. It may be interpreted by standard second-order analysis (see Ioffe and Tihomirov [1979]) as the ratio of the rate of "cost of *incentives* to the principal per unit of disutility," and rate of "*insurance* cost per unit of minimum utility." For further insight, however, we must invoke situation-specific economic parameters. For example, if the principal is risk-neutral $[g(w) = w]$ and the agent's preferences are $u(w) = 2\sqrt{w}$ and $V(a) = a^2$, then from Holmstrom ([1979], p. 79) we know that if $\hat{a}$ is the global optimum [i.e., $(\hat{Z}, \hat{a})$ is the optimal solution to the total optimization problem], then $\mu(\hat{a}, \bar{u}) = \hat{a}^3$ and $4\hat{a}^3 + 2\lambda(\hat{a}, \bar{u}) \cdot \hat{a} = 1$. Then (6.11) implies that (for *any* $\bar{u}$)

$$\hat{a}^3 < \frac{1}{6}$$

Putting this back in (6.11), we may interpret this as showing that at optimality, the cost of insuring the agent's minimum utility is at least twice the cost of incentives for additional disutility for effort.

Observe that $h(x|a^*)$ only differs from $f(x|a^*)$ by an amount $(\mu(a^*)/\lambda) f_a(x|a^*)$ for any $a^* \in A$. If in a particular agency, both $\mu^*(a)$ and $f_a(x|a^*)$ are bounded away from ∞, whereas the Pareto-surface shows λ can take on arbitrarily large values, then for small $\bar{u}$, $h(x|a^*) \approx f(x|a^*)$ and the incentive contract $Z^*(x)$ is in a topological sense (of norm metric) not very different from the first-best risk-sharing contract $\hat{Z}(x)$. Thus, for these agencies, employing first-best risk-sharing contracts would probably reduce the principal's welfare from the second best by a small amount. It is intriguing to speculate whether many fixed-salary contracts, in the presence of moral hazard, are simply practical approximations to more cumbersome contracts whose enforcement costs may far outweigh the marginal benefits to the principal's welfare.

Value of Information in Agency Settings

Consider the agency problem with the principal risk neutral.[6] Suppose the final cash flows x are not directly observable, but instead the agency gets two signals (t, y) correlated with effort, where $\{f(t, y|a) \mid a \in A\}$ denotes the class of joint densities. For example, t = revenues and y = costs (in this case x is indirectly observable as $x = t - y$). As another example, x is net cash flow, but t = cost of materials, and y = cost of factory labor. Observe in this case x is not directly observable.[7]

A question of considerable empirical and theoretical importance (see Hart and Holmstrom [1985]) is the following: Given that the principal wants $a \in A$ implemented, which information system η: $T \times Y \to M_\eta$, where M_η is a set of signals, produces the optimal incentive-compatible contract $Z(\eta(t, y))$ from the principal's perspective?[8] Some of the major results in the agency literature are attempts to answer this question (see, Gjesdal [1982], Holmstrom [1979], [1982], Amershi [1984a], Amershi [1987a], Amershi and Hughes [1987], Amershi, Banker, and Datar [1987], among others). In this literature, system η is called a *monitor* or *performance evaluation measure* for obvious reasons.

Holmstrom ([1979], proposition 3, p. 84) is a major result in the area. It shows that if γ: $T \times Y \to M_\gamma$ is a sufficient statistic (see Amershi [1987a]) for the class $\{f(t, y|a) \mid a \in A\}$, then *no* other monitor η yields a strictly better contract (in expected utility sense) for the principal.

The converse to this result, although initially conjectured by Holmstrom ([1979], p. 84 footnote 21) to be *generically* true, is false as shown in Amershi and Hughes [1987].[9] They show that *only* a partial converse to the result is true in general: *If* the class of densities $\{f(t, y|a)|a \in A\}$ is of the "all a or no a" class, *then* a sufficient statistic γ: $T \times Y \to M_\gamma$ is *strictly better* than every nonsufficient monitor for all $a \in A$.[10] Further, they show that in *no* other class of densities is a sufficient statistic strictly better than all non-sufficient monitors.

Hart and Holmstrom ([1985], p. 15) assert that "the [above converse] sufficient statistic result is *the most powerful result that one can obtain* from the *general agency* model." (Emphasis added.)[11]

Here we provide another argument to show why the converse cannot hold in a general agency. The best contract the principal can create for any a is characterized by the following first-order conditions

$$\frac{1}{u'(Z^*(t, y))} = \lambda + \mu \frac{f_a(t, y|a^*)}{f(t, y|a^*)} \qquad \text{for all } x \tag{6.12}$$

This in turn, as shown in the previous section, can be rewritten as

$$\frac{1}{u'(Z^*(t, y))} = \lambda \frac{h(t, y|a^*)}{f(t, y|a^*)} \tag{6.13}$$

where

$$h(t, y|a^*) = f(t, y|a^*) + \frac{\mu}{\lambda} f_a(t, y|a^*)$$

represents the derived beliefs attributable to the agent. As explained before, (6.13) are the first-order conditions for Pareto optimal risk sharing under heterogeneous beliefs $h(t, y|a^*), f(t, y|a^*)$ at the given a^*.

We know from Amershi [1987a] that a contract $Z^*(t, y)$ is Pareto-optimal under heterogeneous beliefs if and only if it is an invertible function of the minimal sufficient statistic for the heterogeneous beliefs. Since the minimal sufficient statistic for $h(t, y|a^*)$ and $f(t, y|a^*)$ for any fixed a^* is (see Lehmann [1983]) the ratio $h(t, y|a^*)/f(t, y|a^*)$, we see that $Z^*(t, y)$ uses *only* the information partition on $T \times Y$ generated by $h(t, y|a^*)/f(t, y|a^*)$.

Now consider the minimal sufficient statistic for the *class* $\{f(t, y|a)\,|\,a \in A\}$ (see Amershi [1987a] for what this means). Say this is some function γ: $T \times Y \to M_\gamma$.

Proposition 6.3

The sufficient statistic γ is strictly preferred to any nonsufficient monitor η (where nonsufficiency is w.r.t. the class $\{f(t, y|a)\,|\,a \in A\}$) *if and only if* the partitions of γ and $h(t, y|a^*)/f(t, y|a^*)$ on $T \times Y$ are identical.

Proof: If the partitions are identical, then a nonsufficient monitor η produces a coarser partition than γ, and hence h/f. But since Z^* is an invertible function of h/f, Z^*'s partition is identical to γ, and thus Z^* cannot be sustained by η. *Conversely*, from Amershi and Hughes [1987], γ is strictly preferred to any nonsufficient monitor only if Z^* is an invertible function of γ. But Z^* is an invertible function of h/f, and hence the partitions of γ and h/f are identical. Q.E.D.

As shown in Amershi and Hughes [1987], the partition of γ will coincide with the partitions of h/f for all $a \in A$ if and only if the density class $\{f(t, y|a) \mid a \in A\}$ is the "all a or no a" class. Otherwise, for each $a \in A$, h/f *always* produces a coarser parition than γ.

We believe a reason for this is that the density function $h(t, y|a^*)$ is, as shown earlier, not a member of the class $\{f(t, y|a) \mid a \in A\} = C$. Hence a statistic sufficient for the whole class C, if A is infinite, will typically generate more information than is produced by the ratio of $h(t, y|a)$ and $f(t, y|a)$.

Performance Information in Multiagent Agencies: The Suboptimality of Relative Performance Evaluation Measures

In the previous section we used the first-order-conditions approach to derive connections between risk sharing with heterogeneous beliefs and agency contracts under moral hazard. Here we shift focus and use a *global optimization* approach when $A = \{a_1, \ldots, a_n\}$ is a discrete set to show that in multiagent agencies, with continuous densities on performance signals, *all* relative performance evaluation measures with a countable range of possible evaluations are suboptimal. Holmstrom ([1982], p. 336) shows that this is generally the case for independent outputs and rank-order tournament contracts. Our result considerably generalizes the scope of his observation.

For modeling purposes we rely on Amershi [1984b]. In what follows, we lay out the model and some results for the single-agent case to anchor the intuition.

Global Optimization and Value of Information—The Single-Agent Case

While we shall develop the first-order global optimization conditons for the multiagent case in the next section, we believe it is useful to anchor the intuition for the single-agent agency. The development here is not new but borrowed from Amershi ([1984b], [1987b]).[12]

The model consists of a single principal and agent as before, but with the set of effort levels $A = \{a_1, \ldots, a_n\}$ a *finite* set. Other than this, everything else remains the same. Since it is finite, we can give it a much broader interpretation than simply numbers. They could be vectors in $\mathfrak{R}^m$ or, more generally, elements in an infinite-dimensional normed space corresponding to detailed descriptions of *production plans* the agent can implement. To maintain the "stochastic dominance" assumption on the distributions $F(x|a)$, we may order the elements in A by the following economically intuitive procedure:

$$F(x|a_i) \text{ stochastically dominates } F(x|a_j) \Leftrightarrow V(a_i) > V(a_j) \Leftrightarrow a_i > a_j \qquad (6.14)$$

(Recall $V(a)$ is "disutility" for effort a.)

Assumption 6.1: For each $F(x|a)$, $a \in A$, there is a continuously differentiable (in x) density function $f(x|a)$. All densities have identical support.

Assumption 6.2: The principal is risk neutral.[13]

We allow for the possibility of multiple performance signals $s = (y_1, \ldots, y_n)$ on which the principal can base the compensation to the agent. For the risk neutral case under consideration here, it is not necessary that the net cash flows x be observable. Hence x may or may not enter into the compensation scheme of the agent.

Assumption 6.3:

i. For each a, there is a joint density $f(y_1, \ldots, y_n|a) \equiv f(s|a)$ on the space of signals S.
ii. S is the support of each joint density for each $a \in A$.

Assumption 6.3 allows us to invoke a particularly useful characterization of a *minimal sufficient statistic* (see Amershi [1987a]) in the setting here.

Theorem (Lehmann [1983], p. 41)

For any fixed $a^* \in A$, a minimal sufficient for the statistical structure described in assumption 6.3 is the vector function

$$T: S \rightarrow \mathfrak{R}^n$$

given by

$$T_{a^*}(s) = \left[\frac{f(s|a_1)}{f(s|a^*)}, \ldots, \frac{f(s|a_n)}{f(s|a^*)}\right] \qquad (6.15)$$

Remarks: First, observe that $T_{a^*}(s)$ has at most $n-1$ degrees of freedom at $a^* \in A$. Second, note that the information generated by T_{a^*} is simply the partition on S induced by it through the inverse relationship

$$\{T_{a^*}^{-1}(r) \mid r \in \mathfrak{R}^n\}$$

where $T_{a^*}^{-1}(r) = \{s \in S \mid T_{a^*}(s) = r\}$ (see Amershi [1987a], appendix 1A).

Thirdly, the information revealed by T at any $s \in S$ refers to the $a \in A$ that prevails. To be sure, once a particular a^* is contracted upon, if the contract is incentive compatible, the principal knows ex post facto which a^* prevails. However, this does not deny the role of statistical analysis of information structures on S that enable the principal to discriminate among the different contracts that can be used to induce the desired a^*. Put another way, whatever a^* the principal wishes the agent to implement can be implemented by an appropriate compensation contract $Z(\eta(s))$ based on several information structures (not a constant function) $\eta: S \to M_\eta$. However, different information structures produce different contracts, and the principal would prefer some contracts over others, thereby implying a preference order over information structures. The preference arises because different information structures differentially discriminate among which $a \in A$ produced the signals. Hence, *knowledge of the statistical properties of different information structures* in discriminating among the $a \in A$ is *absolutely essential* for the principal to choose the "best" contract. It is precisely for this reason that sufficient statistics produce the best contracts because they are the information systems providing the sharpest discrimination among the $a \in A$.[14]

The agency problem stated in (6.4)–(6.6) may now be restated here as follows:

$$\underset{Z}{\text{maximize:}} \quad E(x - Z(s)|a^*) \qquad (6.16)$$

$$\text{subject to:} \quad E[u(Z(s))|a^*] - V(a^*) \geq \bar{u} \qquad (6.17)$$

$$E[u(Z(s))|a^*] - V(a^*) \geq E[u(Z(s))|a_i] - V(a_i) \qquad (6.18)$$

$$\text{for all } i = 1, \ldots, n$$

Observe that the n (actually only $n-1$) constraints (6.18) have replaced constraint (6.6) because A is finite. For problem (6.16)–(6.18) we do not need to invoke conditions sufficient to convert (6.6) into a differential constraint, as in the local first-order optimization problem used in Mirrlees [1976] and Holmstrom ([1979], [1982]). For this reason, we term (6.16)–(6.18) the *global optimization* approach (which is similar to the approach in Grossman and Hart [1983], though our S is infinite and A is finite).

Assumption 6.4:

i. Problem (6.16)–(6.18) has a solution (Z^*, a^*).
ii. There does not exist a first-best (pure risk-sharing) solution to problem (6.16)–(6.18).

The global optimization approach allows us to use the general Kuhn–Tucker theory of optimization (see Ioffe and Tihomirov [1979], pp. 70–77) under the following assumption.

Assumption 6.5: At an optimal contract (Z^*, a^*), a generalized Kuhn–Tucker constraint qualification holds.

Under assumptions 6.4 and 6.5, the optimal solution (Z^*, a^*) satisfies the following first-order Kuhn–Tucker conditions:

$$\frac{1}{u'(Z^*(s))} = \lambda + \sum_i \mu_i - \sum_i \mu_i \frac{f(s|a_i)}{f(s|a^*)} \qquad \text{for all } s \in S \tag{6.19}$$

where λ is the Lagrange multiplier of constraint (6.17) and μ_i are the Lagrange multipliers of constraints (6.18).

Definition 6.1

The *linear transformation* $L: \mathfrak{R}^n \to \mathfrak{R}$ defined by

$$L(r) = \sum_i \mu_i r_i \qquad r = (r_1, \ldots, r_n)^t \in \mathfrak{R}^n$$

is termed the *incentive multiplier likelihood* (IML) transformation. (The t superscript after vector r denotes transpose, meaning that we consider r a *column vector* in $\mathfrak{R}^n$.)

Remark: It is well known from elementary linear algebra that we can take $L = (\mu_1, \ldots, \mu_n)$ so that $L(r) = \mu r$ for all $r \in \mathfrak{R}^n$.

Amershi ([1984b], [1987b]) shows that the IML plays a decisive role in determining whether the minimal sufficient statistic T_a is informative or not.

In particular, he shows that if $T_{a^*}(S) = B \subseteq \mathfrak{R}^n$ denotes the *image set* (see Amershi [1987a], appendix 1A) of the vector statistic T_{a^*}, then *risk substitution* takes place in the construction of $Z^*(s)$ if the IML transformation L is not invertible on B. That is, if r_1 and r_2 are distinct elements in B, and $T_{a^*}^{-1}(r_1) \subseteq S$, $T_{a^*}^{-1}(r_2) \subseteq S$ are the subsets in the partition on S generated by T_{a^*} on S, then,

$$L(r_1) = L(r_2)$$

implies that the optimal contract

$$Z^*(s) = Z^*(s') \qquad \text{for all } s \in T_{a^*}^{-1}(r_1) \quad \text{and} \quad s' \in T_{a^*}^{-1}(r_2)$$

Consequently Z^* does *not* use all the information provided by T_{a^*}.

Observe that we may write

$$\sum_i \mu_i \frac{f(s|a_i)}{f(s|a^*)} = L(T_{a^*}(s))$$

The IML transformation generates a family of hyperplanes in $\mathfrak{R}^n$ of the form $H_\alpha(L) = \{r \in \mathfrak{R}^n | L(r) = \alpha\}$ as level sets. To say that $Z^*(s)$ does *not* use all the information provided by the statistic $T_{a^*}(s)$ is equivalent to saying that some of the hyperplanes $H_\alpha(L)$ contain more than one element of the image set $T_{a^*}(S) = B$. The economic intuition of this is explained by Amershi ([1984b], [1987b]) in terms of *risk substitution*. For completeness, it is worth reproducing his explanation here.

The intuition parallels the idea of substitution of commodities for consumption by a consumer at a given level of satisfaction. The Lagrange multipliers μ_i have the characteristics of "prices" for incentive. For example, consider some $\mu_i > 0$. From standard second-order optimization-theory sensitivity analysis (see, e.g., Ioffe and Tihomirov [1979], pp. 292–298), if we consider a decrease of Δv utilities in the agent's disutility $V(a_i)$ if he takes action a_i, *ceteris paribus*, then the change in the principal's welfare $\Delta G(Z^*, a^*)$ is such that $\partial G(Z^*, a^*)/\partial U(Z^*, a_i) = -\mu_i$. Hence μ_i equals the price per unit of incentives for a^* over a_i. Let $e \equiv (1, \ldots, 1)^t \in \mathfrak{R}^n$, $\mu \equiv (\mu_1, \ldots, \mu_n)$. Then the inner product $\mu \cdot (e - T_{a^*}(s))$ at each s on the right-hand side of (6.19) denotes the cost to the principal of providing incentives to the agent by purchasing the risk bundle $T_{a^*}(s)$.

Now observe that $T_{a^*}(s)$ is a vector of n component risks $f(s|a_i)/f(s|a^*)$, priced at μ_i. But (6.19) shows (this is vividly clear for an agent with $u(w) = \log w$) that these individual risks do not enter into the compensation; only the linear combination $L(T_{a^*}(s))$ of the risk bundle $T_{a^*}(s)$ affects it. If for any two s_1, s_2, these combination risks lie on the same isocost hyperplane $H_\alpha(L)$ for some α, then these two risk bundles are *perfect substitutes* for each other. If the principal makes different contingent payments on each risk bundle, he imposes *twice* the useful risk, which is counterproductive and leads to a decrease in welfare since higher risk premiums have to be paid to the agent. This leads to the crucial criterion for informativeness: *Perfect risk substitutes do not generate incentive value if used separately.* All results on strict informativeness stem from this *principle of risk substitution.* We shall utilize this intuition in the next section.

Global Optimization—The Multiple-Agent Case and the Suboptimality of Relative Performance Evaluation Measures

Although the preceding development has been conducted in agencies with *one* principal and *one* agent, many of the results also hold for multiagent agencies at an *implementable Nash equilibrium.*[15] At a Nash equilibrium in a noncooperative game in normal form, from his viewpoint, *an agent is essentially playing a single-agent game with the principal.* Thus suppose there are two agents (the case of $K > 2$ two agents has identical results) with A^1 and A^2 as their action sets. Each agent's production process generates signals $s^j \in S^j$, but the probability distributions over S^j may depend on both a^1 and a^2. $S = S^1 \times S^2$. The concept of an optimal *contract* remains identical to that for problem (6.16)–(6.18) with straightforward modifications.

Under assumption 6.3, we can derive a characterization of the sufficient statistics of interest as in Lehmann's theorem. However, here some care is required since subtleties appear. As in the single-agent case, one would think that the family of probability measures of interest in this case is that generated by $\{f(s|a)\,|\,a \in A\}$ where $A = A^1 \times A^2$, but this is *not* true. At *any* optimal Nash equilibrium contract (Z^*, a^*) (where $Z^*(s) = [Z^{*1}(s), Z^{*2}(s)]$, and $a^* = [a^{*1}, a^{*2}]$), given our observation that each agent plays a single-agent game against the principal if all others maintain their Nash strategies, the families of interest are[16]

$$P_A^j = \{f(\cdot\,|a^j, a^{*k})\,|\,a^j \in A^j\} \qquad j, k = 1, 2 \tag{6.20}$$

Thus, we do not have a single sufficient statistic of interest, but *two* of them of the type $T_{a^*}^j(s)$ for each $j = 1, 2$, where $T_{a^*}^j(s)$ is similar to $T_{a^*}(s)$ in Lehmann's theorem (6.15). It is the components of these statistics that appear in Kuhn–Tucker equations like (6.19). The earlier results should be modified with this in mind.

Having explained some of the intricacies, the others should be rather clear, and we shall not (because of space considerations) spell out the details here. We merely assert the following:

All the results of global optimization for the single-agent case hold with $T_{a^*}(s)$ replaced in appropriate places by $T^j_{a^*}(s)$ and μ_k by μ^j_k.

One monitor that has been suggested in the literature (see, e.g., Green and Stokey [1983], Lazear and Rosen [1981], Nalebuff and Stiglitz [1983]) is that serving a *rank-order tournament*.[17] Holmstrom ([1982], theorem 7, p. 335) shows, however, that when the *outputs from the agents are independent*, tournaments *cannot* replace sufficient statistics. Here, using the risk-substitution insights of the previous section, we generalize this point by showing that *all countable*-range relative performance evaluation measures are *strictly* dominated by sufficient statistics in agencies with continuous densities, *whether or not* the outputs are independent.[18, 19] The intuition underlying the result is explained next in the context of tournaments.

Whenever signals are available about each agent's performance in a multiagent context, it is intuitive to expect the principal to relate one agent's performance to another and make rewards contingent on such relative performance evaluation.

Consider, for example, a rank-order tournament among three agents with total net profit $X = X_1 + X_2 + X_3$. Suppose the sample space S of signals is the set of net profit vectors $s = (x_1, x_2, x_3)$. A rank-order tournament monitor $\delta\colon S \to \mathfrak{R}^3$ *only* reports the *ordinal* position of the jth output x_j in s. For the three agents, there are at most 3 distinct values of the monitor $\delta(s)$ in $\mathfrak{R}^3$. Thus, if there is a best contract (Z^*, a^*) based on δ, then $Z^*(s) = [Z^{*1}(s), Z^{*2}(s), Z^{*3}(s)]$ can have *at most* 3 distinct compensation patterns.[20]

Now suppose assumptions 6.1 to 6.5, appropriately modified for the multiagent case, hold. Then for each agent, a first-order Kuhn–Tucker equation similar to (6.19) obtains (simply add superscripts $j = 1, 2, 3$, appropriately). Also keep in mind that on the right-hand side of (6.19) we have now the IML transform $L^j \equiv (\mu^j_1, \ldots, \mu^j_{n_j})$ and the density ratios of the minimal sufficient statistic $T^j_{a^*}$ for the family P^j_A of probability measures.

From this we see that if the *individual IML transforms L^j* acting on the individual image sets of $T^j_{a^*}$ produce d_j distinct images, and if any $d_j > 3$, then the principal *strictly* prefers the vector of sufficient statistics $T_{a^*} = [T^1_{a^*}, T^2_{a^*}, T^3_{a^*}]$ over the tournament monitor δ. Essentially, this says that the tournament monitor δ carries out much more risk substitution in the vector of minimal sufficient statistics T_{a^*} than is optimal. One situation where tournament monitors will be strictly dominated by a sufficient statistic is when any $T^j_{a^*}$ has density ratios made up of continuous densities such as the exponential family of densities.

Theorem 6.1

Suppose the modified assumptions 6.1 to 6.5 hold, and the principal is risk-neutral. Then the principal strictly prefers the vector of minimal sufficient statistics T_{a*} over *a relative performance monitor* δ that has a countable range if at *least one component of sufficient statistic* T_{a*}^{j} is constructed from continuous densities of the family P_A^j on a connected set S, and $a^{*j} \in A_j$ is not the least effort choice by j under Z_j^*.

Proof: Suppose without loss of generality, T_{a*}^{1} is a vector composed of continuous densities as in expression (6.15). For agent 1, the first-order conditions (6.19) at a Nash optimal contract (Z^*, a^*) are

$$\frac{1}{u_1(Z_1^*(s))} = \lambda_1 + \Sigma \mu_i^1 - L^1(T_{a*}^1(s)) \tag{6.21}$$

Since $T_{a*}^1 \colon S \to \mathfrak{R}^{n_1}$ is a continuous function, it follows from standard topological arguments that the image B^1 of S in $\mathfrak{R}^{n_1}$ under the function T_{a*}^1 is a *connected* domain. Further, as $L^1 \colon \mathfrak{R}^{n_1} \to \mathfrak{R}$ is a linear transformation, it is continuous on $\mathfrak{R}^{n_1}$, and hence $L^1(B^1)$, the image of B^1 in $\mathfrak{R}$ under L^1 is also a connected set.

Now $L^1(B^1)$ cannot be a singleton set because if it were, then (6.21) implies that $Z^{*1}(s) = \text{constant} \Rightarrow$ it is not incentive compatible because it will produce the least effort action a_1^1. Therefore, $L^1(B^1)$ has at least two points $\Rightarrow L^1(B^1)$ is a nondegenerate interval of numbers in $\mathfrak{R}$. Since every nondegenerate interval in $\mathfrak{R}$ has an *uncountably* infinite number of elements $\Rightarrow Z^{*1}(s)$ assumes an *uncountably* infinite number of values. This implies that Z^* cannot be a countable range contract, and, thus, the principal strictly prefers the joint minimal sufficient statistic $T_{a*} = [T_{a*}^1, T_{a*}^2, T_{a*}^3]$ over any relative performance monitor δ with a countable range of values. Q.E.D.

Observe that theorem 6.1 holds even if the number of agents becomes large, because the possible relative performance evaluations is still countable.[21]

Concluding Remarks

In this paper we have explored some issues regarding agency contracts under moral hazard in single- and multiple-agent agencies. We found that the standard Holmstrom–Mirrlees one-principal-one-agent first-order conditions can be reinterpreted as the first-order conditions between two partners in a pure risk-sharing venture with heterogeneous beliefs. This discovery yielded interesting insights into the nature of incentive-compatible agency contracts and the role of additional information.

Changing the problem structure to the case of a finite action set available to the agent, we were able to bypass the first-order local optimization conditions requirements, and develop a global optimization approach. This yielded insights into the demand for information from multiple signals at an optimal contract, and borrowing from Amershi ([1984b], [1987b]), we showed that the minimal sufficient statistic is just a vector of density ratios (indexed by $a \in A$). This, in turn yields a *risk-substitution* insight into the use of information, analogous to commodity substitution in consumption. In the multiple-agent case, this insight reveals that all relative performance evaluation measures with a countable range of evaluations are, in most cases of interest, suboptimal. The result generalizes the observation on rank-order tournaments made by Holmstrom [1982] for the case when the agents outputs are independent of each other. Our result holds for all continuous joint density functions over the set of performance signals.

Notes

1. How these heterogeneous beliefs came about is not at issue here. We shall, therefore, take them to be exogenously given. However, under "Second-Best Contracts under Moral Hazard" below, we will show how the heterogeneous beliefs can arise from information asymmetry.

2. The case of n signals $y_1, \ldots, y_n$ is identical and we will not present it here, as no additional insights are generated for our purposes here.

3. As shown in (Amershi [1987a]), the sufficient statistic for the *entire* two classes, say $\{f(t, y|a) \big| a \in A\}$ and $\{h(t, y|a) \big| a \in A\}$ is not necessarily $f(t, y|a)/h(t, y|a)$ for any fixed a. Here we assume that the partnership choice of optimal action $a \in A$ has occurred, and we are merely characterizing the optimal compensation Z for that *particular* $a \in A$. In this case, only the two beliefs $f(t, y|a)$ and $h(t, y|a)$ are of consequence, and it is sufficiency w.r.t to these two beliefs. That the ratio of these two beliefs is sufficient for them follows from a result in Lehmann [1983].

4. The point here is somewhat subtle. The contract having specified and enforced a^*, there is nothing "more" to know about a^* in this sense. The principal is sure that a^* will occur. However, having rewritten (6.7) as (6.9), it is *as if* the principal forms a partnership with a knowledgeable agent who knows more about his actions as reflected in the differential beliefs $h(x|a)$ and $f(x|a)$.

5. It is possible to generalize the findings here to more general "exponential families" (see Lehmann [1983] or Amershi and Hughes [1987]).

6. All the results here can be extended to the risk-averse case. Risk-neutrality is assumed purely for expositional ease.

7. As shown in Amershi [1987a] and Amershi and Hughes [1987], this situation cannot obtain if the principal is risk-averse, and wants to write a "full insurance" second-best contract with the agent. For risk-averse principals, if x is unobservable, the principal can still write a "partial insurance" contract with the agent (see Gjesdal [1982], or Atkinson and Feltham

[1983]). In this case additional information may have value for both insurance and incentive purposes. If x is observed, however, additional information only has incentive value.

8. To be sure, if all systems were costless or of equal cost, obviously the *full reporting* system $\eta(t, y) = (t, y)$ is the best. The examination of this problem in the literature implicitly assumes (but does not model) differential costs for different systems. The reason is that the benefits of an information system are far more difficult to determine as the information works through the decision problem to precipitate the benefits. Costs, on the other hand, are easy to calculate, since they amount to the value of resources sacrificed to run the system. Hence, once the *benefit-ranking* of systems is determined, a *cost-benefit ranking* is a trivial consequence. As an example, consider the standard accounting system, where (t, y) could correspond to basic journal entries (the first-level transactions data), and $\eta(t, y)$ could be considered aggregations of these into financial statements.

9. By "generically true" we mean that Holmstrom ([1979], p. 84, footnote 21) claimed that the cases where the converse does not hold are "exceptional case(s) . . . of little interest." Amershi and Hughes [1987] (see also Amershi [1984a]) provide a counterexample and detailed analysis of the issues. They also show that Holmstrom ([1982] theorem 6, p. 331 on "global insufficiency") does not provide the converse. Amershi, Banker and Datar [1987], working in a general class of probability densities, show that the converse only holds in a subset of Lebesgue measure 0 in the space of production functions giving rise to those densities.

10. The term "all a or no a" was coined by Holmstrom ([1979], footnote 21, p. 84), although he does not provide (neither in [1979] nor in [1982]) the statistical properties of this class nor a well-defined class of such densities. Amershi and Hughes [1987] show that the "all a or no a" class is precisely that class such that the likelihood ratios $f_a(t, y|a)/f(t, y|a)$ are *invertible functions* of the *minimal sufficient statistic* (see Amershi [1987a] for a definition). A well-known such class is the *exponential family of rank one* (see Amershi and Hughes [1987], Lehmann [1983]).

11. As explained in notes 9 and 10, this claim is rather strong. Nevertheless, it is proper to say that Holmstrom's ([1979], p. 84, proposition 3) is a major result for three reasons. First, it is a purely statistical result and hence independent of the preference structure in the agency. Second, it shows that statistical inference has a significant role to play in the comparison of information systems (see Amershi and Hughes [1987] for more details). Third, it is the first substantial result of its kind in the literature.

12. Amershi [1987b]) provides a more detailed exposition of the role of sufficient statistics and information value using the global optimization approach. Since this aproach does not require the stringent justifications for the differentiable local optimization approach, the results derived there are more robust. It is interesting to note that they corroborate the results in Amershi and Hughes [1987] on the role of sufficient statistics in monitoring.

13. This assumption is made here purely for expositional ease, and can be relaxed as shown in Amershi [1984b] and [1987b].

14. It is precisely for this reason that Holmstrom's ([1979], [1982]), results and the results in Amershi [1984a] and Amershi and Hughes [1987], on the value of the information provided by sufficient statistics, are important.

15. Implementability of Nash equilibrium means that given the contract mechanism for the agents, there is no other Nash equilibrium in the agents' subgame that Pareto dominates (weakly or strictly) the Nash equilibrium of actions that the principal wants implemented. Amershi and Cheng [1987] provide a detailed exposition of the issues. *Here we shall assume that the optimal contract is implementable.*

16. As mentioned in Amershi ([1984b], [1987b]), in standard statistical terminology (see, e.g., Zacks [1971]), the a^{*k}, $k \neq j$ appear as "nuisance parameters" in the family of interest P^j_A at a Nash equilibrium. It is important to note that for any particular agency, *only* the particular

implementable Nash equilibrium is of interest; hence, we concentrate on the families $P_A^j, j = 1, 2$ rather than the larger family $P_A = \{f(s|a) \mid a \in A\}$. The sufficient statistic for this larger family contains much redundant information about "off equilibrium" a, which the principal, unless he has incomplete information about the fundamental structure of his agency, does not require to implement the Nash equilibrium. For example if A^1 has 20 actions and A^2 has 30 actions, their individual sufficient statistics T_{a*}^j at any particular Nash equilibrium $[a^{*1}, a^{*2}]$ will have 20 and 30 density ratios each, whereas the optimal sufficient statistic for P^A will have 600 density ratios. This point is elaborated upon here because Holmstrom ([1982], p. 331) and Mookherjee ([1984] p. 435) work with the larger P^A rather than the smaller ones. This is one essential difference between our approach and theirs.

17. In a rank-order tournament, the principal makes payments to the agents only on the basis of the ordinal rank of their outputs. For example, the principal may precommit to a set of prizes, say $\{w_1, w_2\}$. If agent 2 has higher output than agent 1, agent 2 gets w_1 and w_2 goes to 1.

18. By countably valued we mean (see Amershi [1987a], appendix 1A) that the range of values can be put into 1–1 correspondence with a *subset* of the set $N = \{1, 2, \ldots, n, \ldots\}$ of positive integers.

19. In a recent study, Antle and Smith [1986] found only limited empirical support for the use of relative performance measures in executive compensation contracts.

20. A more complex "tournament-like" monitor would report both the agent's number ($j = 1, 2, 3$) and his output's ordinal rank compared to the other outputs. In this case the monitor has 6 different compensation patterns because, for example, agent 1, if he is first in output, will be rewarded differentially depending on whether agent 2 or agent 3 is second.

21. Our intuition suggests that if the relative performance monitor's range is dense in the image set of the IML Transformations, then it may be possible to get arbitrarily close to the best contract by using relative performance evaluation.

APPENDIX 6

Here we shall show that the set

$$A^* = \{a^* \in A \mid \mu(a^*) > 0\}$$

is not empty. First, if $(\hat{Z}, \hat{a})$ is a solution to the total problem, then Holmstrom ([1979], p. 90) shows that $\mu(\hat{a}) > 0$. Further, from the second-order conditions required in proving $\mu(\hat{a}) > 0$, it follows that there is an $\varepsilon > 0$ such that for all $a^* \in (\hat{a} - \varepsilon, \hat{a} + \varepsilon)$, $\mu(a^*) > 0$. Second, if the principal is risk neutral and the likelihood ratios $f_a(x \mid a)/f(x \mid a)$ are monotone increasing in x (i.e., they satisfy the monotone likelihood ratio condition (MLRC)), then (6.7) shows that $\mu(a) > 0$ for all $a \in A$ other than the lowest effort $\bar{a}$. (At this juncture we do not know whether or not A^* equals A for all agencies.)

References

Amershi, A.H. [1984a]. "Informativeness in Agencies: Contractual Sufficiency versus Statistical Sufficiency." Working Paper, University of British Columbia.

Amershi, A.H. [1984b]. "A Theory of Informativeness under Asymmetric Information." Working Paper, University of British Columbia.

Amershi, A.H. [1987a]. "Blackwell Informativeness and Sufficient Statistics with Applications to Financial Markets and Multiperson Agencies." (This volume)

Amershi, A.H. [1987b]. "On the Globally Optimal Informativeness of Sufficient Statistics in Agencies under Moral Hazard." Working Paper, University of Minnesota.

Amershi, A.H., Banker, R., and Datar, S. [1987]. "Economic Sufficiency and Statistical Sufficiency in the Aggregation of Accounting Signals." Working paper, Carnegie-Mellon University.

Amershi, A.H., and Cheng, P. [1987]. "Implementable Equilibria in Accounting Contexts: An Exploratory Study." *Contemporary Accounting Research* (forthcoming).

Amershi, A.H., and Hughes, J. [1987]. "Multiple Signals, Statistical Sufficiency and Pareto-Ordering of Best Agency Contracts." Working Paper, University of British Columbia.

Amershi, A.H., and Stoeckenius, J.H.W. [1983]. "The Theory of Syndicates and Linear Sharing Rules." *Econometrica* 51, 1407–1416.

Antle, R., and Smith, A. [1986]. "An Empirical Investigation of Relative Performance Evaluation of Corporate Executives." *Journal of Accounting Research* 24, 1–39.

Atkinson, A., and Feltham, G.A. [1983]. "Information in Capital Markets: An Agency Theory Perspective." Working Paper, University of British Columbia.

Berge, J.E., Daley, L.A., Dickhaut, J.W., and O'Brien, J. [1986]. "An Examination of the Explanatory Power of the Formal Agency Model." Working Paper, University of Minnesota.

Borch, K. [1962]. "Equilibrium in a Reinsurance Market." *Econometrica* 30, 42–444.

Clarke, F.H., and Darrough, M. [1980]. "Optimal Incentive Schemes: Existence and Characterization." *Economics Letters* 5, 305–310.

Gjesdal, F. [1982]. "Information and Incentives: The Agency Information Problem." *Review of Economic Studies* 49, 373–390.

Green, J., and Stokey, N. [1983]. "A Comparison of Tournaments and Contracts." *Journal of Political Economy* 91, 349–364.

Grossman, S., and Hart, O. [1983]. "An Analysis of the Principal-Agent Problem." *Econometrica* 51, 7–46.

Hart, O., and Holmstrom, B. [1985]. "The Theory of Contracts." Working Paper, MIT.

Holmstrom, B. [1979]. "Moral Hazard and Observability." *Bell Journal of Economics* 10, 74–91.

Holmstrom, B. [1982]. "Moral Hazard in Teams." *Bell Journal of Economics* 13, 324–340.

Ioffe, A.D., and Tihomirov, V.M. [1979]. *Theory of Extremal Problems.* New York: North Holland.

Lazear, E.P., and S. Rosen, [1981]. "Rank-Order Tournaments as Optimum Labour Contracts." *Journal of Political Economy* 89, 841–864.

Lehmann, E. [1983]. *Theory of Point Estimation.* New York: John Wiley.

Mirrlees, J. [1976]. "The Optimal Structure of Incentives and Authority within an Organization." *Bell Journal of Economics* 7, 105–131.

Mookherjee, D. [1984]. "Optimal Incentive Schemes with Many Agents." *Review of Economic Studies* 51, 433–446.

Nalebuff, B., and Stiglitz, J. [1983]. "Prizes and Incentives: Towards a General Theory of Compensation and Competition." *Bell Journal of Economics* 14, 21–43.

Rogerson, W.P. [1985]. "The First-Order Approach to the Principal Agent Problem." *Econometrica* 53, 1357–1367.

Zacks, S. [1971]. *The Theory of Statistical Inference*. New York: John Wiley.

7 SEQUENTIAL CHOICE UNDER MORAL HAZARD*

Ella Mae Matsumura

Introduction

Consider a production manager who is hired by a firm to ensure that daily operations run smoothly and efficiently. The manager receives intermediate cost reports during each month for control purposes, and is evaluated on the basis of monthly summary cost reports. The manager may wish to adjust his or her daily control effort based on the information in the intermediate cost reports.

Consider also a traveling salesperson who spends time selling a firm's product in several territories before being paid at the end of each month. The

* This paper is based on part of the author's Ph.D. dissertation at the University of British Columbia. Special thanks are due to Gerald Feltham, who supervised the dissertation, for his comments and discussions related to the dissertation and for his detailed comments on this paper. Thanks are also due to John Butterworth for discussions related to the dissertation, and to Kam-Wah Tsui for his comments on this paper. The research was partially supported by the Research Center for Managerial Economics and Public Policy at the University of California, Los Angeles.

salesperson attempts to sell in one territory and observes the amount of the resultant sales there before attempting to sell in the next territory. The time (effort) spent by the salesperson in a territory may be influenced by sales information from previously visited territories.

Both these situations involve sequential decisions within a period by an employee who is compensated at the end of the period. Since the employee's effort is not continuously monitored, a moral hazard problem may exist. That is, the employee may exert less effort than agreed upon.

This paper uses agency theory to study one-period sequential choice under moral hazard. The basic agency theoretic framework (see, e.g., Harris and Raviv [1979] and Holmstrom [1979]), involves a principal (employer) who delegates an action choice to an agent (employee). The agent's action and a random state of nature jointly determine the monetary outcome. Generally, neither the agent's action nor the state of nature are observable by the principal. The agent can therefore blame a poor outcome on a bad state of nature rather than a bad action.

The choices of the two individuals are modeled using expected utility theory. The principal is assumed to have utility only for wealth, while the agent is assumed to have utility for wealth and disutility for work. The principal offers a compensation schedule which provides the agent with as much expected utility as he or she could obtain from any alternative employment. The compensation can be based only on what is jointly observable to the principal and the agent. For simplicity, in this paper, the compensation will be assumed to depend on monetary outcomes.

The agent's actions (efforts) will be denoted a_i. It will be assumed that each effort a_i corresponds to a monetary outcome x_i. The compensation schedule (sharing rule) is denoted $s(\cdot)$. With these definitions, the one-period two-sequential-effort choice-problem can be depicted as follows:

Principal chooses $s(x_1, x_2)$	Agent exerts a_1	Agent observes x_1	Agent exerts $a_2(\cdot)$	Agent observes x_2; principal observes x_1 and x_2 and pays $s(x_1, x_2)$ to the agent.

This differs from the two-period model, in which the first outcome is jointly observed and the first compensation is paid before the second effort is exerted. The two-period model can be depicted as follows:

Principal chooses $s_1(x_1)$ and $s_2(x_1, x_2)$	Agent exerts a_1	Principal and agent observe x_1; principal pays $s_1(x_1)$ to the agent.	Agent exerts $a_2(\cdot)$	Principal and agent observe x_2; principal pays $s_2(x_1, x_2)$ to the agent.

The one-period sequential model can be thought of as the special case of the fully general two-period model in which the periods are very short, so that the principal's and the agent's expected utilities depend only on their total return for the entire horizon. The one-period model can incorporate some of the elements of the fully general two-period model while providing a somewhat simplified structure for analysis. For example, in both models, the first outcome, which is first-stage postdecision information, can be used as predecision information for the second-effort choice. The agent's precommitment to stay for the entire time horizon is not a major problem in the one-period model, since the agent is not paid until all the efforts have been exerted.

In this paper, the simplified structure in the one-period sequential model is used to explore the impact of correlation of outcomes in first-best and second-best situations. The analysis will focus on aspects that were not addressed in the predecision information literature or in previous multiperiod agency analyses. Before proceeding to the analysis, a brief review of the existing results on predecision information will be given and the multiperiod agency results of Lambert [1983], Rogerson [1985a], and Holmstrom and Milgrom [1985] will be summarized.

Predecision Information

Baiman comments as follows on the increased complexity with predecision information:

> The role and value of a pre-decision information system is more complex than that of a post-decision information system. Expanding a post-decision information system to report an additional piece of information will always result in at least a weak Pareto improvement, since the principal and agent can always agree to a payment schedule that ignores the additional information. However, expanding a pre-decision information system to report an additional piece of information may not result in even a weak Pareto improvement. The agent generally cannot commit himself to ignore the additional information, and

> therefore the optimal employment contract without the additional pre-decision information is no longer necessarily self-enforcing given the additional information. This is true whether the additional pre-decision information is privately reported or publicly reported. (Baiman [1982], p. 192)

Some of the research concerning predecision information focuses on the following question: Given that the agent has private predecision information, what is the value of public postdecision information systems? Holmstrom [1979] showed that an informativeness criterion ($f(x, y, z; a) \neq g(x, y)\, h(x, z; a)$, where z is the predecision signal and f, g, and h represent probability density functions) is necessary for the postdecision information system which reports a public signal, y, in addition to x, the outcome, to provide a Pareto improvement over the information system which reports only x. Christensen [1982] expanded Holmstrom's [1979] model by allowing the agent to communicate to the principal a message m about the private predecision signal. The agent is assumed to select the message that maximizes his or her expected utility. In Christensen's model, a generalization of Holmstrom's [1979] informativeness criterion is necessary for the postdecision information system which reports y, in addition to x and m, to provide a Pareto improvement over the information system that reports only x and m. Here, the public postdecision signal is a signal about the agent's effort and the agent's private predecision information signal.

Another direction of the research on predecision information has been the value of predecision information systems. There are both positive and negative effects of private predecision information for the agent. On one hand, the agent has more information before choosing an action, and hence should make "better" decisions. On the other hand, more information may reduce the risk the agent faces, and hence reduce the motivation for the agent to exert effort. Christensen [1981] provides an example which shows that the principal may be worse off when the agent has private predecision information (with or without communication of a message), and also provides an example that shows that the principal may be better off when the agent has private predecision information and communicates a message to the principal. Christensen's examples illustrate the difficulty in obtaining a general preference-ordering rule over predecision information systems.

A third direction of research on private predecision information has been the value of communication of a message about the private information from the agent to the principal, given the existence of the private predecision information system. In the accounting context, the focus is on the value of communication of private information in the process of participative budgeting. The major result in this area is that of Baiman and Evans [1983], who provided necessary and sufficient conditions for communication to result in a Pareto improvement. Baiman summarizes the result as follows:

> If the agent's private pre-decision information is perfect, then communication has no value. Observing the firm's output in that case allows the principal to infer all he needs to know about the agent's private pre-decision information. However, if the agent's private pre-decision information is imperfect, a necessary and sufficient condition for communication to be strictly valuable is for the honest revelation of the agent's private pre-decision information to be strictly valuable. That is, if any value can be achieved with the information being honestly revealed to *all*, then a strictly positive part of that value can be achieved by giving the agent sole direct access to the information and letting him communicate in a manner that maximizes *his* expected utility. (Baiman [1982], p. 204)

Finite-Horizon Multiperiod Agency Analyses

Lambert [1983] has examined a special case of the finite-horizon multiperiod agency problem. He assumed that both the principal and the agent have utility functions (and that the agent has a disutility function) which are separable across time. He further assumed that the state variables are independently distributed across time, and that effort in one period does not influence the monetary outcome in any other period. Under these conditions, Lambert showed that the agent's compensation in a given period will depend on the outcomes in previous periods as well as on the outcome in the present period. He further showed that the incentive problems associated with the agent's effort choices in each period are not eliminated.[1]

Rogerson [1985a] used an alternative method to analyze the multiperiod (finitely or infinitely repeated) agency problem. He assumed that the principal is risk-neutral and that the agent is risk averse and discounts future consumption. As Lambert [1983] did, Rogerson assumed that the outcomes are independently distributed over time and that effort in any period influences the outcome of only that period. One result shows that if an outcome is part of the basis for compensation in the current period, then it is part of the basis for compensation in the future. Another result shows that whether the agent's expected compensation will increase or decrease over time depends on the shape of the agent's marginal utility. Finally, Rogerson shows that it is necessary to restrict the agent's access to credit in order to achieve a Pareto optimal outcome.

Holmstrom and Milgrom [1985] took a dynamic programming approach to a finite-horizon multiperiod agency problem in which the agent's utility is evaluated only at the end of the horizon. The agent is assumed to have an exponential utility function, and the cost of the agent's actions is expressed in monetary terms. Neither the principal nor the agent has private information before contracting. Under these restrictions, it is shown that in a discrete-time, discrete-outcome model, the optimal compensation scheme depends linearly on time aggregates of the outcomes (the number of times each outcome occurs during the time horizon). Related results are developed for continuous-time approximations of the discrete-time model. In the continuous-time model, the agent is assumed to control the drift but not the variance of a Brownian motion.

The remainder of this paper analyzes the one-period sequential-effort choice problem. The cooperative, or first-best case is first considered, and the behavior of the agent's second-stage effort choice strategy is characterized. The second-best case is then analyzed. The optimal sharing rule is derived and discussed, as is the behavior of the agent's second-stage choice strategy. The agent's second-stage strategy may depend on the first outcome because of a "wealth" effect or an "information" effect. In a situation where the first outcome conveys no state information about the second outcome to the agent, the agent's strategy is decreasing in the first outcome. At the other extreme, in a situation where the first outcome conveys perfect state information about the second outcome to the agent, the agent's strategy is increasing in the first outcome. With imperfect state information, the agent's strategy is more complex.

Notation and First-best Analysis

The following assumptions and notation will be used. For expositional simplicity, the agent will choose two nonnegative efforts, a_1 and a_2, which in conjunction with random states of nature result in corresponding sequential real-valued monetary outcomes, x_1 and x_2. The principal and the agent initially have identical beliefs about the probability distributions. It is assumed that the supports of the probability distributions conditional on effort do not vary as effort varies, and that the partial derivatives of the distributions with respect to effort exist and are nondegenerate. Furthermore, $F_i(x_i|a_i)$, the cumulative distribution function of the outcome x_i conditional on effort a_i, is assumed to satisfy first-order stochastic dominance, $i = 1, 2$. That is, $\partial F_i(x_i|a_i)/\partial a_i \leq 0$, $i = 1, 2$. It is assumed that there is sufficient regularity to allow differentiation with respect to effort through the integration signs of the expected utilities.

The sharing rule $s(\cdot)$ is a bounded, measurable, real-valued function. The principal's utility for wealth is $W(\cdot)$, where $W' > 0$ and $W'' \leq 0$. As in much of the agency literature, the agent's net utility function is assumed to be additively separable in wealth and effort. That is, the agent's net utility is $U(s) - V(a_1, a_2)$, where $U' > 0$, $U'' \leq 0$, $\partial V/\partial a_i > 0$, and $\partial^2 V/\partial a_i^2 > 0$, $i = 1, 2$. Finally, $\bar{u}$ denotes the agent's minimum acceptable expected utility level.

In the first-best case, the principal's problem is

$$\underset{s(\cdot), a_1, a_2(\cdot)}{\text{maximize:}} \quad \int\int W(x - s(x_1, x_2))\phi(x_1, x_2 | a_1, a_2(\cdot))dx_2 dx_1$$

$$\text{subject to:} \quad \int\int \{U(s(x_1, x_2)) - V(a_1, a_2(\cdot))\}\phi(\cdot)dx_2 dx_1 \geq \bar{u}$$

where $\phi(x_1, x_2 | a_1, a_2(\cdot)) = f(x_1 | a_1)g(x_2 | x_1, a_1, a_2(\cdot))$ is the joint distribution of the outcomes conditional on the efforts, and $a_2(\cdot)$ indicates that the agent's second-stage effort is in general not a constant, but rather can depend on any information available at the time of choice. Letting λ be the multiplier for the agent's expected utility constraint and differentiating the Hamiltonian with respect to $s(\cdot)$ for every (x_1, x_2) yields

$$\frac{W'(x - s(x_1, x_2))}{U'(s(x_1, x_2))} = \lambda$$

for almost every (x_1, x_2). This implies that if one person is risk-neutral and the other is risk averse, then the risk-neutral person will bear the risk. That is, if the principal is risk-neutral and the agent is risk averse, then the optimal sharing rule is constant; if the principal is risk averse and the agent is risk-neutral, then the principal's return is k, a constant, and the agent receives $x_1 + x_2 - k$. If both individuals are risk averse, then the risk is shared; the optimal sharing rule is a function of $(x_1 + x_2)$. Furthermore, $\partial s/\partial x_i$ is positive for $i = 1, 2$. Finally, if both are risk neutral, then the optimal sharing rule is $s = \bar{u} + V(a_1, a_2(\cdot))$.

In this scenario, there are no signals on which the choice of a_1 can be based. Whether or not a_2 is a function of x_1 depends on the risk attitudes of the individuals and the joint distribution $\phi(x_1, x_2 | a_1, a_2(\cdot))$. If at least one of the individuals is risk neutral and $\phi(x_1, x_2 | a_1, a_2(\cdot)) = f(x_1 | a_1)g(x_2 | a_2(\cdot))$, then the optimal $a_2(\cdot)$ is independent of x_1.[2] In this case, the risk neutral person essentially owns the output of the firm, and thus bears all the risk associated with the uncertainty of x_1. Furthermore, x_1 conveys no information about x_2.

If both of the individuals are risk averse or if $\phi(\cdot)$ is the more general $f(x_1 | a_1)g(x_2 | x_1, a_1, a_2(\cdot))$, then the optimal $a_2(\cdot)$ will generally depend on

x_1.[3] In the first case, the change from the situation where one individual is risk neutral occurs because each risk averse individual's marginal utility depends on the first outcome, since it determines where on his or her utility curve the individual is; a risk neutral individual's marginal utility, on the other hand, would be the same no matter what the value of x_1 is. This first effect of x_1 can be termed the *wealth* or *risk aversion* effect. In the second case, if x_1 and x_2 are dependent, then expectations for x_2 may change according to the first outcome, x_1. The principal may therefore wish to induce the agent to choose $a_2(\cdot)$ as an increasing or decreasing function of x_1, depending on the risk attitudes of the principal and the agent, the agent's disutility for effort, and the nature of the correlation between x_1 and x_2. This second effect of x_1 can be termed the *information* effect. The information effect of x_1 is made more precise in the proposition below.

Proposition 7.1

Suppose that in the first-best case, the principal is risk neutral, the agent is risk averse, and $\phi(\cdot) = f(x_1|a_1)g(x_2|x_1, a_1, a_2(\cdot))$. In this case, the optimal second effort strategy $a_2^*(\cdot)$ will depend on x_1. Let $M_2(x_1, a_1, a_2(\cdot))$ denote the conditional mean of x_2 with respect to $g(\cdot)$. Let the second and third subscripts of j on M_2 denote partial differentiation of M_2 with respect to the jth argument of $M_2(x_1, a_1, a_2(\cdot))$. Then

$$a_2^{*\prime}(x_1) = \frac{-M_{231}}{M_{233} - \lambda[\partial^2 V(\cdot)/\partial a_2^2]}$$

For example, suppose $M_2(x_1, a_1, a_2(\cdot)) = x_1 a_2(x_1)/a_1$ and $V(\cdot) = (a_1 + a_2)^2$. Then $a_2^{*\prime}(x_1) = 1/(2a_1^*\lambda) > 0$. In this case, $a_2^*(x_1)$ increases linearly in x_1.

The effect of the nature of the correlation between x_1 and x_2 is captured in the derivatives of $M_2(\cdot)$, and the effect of the disutility function is captured in the $\partial^2 V/\partial a_2^2$ term. Note that $a_2^*(x_1)$ does not depend on the agent's utility function for wealth. This is because the risk averse agent receives a constant wage in the first-best case, and hence the agent's utility for the wage is constant. Note further that because the principal is risk neutral and no risk is imposed on the risk averse agent, the impact of the uncertainty of the second outcome on $a_2(\cdot)$ is completely captured by the mean of the second outcome. Finally, if M_2 depends only on $a_2(\cdot)$, then a_2^* is constant.

Proposition 7.1 and the discussion preceding it focused on the second effort choice's dependence on x_1, the first outcome. The second effort choice, $a_2(\cdot)$, might seem to also depend on the *first* effort choice, a_1. However, the agent chooses the effort a_1 and the effort strategy $a_2(\cdot)$ simultaneously at the beginning of the time horizon. The second effort choice is therefore not viewed as a function of a_1, although there is implicit recognition that a_1 and $a_2(\cdot)$ are chosen jointly and therefore influence one another. However, since the first outcome is unknown at the beginning of the time horizon, the second effort choice can potentially depend on the first outcome.

Second Best

In this section, the general formulation of the one-period sequential model is first presented. Subsequently, the two extremes of independent outcomes and perfectly correlated outcomes are examined. In the first case, knowledge of x_1 reveals no information about x_2; in the second case, x_1 reveals perfect information about x_2. The behavior of the agent's second effort strategy is illustrated in the two extreme cases, and also for the intermediate case of imperfectly correlated outcomes.

General Formulation of the Second-Best Problem

In order to focus on motivational issues, it will be assumed that the principal is risk neutral and the agent is risk averse. The principal's problem is

$$\underset{s(\cdot),a_1,a_2(\cdot)}{\text{maximize:}} \quad \int\int (x - s(x_1, x_2))\phi(x_1, x_2 | a_1, a_2(\cdot))\, dx_2\, dx_1$$

subject to:

$$\int\Big[\int U(s(x_1, x_2)) g(x_2 | x_1, a_1, a_2(\cdot))\, dx_2 - V(a_1, a_2(\cdot))\Big] f(x_1 | a_1)\, dx_1 \geq \bar{u}$$

$$\int\int U(s(\cdot))[g_{a_1} f + g f_{a_1}]\, dx_2\, dx_1 - \int (V_{a_1} f + V f_{a_1})\, dx_1 = 0$$

$$\Big\{\int U(s(\cdot)) g_{a_2}(\cdot)\, dx_2 - V_{a_2}(\cdot)\Big\} f(x_1 | a_1) = 0 \qquad \text{for almost every } x_1$$

where $\phi(x_1, x_2 | a_1, a_2(\cdot)) = f(x_1 | a_1) g(x_2 | x_1, a_1, a_2(\cdot))$, and differentiation with respect to a_2 is pointwise for each x_1. The second and third constraints are the agent's first-order conditions, which reflect the principal's assumption that the agent will act in his or her own best interest. It is assumed here that these conditions are sufficient (see Rogerson [1985b] for identification of contexts in which these conditions are sufficient). The interior portion of the optimal sharing rule is characterized by

$$\frac{1}{U'(s(\mathbf{x}))} = \lambda + \frac{\mu_1 \phi_{a_1}}{\phi} + \frac{\mu_2(x_1)\phi_{a_2}}{\phi} \qquad \text{for almost every } \mathbf{x} = (x_1, x_2)$$

where λ, μ_1, and $\mu_2(x_1)$ are multipliers for the three constraints above. Here $\phi_{a_1}/\phi = f_{a_1}/f + g_{a_1}/g$ and $\phi_{a_2}/\phi = g_{a_2}/g$. If a_1 does not influence x_2, then $\phi_{a_1}/\phi = f_{a_1}/f$.

In general, $a_2^*(\cdot)$ depends on x_1.[4] However, if the agent is risk neutral and $\phi(x_1, x_2|a_1, a_2(\cdot)) = f(x_1|a_1)g(x_2|a_2(\cdot))$, then $a_2^*(\cdot)$ does *not* depend on x_1. If the x_i's are conditionally correlated, then $a_2^*(\cdot)$ will depend on x_1 even if the agent is risk neutral. These results are direct consequences of the achievability of the first-best solution in the second-best case if the agent is risk neutral (see Shavell [1979]).

Independent Outcomes

The proposition below describes aspects of the second stage problem for a particular utility function (necessitated because of mathematical tractability) for the agent, and for several commonly used distributions for the independent outcomes.

Proposition 7.2

Suppose that in the second best-case, the principal is risk neutral, and the agent's utility function for wealth is $U(s) = 2\sqrt{s}$. Suppose also that $\phi(\cdot) = f(x_1|a_1)g(x_2|a_2(\cdot))$, where $f(\cdot)$ and $g(\cdot)$ are in Q_1, the class consisting of the exponential, gamma, and Poisson distributions represented in appendix 7A. Define a_1 and a_2 so that the mean of $f(x_1|a_1)$ is a_1 and the mean of $g(x_2|a_2)$ is a_2. Then, assuming that the optimal efforts are nonzero,

i. if $\partial V/\partial a_2$ is positive at $\mathbf{a}^* = (a_1^*, a_2^*(\cdot))$ then $\mu_2(x_1)$ is positive; and
ii. if μ_1 is positive, then
   (a) the agent's expected second-stage utility for the pecuniary return, $E\{U(s(\mathbf{x}))|x_1\}$, is an increasing function of x_1,
   (b) a sufficient condition for the agent's expected second-stage net utility to be increasing in x_1 is that $a_2^*(\cdot)$ be a decreasing function of x_1; and
   (c) the conditions $V_2 > 0$, $V_{22} \geq 0$, $V_{222} \geq 0$, and $V_{122} \geq 0$ are jointly sufficient for $a_2^*(\cdot)$ to be a decreasing function of x_1. Here, subscripts j on V represent partial differentiation with respect to the jth effort variable.

The condition that $\partial V/\partial a_2$ be positive is a standard one, and is non-restrictive. A number of general forms of disutility functions satisfy the conditions in ii(c), for example:

$$V(a_1, a_2) = h(a_1) + a_2^m, \qquad \text{where } m \geq 1 \text{ and } a_2 > 0$$

$$V(a_1, a_2) = a_1^2 a_2^2, \qquad \text{where } a_1 \geq 0 \text{ and } a_2 \geq 0$$

$$V(a_1, a_2) = h(c_1 a_1 + c_2 a_2), \qquad \text{where } h' > 0,\ h'' \geq 0,\ h''' \geq 0, \text{ and the constants } c_1 \text{ and } c_2 \text{ are positive}$$

If μ_1 is zero (there is no incentive problem with respect to a_1), then a_2 does not depend on x_1.[5] This is consistent with the first-best results with a risk neutral principal, a risk averse agent, and independence of the outcomes. There is neither an incentive problem nor an information effect to induce the dependence of a_2 on x_1.

In general, though, a_2 will depend on x_1. Proposition 7.2 states that in some particular settings, the optimal second-stage effort will decrease as the first outcome increases. Recall that x_1 determines a point on the utility curve for the agent before the second-stage effort is chosen. Because the agent's marginal utility for wealth is a decreasing function and the agent's marginal disutility for effort is an increasing function, it is more costly for the principal to induce a given level of a_2, the higher x_1 is. The result that a_2 is decreasing in x_1 should thus hold for other concave utility functions for wealth, coupled with convex disutility functions, *even if the outcomes are completely independent.*

Proposition 7.2 also provides conditions under which the agent's second stage expected utility will increase as the outcome increases. Under the given conditions, $E[U(s(\mathbf{x}))|x_1]$ is increasing in x_1, and $-V(a_1, a_2(x_1))$ is increasing in x_1 because a_2 is decreasing in x_1. Thus, the agent's expected second stage net utility is increasing in x_1.

Illustration of Second-Best Results

To illustrate the second-best results, suppose that the principal is risk neutral and the agent's utility for wealth is $2\sqrt{s}$. Suppose further that $x_1|a_1$ and $x_2|a_2$ are independent, $f(\cdot)$ is exponential with mean a_1, and $g(\cdot)$ is exponential with mean $a_2(x_1)$. Then the interior portion of the optimal sharing rule is characterized by $s(x_1, x_2) = P(\mathbf{x})^2$, where

$$P(\mathbf{x}) = \lambda + \mu_1 \left[\frac{x_1 - a_1^*}{(a_1^*)^2} \right] + \mu_2(x_1) \left[\frac{x_2 - a_2^*(x_1)}{a_2^*(x_1)^2} \right] \tag{7.1}$$

$P(\mathbf{x})$ must be strictly positive in order to satisfy the first-order condition $1/U' = P(\mathbf{x})$. In the proof of proposition 7.2, it is shown that

$$\mu_2(x_1) = (\partial V(\mathbf{a}^*)/\partial a_2) a_2^*(x_1)^2/2, \tag{7.2}$$

which is positive under the usual assumption that the agent's disutility function is increasing in the second effort. Furthermore, it is easily seen that $\mu_2'(x_1) < 0$ under the assumptions in proposition 7.2, ii(c). Intuitively, the higher the first outcome is, the less concerned the risk neutral principal is about motivating a high choice of a_2. This is because the higher the outcome x_1 is, the costlier it becomes to induce a given level of a_2. The principal therefore induces a strategy $a_2(x_1)$ which is decreasing in x_1.

To examine the behavior of the sharing rule, note first that $\partial s/\partial x_2 = 2P(\mathbf{x}) (\mu_2(x_1)/a_2^*(x_1)^2) > 0$ since $P(\mathbf{x})$ and $\mu_2(x_1)$ are strictly positive. The monotonicity of $\partial s/\partial x_2$ is to be expected, since at the time of the second effort choice, the first outcome is known, so the agent is at that point essentially faced with a one-stage, one-period choice problem. With the exponential distribution assumption, the one-stage, one-period sharing rule would be strictly increasing in the outcome. The behavior of $s(\cdot)$ as x_1 varies is considerably more complicated because of future-period effects of x_1. Substituting equation (7.2) into equation (7.1) and differentiating shows that

$$\frac{\partial s}{\partial x_1} = 2P(\mathbf{x})\left[\frac{\mu_1}{(a_1^*)^2} + \left(\frac{x_2 - a_2^*(\cdot)}{2}\right)(a_2^*)' V_{a_2a_2}(\cdot) - (a_2^*)' V_{a_2}(\cdot)/2\right]$$

If μ_1 is positive and the conditions in proposition 7.2, ii(c) hold, the first and third terms in the brackets are positive. The additional condition that $x_2 \leq a_2^*(x_1)$ is sufficient for the sharing rule to be increasing in the first outcome. However it is clearly possible that $\partial s/\partial x_1$ is increasing in x_1 even if $x_2 > a_2^*(x_1)$. Although it is unclear how $s(\cdot)$ varies as x_1 varies, a statement can be made about the impact on the agent of variations in x_1. If the conditions in proposition 7.2 hold, then the agent's expected second-stage utility for wealth and the agent's expected second-stage net utility are increasing in x_1. On average, the higher x_1 is, the greater is the agent's net utility.

Perfectly Correlated Outcomes

The independence of x_1 and x_2 in proposition 7.2 means that there is no information effect of x_1. If x_1 and x_2 are correlated, then the behavior of $a_2^*(\cdot)$ would depend additionally on the nature of the correlation. In order to examine the information effect of x_1, the extreme case of perfect correlation of the outcomes will next be analyzed. When the outcomes are perfectly correlated, a joint density for x_1 and x_2 does not exist. Since the lack of a joint density precludes using the previous analysis directly, a modified approach must be taken in order to examine the nature of the sharing rule and the agent's second-stage effort choice when the outcomes are perfectly correlated.

Let $x_i = x_i(\theta, a_i)$, where θ is an uncertain state that influences both the outcomes. It will be assumed that for any fixed a_1, x_1 can be inverted to obtain $\theta = \theta(x_1, a_1)$. The principal's and the agent's common beliefs about the outcomes will be expressed as $\phi(x_1, x_2 | a_1, a_2(\cdot)) = f(x_1 | a_1)$ if $x_2 = x_2(\theta, a_2(x_1))$ and $\theta = \theta(x_1, a_1)$; otherwise, $\phi(\cdot) = 0$.

In order to describe the sharing rule, let a_1^* be the agent's first-stage effort choice induced by the sharing rule, and let $a_2^*(x_1)$ be the agent's second-stage effort strategy induced if x_1 is observed and it is assumed that $a_1 = a_1^*$. Because of the perfect correlation between x_1 and x_2, the sharing rule $\hat{s}(x_1, x_2)$ can be viewed as being of the following form: $\hat{s}(x_1, x_2) = s(x_1)$ if $x_2 = x_2(\theta, a_2^*(x_1))$ and $\theta = \theta(x_1, a_1^*)$; otherwise, $\hat{s}(\cdot)$ is a penalty wage which is possibly negative.

The sharing rule can be viewed as being dichotomous with respect to x_2 and varying continuously only with x_1. Alternatively, the sharing rule can be viewed as being a function of the total output, $x_1 + x_2$, subject to the condition that the observed x_2 is in agreement with the observed value of x_1 and the inferred value of θ. In either view of the sharing rule, lack of agreement between the observed values of x_2 and x_1 is taken as evidence of shirking; accordingly, a penalty is imposed in such situations. If the penalty is sufficiently severe, the penalty need never be imposed, since the agent will choose to avoid the penalty by choosing $a_2^*(x_1)$. Determination of the optimal sharing rule can hence be confined to determination of the optimal function $s(x_1)$; furthermore, no first-order condition is required in order to induce $a_2^*(x_1)$, as long as a_1^* is properly induced.

The principal's problem can therefore be written as follows:

$$\underset{s(x_1), a_1, a_2(x_1)}{\text{maximize:}} \quad \int W[x_1 + x_2(\theta(x_1, a_1), a_2(x_1)) - s(x_1)] f(x_1 | a_1) \, dx_1$$

$$\text{subject to:} \quad \int [U(s(x_1)) - V(a_1, a_2(x_1))] f(x_1 | a_1) \, dx_1 \geq \bar{u}$$

$$\int [U(s(x_1)) - V(a_1, a_2(x_1))] f_{a_1}(x_1 | a_1) \, dx_1 - \int V_{a_1}(a_1, a_2(x_1)) f(x_1 | a_1) \, dx_1 = 0$$

In order to determine the first-order conditions, let λ and μ be the Lagrangian multipliers for the first and second constraints, respectively, and form the Hamiltonian H in the usual way. If the principal is risk neutral, as is commonly assumed in order to focus on motivational rather than risk-sharing issues, then the first-order conditions reduce to

$$\frac{1}{U'(s(x_1))} = \lambda + \mu \frac{f_{a_1}(x_1 | a_1)}{f(x_1 | a_1)} \tag{7.3}$$

$$\begin{aligned}
&\int \frac{\partial x_2}{\partial \theta} \frac{\partial \theta}{\partial a_1} f(x_1 | a_1)\, dx_1 + \int W(\cdot) f_{a_1}(x_1 | a_1)\, dx_1 \\
&+ \mu \int \{[U(s(x_1)) - V(a_1, a_2(x_1))] f_{a_1 a_1}(x_1 | a_1)\, dx_1 \\
&\qquad - 2V_{a_1}(a_1, a_2(x_1)) f_{a_1}(x_1 | a_1) \\
&\qquad - V_{a_1 a_1}(a_1, a_2(x_1)) f(x_1 | a_1)\}\, dx_1 = 0
\end{aligned} \tag{7.4}$$

and

$$\begin{aligned}
&\frac{\partial x_2}{\partial a_2} f(x_1 | a_1) - \lambda V_{a_2}(a_1, a_2(x_1)) f(x_1 | a_1) \\
&\qquad - \mu [V_{a_2}(a_1, a_2(x_1)) f_{a_1}(x_1 | a_1) \\
&\qquad + V_{a_1 a_2}(a_1, a_2(x_1)) f(x_1 | a_1)] = 0
\end{aligned} \tag{7.5}$$

Dividing equation (7.5) by $f(x_1 | a_1)$ and rearranging yields

$$\frac{\partial x_2}{\partial a_2} = \left[\lambda + \mu \frac{f_{a_1}(x_1 | a_1)}{f(x_1 | a_1)}\right] V_{a_2}(a_1, a_2(x_1)) + \mu V_{a_1 a_2}(a_1, a_2(x_1)) \tag{7.6}$$

In order to interpret (7.6), equation (7.3) can be substituted into equation (7.6) to obtain

$$\frac{\partial x_2}{\partial a_2} = \frac{1}{U'(s(x_1))} V_{a_2}(a_1, a_2(x_1)) + \mu V_{a_1 a_2}(a_1, a_2(x_1)) \tag{7.7}$$

The right-hand side of (7.7) captures the tradeoff between the agent's marginal utility for wealth and marginal disutility for second-stage effort, and the interaction between the effort levels in the two stages. If there is no interaction between the effort levels, equation (7.7) can be thought of as requiring a balancing of the "information" and "wealth" effects of x_1.

It is easily seen that if equation (7.6) is to hold for almost every x_1, then $a_2(\cdot)$ must in general vary with x_1. The precise behavior of a_2^* as x_1 varies can be determined by differentiating equation (7.6) with respect to x_1. This will be illustrated for two special cases: (i) $x_i = \theta + a_i$, where θ is purely noise, and (ii) $x_i = \theta a_i$, where θ reveals information about the production technology. In case (i), the marginal output per unit of effort is one, regardless of the value of θ. In case (ii), however, the marginal output per unit of effort is θ. To illustrate the results, suppose that $V(\cdot) = a_1^2 a_2^2$.

Pure Noise. For case (i), assume that $\theta \sim N(0, \sigma^2)$. Then $x_1 \sim N(a_1, \sigma^2)$ and $f_{a_1}/f = (x_1 - a_1)/\sigma^2$. Solving for $a_2(x_1)$ directly from (7.6) provides

$$a_2^*(x_1) = [2a_1^2(\lambda + \mu(x_1 - a_1)/\sigma^2) + 4\mu a_1]^{-1}$$

Differentiating with respect to x_1,

$$(a_2^*)'(x_1) = -2\mu a_1^2 a_2^2/\sigma^2$$

Therefore, $(a_2^*)'(x_1) < 0$, provided that $\mu > 0$.

In this case, the sign of $(a_2^*)'$ is the same as in the independent outcome situation described in proposition 7.2, where there was no information about x_2 to be gained from x_1. The case (i) result here might be interpreted as indicating that the wealth effect of x_1 dominates any information effect that exists through perfect correlation of the outcomes. It should be noted, however, that the only information provided in this case is information about the random noise, not about the agent's marginal productivity. Assuming that the θ's are ordered so that $\partial x_i/\partial\theta > 0$, a high value of x_1 given a_1^* reveals that θ was relatively high. This in turn implies that for any given value of a_2, x_2 will be relatively high. The result is that the higher the value of x_1, the less effort the agent is required to exert in the second stage.

Production Technology Information. For case (ii), assume $\theta \sim \exp(1)$. Then $x_1 \sim \exp(a_1)$ and $x_2 = x_1 a_2(x_1)/a_1$. Substituting $\partial x_2/\partial a_2 = \theta = x_1/a_1$ into (7.6) and solving for $a_2(x_1)$ provides

$$a_2^*(x_1) = x_1\{2a_1^2[a_1(\lambda + \mu(x_1 - a_1)/a_1^2) + 2\mu]\}^{-1}$$

Differentiating with respect to x_1, for $x_1 > 0$,

$$(a_2^*)'(x_1) = 2(a_1\lambda + \mu)a_1^2 a_2^2/x_1^2$$

Therefore, $(a_2^*)'(x_1) > 0$, provided that $\lambda, \mu > 0$.

Although θ is purely noise in case (i), risk is imposed on the agent for motivational purposes in order to induce a Pareto optimal choice of a_1. The effort strategy $a_2(x_1)$ is primarily determined by the wealth effect of x_1, leading to a decreasing function of x_1 just as in the case when the outcomes were assumed to be independent (see proposition 7.2). In case (ii), where the marginal output per unit of effort is θ, the agent receives perfect information about the production technology that was not relevant in case (i). If x_1 and hence θ are large in case (ii), then the agent's marginal productivity is large, and it is profitable for the principal to induce a relatively high level of a_2. The information effect of x_1 now overrides the wealth effect, so that a_2^* is an increasing function of x_1.

Illustration of Imperfect Correlation

A general analysis of imperfect correlation between $x_1|a_1$ and $x_2|a_2$ is hampered by the dependence of the results on the specific form of the joint distribution $\phi(\cdot)$, as shown below. Some insight can be gained by considering the following examples, chosen to facilitate comparison with the independent and perfect correlation examples given earlier.

Suppose that $g(x_2|x_1, a_2(x_1))$ is exponential with mean $M_2(x_1) = x_1^b a_2(x_1)$. Since the exponential distribution is a one-parameter distribution, we may write $g(x_2|x_1, a_2(x_1)) = g(x_2|M_2(x_1))$, and proposition 7.2 can be applied. For concreteness, suppose as before that $V(a_1, a_2) = a_1^2 a_2^2$. Then $V_2 = 2a_1^2 a_2 > 0$, $V_{22} = 2a_1^2 > 0$, $V_{222} = 0$, and $V_{122} = 4a_1 > 0$, so that the conditions in proposition 7.2, ii(c) are satisfied. Substituting $a_2(x_1) = M_2(x_1)/x_1^b$ into the expression for V_2 yields $V_2 = 2a_1^2 M_2(x_1)/x_1^b$, which is still positive. Therefore, if μ_1 is positive, then $M_2(x_1) = x_1^b a_2(x_1)$ is decreasing in x_1. That is,

$$bx^{b-1} a_2(x_1) + x_1^b a_2'(x_1) < 0 \tag{7.8}$$

If b is positive, then it is easily seen that $a_2(x_1)$ is decreasing in x_1, as when b is zero (the "independent" case). In this situation, as when there is perfect correlation with the normal distribution in case (i), the wealth effect of x_1 is dominant. Recall that case (ii) of the perfect-correlation analysis assumed that $x_i = \theta a_i$, so that $x_2 = x_1 a_2(x_1)/a_1$. This seems similar to the imperfect correlation example in which $M_2(x_1) = x_1 a_2(x_1)$. However, the signs of $(a_2^*)'(x_1)$ are opposite in these perfect and imperfect correlation cases. This can be interpreted as follows: in the presence of information related to the production technology, the wealth effect of x_1 is dominant if the correlation is imperfect; the information effect of x_1 is dominant only if the correlation is perfect.

If b is negative, then the behavior of $a_2(x_1)$ is potentially much more complex. Now the first term in (7.8) is negative, so that $a_2'(x_1)$ may be positive or negative. It could be, for example, that because of the interactions of the wealth and information effects of x_1, $a_2(x_1)$ is increasing for low values of x_1 and decreasing for high values of x_1.

Summary and Discussion

This paper examined the problem of sequential effort decisions within one period. The sequential aspect arose because the agent observed an outcome affected by the first effort choice before making the second effort choice, which affected a second outcome. The agent was paid only after both efforts were exerted and both outcomes were observed.

In the first-best case, if one person is risk neutral and the other is risk averse, then the risk neutral person bears the risk. If both the principal and the agent are risk averse, then the risk is shared, with the sharing rule a function of the sum of the outcomes.

If both of the individuals are risk averse, then the optimal second-stage effort strategy will depend on x_1, the first outcome. The second-stage effort strategy will also depend on x_1 if the joint density of the two outcomes given the actions is $f(x_1|a_1)g(x_2|x_1, a_1, a_2(\cdot))$. However, if at least one of the individuals is risk neutral and the joint density of the two outcomes given the actions is $f(x_1|a_1)g(x_2|a_2(\cdot))$ then the optimal second-stage effort strategy will be independent of x_1.

The second-stage effort strategy may depend on x_1 because of a wealth (risk aversion) effect, or because of an information effect. The wealth effect occurs when both individuals are risk averse, because a risk averse individual's marginal utility varies at different points of the utility curve. The first outcome determines where on the utility curve the individual is, so the individual will want the second-stage effort adjusted according to the value of the first outcome. The information effect occurs when the two outcomes are dependent. Depending on the nature of the correlation between the two outcomes, the principal may wish to induce the agent to choose the second-stage effort strategy to be an increasing or decreasing function of the first outcome. Proposition 7.1 provides a precise expression for the derivative of the second-stage effort strategy with respect to the first outcome.

The behavior of the second effort strategy can be related to income-smoothing. Lambert [1984] discussed income-smoothing as optimal equilibrium behavior, drawing on his [1983] two-period agency analysis with independent outcomes. His discussion centered on "real" smoothing (involving production and investment decisions, as opposed to choice of accounting techniques) across two periods toward the ex ante expected income for the two periods. He concludes that with independent outcomes, a square-root utility function for the agent, and utility functions that are additively separable across time periods, the optimal second-period effort is decreasing in the first-period outcome. In Lambert's context, this is *income-smoothing*. Proposition 7.2 provides a similar result in the one-period sequential choice setting.

The optimality of income-smoothing becomes a more complex question when correlation of the outcomes is introduced. The analysis in the second-best case allowed for nonindependence of the outcomes. As usual, the principal was assumed to be risk neutral and the agent was assumed to be risk averse. It was shown in an example that with perfect correlation and a state that represents random noise, the second effort strategy is decreasing in the first outcome. In another example, it was shown that with perfect correlation and a state that reveals the marginal productivity of the agent, the second effort strategy is *increasing* in the first outcome. With imperfect correlation, the behavior of the second effort strategy is highly dependent on the specific form of the joint distribution of the outcomes.

Notes

1. In the notation introduced later in the paper, the result can be stated as (i) $\mu_1 > 0$, and (ii) $\mu_2(x_1) > 0$ for almost every x_1.

2. Suppose that the principal is risk neutral and the agent is risk averse. Since the optimal sharing rule is constant, the function to be maximized (ignoring constants) is

$$\int [\![x_1 + \{ \int [x_2 - \lambda V(a_1, a_2(\cdot))] g(x_2|a_2(\cdot)) dx_2 \}]\!] f(x_1|a_1) dx_1 \tag{7N.1}$$

For each fixed x_1, maximizing the expression inside the braces with respect to a_2 will maximize (7N.1) with respect to a_2. Since the expression depends on x_1 only through a_2, $a_2(\cdot)$ is the same for almost every x_1. That is, a_2 does not depend on x_1. A similar analysis can be done for the case where the principal is risk averse and the agent is risk neutral.

3. The function to be maximized is

$$\int [\int W(x - s(\mathbf{x})) g(x_2|x_1, a_1, a_2(\cdot))\, dx_2] f(x_1|a_1) dx_1$$
$$+ \lambda [\int \{ \int U(s(\mathbf{x})) g(x_2|x_1, a_1, a_2(\cdot)) dx_2 - V(a_1, a_2(\cdot)) \} f(x_1|a_1) dx_1]$$

In this case, $a_2(\cdot)$ will generally depend on x_1.

4. Differentiating the Hamiltonian with respect to a_2 for every fixed x_1 and evaluating at $\mathbf{a} = \mathbf{a}^*$ yields

$$\int (x - s(x_1, x_2)) \phi_{a_2}(\cdot) dx_2$$
$$+ \mu_1 \{ \int U(s(\cdot)) [g_{a_1 a_2} f + g_{a_2} f_{a_1}] \mathrm{d}x_2 - (V_{a_1 a_2} f + V_{a_2} f_{a_1}) \}$$
$$+ \mu_2(x_1) \{ \int U(s(\cdot)) g_{a_2 a_2}(\cdot) dx_2 - V_{a_2 a_2}(\cdot) \} f(x_1|a_1) = 0$$

Clearly, the strategy $a_2^*(\cdot)$ depends on x_1 in general.

5. See the proof of ii (c) in appendix 7B.

APPENDIX 7A
Properties of Distributions in Q

$$f(x|a) = \exp[z(a)x - B(z(a))]\,h(x)$$

	Exponential	*Gamma*	*Poisson*
$f(x\|a)$	$\frac{1}{M(a)}\exp\left[\frac{-x}{\hat{M}(a)}\right]$	$\frac{\lambda^n x^{n-1} e^{-\lambda x}}{\Gamma(n)}$	$\exp[-M(a)]\frac{(M(a))^x}{x!}$
$E(x\|a)$	$M(a)$	$M(a)\ (= n/\lambda)$	$M(a)$
$\mathrm{var}\,(x\|a)$	$M^2(a)$	$\frac{M^2(a)}{n}$	$M(a)$
$z(a)$	$-\frac{1}{M(a)}$	$-\frac{n}{M(a)}$	$\ln M(a)$
$B(z)$	$-\ln(-z)$	$n\ln\left(-\frac{n}{z}\right)$	$\exp(z)$

	Exponential	*Gamma*	*Poisson*
$B'(z)$	$-\frac{1}{z}$	$-\frac{n}{z}$	$\exp(z)$
$B''(z)$	$\frac{1}{z^2}$	$\frac{n}{z^2}$	$\exp(z)$
f_a/f	$\frac{M'(a)}{M^2(a)}(x - M(a))$	$\frac{nM'(a)}{M^2(a)}(x - M(a))$	$\frac{M'(a)}{M(a)}(x - M(a))$

APPENDIX 7B

Proof of Proposition 7.1

Under the given assumptions, $a_2(\cdot)$ will depend on x_1. Let $M_1(a_1)$ denote the mean of x_1 given a_1, and let $M_2(x_1, a_1, a_2(\cdot))$ denote the conditional mean of x_2 with respect to $g(\cdot)$. The function to be maximized is

$$\begin{aligned}&\textstyle\iint (x_1 + x_2)\phi(\cdot)dx_2dx_1 - \lambda\iint V(a_1, a_2(\cdot))\phi(\cdot)dx_2dx_1\\ &\quad = \textstyle\int x_1 f(x_1|a_1)dx_1 + \int M_2(\cdot)f(x_1|a_1)dx_1 - \lambda\int V(\cdot)f(x_1|a_1)dx_1\\ &\quad = M_1(a_1) + E_1 M_2(\cdot) - \lambda E_1 V(\cdot)\end{aligned}$$

where E_1 represents expectation with respect to $f(\cdot)$. The first-order condition with respect to $a_2(\cdot)$ is then

$$\frac{\partial M_2(\cdot)}{\partial a_2} = \lambda\frac{\partial V(\cdot)}{\partial a_2} \tag{7B.1}$$

for almost every x_1 and for $a_1 = a_1^*$. The sign of $(a_2^*)'(x_1)$ can be determined by taking the derivative of (7B.1) with respect to x_1. Let the second and third subscripts of j on M_2 denote partial differentiation of M_2 with respect to the

jth argument of $M_2(x_1, a_1, a_2(\cdot))$. Taking the derivative of (7B.1) with respect to x_1 results in

$$M_{233}(a_2^*)' + M_{231} = \lambda[\partial^2 V(\cdot)/\partial a_2^2](a_2^*)'$$

or

$$(a_2^*)'(x_1) = \frac{-M_{231}}{M_{233} - \lambda[\partial^2 V(\cdot)/\partial a_2^2]} \qquad \text{Q.E.D.}$$

Proof of Proposition 7.2

Since $f(\cdot)$ and $g(\cdot)$ are in Q they can be written as

$$f(x_1|a) = \exp[z_1(a)x_1 - B_1(z_1(a))]h_1(x_1)$$

and

$$g(x_2|a) = \exp[z_2(a)x_2 - B_2(z_2(a))]h_2(x_2)$$

We have $a = E(x_i|a) = B_i'(z_i(a))$, $\text{var}(x_i|a) = B_i''(z_i(a))$, and $f_a/f = z_1'(a)(x_1 - a_1)$. Let $C_i = \mu_i z_i'(a_i^*)(x_i - a_i^*)$, where μ_2 denotes $\mu_2(x_1)$. Then $s(x) = (\lambda + C_1 + C_2)^2$.

Some helpful quantities will first be calculated.

$$\begin{aligned}&\iint (x_1 + x_2) f(x_1|a_1) g(x_2|a_2(x_1)) dx_1\, dx_2\\ &\quad = x_1 f(x_1|a_1)dx_1 + \int[\int x_2 g(x_2|a_2(x_1))dx_2] f(x_1|a_1)dx_1\\ &\quad = a_1 + \int a_2(x_1) f(x_1|a_1)dx_1 \end{aligned} \qquad (7B.2)$$

$$\begin{aligned}&\iint s(x_1, x_2) f(x_1|a_1) g(x_2|a_2(x_1)) dx_1\, dx_2\\ &\quad = \iint (D + F + G) f(x_1|a_1) g(x_2|a_2(\cdot)) dx_1\, dx_2\end{aligned} \qquad (7B.3)$$

where $D = (\lambda + C_1)^2$, $F = 2(\lambda + C_1)C_2$, and $G = C_2^2$.

$$\begin{aligned}E(D) &= \iint [\lambda^2 + 2\lambda\mu_1 z_1'(a_1^*)(x_1 - a_1^*)\\ &\quad + \mu_1^2 z_1'(a_1^*)^2(x_1 - a_1^*)^2] f(x_1|a_1) g(x_2|a_2(\cdot)) dx_1\, dx_2\\ &= \lambda^2 + 2\lambda\mu_1 z_1'(a_1^*)(a_1 - a_1^*)\\ &\quad + \mu_1^2 z_1'(a_1^*)^2(\text{var}(x_1|a_1) + a_1^2 - 2a_1^* a_1 + (a_1^*)^2]\end{aligned}$$

since $E(x - a^*)^2 = \text{var}(x) + (Ex)^2 - 2a^* Ex + (a^*)^2$.

$$\begin{aligned}E(F) &= 2\lambda \iint \mu_2(x_1) z_2'(a_2^*)[x_2 - a_2^*(\cdot)] f(x_1|a_1) g(x_2|a_2(\cdot)) dx_1\, dx_2\\ &\quad + 2\mu_1 \iint z_1'(a_1^*)(x_1 - a_1^*)\mu_2(x_1) z_2'(a_2^*(\cdot))\\ &\quad \times (x_2 - a_2^*(\cdot)) f(\cdot) g(\cdot) dx_1\, dx_2\\ &= 2\lambda \int \mu_2(x_1) z_2'(a_2^*)[a_2(x_1) - a_2^*(x_1)] f(x_1|a_1)\, dx_1\\ &\quad + 2\mu_1 z_1'(a_1^*) \int z_2'(a_2^*(\cdot))\mu_2(x_1)(x_1 - a_1^*)(a_2(\cdot) - a_2^*(\cdot)) f(\cdot) dx_1\end{aligned}$$

$$E(G) = \iint \mu_2^2(x_1) z_2'(a_2^*)^2(\cdot)(x_2 - a_2^*(\cdot))^2 f(\cdot) g(\cdot) dx_1 dx_2$$
$$= \int z_2'(a_2^*)^2(\cdot)\mu_2^2(x_1)[\text{var}(x_2|a_2(\cdot))$$
$$+ a_2^2(\cdot) - 2a_2^*(\cdot)a_2(\cdot) + (a_2^*)^2(\cdot)] f(\cdot) dx_1$$

$$\iint 2\sqrt{s(x)}\, f(x_1|a_1) g(x_2|a_2(\cdot)) dx_1 dx_2 - \int V(a_1, a_2(\cdot)) f(x_1|a_1) dx_1$$
$$= 2\iint [\lambda + \mu_1 z_1'(a_1^*)(x_1 - a_1^*)$$
$$+ \mu_2(x_1) z_2'(a_2^*(\cdot))(x_2 - a_2^*(\cdot))] f(\cdot) g(\cdot) dx_1 dx_2$$
$$- \int V(a_1, a_2(\cdot)) f(x_1|a_1) dx_1$$
$$= 2\lambda + 2\mu_1 z_1'(a_1^*)(a_1 - a_1^*)$$
$$+ 2\int \mu_2(x_1) z_2'(a_2^*(\cdot))[a_2(\cdot) - a_2^*(\cdot)] f(\cdot) dx_1$$
$$- \int V(a_1, a_2(\cdot)) f(x_1|a_1) dx_1 \qquad (7B.4)$$

$$\frac{\partial(7B.4)}{\partial a_1} = 2\mu_1 z_1'(a_1^*) + 2\int \mu_2(x_1) z_2'(a_2^*(\cdot))[a_2(\cdot) - a_2^*(\cdot)] f_{a_1} dx_1$$
$$- \int V_{a_1} f(x_1|a_1) dx_1 - \int V(\cdot) f_{a_1}(x_1|a_1) dx_1 \qquad (7B.5)$$

Fix x_1: $$\frac{\partial(7B.4)}{\partial a_2} = 2\mu_2(x_1) z_2'(a_2^*(\cdot)) f(x_1|a_1) - V_{a_2}(\cdot) f(x_1|a_1) \qquad (7B.6)$$

Result i

Setting (7B.6) equal to zero and solving for $\mu_2(x_1)$ yields

$$\mu_2(x_1) = \frac{V_{a_2}(\mathbf{a}^*)}{2z_2'(a_2^*(x_1))} \qquad (7B.7)$$

Recall that $B_2'(z_2(a)) = a$, so that $B_2'' z_2' = 1$. Since B_2'' is a variance, z_2' must be positive. Therefore, $\mu_2(x_1) > 0$ if $V_{a_2}(\cdot) > 0$.

Results ii(a) and ii(b)

After x_1 is realized, the agent's expected utility given x_1 and $a_2^*(x_1)$ is

$$2\int \sqrt{s(x)}\, g(x_2|a_2^*(x_1)) dx_2 - V(a_1^*, a_2^*(x_1))$$
$$- 2\int [\lambda + \mu_1 z_1'(a_1^*)(x_1 - a_1^*) + \mu_2(x_1) z_2'(a_2^*(x_1))$$
$$\times (x_2 - a_2^*(x_1))] g(x_2|\cdot) dx_2 - V(a_1^*, a_2^*(x_1))$$
$$= 2[\lambda + \mu_1 z_1'(a_1^*)(x_1 - a_1^*)] - V(a_1^*, a_2^*(x_1))$$

Differentiating with respect to x_1 yields

$$2\mu_1 z_1'(a_1^*) - V_{a_2}(\cdot)(a_2^*)'(x_1)$$

The agent's expected utility for the second-stage *pecuniary* return (i.e., $s(\mathbf{x})$) is an increasing function of x_1 (assuming $\mu_1 > 0$). This establishes result ii(a). Assuming further that $V_{a_2}(\cdot) > 0$, a sufficient condition for the agent's expected second-stage *net* utility to be increasing in x_1 is that $a_2^*(x_1)$ be a decreasing function of x_1. This establishes result ii(b).

Result ii(c)

Fix x_1 and let a_2 denote $a_2(x_1)$, and f denote $f(x_1|a_1)$. Using (7B.2) through (7B.6),

$$\begin{aligned}\frac{\partial H}{\partial a_2} &= f - 2\lambda\mu_2(x_1)z_2'(a_2^*)f - 2\mu_1 z_1'(a_1^*)z_2'(a_2^*)\mu_2(x_1)(x_1 - a_1^*)f \\ &\quad - z_2'(a_2^*)^2\mu_2^2(x_1)[B_2'''(z_2(a_2))z_2'(a_2) + 2a_2 - 2a_2^*]f \\ &\quad + \mu_1[2\mu_2(x_1)z_2'(a_2^*)f_{a_1} - V_{a_1a_2}f - V_{a_2}(\cdot)f_{a_1}] - \mu_2(x_1)V_{a_2a_2}(\cdot)f \\ \frac{1}{f}\cdot\frac{\partial H}{\partial a_2}\bigg|_{a^*} &= 1 - 2\mu_2(x_1)\left[\lambda z_2'(a_2^*) + \frac{V_{a_2a_2}}{2}\right] - \frac{\mu_1 V_{a_2}f_{a_1}}{f}\bigg|_{a^*} \\ &\quad - \mu_1 V_{a_1a_2} - \mu_2^2(x_1)z_2'(a_2^*)^3 B_2'''(z_2(a_2^*)) = 0\end{aligned}$$

(Note that $f_{a_1}/f|_{a^*} - z_1'(a_1^*)(x_1 - a_1^*) = 0$.)

Substituting the expression for $\mu_2(x_1)$ from (7B.7) above and letting subscripts j on V represent partial differentiation with respect to the jth effort variable yields

$$1 - \lambda V_2 - \frac{V_2 V_{22}}{2z_2'} - \mu_1 V_2 z_1'(x_1 - a_1) - \mu_1 V_{12} - \frac{V_2^2 z_2' B_2'''}{4} = 0$$

Differentiating with respect to x_1,

$$\begin{aligned}&-\lambda V_{22}a_2' - \frac{a_2'}{2}\left[\frac{V_{22}^2 + V_2 V_{222}}{z_2'} - \frac{V_2 V_{22} z_2''}{(z_2')^2}\right] \\ &- \mu_1[V_{122}a_2' + V_{22}a_2' z_1'(x_1 - a_1) + V_2 z_1'] \\ &- \frac{a_2'}{4}[2V_2 V_{22} z_2' B_2''' + V_2^2 z_2'' B_2''' + V_2^2(z_2')^2 B_2''''] = 0\end{aligned}$$

Rearranging,

$$a_2'(x_1) = -\mu_1 V_2 z_1'/L$$

where

$$L = \left(\lambda + \mu_1 \frac{f_{a_1}}{f}\right) V_{22} + \frac{V_{22}^2 + V_2 V_{222}}{2z_2'} - \frac{V_2 V_{22} z_2''}{(2z_2')^2}$$

$$+ \mu_1 V_{122} + \frac{V_2 V_{22} z_2' B_2'''}{2} + \frac{V_2^2 (z_2'' B_2''' + (z_2')^2 B_2'''')}{4}$$

Recall that it is assumed that $V_2 > 0$, $V_{22} \geq 0$, $V_{222} \geq 0$, and $V_{122} \geq 0$. It is easily checked that for the exponential, gamma, and Poisson distributions in Q, $z' > 0$, $z'' < 0$, $B'''' > 0$, and $z'' B''' + (z')^2 B'''' \geq 0$. These facts, plus the first-order condition requiring that $\lambda + \mu_1 f_{a_1}/f$ be positive, guarantee that the denominator of $a_2'(x_1)$ is positive. The sign of the numerator is the same as the sign of μ_1. Hence, if $\mu_1 > 0$, then $a_2^*(\cdot)$ is a decreasing function of x_1. This establishes result ii(c). Q.E.D.

References

Baiman, S. [1982]. "Agency Research in Managerial Accounting: A Survey." *Journal of Accounting Literature* 1, 154–213.

Baiman, S., and Evans, III, J. [1983]. "Pre-Decision Information and Participative Management Control Systems." *Journal of Accounting Research* 21, 371–395.

Christensen, J. [1981]. "Communication in Agencies." *Bell Journal of Economics* 12, 661–674.

Christensen, J. [1982]. "The Determination of Performance Standards and Participation." *Journal of Accounting Research* 20, 589–603.

Harris, M., and Raviv, A. [1979]. "Optimal Incentive Contracts with Imperfect Information." *Journal of Economic Theory* 20, 231–259.

Holmstrom, B. [1979]. "Moral Hazard and Observability." *Bell Journal of Economics* 10, 74–91.

Holmstrom, B., and Milgrom, P. [1985]. "Aggregation and Linearity in the Provision of Intertemporal Incentives." Technical Report No. 466, IMSSS, Stanford University.

Lambert, R. [1983]. "Long-Term Contracts and Moral Hazard." *Bell Journal of Economics* 14, 441–452.

Lambert, R. [1984]. "Income Smoothing as Rational Equilibrium Behavior." *Accounting Review* 59, 604–617.

Rogerson, W. [1985a]. "Repeated Moral Hazard." *Econometrica* 53, 69–76.

Rogerson, W. [1985b]. "The First-Order Approach to Principal-Agent Problems." *Econometrica* 53, 1353–1367.

Shavell, S. [1979]. "Risk Sharing and Incentives in the Principal and Agent Relationship." *Bell Journal of Economics* 10, 55–73.

8 RISK SHARING AND VALUATION UNDER MORAL HAZARD*

Patricia J. Hughes

Jensen and Meckling [1976] describe an agency problem between a firm's utility-maximizing manager and shareholders that arises because the firm's value can be reduced through the unobservable actions of the manager. Investors infer that the manager will undertake actions that maximize the manager's own welfare rather than the value of the firm and they price the firm's securities accordingly. In order to raise sufficient capital in the securities market, the manager voluntarily bonds himself to the shareholders' interests.

This paper provides a formal analysis of the Jensen–Meckling problem by following from the Ross [1973] and Holmstrom [1979] agency literature in which a principal seeks to share the risk of an outcome with an agent where the outcome depends upon both the realization of a random variable and an

* This paper is based upon a portion of my doctoral dissertation written at the University of British Columbia. I would like to thank Jerry Feltham and Rob Heinkel for helpful discussions and Deloitte, Haskins & Sells for financial support. I am grateful to Brett Trueman for helpful comments on this paper.

unobservable action of the agent. The primary distinction between the two approaches is that the normative Ross–Holmstrom literature derives optimal contracts and the positive Jensen–Meckling literature seeks to explain existing contractual arrangements. A limitation of the analysis of this paper is that the solution is restricted to linear risk sharing contracts. However, the analysis does embody important risk sharing features of the capital market that are absent in the Ross–Holmstrom literature.

It will be shown in this paper that the contracts actually observed between managers and shareholders may be the optimal response of a manager to suboptimal risk sharing. The analysis of the paper leads to the same empirical prediction as the financial signaling model of Leland and Pyle [1977], i.e., the market value of a firm will be positively related to managerial ownership in the firm. This suggests that the effects of asymmetric information about endogenous behavior and exogenous value may be similar, and that it may be difficult to distinguish between them empirically.

A discussion of the principal/agent problem in a securities-market setting appears in the next section. The problem is then formulated and the impacts on firm value and risk sharing between investors and a manager are analyzed. Additional restrictions are then imposed on the model so that explicit risk sharing and valuation solutions can be derived. A summary concludes the paper.

The Principal/Agent Problem in a Securities Market

In the two-person agency problem, the agent has a dual role: to undertake a productive action and to share risks with the principal. However, the securities market provides an opportunity for investors (principals) to share the risks of ownership in risky firms. Since well-diversified investors can perfectly share risks in the market, the primary role of a manager (agent) must be to provide some expertise in production. Pareto-optimal contracts would entail risk sharing among principals in the securities market and contracting with and compensating an agent for productive acts. However, such contracts are not feasible under moral hazard because the agent's actions are not observable. Therefore, as with the two-person problem, risk may be imposed upon the agent for incentive purposes despite the fact that perfect risk sharing is attainable in the market.[1]

The analysis of the principal/agent problem in a securities market has complexities that do not arise in the two-person problem. Specific issues include

1. The risk-sharing capabilities of the capital market are available to the agent as well as the principal. Consequently, the agent may select an investment portfolio that reduces the risk imposed on him for incentive purposes without altering the incentive aspects of the return he receives from his own firm.
2. Nondiversifiable market risk can serve as information about the variations in the firm's return that are due to factors beyond the agent's control.
3. Opportunities may exist for the manager to reduce the risk he must bear by altering the variance of cash flows generated by the firm's capital investments through selection of the firm's investment projects.
4. The agent's reservation level of expected utility can no longer be taken as exogenous, due to the existence of a market for managerial labor.
5. Coordination and contracting may be complex and costly due to the existence of many shareholders/principals and a possible hierarchy of agents.

Some of these additional issues have been addressed by Diamond and Verrecchia [1982], Marcus [1982], Beck and Zorn [1982], Campbell and Kracaw [1985], and Ramakrishnan and Thakor [1982]. However, the studies have been partial equilibrium analyses because the determination of the manager's market price has not been addressed.

An approach that eliminates the need to determine the market price for managerial expertise is to invert the usual principal/agent formulation to one in which (a) the manager offers to investors the investment contract that maximizes the manager's expected utility and (b) shareholders accept the contract if it provides a return equal to that of similar investment opportunities available in the market. Such an approach is used by Atkinson and Feltham [1983], wherein a risk-averse manager is endowed with capital and a productive technology requiring a capital investment in order to generate a return. The manager offers securities to the market in order to raise external capital, invests in the capital market and in the productive technology, and earns risky returns from both investments. A moral hazard problem arises because the manager's utility is defined over wealth and effort, and cash flows generated by the productive investment are dependent upon unobservable managerial effort.

An approach similar to that of Atkinson and Feltham is that of Jensen and Meckling [1976]. A risk-neutral owner/manager of a firm is endowed with a productive technology and seeks to raise capital in the market because he has insufficient wealth to finance the capital investment necessary to realize a return from the technology. A moral hazard problem arises because managerial actions are not observable and the manager can divert assets of the firm for personal consumption. Jensen and Meckling describe the behavior, which is suboptimal from the viewpoint of shareholders, as consumption of perquisites. However, such behavior may in effect be the same as shirking or reducing effort expenditure if both reduce the expected value of cash flows and are unobservable. When the owner/manager owns 100% of the equity in a firm, he receives 100% of the benefits of perquisite consumption and bears 100% of the cost. As his proportion of ownership declines, he bears less than 100% of the cost of his behavior while continuing to receive all the benefit. Nonmanaging prospective shareholders know the manager's utility function, can rationally infer the manager's behavior as his ownership declines, and will price the equity accordingly. The manager selects his proportion of firm ownership in order to maximize his return, where the market valuation of the equity sold is increasing in his proportionate ownership and his perquisite consumption is decreasing. Since Jensen and Meckling's manager is risk neutral, the additional cost arising from risk aversion does not enter their model.

Jensen and Meckling state that their approach differs fundamentally from the existing agency-theory literature.[2] However the two approaches are not substantially different if risk aversion is added to the Jensen–Meckling model and it is compared to the Atkinson–Feltham model. When the agent is risk averse, his ownership in his own firm clearly represents suboptimal risk sharing, which he selects in order to precommit his behavior to the market. The manager selects a compensation package composed of unobservable nontradeable riskless perquisites and observable nontradeable risky shares in order to maximize his expected utility. Jensen and Meckling are indirectly determining an optimal linear compensation contract in which a portion of the manager's compensation consists of returns from his own firm, which is a nontradeable asset and which imposes risk on him, in order to motivate him to act in the best interests of the owners of his firm.

The Entrepreneur's Decision Problem

In the problem at hand, an entrepreneur is endowed with a productive technology and can acquire the capital necessary for investment in the technology through the sale of equity in the future cash flows to be generated by the investment. In a capital market, Pareto optimal risk sharing among investors is attained when firm-specific risks are eliminated through portfolio diversification and aggregate market risk is shared by all investors according to their relative aversion to risks. Therefore, in the absence of any market imperfections, Pareto optimal risk sharing is attainable when the entrepreneur sells all of the equity in the risky cash flows and invests in a well-diversified market portfolio.

Investors and the entrepreneur have homogeneous beliefs about the exogenous distribution of cash flows generated by the capital investment. However, the entrepreneur can alter the distribution of cash flows through managerial actions that are unobservable by outside investors. The value of the firm thus becomes endogenous and unknown to investors. An information asymmetry between investors and the entrepreneur has been created under which Pareto optimal risk sharing may not be attainable.

The entrepreneur chooses his ownership in his firm, α, and his actions in order to maximize his expected utility. He can reduce cash flows in every state by (i) shirking, or reducing the amount of effort expended in managing the firm, and (ii) taking nonpecuniary benefits, or diverting assets of the firm to his personal use (e.g., supplying himself with a company car, or using the corporate jet for recreational travel). Perquisite consumption reduces cash flows by at least the cost of the assets consumed and shirking will result in reduced cash flows to the extent that they are dependent upon managerial actions. The reduction in cash flows in every state due to shirking and perquisite consumption will be denoted F.[3] Since perquisites affect only the expected value of cash flows, they are riskless to the entrepreneur. When α is equal to the Pareto optimal value of zero, the manager will receive 100% of the benefit of F while the firm's shareholders will bear 100% of the cost. When $\alpha > 0$, the manager continues to receive 100% of the benefit of F, but also bears the proportion α of the cost. Therefore as α increases, the manager's propensity to consume perquisites should decrease.

The problem of the entrepreneur is to select observable α and unobservable F along with investments in the market portfolio, β, and the riskless asset, Y, in order to maximize expected utility of end-of-period wealth, or

$$\underset{\alpha,\beta,F,Y}{\text{maximize}}\ E\{U(\tilde{W}_1, F)\} \tag{8.1}$$

subject to

$$W_0 + (1-\alpha)V(\alpha) - I - \beta V_m - Y = 0 \tag{8.2}$$

where

$$\tilde{W}_1 = \alpha(\tilde{x} - F) + \beta\tilde{M} + (1+r)Y \tag{8.3}$$

In (8.1) the entrepreneur derives utility from end-of-period wealth W_1 and perquisites F. Equation (8.2) is the budget constraint in which the entrepreneur has an initial wealth W_0 and sells a proportion $1-\alpha$ of ownership in the cash flows to be generated by the project after the capital investment I. For a proportional ownership of $1-\alpha$ in the future cash flows, investors are willing to pay $1-\alpha$ times the value of the project which they infer from observation of α, where $V(\alpha)$ is the inferred value of the project. Wealth remaining after the capital expenditure I is invested in the market portfolio and the riskless asset, where V_m is the market value of the market portfolio, β is the proportion of the market portfolio owned by the entrepreneur, and Y is the amount invested in the riskless asset. In equation (8.3), end-of-period wealth is composed of returns on the investment portfolio selected at the beginning of the period: $\tilde{x}$ is the firm's (i.e., capital investment's) end-of-period cash flow, $\tilde{M}$ is the cash flow on the market, and r is the risk-free rate of interest. A linear sharing rule, which is not likely to be optimal under moral hazard, is being assumed in this analysis. The consequent loss in generality is being accepted for analytical simplification.

In a perfect market, the value of a firm derived from the capital asset pricing model is the risk-adjusted present value of future cash flows, or

$$V = \frac{\mu - \lambda^0 \mathrm{cov}(\tilde{x}, \tilde{M})}{1+r}$$

where

$$\lambda^0 = \frac{\bar{M} - (1+r)V_m}{\sigma_m^2}$$

or

$$V = \frac{\mu - \lambda}{1+r}, \qquad \text{letting } \lambda = \lambda^0 \mathrm{cov}(\tilde{x}, \tilde{M}) \tag{8.4}$$

Since the effect of the entrepreneur's actions on the firm is a reduction in the expected value of cash flows μ, the entrepreneur's valuation of the firm becomes

$$V = \frac{\mu - F^* - \lambda}{1+r}$$

where F^* is the entrepreneur's choice of perquisites. An additional constraint on the optimization problem is the market rationality constraint that the market's inference is correct in equilibrium,

$$V(\alpha^*) = \frac{\mu - F(\alpha^*) - \lambda}{1+r} = \frac{\mu - F^* - \lambda}{1+r} = V \tag{8.5}$$

The entrepreneur is assumed to have a negative exponential utility function,

$$U(\tilde{W}_1) = -e^{-b\tilde{W}_1}$$

in which b is his coefficient of risk aversion. This assumption, together with that of normally distributed cash flows on all securities, simplifies the objective function to

$$\max_{\alpha, \beta, F, Y} \bar{W}_1 - \frac{b}{2}\sigma^2_{w_1}$$

where $\bar{W}_1$ is the expected value of $\tilde{W}_1$, and $\sigma^2_{w_1}$ is the variance of $\tilde{W}_1$.

In the entrepreneur's objective function, perquisites, F, is separated from wealth because utility is derived from the consumption of nonmarketable benefits such as perquisites or shirking. In the usual formulation of a two-person agency problem, the agent's utility is assumed to be additively separable in wealth and effort. Similarly here, a separate utility function for perquisites could be defined so that the objective function becomes $E\{U(\tilde{W}_1) + G(F)\}$. However, in order to maintain the analytical simplification provided by the combination of a normal distribution and negative exponential utility function, the approach to be taken is to transfer the benefits of F into equivalent dollars of wealth.

The transformation of F into equivalent dollars of wealth is accomplished by introducing a transformation function $T(F)$ which satisfies the following conditions:

i. $T(0) = 0$.
ii. $T(F) > 0$ for $F > 0$ because benefits are derived from any positive level of perquisites or shirking.
iii. $0 < T'(F) < 1$ since more perquisites are preferred to less and they are not tradeable.

Additional conditions which impose sufficient regularity on $T(F)$ in order to satisfy the second-order conditions of the problem are

iv. $T''(F) < 0$.
v. $T'''(F) > 0$.

Thus $T(F)$ is a type of "utility" function which transforms F to dollars of wealth rather than utiles. Figure 8–1 depicts an acceptable transformation.

$T(F)$ is measured in the same units as wealth and can therefore be combined with wealth in a single utility function:

$$U(\tilde{W}_1, F) = -e^{-b(\tilde{W}_1 + T(F))}$$

Therefore, because F is riskless, the entrepreneur's objective function can be rewritten as

$$\underset{\alpha, \beta, F, Y}{\text{maximize}}\ \bar{W}_1 - \frac{b}{2}\sigma^2_{w_1} + T(F)$$

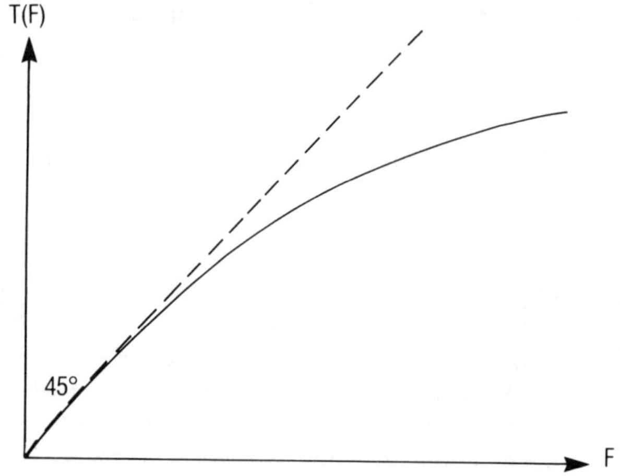

Figure 8–1. Perquisite Transformation Function

After elimination of Y by combining (8.2) and (8.3), end-of-period wealth becomes

$$\tilde{W}_1 = \alpha(\tilde{x} - F) + \beta\tilde{M} + (1+r)[W_0 + (1-\alpha)V(\alpha) - I - \beta V_m] \quad (8.6)$$

After substitution for $V(\alpha)$ using (8.5) and simplification, (8.6) becomes

$$\tilde{W}_1 = \alpha[\tilde{x} - F - \mu + F(\alpha) + \lambda] + \beta[\tilde{M} - (1+r)V_m] + \mu - F(\alpha) - \lambda + (1+r)(W_0 - I) \quad (8.7)$$

The expected value and variance of (8.7) are

$$\bar{W}_1 = \alpha[\mu - F - \mu + F(\alpha) + \lambda] + \beta[\bar{M} - (1+r)V_m] + \mu - F(\alpha) - \lambda + (1+r)(W_0 - I) \quad (8.8)$$

$$\sigma^2_{w_1} = \alpha^2\sigma^2 + \beta^2\sigma^2_m + 2\alpha\beta\,\mathrm{cov}(\tilde{x}, \tilde{M}) \quad (8.9)$$

where σ^2 and σ^2_m are the variances of $\tilde{x}$ and $\tilde{M}$, respectively.

Let

$$H(\alpha, \beta, F) \equiv \bar{W}_1 - \frac{b}{2}\sigma^2_{w_1} + T(F)$$

The first-order conditions to the problem are

$$\frac{\partial H}{\partial \alpha} = \mu - F - \mu + F(\alpha) + \lambda + (\alpha - 1)F_\alpha - \alpha b\sigma^2 - \beta b\,\mathrm{cov}(\tilde{x}, \tilde{M}) = 0 \quad (8.10)$$

$$\frac{\partial H}{\partial \beta} = \bar{M} - (1+r)V_m - \beta b \sigma_m^2 - \alpha b \operatorname{cov}(\tilde{x}, \tilde{M}) = 0 \qquad (8.11)$$

$$\frac{\partial H}{\partial F} = -\alpha + T'(F) = 0 \qquad (8.12)$$

In order to eliminate β from the problem, (8.11) is solved for βb and then substituted into (8.10):

$$-F + F(\alpha) + (\alpha - 1)F_\alpha - \alpha b\left[\frac{\sigma^2\sigma_m^2 - \operatorname{cov}(\tilde{x}, \tilde{M})^2}{\sigma_m^2}\right] = 0 \qquad (8.13)$$

The market rationality condition (8.5) is combined with (8.13) to arrive at

$$(\alpha - 1)F_\alpha = \alpha b\left[\frac{\sigma^2\sigma_m^2 - \operatorname{cov}(\tilde{x}, \tilde{M})^2}{\sigma_m^2}\right] \qquad (8.14)$$

Equation (8.12) is rewritten as

$$T'(F) = \alpha \qquad (8.15)$$

Equations (8.14) and (8.15) are the necessary equilibrium conditions, each equating marginal benefit and marginal cost for a choice variable. In (8.14) the benefit of communication through ownership in the firm is the increase in proceeds $(\alpha - 1)F_\alpha$ and the cost is the loss of a diversified investment portfolio. The entrepreneur must bear firm-specific risk, which is the term within brackets in (8.14), in order to "signal" his behavior. In (8.15) the benefit of perquisite consumption is the marginal increase in the wealth equivalent of perquisites $T'(F)$ and the cost of F is α, the entrepreneur's share of the cost of F. Figure 8–2 illustrates that the level of perquisite consumption selected is determined by the choice of α in that the slope of the transformation function at F^* is equal to α^*. Thus the market infers F from observation of α and the entrepreneur does indeed select F on the basis of α. It also is clear that the condition that $0 < T'(F) < 1$ is satisfied ensures that $0 < \alpha < 1$.

It was suggested earlier in this section that the manager's propensity to consume perquisites or to shirk should decrease as α increases. In order to verify this conjecture, totally differentiate (8.15) with respect to F and α:

$$T''(F)\,dF = d\alpha$$

or

$$\frac{dF}{d\alpha} = \frac{1}{T''(F)} < 0 \qquad (8.16)$$

from condition iv on $T(F)$. Therefore it is true that F is decreasing in α. The choice of F as a function of α is illustrated in figure 8–3. Convexity is proved

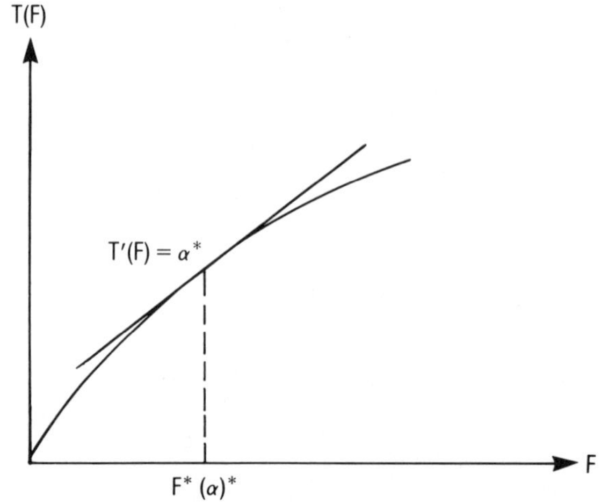

Figure 8–2. Choice of $F(\alpha^*)$

by differentiating (8.16) with respect to α:

$$\frac{d^2F}{d\alpha^2} = -\frac{1}{[T''(F)]^2} T'''(F) F_\alpha > 0 \tag{8.17}$$

follows from $T''' > 0$ and $F_\alpha < 0$. Since the market's inference is assumed to be rational, in equilibrium the market's inference schedule will also look like figure 8–3, and (8.16) can be substituted into (8.14) to arrive at the single necessary equilibrium condition:

$$\frac{(\alpha - 1)}{T''(F)} = \alpha b \left[\frac{\sigma^2 \sigma_m^2 - \operatorname{cov}(\tilde{x}, \tilde{M})^2}{\sigma_m^2} \right] \tag{8.18}$$

which has replaced the market's inference F_α with the entrepreneur's choice $F_\alpha = [1/T''(F)]$. Equation (8.18) relates choices of α and F to exogenous parameters. Calculations omitted from this paper establish that the second-order conditions are satisfied. Proofs of the following propositions appear in the appendix.

Proposition 8.1

An increase in firm specific risk will result in a decrease in equilibrium α^* and a corresponding increase in F^*.

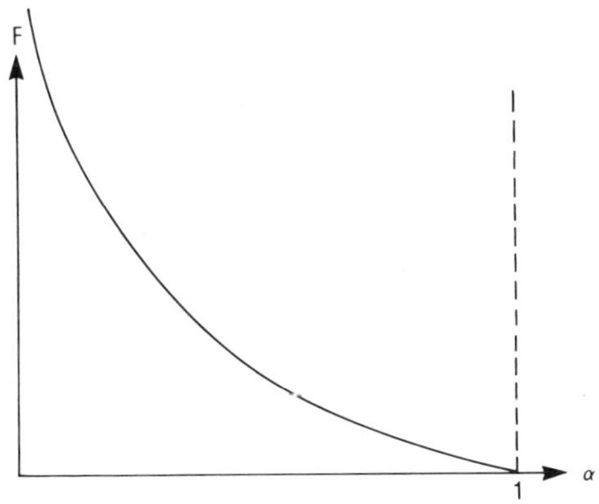

Figure 8–3. The Entrepreneur's $F(\alpha)$ Choice

Systematic risk can be efficiently shared in the capital market and, under perfect information, nonsystematic risk will be borne by well-diversified investors who do not demand a risk premium for bearing firm-specific risks. However, here the risk-averse agent accepts costly firm-specific risk in order to precommit his behavior to the market. If firm-specific risk increases, "signaling" with α becomes more costly and the entrepreneur increases his welfare by substituting riskless F for risky α. Because of this ability to select both the riskless and risky components of return from his own firm, perquisites serve as a substitute for increases in risk.

Proposition 8.2

An increase in the risk-aversion parameter b will result in a decrease in equilibrium α^* and a corresponding increase in F^*.

This result is similar to proposition 8.1. If b increases, communicating through α becomes more costly and therefore risky α is exchanged for riskless F.

Leland and Pyle [1977] reached the same conclusions as these propositions in their proposition II where α served as a signal of μ. Subsequent empirical tests of the Leland and Pyle model by Downes and Heinkel [1982] and Ritter [1984] found a statistically significant positive relationship between α and firm value. However, as proved in this paper, and suggested by Ritter, such a positive relationship can be explained by the existence of a moral hazard problem rather than the adverse selection problem addressed by Leland and Pyle.

Many of the studies cited earlier show how a manager may be motivated to reduce the variance of cash flows through the firm's investment policy, which he controls, in order to reduce the risk he must bear for incentive reasons. Diamond and Verrecchia [1982] describe systematic risk as being "observable" and conclude that reduction of firm-specific risk should result in improved risk sharing between a risk-averse agent and risk-neutral principal because effort is more easily detectable. It can be seen from (8.18) that firm-specific risk can be reduced if σ^2 is decreased or cov is increased. The following proposition formalizes the Diamond–Verrecchia conjecture.

Proposition 8.3

A reduction in firm-specific risk achieved through an ex ante anticipated reduction in σ^2 results in a greater expected utility for the entrepreneur and an increase in the market value of the firm *for a given covariance.*

A decrease in σ^2 reduces $\sigma^2_{w_1}$ and therefore improves the welfare of the entrepreneur in that the cost of communicating F by α has decreased. Market valuation increases because $F(\alpha)$ decreases as a result of a decrease in σ^2. In a perfect market, firm value is a function of systematic risk and changes in firm-specific risk should have no effect on valuation. However, when moral hazard is present and the manager must bear firm-specific risk as an agency cost, changes in that risk result in changes in his behavior and therefore in firm valuation that depends upon his behavior. Therefore, more efficient risk sharing does result when firm-specific risk is reduced, and the manager is better off.[4]

Shareholders are indifferent to the value of and changes in σ^2 ex ante because they correctly infer managerial behavior, and value the firm based upon observation of α; while the manager does gain by ex ante reduction in σ^2 as shown in part (i) of the proof (see appendix). On the other hand, ex post reduction of σ^2 does benefit shareholders as well as the manager because the value of the firm will increase despite no changes in the expected value and systematic risk of cash flows.

As shown in the appendix, firm-specific risk can be expressed as

$$\sigma^2_\varepsilon = \frac{\sigma^2 \sigma^2_m - \operatorname{cov}(\tilde{x}, \tilde{M})^2}{\sigma^2_m}$$

It is seen from equation (8A.1) in the appendix that α will approach the value of 1 as σ_ε^2 becomes very small because the costs of α become very small. If $\sigma_\varepsilon^2 = 0$, the firm's cash flows are perfectly correlated with those of the market portfolio so that the entrepreneur's investment in his own firm is a perfect substitute for an investment in the market. Therefore no moral hazard problem will exist if $\sigma_\varepsilon^2 = 0$: the entrepreneur will own 100% of the equity in future cash flows, will hold an investment in the market portfolio that complements the systematic risk in his firm, and hence will bear 100% of the cost of his behavior. Therefore, it is indeed true that the agency problem is minimized if firm-specific risk is very small.

Proposition 8.4

An anticipated decrease in $\text{cov}(\tilde{x}, \tilde{M})$, given constant σ_v^2, results in greater expected utility for the entrepreneur, *even if it results in greater firm-specific risk*. The effect on market value has two components and depends upon the sign of the covariance.

As shown in appendix equation (8A.3), (in the proof of proposition 8.4), if $\text{cov}(\tilde{x}, \tilde{M})$ decreases, the increase in the entrepreneur's expected utility has two sources: an increase in wealth due to the direct increase in the value of the firm and a reduction in the risk of his investment portfolio. From the first-order condition (8.11), the choice of β simplifies to:

$$\beta^* = \frac{\lambda^0}{b} - \frac{\alpha \,\text{cov}(\tilde{x}, \tilde{M})}{\sigma^2}$$

It can easily be shown that the optimal choice of α and β in a perfect market are

$$\alpha^0 = 0$$

$$\beta^0 = \frac{\lambda^0}{b}$$

β^0 is the optimal investment in the market portfolio for an investor with a coefficient of risk aversion b in order to bear an optimal amount of systematic market risk. If $\text{cov}(\tilde{x}, \tilde{M}) = 0$, then $\beta^* = \beta^0$ regardless of the level of α: if the firm is uncorrelated with the market, the entrepreneur will bear the optimal amount of systematic risk through his investment in the market portfolio. If $\text{cov}(\tilde{x}, \tilde{M}) > 0$, some systematic risk is held through the investment in his own firm and therefore the entrepreneur reduces his investment in the market by $\alpha \,\text{cov}(\tilde{x}, \tilde{M})$. If $\text{cov}(\tilde{x}, \tilde{M}) < 0$, the entrepreneur is "selling short" systematic risk through his investment α and therefore increases his investment in the market so as to acquire the desired amount of market risk. Therefore the choices of β^* in the present problem are

$$\beta^* < \beta^0 \quad \text{if } \operatorname{cov}(\tilde{x}, \tilde{M}) > 0$$

$$\beta^* > \beta^0 \quad \text{if } \operatorname{cov}(\tilde{x}, \tilde{M}) < 0$$

$$\beta^* = \beta^0 \quad \text{if } \operatorname{cov}(\tilde{x}, \tilde{M}) = 0$$

If the covariance changes while σ^2 is constant, firm-specific risk changes and therefore α will change. As both the covariance and α change, the entrepreneur will adjust β^* so that he continues to hold the optimal amount of systematic risk.

If $\operatorname{cov}(\tilde{x}, \tilde{M}) > 0$, a decrease in $\operatorname{cov}(\tilde{x}, \tilde{M})$ has the following effects:

Increase in $\sigma_\varepsilon^2 \rightarrow$	decrease in α^* because the signal α has become more costly.
Decrease in cov Decrease in α $\Big\} \rightarrow$	increase in β^* because less market risk is held through α. Less wealth is invested in a nontradeable asset (i.e., his firm) with systematic risk and therefore a greater investment will be made in the market so that β^0 is reattained.
Increase in $E\{U\}$	because of the direct increase in the value of the firm and the reduction in risk.

If $\operatorname{cov}(\tilde{x}, \tilde{M}) < 0$, a decrease in $\operatorname{cov}(\tilde{x}, \tilde{M})$ has the following effects:

Decrease in $\sigma_\varepsilon^2 \rightarrow$	increase in α^* because the signal α has become less costly.
Decrease in cov Increase in α $\Big\} \rightarrow$	increase in β^*. Because of the negative correlation, not only does a decrease in the covariance mean that less market risk is held, but also the increase in α means that more is sold short. Therefore a greater investment is made in the market.
Increase in $E\{U\}$	because of the direct increase in the value of the firm and the reduction in risk.

The inconclusive result on market value from a changed covariance arises because the change in value, as seen in (8A.4) in the appendix, has two terms: one representing a direct exogenous effect which is a change in the risk priced by the market, and the second an indirect endogenous effect resulting from managerial behavior. In a perfect market, only the first effect would result from a change in the covariance.

If $\operatorname{cov}(\tilde{x}, \tilde{M}) > 0$, a decrease in $\operatorname{cov}(\tilde{x}, \tilde{M})$ has the two following effects on firm value:

> Increase in $\sigma_\varepsilon^2 \to$ decrease in $\alpha \to$ increase in $F \to$ lower value.
> Decrease in risk adjustment $\to$ higher value.

If $\operatorname{cov}(\tilde{x}, \tilde{M}) < 0$, a decrease in $\operatorname{cov}(\tilde{x}, \tilde{M})$ has the two following effects on firm value:

> Decrease in $\sigma_\varepsilon^2 \to$ increase in $\alpha \to$ decrease in $F \to$ higher value.
> Decrease in risk adjustment $\to$ higher value.

Therefore the effect on firm value if $\operatorname{cov}(\tilde{x}, \tilde{M}) > 0$ depends upon the relative sizes of the exogenous and endogenous changes.

Propositions 8.3 and 8.4 illustrate the complexity of the principal/agent problem in a market in which the agent may make decisions other than how much effort to expend or perquisites to consume. Proposition 8.3 shows that all market participants are better off if the variance of cash flows is reduced. Proposition 8.4 shows that the manager can reduce his risk through adjustment of his personal investment portfolio as well as through the firm's investment policy. Investors in the market are assumed to be rational and can infer that the manager will undertake any feasible action that maximizes his welfare. Therefore securities will be priced rationally and the entrepreneur will bear the costs of his actions. Due to the cost of suboptimal risk bearing, the entrepreneur may be motivated to undertake or implement alternative bonding and monitoring activities, such as those suggested by Jensen and Meckling, in order to reduce risk.

An Example

The solution to the entrepreneur's problem in the previous section was in the form of an implicit function of α. A closed-form solution was not attainable without a specification of the form of $T(F)$. Criteria that $T(F)$ is assumed to satisfy were described earlier. The following negative exponential function satisfies these criteria and contains the parameter γ which describes the attitude of the individual toward shirking or consumption of perquisites:

$$T(F) = \frac{1}{\gamma} - \frac{1}{\gamma} e^{-\gamma F} \tag{8.19}$$

where $\gamma > 0$ is the coefficient of the propensity to consume perquisites.[5]

The equilibrium conditions, which were derived in the preceding section and the appendix, are

$$T'(F) = \alpha \tag{8.15}$$

$$(\alpha - 1)F_\alpha = \alpha b \sigma_\varepsilon^2 \tag{8A.1}$$

To solve for F^*, substitute for $T'(F)$ in (8.15)

$$e^{-\gamma F} = \alpha \tag{8.20}$$

Taking logarithms of (8.20),

$$-\gamma F = \ln \alpha$$

or

$$F^* = -\frac{\ln \alpha}{\gamma} > 0 \qquad \text{since } 0 < \alpha < 1 \tag{8.21}$$

and

$$F_\alpha = -\frac{1}{\alpha\gamma} < 0 \tag{8.22}$$

$$F_\gamma = \frac{\ln \alpha}{\gamma^2} > 0 \tag{8.23}$$

Expressions (8.21)–(8.23) describe the entrepreneur's choice of F as decreasing in α and increasing in γ. From (8.21) it is seen that

$$\lim_{\alpha \to 0} F = \infty \qquad \text{and} \qquad \lim_{\alpha \to 1} F = 0$$

The manager will consume zero perquisites if he owns the entire firm because he bears all the cost and his benefit is less than the cost (from $T(F) < F$). Since he will consume all cash flows if no equity in the firm is held, investors will not purchase 100% of the equity in the project. His propensity to consume perquisites is described by γ, in that F is increasing in γ.

The market knows the manager's perquisite transformation function, observes α^* and can perfectly infer F^*:

$$F(\alpha^*) = F^* \tag{8.24}$$

Substituting for F^* from (8.21)

$$F(\alpha^*) = -\frac{\ln \alpha}{\gamma}$$

In order to derive α^*, substitute for F_α in equation (8A.1) using (8.22):

$$\frac{-(\alpha - 1)}{\alpha\gamma} = \alpha b \sigma_\varepsilon^2 \qquad \text{or} \qquad \alpha^2 \gamma b \sigma_\varepsilon^2 + \alpha - 1 = 0 \tag{8.25}$$

The solution to (8.25) is

$$\alpha^* = \frac{-1 + \sqrt{1 + 4\gamma b \sigma_\varepsilon^2}}{2\gamma b \sigma_\varepsilon^2} \tag{8.26}$$

Market valuation of the firm obtains by substituting for $F(\alpha)$ in the valuation function

$$V(\alpha) = \frac{\mu - F(\alpha) - \lambda^0 \operatorname{cov}(\tilde{x}, \tilde{M})}{1+r}$$

so that

$$V(\alpha) = \frac{\mu + \dfrac{\ln \alpha}{\gamma} - \lambda^0 \operatorname{cov}(\tilde{x}, \tilde{M})}{1+r} \tag{8.27}$$

Both α and γ enter into valuation because both are determinants of F.

Proposition 8.5

An increase in the propensity to consume perquisites γ will result in a decrease in α.

The entrepreneur's compensation package has two components: risky return from the firm and riskless perquisites. As the propensity to consume perquisites increases, a higher F follows for a given α. However, the higher riskless return is accompanied by a reduction in risky α. This effect could be viewed as a substitution effect.

Proposition 8.6

The choice of α^* will always strictly satisfy $0 < \alpha < 1$.

The entrepreneur must own some proportion of his firm for incentive purposes, and he will always choose to share some of this risk with investors.

Summary

In the Pareto optimal risk-sharing contract between a risk-averse agent and a risk-neutral principal, all risk is borne by the principal. When the principal hires an effort-averse agent whose unobservable behavior affects the risky outcome, the principal must impose risk upon the agent for incentive purposes. In this paper, the agent offers a contract to investors in which he voluntarily accepts risk in order to precommit his behavior to investors. The agent, however, can improve upon such suboptimal risk sharing through his personal investment portfolio or through his investment decisions for the firm. The existence of alternative bonding contracts—such as management compensation plans—or monitoring contracts—such as cost accounting systems—may be explained by the agent's attempt to minimize the cost of revealing his behavior.

Notes

1. The direct analogue here in the two-person problem is that risk is imposed upon the agent even if the principal is risk neutral.

2. "Our approach to the agency problem here differs fundamentally from most of the existing literature. That literature focuses almost exclusively on the normative aspects of the agency relationship; that is how to structure the contractual relation (including compensation incentives) between the principal and agent to provide appropriate incentives for the agent to make choices which will maximize the principal's welfare given that uncertainty and imperfect monitoring exist" (Jensen and Meckling [1976, p. 309]).

3. The moral hazard problem disappears if the distribution of the outcome has a moving support. Since cash flows are here assumed to be normally distributed, the trivial forcing solution does not exist.

4. Leland and Pyle's proposition III states that a reduction in firm-specific risk results in a reduction of expected utility. However, Diamond [1984] later corrected an error in their proof, thus showing the same results as proposition 8.3 in this paper.

5. To show that (8.19) satisfies the five criteria listed above,

i. $T(F) = \frac{1}{\gamma} - \frac{1}{\gamma} e^{-\gamma F} = 0 \qquad \text{when } F = 0$

ii. $T(F) > 0 \qquad \text{for } F > 0$

$$\text{since } \frac{1}{\gamma}[1 - e^{-\gamma F}] > 0$$

$$\text{follows from } e^{-\gamma F} < 1 \quad \text{for } \gamma F > 0$$

iii. $T'(F) = e^{-\gamma F} = 1 \qquad \text{when } F = 0$

$T'(F) > 0 \qquad \text{since } e^{-\gamma F} > 0$

$T'(F) < 1 \qquad \text{since } e^{-\gamma F} < 1 \text{ for } \gamma F > 0$

iv. $T''(F) = \gamma e^{-\gamma F} < 0$

v. $T'''(F) = \gamma^2 e^{-\gamma F} > 0$

APPENDIX 8

Proof of Proposition 8.1

It is easily derived from the capital asset pricing model that

$$\frac{\sigma^2 \sigma_m^2 - \text{cov}(\tilde{x}, \tilde{M})^2}{\sigma_m^2} = \sigma_\varepsilon^2 \qquad \text{(firm-specific risk)}$$

Equation (8.14) can be rewritten replacing $[\cdot]$ with σ_ε^2:

$$(\alpha - 1) F_\alpha = \alpha b \sigma_\varepsilon^2 \tag{8A.1}$$

The total derivative of (8A.1) with respect to α and σ_ε^2 is

$$(\alpha - 1) F_{\alpha\alpha} d\alpha + F_\alpha d\alpha = b\sigma_\varepsilon^2 \, d\alpha + \alpha b d\sigma_\varepsilon^2$$

or

$$\frac{d\alpha}{d\sigma_\varepsilon^2} = \frac{\alpha b}{(\alpha - 1) F_{\alpha\alpha} + F_\alpha - b\sigma_\varepsilon^2} < 0 \tag{8A.2}$$

since $(\alpha - 1) < 0$

$$F_{\alpha\alpha} > 0$$

$$F_{\alpha} < 0$$

$$b\sigma_{\varepsilon}^2 > 0$$

Q.E.D.

Proof of Proposition 8.2

The total derivative of (8A.1) with respect to α and b is

$$(\alpha - 1) F_{\alpha\alpha} d\alpha + F_{\alpha} d\alpha = b\sigma_{\varepsilon}^2 \, d\alpha + \alpha\sigma_{\varepsilon}^2 \, db$$

or

$$\frac{d\alpha}{db} = \frac{\alpha\sigma_{\varepsilon}^2}{(\alpha - 1) F_{\alpha\alpha} + F_{\alpha} - b\sigma_{\varepsilon}^2} < 0 \qquad \text{Q.E.D.}$$

Proof of Proposition 8.3

(i) When a negative exponential utility function is combined with a normally distributed random variable, the objective function simplifies to $\max e^{bH}$, where $H = \bar{W} - (b/2)\ \sigma_w^2$. Since $G(H) = e^{bH}$ is a monotonically increasing function of H,

$$\text{sign} \frac{dE\{U\}}{d(\text{parameter})} = \text{sign} \frac{dH}{d(\text{parameter})}$$

as long as the parameter is not b, since it appears in G.

$$\frac{dH^*}{d\sigma^2} = \frac{\partial H^*}{\partial \sigma^2} + \frac{\partial H^*}{\partial \alpha} \cdot \frac{\partial \alpha}{\partial \sigma^2} + \frac{\partial H^*}{\partial F} \cdot \frac{\partial F}{\partial \alpha} \cdot \frac{\partial \alpha}{\partial \sigma^2}$$

$$= \frac{\partial H^*}{\partial \sigma^2} \qquad \text{by the envelope theorem}$$

Using (8.9),

$$\frac{dH}{d\sigma^2} = -\frac{b}{2}\alpha^2 < 0$$

(ii) To show that the market value increases, differentiate $V(\alpha)$ in (8.5) with respect to σ^2:

$$\frac{dV(\alpha)}{d\sigma^2} = \frac{\partial V}{\partial F} \cdot \frac{\partial F}{\partial \alpha} \cdot \frac{\partial \alpha}{\partial \sigma^2} < 0 \qquad \text{since each term} < 0 \qquad \text{Q.E.D.}$$

Proof of Proposition 8.4

(i) By use of the envelope condition as in the proof of proposition 8.3,

$$\frac{dH^*}{d\,\mathrm{cov}} = \frac{\partial H^*}{\partial\,\mathrm{cov}}$$

$$= \lambda^0(\alpha - 1) - \alpha b\beta < 0 \tag{8A.3}$$

where

$$\lambda^0 = \frac{\bar{M} - (1+r)V_m}{\sigma_m^2}$$

is the market price of risk.

(ii) In order to prove the effect on market value, (8.5) is rewritten as

$$V(\alpha) = \frac{\mu - F(\alpha) - \lambda^0 \,\mathrm{cov}(\tilde{x}, \tilde{M})}{1+r}$$

which is then differentiated with respect to $\mathrm{cov}(\tilde{x}, \tilde{M})$:

$$\frac{dV}{d\,\mathrm{cov}} = \frac{\partial V}{\partial\,\mathrm{cov}} + \frac{\partial V}{\partial F}\cdot\frac{\partial F}{\partial\alpha}\cdot\frac{\partial\alpha}{\partial\,\mathrm{cov}} \tag{8A.4}$$

All of the above partial derivatives are negative, with the exception of $\partial\alpha/\partial\,\mathrm{cov}$, which depends upon the sign of the covariance (see (8A.2)):

$$\frac{\partial\alpha}{\partial\,\mathrm{cov}} \begin{cases} > 0 \\ < 0 \end{cases} \quad \text{if cov} \begin{cases} > 0 \\ < 0 \end{cases}$$

Therefore

$$\frac{dV}{d\,\mathrm{cov}} \begin{cases} < 0 & \text{if cov} < 0 \\ \lesseqqgtr 0 & \text{if cov} > 0 \end{cases} \qquad \text{Q.E.D.}$$

Proof of Proposition 8.5

Propositions 8.1 and 8.2 indicate that increases in b or σ_ε^2 would result in a decrease in α. In expression (8.26), γ, b, and σ_ε^2 appear multiplicatively.

Totally differentiate (8.25) with respect to α and $(\gamma b\sigma_\varepsilon^2)$:

$$\alpha^2 d(\gamma b\sigma_\varepsilon^2) + 2\alpha(\gamma b\sigma_\varepsilon^2)\,d\alpha + d\alpha = 0$$

or

$$\frac{d\alpha}{d(\gamma b\sigma_\varepsilon^2)} = -\frac{\alpha^2}{2\alpha(\gamma b\sigma_\varepsilon^2) + 1} < 0 \qquad \text{Q.E.D.}$$

Proof of Proposition 8.6

(i) Verification that $\alpha > 0$: From (8.26) it is clear that $\alpha^* > 0$ since $4\gamma b\sigma_\varepsilon^2 > 0$.

(ii) Verification that $\alpha < 1$: To be proved:

$$-1 + \sqrt{1 + 4\gamma b\sigma_\varepsilon^2} < 2\gamma b\sigma_\varepsilon^2 \qquad \text{or} \qquad \sqrt{1 + 4\gamma b\sigma_\varepsilon^2} < 1 + 2\gamma b\sigma_\varepsilon^2$$

Squaring both sides,

$$1 + 4\gamma b\sigma_\varepsilon^2 < 1 + 4\gamma b\sigma_\varepsilon^2 + 4(\gamma b\sigma_\varepsilon^2)^2$$

which is clearly true since $4(\gamma b\sigma_\varepsilon^2)^2 > 0$. Q.E.D.

References

Atkinson, A. and Feltham, G. [1983]. "Information in Capital Markets: An Agency Theory Perspective." Working Paper, University of British Columbia.

Beck, P., and Zorn, T. [1982]. "Managerial Incentives in a Stock Market Economy." *Journal of Finance* 37, 1151–1167.

Campbell, T., and Kracaw, W. [1985]. "The Market for Managerial Labor Services and Capital Market Equilibrium." *Journal of Financial and Quantitative Analysis* 20, 277–297.

Diamond, D. [1984]. "Financial Intermediation and Delegated Monitoring." *Review of Economic Studies* 51, 393–414.

Diamond, D., and Verrecchia, R. [1982]. "Optimal Managerial Contracts and Equilibrium Security Prices." *Journal of Finance* 37, 275–287.

Downes, D., and Heinkel, R. [1982]. "Signaling and the Valuation of Unseasoned New Issues." *Journal of Finance* 37, 1–10.

Holmstrom, B. [1979]. "Moral Hazard and Observability." *Bell Journal of Economics* 10, 74–91.

Jensen, M., and Meckling, W. [1976]. "Theory of the Firm: Managerial Behavior, Agency Costs and Ownership Structure." *Journal of Financial Economics* 3, 305–360.

Leland, H., and Pyle, D. [1977]. "Informational Asymmetries, Financial Structure, and Financial Intermediation." *Journal of Finance* 32, 371–387.

Marcus, A. [1982]. "Risk Sharing and the Theory of the Firm." *Bell Journal of Economics* 13, 369–378.

Ramakrishnan, R., and Thakor, A. [1982]. "Moral Hazard, Agency Costs, and Asset Prices in a Competitive Equilibrium." *Journal of Financial and Quantitative Analysis* 17, 503–532.

Ritter, J. [1984]. "Signaling and the Valuation of Unseasoned New Issues: A Comment." *Journal of Finance* 39, 1231–1237.

Ross, S. [1973]. "The Economic Theory of Agency: The Principal's Problem." *The American Economic Review* 63, 134–139.

PART IV: CONTRACTING IN AGENCIES WITH PRIVATE INFORMATION

9 COMMUNICATION OF PRIVATE INFORMATION IN CAPITAL MARKETS: *Contingent Contracts and Verified Reports**

Gerald A. Feltham
John S. Hughes

Considerable interest has developed in accounting and finance in the communication properties of capital investment contracts. In the typical setting, an agent with private information seeks to raise capital from investors and to share risks with them. Our examination of this *investment game* has two major purposes: (1) to characterize the equilibria that may emerge under alternative concepts of rational behavior, and (2) to identify conditions under which verified reports concerning the agent's private information may have value. A key issue in the characterization of equilibria is whether agents with better news always design contracts to "separate" themselves from agents with worse news, or whether there are conditions under which they choose to

* We wish to express our appreciation for helpful comments provided on earlier drafts by Amin Amershi, Joel Demski, and faculty who attended seminars at the University of British Columbia, Brown University, Duke University, the University of Maryland, the University of Washington, and the Stanford University Summer Workshop. We also wish to express our appreciation for financial support for Jack Hughes from the Center for Accounting, Fuqua School of Business, Duke University.

"pool." The answer to this question has significant implications for the value of verified reports.

The investment game we examine is similar to the *insurance game* examined by Rothschild and Stiglitz [1976], Wilson [1977], and others. In the insurance game, the primary players are the competing insurance companies who simultaneously offer contracts to insurees. The insurees, who have private knowledge of their propensity for losses, passively select from among the offered contracts. Rothschild and Stiglitz [1976] apply the traditional Nash equilibrium concept and demonstrate that an insurance game either has a "separating" Nash equilibrium or no Nash equilibrium. To deal with situations that result in no Nash equilibrium, Wilson introduces the concept of an anticipatory equilibrium. He establishes that if there is no Nash equilibrium, then there is at least one "pooling" anticipatory equilibrium.

Our investment game differs from the insurance game primarily because, under our assumptions, agents (insurees) offer contracts to investors (insurers), who may accept or reject them. The change from simultaneous play among investors (insurees) to sequential play between agents (insurees) and investors (insurers) results in a game in which multiple Nash equilibria always exist. Hence, the focus shifts from seeking alternatives to the Nash equilibrium concept to seeking criteria for choosing from among alternative Nash equilibria.

We find that separating equilibria are *sequentially rational*, in the sense of Kreps and Wilson [1982], and uniquely satisfy a "stability" criterion proposed by Cho and Kreps [1987]. The Cho and Kreps stability criterion precludes pooling equilibria, even in circumstances in which such equilibria might be viewed as equally or more plausible than the separating equilibria. We provide an alternative stability criterion under which either separating or pooling equilibria may occur, depending on the circumstances. A shortcoming of our criterion is that it restricts the class of contracts that agents can expect investors to accept. Thus, both stability criteria have weaknesses and the identification of an equilibrium in some circumstances depends on which criterion is viewed as the more plausible.

With respect to verified reports, we consider reports issued both before and after contracting. Reports issued before contracting are viewed as the consequence of audits which may vary in quality, enabling us to examine the auditor's value as a function of that quality. The analysis of reports issued after contracting is similar to Holmstrom's [1979, 1982] analysis of information in a moral hazard setting; accordingly, we are able to demonstrate a correspondence between informativeness and value in contracting. An interesting result is that we find it possible for reports issued later to be more valuable than reports issued earlier.

While agents (managers) usually possess information not available to investors, they do have some control over the relative timing of their contract offers and their acquisition of private information. We consider the effects of presignal contracting on the agent's welfare and his demand for information. The results are similar to those of Hakansson, Kunkel, and Ohlson [1982], Kunkel [1982], and Ohlson and Buckman [1981]. Basically, given homogeneous beliefs and efficient risk sharing, risk sharing is improved by contracting before the receipt of private signals and information has value to the agent if, and only if, production decisions are affected by its receipt.

The remainder of this paper is organized as follows. First, the model is described; this includes descriptions of the agent and his firm, the market in which firm securities are priced, and the strategies and payoffs for both agents and investors. Separating equilibria are considered next, applying the concepts of sequential rationality and the Cho and Kreps stability criterion. Then pooling equilibria are considered and an alternative stability criterion is introduced. The impact of pre- and postcontract audited reports is examined next, with attention to audit quality. Contracting before agents receive information is examined last, with emphasis on the role of precommitment.

Basic Model

The Agent and His Firm

In the following analysis an agent issues publicly tradeable securities in order to obtain capital from and to share risks with investors. The market value of those securities, denoted V, depends on the investors' beliefs with respect to the dividends they will receive. The agent is endowed with capital, denoted e, as well as ownership of the firm. The capital available to the agent, $e + V$, is either invested in the firm, an amount q, or invested in securities of other firms. an amount I. Hence,

$$e + V = q + I.$$

The firm's output is denoted x, the dividend paid to investors is d, the return provided by investment in the securities of other firms is r, and the net available to the agent for his own consumption is c. Hence,

$$c = x - d + r$$

The agent's preferences are represented by a von Neumann–Morgenstern utility function defined over his end-of-period consumption. That function, denoted $u(c)$, is twice differentiable and strictly concave, reflecting the fact that he is strictly risk averse.

The firm's output is influenced by uncertain events and the capital invested. The investors have homogeneous beliefs with respect to the uncertain events, but they realize that the agent has *private information* about those events. The investors do not know the specific private signal received by the agent, but they believe that it comes from a set $H = \{h\}$ with probability $p(h)$. Furthermore, both the investors and the agent believe that the conditional probability function over the outcome x given investment q and private signal h is $\phi(x|q, h)$. The set of possible output levels from a given investment level q, denoted $X(q)$, is assumed to be independent of the private signal h. The set of possible investment levels is $Q = \{0, k\}$, with $k > e$ and $X(0) = \{0\}$. That is, the agent must choose between zero capital investment, which will produce zero output, and capital investment k, which exceeds his endowment.

We assume that the signals can be ordered such that the following two conditions hold.

Monotone Likelihood Ratio Condition (*MLRC*): If $h_1 < h_2$, then for all $x_1 < x_2$, $x_1, x_2 \in X(k)$,

$$\frac{\phi(x_1|k, h_1)}{\phi(x_1|k, h_2)} \geq \frac{\phi(x_2|k, h_1)}{\phi(x_2|k, h_2)}$$

with strict inequality for some x_1, x_2.

Spanning Condition (*SC*): There exists a function $w(h)$ defined on H and two probability functions $\underline{\phi}(x)$ and $\bar{\phi}(x)$ defined on $X(k)$ such that

a. $\underline{\phi}(x)/\bar{\phi}(x)$ satisfies MLRC.
b. $\phi(x|k, h) = w(h) \cdot \bar{\phi}(x) + (1 - w(h)) \cdot \underline{\phi}(x)$ for all $x \in X(k)$, $h \in H$.
c. $w(h)$ is increasing in h and $0 \leq w(h) \leq 1$.

The monotone likelihood ratio condition implies that there is a first-order stochastic dominance relationship among the signals and, hence, there is a clear concept of good news (h_2) and bad news (h_1) when comparing any two signals.[1] The spanning condition imposes additional regularity to ensure that the optimal incentive contract is increasing in output. It is essentially the same as that used by Grossman and Hart [1983] in their analysis of incentive contracts in a setting in which an agent's actions are unobservable.

Market Value

The events influencing any firm's output and dividends are assumed to be specific to that firm and investors are assumed to be well diversified. Consequently, the investors act as if they are risk neutral and set a firm's market value equal to the expected value of its dividends discounted at the risk-free interest rate. We assume (without loss of generality) that the risk-free interest rate is zero and, hence, V is equal to the expected value of d. A key issue in the following analysis is the identification of the beliefs held by the investors when they determine the expected dividend.

The agent, like any investor, can hold a well-diversified portfolio and thereby avoid the firm-specific risks associated with the securities issued by other firms. Hence, the return on his investment portfolio is equal to the amount invested plus the risk-free return; our assumption of a zero risk-free interest rate implies that

$$r = I$$

We could introduce systematic risk in the form of general economic events that influence the outcomes of many firms, but that would increase notational complexity and provide only limited additional insight.

Strategies and Payoffs

At the start of the period the agent issues securities based on a contract that specifies the capital investment q and the dividend $d(x, q)$ that investors are to receive conditional on a verified report of the investment q and the output x. The agent uses his endowment e and the proceeds from the sale of securities V to invest q in production and $I = e + V - q$ in the market. Observe that the agent has two forms of exchange with the market: he issues securities and invests in the securities of other firms. Our notation is simplified if we express their combined effect in terms of the agent's end-of-period consumption:

$$c(x, q) = x - d(x, q) + r$$

where $r = I = e + V - q$ is the agent's return from his investment in the market. Now, instead of viewing the agent as offering investors securities with dividends $d(\cdot)$ and then investing $e + V - q$ in the market, we can view the agent as offering a consumption function $c(\cdot)$ which the market can choose to accept or reject. The contract is denoted $z = (q, c(\cdot))$.

The specific instruments for implementing consumption function $c(x, q)$ are not considered here; but they could include wages, bonus payments, dividends from securities held by the agent, gains from stock options, etc. It is assumed, however, that the agent is precluded from trading in the securities he issues to investors.[2]

The agent is assumed to implement whatever capital investment level he "promises" (q is reported at the end of the period and there are sufficiently severe penalties to deter nonimplementation). Bankruptcy is precluded by requiring consumption functions to be nonnegative. Therefore, the *set of possible contracts* that the agent can offer is

$$Z = \{z = (q, c(\cdot)) | c(x, q) \geq 0, \quad q \in Q\}$$

The agent can choose to offer any contract in the set Z. But if his offer is rejected he is assumed to implement the *null contract*, $(0, e)$, in which the agent makes no investment in production, and to invest his endowment in the market, which results in a certain consumption of e. Let $\pi = (\pi_a, \pi_i)$ denote the vector of the agent's and investors' *strategies*, where $\pi_a = [\pi_a(z|h)]_{Z \times H}$ is the probability the agent will offer contract z given that he observes h and $\pi_i = [\pi_i(\delta|z)]_{Z \times \Delta}$, $\Delta = \{0, 1\}$, is the probability that the investors will accept $(\delta = 1)$ or reject $(\delta = 0)$ contract z if it is offered.

The agent's expected utility given strategy vector π and signal h is

$$U(\pi, h) = \sum_{z \in Z} \sum_{\delta \in \Delta} [\delta \cdot U(z, h) + (1 - \delta) \cdot u(e)] \cdot \pi_i(\delta|z) \cdot \pi_a(z|h)$$

where

$$U(z, h) = \sum_{x \in X(q)} u(c(x, q)) \cdot \phi(x|q, h)$$

The agent obtains $q - e$ units of capital from investors in return for a promise to pay $x - c(x, q)$ if x is observed. Consequently, given output x and contract $z = (q, c(\cdot))$, the investors' net return if they accept the contract is $x - c(x, q) + e - q$. If they reject the contract, their net return is zero. Therefore, the investors' expected net return given strategy vector π is

$$B(\pi) = \sum_{h \in H} \sum_{z \in Z} B(z, h) \cdot \pi_i(1|z) \cdot \pi_a(z|h) \cdot p(h)$$

where

$$B(z, h) = \sum_{x \in X(q)} [x - c(x, q)] \cdot \phi(x|q, h) + e - q$$

Separating Equilibria

Following Harsanyi's [1968] approach to games with incomplete information, the agent is depicted as choosing a strategy $\pi_a(\cdot|h)$ for each signal he might receive; if he employs a pure strategy, it is denoted

$$\mathbf{z} = (z_1, \ldots, z_H)$$

where z_h is the agent's contract choice if he observes h. The investors choose the strategy π_i and, if they employ pure strategies, the set of contracts they will accept is denoted A. The basic question to be addressed in this section is:

Which set of strategy vectors $\pi = (\pi_a, \pi_i)$ (or $\pi = (\mathbf{z}, A)$) constitute "rational" equilibria? We establish that under rationality conditions suggested by Cho and Kreps [1987], there is a unique rational separating equilibrium (i.e., one in which each signal that induces the investment of k induces the offering of a different contract). In the following section, we explore some alternative rationality conditions that can result in pooling equilibria (i.e., more than one signal induces the offering of a particular contract).

Our investment game is similar to the insurance game analyzed by Rothschild and Stiglitz [1976]. In the insurance game, the *insurers* (investors) *simultaneously* offer a set of contracts, A, from which the insurees (agents) choose—i.e., the insurees play a purely passive role. To be a Nash equilibrium, the acceptance set A must be such that no insurance company would benefit from refusing to offer any of the contracts in A and no insurance company would benefit from offering some contract not in A. Restricting their considerations to pure strategies, Rothschild and Stiglitz [1976] demonstrate that there are situations in which there are *unique* Nash equilibria and there are situations in which there are *no* Nash equilibria. To deal with these latter situations, Wilson [1977] proposes an alternative equilibrium concept, that of an *anticipatory* equilibrium. Dasgupta and Maskin [1986], on the other hand, demonstrate that there always exists a mixed-strategy Nash equilibrium in the insurance game.

In our investment game, the *sequential* play of the game is important. The *agent moves first* and offers a contract to the investors who then accept or reject it. There are *no precommitments* by either the agent or the investors. The agent chooses his contract offer after he observes his signal, and the investors accept or reject a contract after it has been offered. Hence, we have a game in which both the agent and the investors are key players. The following analysis examines the equilibria in this game, relating it, where appropriate, to the above-mentioned analyses of the insurance game.

Nash Equilibria

In the investment game, π is a *Nash equilibrium*[3] if neither the agent (given any signal) nor the investors would benefit from changing their strategy given the strategy of the others—i.e., for all $h \in H$,

$$U(\pi, h) \geq U\big((\pi_a'^h, \pi_a^{-h}), \pi_i, h\big) \qquad \text{all } \pi_a'^h \tag{9.1}$$

and

$$B(\pi) \geq B(\pi_a, \pi_i') \qquad \text{all } \pi_i' \tag{9.2}$$

where π_a^h is column h of π_a and π_a^{-h} is π_a excluding column h.

To illustrate various issues, we introduce a *special case* that can be depicted graphically. There are two possible outcomes, $X(k) = \{x_1, x_2\}$ with $x_1 < x_2$, and two possible signals, $H = \{1, 2\}$ with $\phi_{21} < \phi_{22}$, where $\phi_{jh} = \phi(x_j|k, h)$. Production is profitable if, and only if, the agent receives good news—i.e., $x_1 \cdot \phi_{11} + x_2 \cdot \phi_{21} < k < x_1 \cdot \phi_{12} + x_2 \cdot \phi_{22}$. Figure 9–1 depicts the set of possible consumption levels, where $\mathbf{c} = (c_1, c_2)$ and c_j is the consumption level if x_j occurs. The agent's expected utility and the investors' expected return (given $q = k$) are expressed as functions of the consumption vector $\mathbf{c}$ and the agent's signal h:

$$U(\mathbf{c}, h) = u(c_1) \cdot \phi_{1h} + u(c_2) \cdot \phi_{2h}$$

$$B(\mathbf{c}, h) = [x_1 - c_1] \cdot \phi_{1h} + [x_2 - c_2] \cdot \phi_{2h} + e - k$$

The investors' expected return given their prior beliefs about $h \in H$ is denoted

$$B(\mathbf{c}, H) = B(\mathbf{c}, 1) \cdot p(1) + B(\mathbf{c}, 2) \cdot p(2) + e - k$$

The agent's and investors' indifference curves are both flatter for $h = 2$ than for $h = 1$ because $\phi_{22} > \phi_{21}$.

The agent's indifference curves are strictly convex due to his strict risk aversion, while the investors' indifference curves are linear due to their risk

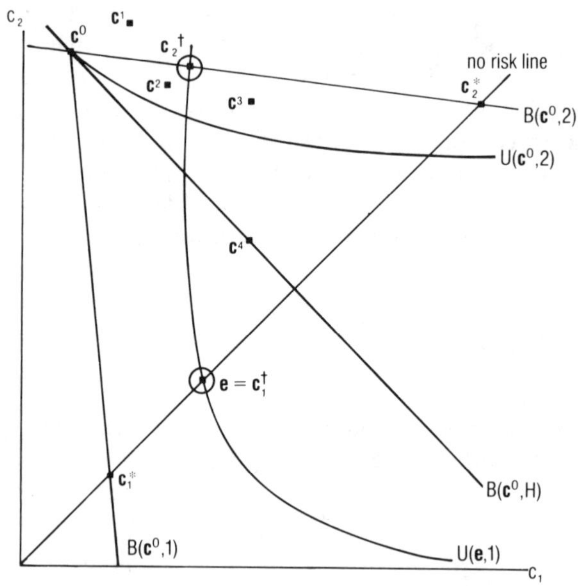

Figure 9–1. Alternative Contracts

neutrality with respect to the agent's risks.[4] Consumption plan $\mathbf{c}_h^* = (c_h^*, c_h^*)$ is the agent's optimal (riskless) contract if both he and the investors have observed h and $q = k$—i.e., $c_h^* = \Sigma_x x \cdot \pi(x|k,h) + e - k$, whereas $\mathbf{e} = (e, e)$ is the agent's consumption plan if he does not invest in the project. Consumption plan $\mathbf{c}^0$ is the contract in which the agent bears all the risk and borrows the required capital $k - e$—i.e., $c_j^0 = x_j + e - k$. Under that contract the investors' net return is zero no matter what signal the agent has observed. The investors' indifference curve denoted $B(\mathbf{c}^0, h)$ represents all consumption plans that provide investors' with an expected return of zero if they believe that the agent has observed h. Similarly, $B(\mathbf{c}^0, H)$ represents all consumption plans that provide investors' with an expected return of zero based on their prior beliefs about $h \in H$. These indifference curves can be viewed as the agent's *budget constraint* given the investors' beliefs about his signal. For example, if investors believe that the agent has received signal h, then all consumption plans $\mathbf{c}$ in the region bounded above by $B(\mathbf{c}^0, h)$ are acceptable to the investors.

In the investment game, unlike the insurance game, there are numerous pure-strategy Nash equilibria. Several contracts are depicted in figure 9–1 and the following are pure-strategy Nash equilibria (given appropriate acceptance sets A):

$$\mathbf{z}^\dagger = ((0, \mathbf{e}), (k, \mathbf{c}_2^\dagger)), \qquad \mathbf{z}^2 = ((0, \mathbf{e}), (k, \mathbf{c}^2)), \quad \mathbf{z}^4 = ((k, \mathbf{c}^4), (k, \mathbf{c}^4))$$

Neither $\mathbf{c}^1$, $\mathbf{c}^3$, $\mathbf{c}_1^*$, nor $\mathbf{c}_2^*$ can be part of a Nash equilibrium. Investors will reject $\mathbf{c}^1$ since it will provide a negative expected return even if $h = 2$ (i.e., it is above $B(\mathbf{c}^0, 2)$). While $\mathbf{c}^3$ and $\mathbf{c}_2^*$ would yield non-negative returns if offered only when $h = 2$, they would also be offered if $h = 1$ and that makes them unacceptable to investors (i.e., they are above $B(\mathbf{c}^0, H)$). Assuming that $(0, \mathbf{e}) \in A$, the agent would never offer $\mathbf{c}_1^*$ since it is less preferred than $\mathbf{e}$ for both $h = 1$ and $h = 2$.[5]

In the following subsections we argue that only $\mathbf{z}^\dagger$ is a rational equilibrium. All other Nash equilibria, including $\mathbf{z}^2$ and $\mathbf{z}^4$, involve noncredible rejection threats.

Sequential Equilibria

There is no mechanism by which the investors can precommit to an acceptance set. They decide whether to accept or reject a contract *after* they have observed the contract offered by the agent. The Nash equilibrium concept gives no explicit consideration to this sequential aspect of the game. As a result, some Nash equilibria involve noncredible rejection threats. But how do we distinguish between credible and noncredible rejection threats? One approach is to require an equilibrium to satisfy the requirements of what Kreps and Wilson [1982] have termed a sequential equilibrium.[6] The following discussion applies the sequential equilibrium concept to our investment game.[7]

We denote investor posterior beliefs by $P = [p(h|z)]_{H \times Z}$, where $p(h|z)$ is their posterior belief that the agent has observed h if he has offered $z \in Z$. These beliefs plus the players' strategies constitute an *assessment* $\gamma = (P, \pi)$.

Definition

An assessment γ is *sequentially rational* if

1. For all $h \in H$,

$$U(\pi, h) \geq U\big((\pi_a'^h, \pi_a^{-h}), \pi_i, h\big) \qquad \text{all } \pi_a'^h$$

2. For all $z \in Z$,

$$\sum_{h \in H} B(z,h) \cdot \pi_i(1|z) \cdot p(h|z) \geq \sum_{h \in H} B(z,h) \cdot \pi_i'(1|z) \cdot p(h|z) \qquad \text{all } \pi_i'$$

That is, the agent selects his best action given the signal he has observed and the investors' anticipated response. The investors, on the other hand, select their best action given their beliefs about h, conditional on the contract that has been offered. The remaining question is: What investor beliefs are rational?

Let Π^0 denote the set of strategies such that $\pi_a(z|h) > 0$ for all $z \in Z$ and $h \in H$, and let Γ^0 denote the set of assessments such that $\pi \in \Pi^0$ and P is obtained by Bayes' theorem, i.e.,

$$p(h|z) = \pi_a(z|h) \cdot p(h) / \bar{\pi}_a(z)$$

where

$$\bar{\pi}_a(z) = \sum_{h \in H} \pi_a(z|h) \cdot p(h)$$

Definition

Assessment γ is *consistent* if there exists a sequence $\gamma_n \in \Gamma^0$ such that

$$\lim_{n \to \infty} \gamma_n = \gamma$$

This condition ensures that the investors compute $p(h|z)$ by Bayes' theorem if they can (i.e., if $\pi_a(z|h) > 0$ for some h), and if that is not possible then they hypothesize some process (a "trembling hand") that might explain how a contract z could have been offered even though it was not supposed to be.

Definition

A *sequential equilibrium* is an assessment $\gamma = (P, \pi)$ that is both consistent and sequentially rational.

Rational investors will accept any contract z such that $B(z, 1) \geq 0$ *and* $B(z, 2) \geq 0$, since that contract provides a non-negative expected return for all beliefs p. Consequently, in figure 9–1, rational investors will always accept $(k, \mathbf{c}^0)$. Since the agent prefers $(k, \mathbf{c}^0)$ to $(k, \mathbf{c}^4)$ if he observes $h = 2$, it follows that he will not offer the latter and Nash equilibrium $\mathbf{z}^4$ is *not sequentially rational.*

Nash equilibria $\mathbf{z}^\dagger$ and $\mathbf{z}^2$, on the other hand, are *sequentially rational*; for example, they are supported by the consistent beliefs[8]

$$P^\dagger = [p(1|z) = 1, \text{ for all } z \neq z_2^\dagger = (k, \mathbf{c}_2^\dagger), \quad \text{and} \quad p(1|z_2^\dagger) = 0]$$

and

$$P^2 = [p(1|z) = 1, \text{ for all } z \neq z^2 = (k, \mathbf{c}^2), \quad \text{and} \quad p(1|z^2) = 0]$$

Stable Equilibria

While both $\mathbf{z}^\dagger$ and $\mathbf{z}^2$ are sequential equilibria, $\mathbf{z}^2$ is sustained by a non-credible rejection threat. If the agent observes $h = 2$, he prefers $\mathbf{c}_2^\dagger$ to $\mathbf{c}^2$. In fact, the agent prefers $\mathbf{c}_2^\dagger$ to all other contracts in the set

$$\{\mathbf{c} | U(\mathbf{c}, 1) \leq U(\mathbf{e}, 1) \quad \text{and} \quad B(\mathbf{c}, 2) \geq B(\mathbf{c}^0, 2)\}$$

which is the set of contracts that would not be offered by the agent if $h = 1$ and would be acceptable to investors if $h = 2$.[9] The investors would prefer $\mathbf{c}^2$, but it will not be rational for them to reject $\mathbf{c}_2^\dagger$. In effect, by moving first and having his choice observable to investors, an agent can dictate which equilibrium will be played.

Cho and Kreps [1987] introduce an intuitive stability criterion which formalizes the above argument.[10] In our context, the following definition is essentially equivalent to that of Cho and Kreps, but it is stated slightly differently.

Definition

Consider a sequential equilibrium $(\mathbf{z}, A)$. For each out-of-equilibrium contract $z \in Z$ (i.e., $z \neq z_h$, all $h \in H$), form the set

$$H(z) = \{h \,|\, U(z,h) \geq U(z_h, h), h \in H\}$$

The equilibrium *fails to satisfy the Cho and Kreps intuitive stability* (CK-stability) *criterion* if for any out-of-equilibrium contract $z \in Z$,

1. $U(z,h) > U(z_h, h)$ for *some* signal $h \in H(z)$, and
2. $B(z,h) \geq 0$ for *all* signals $h \in H(z)$

The set $H(z)$ consists of all signals for which the agent would weakly prefer contract z to his equilibrium contract, if the investors would accept z. The first condition then assesses whether there is some signal $h \in H(z)$ for which the agent would strictly prefer contract z to his equilibrium contract, while the second condition assesses whether the investors would be willing to accept that contract no matter which of the signals in $H(z)$ the agent has received. The failure to satisfy the stability criterion implies that there is a contract z which the agent would prefer to offer (given some signal h) and which the investors "should not" reject.

In figure 9–1, $\mathbf{z}^\dagger$ is the *only sequential equilibrium satisfying* the *CK-stability criterion.*[11] It is referred to as a *separating equilibrium* since the agent offers a different contract if he observes $h = 2$ than if he observes $h = 1$.

Generalization

The preceding discussion has demonstrated the implications of sequential rationality and the CK-stability criterion in the simple two-signal/two-outcome example in figure 9–1. We now consider the multisignal/multi-outcome case.

In this case it is useful to let $H^* \subset H$ denote the set of signals that indicate that the investment project is profitable, i.e.,

$$H^* = \{h \,|\, \bar{x}(k,h) = \sum_{x \in X(q)} x \cdot \phi(x|k,h) > k\}$$

Proposition 9.1[12]

There is only one sequential equilibrium, denoted $(\mathbf{z}^\dagger, A^\dagger)$, that satisfies the CK-stability criterion and it satisfies the following conditions:

(a) For all $h \in H \setminus H^*$, $z_h^\dagger = (0, \mathbf{e})$.
(b) For all $h \in H^*$, $z_h^\dagger = (k, \mathbf{c}_h^\dagger)$, where $\mathbf{c}_h^\dagger$ is characterized by the following first-order condition (assuming an interior solution):

$$u'\left(c_h^\dagger(x, k)\right) = \lambda_h \cdot \left[1 - \mu_h \cdot \frac{\phi(x | k, h-1)}{\phi(x | k, h)}\right]^{-1} \qquad \text{all } x \in X(k)$$

where λ_h and μ_h are positive multipliers (except that $\mu_h = 0$ if $h = 1$).

Observe that the above contract has a form similar to the optimal incentive contract in the moral hazard problem analyzed by Grossman and Hart [1983].[13] The incentives required to induce an agent to tell the truth are essentially the same as those required to induce him to provide effort. However, unlike the moral hazard case, in the signaling context the monotone likelihood ratio and spanning conditions are sufficient for the equilibrium separating contract to be characterized by the likelihood ratio between h and $h-1$, for $h \in H^*$. That is, if the agent bears sufficient risk to convince investors that he has not received the next-worst signal, then that is also sufficient to convince them that he has not received any inferior signal. The more favorable the signal the more risk the agent bears, and hence we have a *separating equilibrium* (except for $h \in H \setminus H^*$).

This type of equilibrium is similar to that derived by Leland and Pyle [1977], except they consider a continuum of signals and restrict consumption to be a linear function of x. The latter is a nontrivial restriction in that the optimal consumption function is in general not linear, even if the likelihood ratio is a linear function of x.

Pooling Equilibria

Instability in Stable Equilibria

The equilibrium depicted in figure 9–1 is essentially the same as the unique Nash equilibrium in the insurance game. In that game, the key factor determining the existence of a Nash equilibrium is the insurers' prior beliefs $p(h)$, which determine the location of $B(\mathbf{c}^0, H)$. In figure 9–1, $p(1)$ is sufficiently large that $B(\mathbf{c}^0, H)$ does not intersect $U(\mathbf{c}_2^\dagger, 2)$. Under these conditions, if the agent has good news ($h = 2$) then it is in his best interests to absorb considerable risk ($\mathbf{c}_2^\dagger$ is far from the no-risk line) in order to convince investors that he does not have bad news ($h = 1$).

Figure 9–2 depicts the same example shown in figure 9–1 except that $p(1)$ is sufficiently small that $B(\mathbf{c}^0, H)$ intersects $U(\mathbf{c}_2^\dagger, 2)$. In the investment game

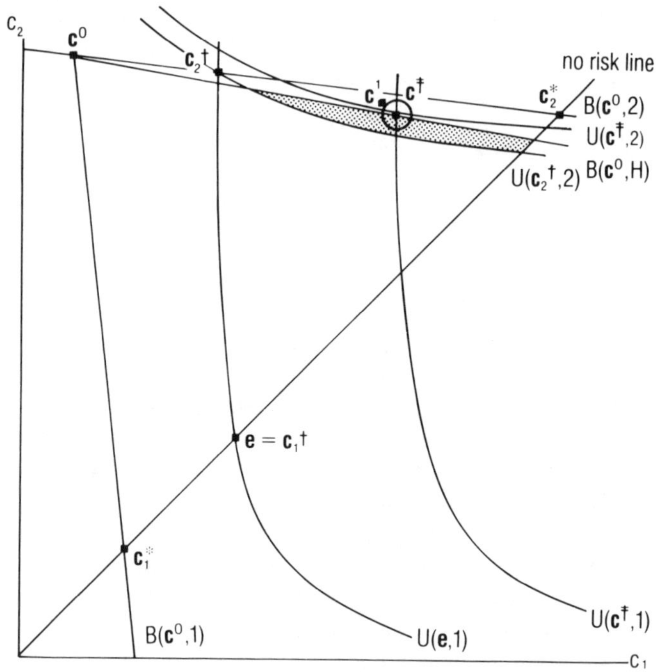

Figure 9–2. Pooling Equilibria

there are many Nash and sequential equilibria, and the separating equilibrium $\mathbf{z}^\dagger = ((0, \mathbf{e})), (k, \mathbf{c}_2^\dagger))$ is again the only sequential equilibrium that satisfies the CK-stability criterion. However, all consumption plans in the shaded region of figure 9–2 are preferred by the agent to $\mathbf{z}^\dagger$, whether he observes $h = 1$ or $h = 2$, and a contract with consumption in the shaded region provides investors with a non-negative expected return if their posterior signal beliefs $p(h|z)$ for that contract are equal to their prior signal beliefs. The existence of these Pareto preferred plans does not cause $\mathbf{z}^\dagger$ to fail the CK-stability criterion.[14] Their existence does imply, however, that $\mathbf{z}^\dagger$ is *not a perfect sequential equilibrium* (Grossman and Perry [1986]).

An assessment $\gamma = (P, \pi)$ is a *perfect sequential equilibrium* if the strategy vector π is *sequentially perfect* with respect to posterior beliefs P and the posterior beliefs P are *credible* with respect to the strategy vector π. The sequential perfectness requirement is essentially the same as the sequential rationality requirement stated earlier.[15] The key requirement for our purposes is the restriction imposed on some out-of-equilibrium posterior beliefs. We will not state the credibility requirement here. Instead, we provide a stability criterion which is derived from those requirements and which, if not satisfied, implies that a proposed equilibrium is not a perfect sequential equilibrium.

Definition

Consider a sequential equilibrium $(\mathbf{z}, A)$. For each out-of-equilibrium contract $z \in Z$ (i.e., $z \neq z_h$, all $h \in H$), form the set

$$H(z) = \{h \mid U(z,h) \geq U(z_h,h), \quad h \in H\}$$

The equilibrium is *not a perfect sequential equilibrium* (fails to satisfy the "perfect-stability" criterion) if for any out-of-equilibrium contract $z \in Z$,

1. $U(z,h) > U(z_h,h)$ for some signal $h \in H(z)$, and
2. $\sum_{h \in H(z)} B(z,h) \cdot g(h) \geq 0$ for all $g(h)$ such that

$$g(h) \begin{cases} = p(h) & \text{if } U(z,h) > U(z_h,h) \\ \in [0, p(h)] & \text{if } U(z,h) = U(z_h,h) \end{cases}$$

The above criterion has been stated in a manner directly parallel to our statement of the CK-stability criterion. The key difference in the two criteria is the specification of the restrictions on posterior beliefs that investors can use to *reject* an out-of-equilibrium contract. The perfect-stability criterion requires those beliefs to be based on investors' prior beliefs over the set of signals for which the agent would weakly prefer the out-of-equilibrium contract. The CK-stability criterion, on the other hand, permits investors to hold very pessimistic beliefs over that same set. (In particular, investors can assign probability one to the worst signal for which the agent would weakly prefer the out-of-equilibrium contract.) Hence, as is illustrated in figure 9–2, an equilibrium that does not fail the CK-stability criterion can still fail the perfect-stability criterion.

In figure 9–1, $\mathbf{z}^\dagger$ is a perfect sequential equilibrium (the only one), but in figure 9–2 there are *no perfect sequential equilibria*. The contract $\mathbf{z}^\ddagger = ((k, \mathbf{c}^\ddagger), (k, \mathbf{c}^\ddagger))$, for example, fails the perfect-stability criterion because $H(z) = \{2\}$ for $z = (k, \mathbf{c}^1)$, and this contract is such that $U(z,2) > U(z_2,2)$ and $B(z,2) > 0$.[16]

Sequential Stability

In the insurance game, which focuses on the simultaneous play of the insurers, there is no pure-strategy Nash equilibrium in the situation depicted in figure 9–2. This led Wilson [1977] to propose an alternative equilibrium concept. He suggested that $\mathbf{c}^{\ddagger}$ is an *anticipatory* equilibrium since it satisfies the following condition:

> There is no alternative contract that an insurance firm could offer which would be profitable after all contracts which become unprofitable as a result of the new entry are dropped.

For example, if $\mathbf{c}^1$ were offered, $\mathbf{c}^{\ddagger}$ would be dropped and all insurees would accept $\mathbf{c}^1$, making it unprofitable (since it is above $B(\mathbf{c}^0, H)$).

In the investment game, $\mathbf{z}^{\ddagger}$ is a Nash equilibrium and hence we do not need an alternative to the Nash concept. The issue here is the appropriate criterion for selecting from among the alternative sequential (Nash) equilibria. In particular, how will investors react to an offer of $(k, \mathbf{c}^1)$? If they would accept it, then that implies they would reject $(k, \mathbf{c}^{\ddagger})$, since it would be offered only if the agent observed $h = 1$. However, if the agent anticipates this, he would offer a contract such as $(k, \mathbf{c}^1)$ even if $h = 1$, since it is preferred to $(0, \mathbf{e})$, which would now make $(k, \mathbf{c}^1)$ unacceptable to investors. These arguments describe why $\mathbf{z}^{\ddagger}$ is not a perfect sequential equilibrium, but they also suggest an alternative stability concept, which we term sequential stability.

Definition

A sequential equilibrium $\mathbf{z}$ is *sequentially stable* if there does not exist a signal $l \in H$ and another sequential equilibrium contract $\mathbf{z}'$ such that

1. $U(z'_l, l) > U(z_l, l)$
2. $U(z'_h, h) \geq U(z_h, h) \qquad \text{all } h > l,\ h \in H$

This criterion restricts potential "defections" to alternative sequential equilibria, which implies that investors would reject contracts for which there does not exist a set of consistent beliefs that would support those contracts in equilibrium. The criterion also recognizes that an agent with signal l is in a subordinate position with respect to an agent with a better signal, and he is in a superior position relative to an agent with a worse signal. For example, the agent with signal l might prefer to pool with an agent with a better signal, but that will not be part of a sequentially stable equilibrium unless it is in the best interests of the agent with a better signal to offer the same contract as the agent with signal l. Furthermore, given that pooling occurs, the agent with the best signal in the pool determines which pooling contract will be offered. The agent with signal l must either mimic the agent with a better signal or reveal to investors that he has a worse signal.

Characteristics of Sequentially Stable Equilibria

To facilitate characterization of sequentially stable equilibria we explicitly recognize the possibility of pooling. The equilibrium pools are represented by $H_1, \ldots, H_Y$, the coarsest partition on H such that if $h_1, h_2 \in H_y$, then $z_{h_1} = z_{h_2} = z_y$. That is, H_y is a pool of agent signals that result in the same contract offer z_y. If investors know only that the agent has observed a signal in pool y, then their outcome beliefs are

$$\phi(x|k, y) \equiv \sum_{h \in H_y} \phi(x|k, h) \cdot p(h|H_y)$$

Let h_y denote the most desirable signal in the set H_y.

In both figure 9–1 and figure 9–2 there are unique sequentially stable equilibria. In figure 9–1 it is the separating equilibrium $\mathbf{z}^{\dagger}$, and in figure 9–2 it is the pooling equilibrium $\mathbf{z}^{\ddagger}$. These are similar to Wilson's anticipatory equilibria in the insurance game.

Generalizing to the case of multiple outcomes and multiple signals is relatively straightforward if the equilibrium pools are *convex*:

Definition

The pools $H_1, \ldots, H_Y$ are *convex* if for any three signals $h_1 < l < h_2$, $h_1, h_2 \in H_y$, for some y, implies that $l \in H_y$.

The monotone likelihood ratio and spanning conditions are sufficient for sequentially stable equilibrium pools to be convex.[17]

Proposition 9.2

There is only one sequential equilibrium, denoted $(\mathbf{z}^{\ddagger}, A^{\ddagger})$, that satisfies the sequential stability criterion. In that equilibrium the pools are convex and the contracts satisfy the following conditions:

(a) If $H_y \cap H^* = \varnothing$, then $z_y = (0, \mathbf{e})$.

(b) If $H_y \cap H^* \neq \varnothing$, then $z_y = (k, \mathbf{c}_y)$ and $\mathbf{c}_y$ is characterized by the following first-order condition for all $x \in X(k)$:

$$u'(c_y(x, k)) = \lambda_y \cdot \frac{\phi(x|k, H_y)}{\phi(x|k, h_y)} \cdot \left[1 - \mu_y \cdot \frac{\phi(x|k, h_{y-1})}{\phi(x|k, h_y)}\right]^{-1}$$

where λ_y and μ_y, are positive multipliers (except that $\mu_y = 0$ if $y = 1$).

The contract for a pool is the optimal contract from the perspective of the best signal in the pool. All other signals in the pool induce the agent to disguise his information.

The term in the square brackets $[\cdot]$ ensures that the contract for pool H_y efficiently differentiates between signal h_y and the next worst signal not in pool H_y. It is the same as in the separating case if H_y is a singleton.

The more interesting term is the likelihood ratio $\phi(x|k, H_y)/\phi(x|k, h_y)$. This ratio equals one in the separating equilibrium case, but it is *decreasing in x* for all y that contain more than one signal. The numerator is the investors' belief with respect to x (given z_y) and the denominator is the agent's belief (given h_y). The agent has superior information and engages in *side-betting* with the investors. This interpretation is particularly clear if there is only one pool, as in figure 9–2. The left-hand side is the ratio of the agent's marginal utility to the investors' marginal utility (which equals one) and the right-hand side is the ratio of their beliefs. Hence, the form of the optimal contract is exactly the same as in the case where there is no private information but the contracting parties have heterogeneous beliefs. In figure 9–2 this is reflected in the fact that $U(\mathbf{c}^{\ddagger}, 2)$ is tangent to $B(\mathbf{c}^{0}, H)$.

First-order condition (b) and the monotone likelihood ratio condition imply that equilibrium consumption is increasing in x. In particular, both the side-betting and incentive components of (b) imply that $c_y(x, k)$ increases whenever an increase in x results in a decrease in the likelihood ratio relative to h_y for either signals in the pool H_y or for the next-worst signal outside the pool.

The investors' prior signal beliefs significantly affect which signals are pooled together and it is difficult to provide any general characterization of these pools.

Which Equilibrium?

If there are no mechanisms to enforce precommitment by agents not to propose nonsequentially rational contracts, or by investors not to revise their beliefs and accept such contracts, then incentives to engage in this behavior exist. Thus, any attempts to establish existence of an equilibrium in settings where there are no perfect sequential equilibria are somewhat lacking in appeal. Only in the case where there is a perfect sequential equilibrium do we have an equilibrium that is totally satisfactory.

In cases where there are no perfect sequential equilibria we can view the above analysis as providing two competing hypotheses of rational agent and investor behavior. If the CK-stability criterion is employed, then a separating equilibrium is predicted in every case. If the sequential stability criterion is employed, then either a separating or a pooling equilibrium may occur, depending on the prior beliefs of investors.

The next section examines the impact of audited reports which accompany contracts between agents and investors. If a report changes investor beliefs about the agent's private signal, then it may change the contract used to communicate that signal. However, the impact of an audited report depends on both the investors' revised beliefs and the stability criterion employed. If the CK-stability criterion is employed, then an audited report has no impact unless it causes investors to attach zero probability to some agent signals to which they had previously attached a positive probability. On the other hand, if the sequential stability criterion is employed, an audited report can have an impact by merely shifting investor beliefs. The key difference is that pooling equilibria are influenced by investor beliefs, whereas separating equilibria are influenced only by the support of the investors' beliefs (i.e., the set of signals to which investors assign a positive probability) and not by the specifics of those beliefs. Hence, the type of equilibria predicted to occur is an important ingredient in the predicted impact of audited reports.

Analysis cannot determine which of the two competing hypotheses of rational agent and investor behavior is most appropriate. This is an empirical issue. While there is no empirical evidence regarding the contracts offered by agents in our investment game, Berge, Dickhaut, and Senkow [1986] have used experiments to examine the equilibria that occur when principals offer competing wage contracts in a context similar to the insurance game. In their experiments the agents signal their productivity by the contracts they choose. In some preliminary experiments the principals offered separating contracts when they constituted a Nash equilibrium and almost always selected the pooling equilibrium when there was no Nash equilibrium. However, subsequent experiments have obtained mixed results in the latter case. That is, while some principals made choices consistent with the Wilson's [1977] hypothesis that they would implement an anticipatory equilibrium, others did not.

Verified Ex Ante Information

Contracts between agents and investors are usually accompanied by information supplied by the agent, some of which may be verified by an independent auditor. In this section we examine the agent's incentives to provide audited reports that at least partially reveal his private signal to investors prior to their acceptance or rejection of the contract he offers.

Perfect Ex Ante Information

The simplest case to consider is that in which the agent is able to *costlessly* provide a verified report of his private signal. This case serves as a useful benchmark for subsequent information analyses.

The basic result here is straightforward.

Proposition 9.3

If the agent can costlessly provide a verified report of his private signal, then there exists an equilibrium $(\mathbf{z}^*, A^*)$ where

$$z_h^* = \begin{cases} (0, e) & \text{if } h \in H \backslash H^* \\ (k, c_h^*) & \text{if } h \in H^* \end{cases}$$

$$A^* = \{z \mid z = z_h^*, \quad \text{some } h \in H, \quad \text{or} \quad B(z, h) \geq 0, \quad \text{all } h \in H\}$$

$$c_h^* = \sum_{x \in X(k)} x \cdot \phi(x \mid k, h) + e - k$$

That is, if the agent is able to verify his private signal, then he will do so in order to convince investors that he does not have a worse signal. The only time he will not be motivated to provide this report is if he has observed $h = 1$ (the worst signal) or if $h \in H \backslash H^*$ (the signal indicates that the project is not profitable).

Observe that with costless verification of the agent's private signal, the agent bears no risk. His consumption is independent of the outcome and is equal to the expected value of the output plus his endowment minus the project investment.

Now compare the agent's expected utility in the case of costless signal verification to the case of no signal verification. Let $(\mathbf{z}, A)$ denote the equilibrium if there is no verification. If $(\mathbf{z}, A)$ is a separating equilibrium, then the agent is never worse off under costless verification. In fact, he will be strictly better off if $h \in H^*$ and $h > 1$. If $(\mathbf{z}, A)$ is a pooling equilibrium, the agent is always better off with verification if he has the best signal in a pool (i.e., h_y), but he may be worse off if he benefits from disguising his signal in a pool containing "better" signals (i.e., $h < h_y$ and $h \in y$). In the latter case, the verified reports "break" the pool and force the agent to reveal that he has observed h. More formally,

Proposition 9.4

Let $(\mathbf{z}, A)$ and $(\mathbf{z}^*, A^*)$ denote the equilibria in the no-verification and costless verification cases, respectively:

(a) If $(\mathbf{z}, A)$ is a separating equilibrium, then

$$U(z_h, h) = U(z_h^*, h) \qquad \text{if } h \in H \backslash H^* \quad \text{or } h = 1$$
$$U(z_h, h) < U(z_h^*, h) \qquad \text{if } h \in H^* \text{ and } h > 1$$

(b) If $(\mathbf{z}, A)$ is a pooling (sequentially stable) equilibrium, then

$$U(z_h, h) \geq U(z_h^*, h) \qquad \text{if } h \in H \backslash H^* \text{ or } h = 1$$
$$U(z_h, h) < U(z_h^*, h) \qquad \text{if } h \in H^* \text{ and } h = h_y, \text{ some } y \in Y$$

and for other signals the inequality can be in either direction.

Imperfect Ex Ante Information

While auditors can verify some of the information that might accompany a contract offer, verifiable information may not fully reveal what the agent knows about the profitability of his project. However, imperfect verified information will change the investors' beliefs with respect to $h \in H$.

We assume that the agent knows his private signal h when he hires the auditor, but he does not know what representations of his financial status and other prospectus information will be acceptable to the auditor. We further assume that if an auditor is hired, then the audited report must be included with the contract offer no matter what it contains. The agent knows the contents of the audited report before he chooses the contract to be offered.

The auditor is best referred to as an audit technology in that he operates mechanistically and is not modeled as a rational player in the game. That technology provides no additional information about the agent's outcome[18] and is described by the likelihood function $\phi(\psi | h)$, which specifies the probability that that ψ will be reported given private signal h. The investors' posterior signal beliefs given report ψ are

$$p(h | \psi) = \phi(\psi | h) \cdot p(h) / \phi(\psi)$$

where

$$\phi(\psi) = \sum_{h \in H} \phi(\psi | h) \cdot p(h)$$

The set of possible audited reports given that the agent has observed h is denoted $\Psi(h)$ and the set of possible private signals h, given report ψ, is denoted $H(\psi)$. The latter is particularly important in subsequent analysis and is termed the support of ψ in H. It includes only those signals that have a strictly positive posterior probability given report ψ, that is,

$$H(\psi) = \{h | p(h|\psi) > 0, \quad h \in H\} = \{h | \psi \in \Psi(h), \quad h \in H\}$$

If the agent observes h and hires an audit technology, then he has chosen a gamble whose outcome (the audited report) determines which signaling game he will play when he offers his contract to the investors. If ψ is reported, then the signaling game is characterized by the set $H(\psi)$ and investor beliefs $p(h|\psi)$. Let $(\mathbf{z}(\psi), A(\psi))$ denote an equilibrium for that game. We now address the question: Under what conditions does such a gamble have positive value to the agent and how is that value influenced by the quality of the audit technology?

The answer to the above question depends to some extent on whether we employ the CK- or sequential-stability criterion. We first consider the case where the CK-stability criterion is employed and, hence, the equilibrium is always a separating equilibrium.[19]

If the equilibrium is always a separating equilibrium, then the audited report has zero value to an agent who has observed h unless there are some worse signals that could not result in that report. The key issue here is that the *separating equilibrium* depends on $H(\psi)$, but it is *independent of* the *investors' beliefs* over that set. Therefore, a report has zero value to the agent if $H(\psi) = H$, that is, the report only changes the investors' beliefs over the set H but does not exclude the possibility of any signal. Furthermore, it has zero value, given a particular signal h, if the report merely informs investors that they could not have observed a better signal.

Proposition 9.5

If equilibria $(\mathbf{z}, A)$ and $(\mathbf{z}(\psi), A(\psi))$, $\psi \in \Psi(h)$, are all *separating equilibria*, then, given $h \in H^*$, an *audit technology has positive value* if, and only if, for at least one report $\psi \in \Psi(h)$, there is at least one signal $l \in H$ such that $l \notin H(\psi)$ and either,

(a) $l \in H^*$ and $l < h$, or
(b) l is the best signal such that $l \in H \setminus H^*$.

Figure 9–3 illustrates the impact of audited reports when the CK-stability criterion is employed. In this example, $H = \{1, 2, 3\}$ and the consumption contracts offered in the separating equilibrium, given no report, are $\mathbf{z}^\dagger = \big((0, \mathbf{e}), (k, \mathbf{c}_2^\dagger), (k, \mathbf{c}_3^\dagger)\big)$. Now consider an audit technology which will issue one of two reports, ψ_1 or ψ_2, such that $H(\psi_1) = \{1,2\}$ and $H(\psi_2) = \{2, 3\}$. That is, the agent knows the good report (ψ_2) will be issued if he has observed $h = 3$, but it might also be issued if $h = 2$. The bad report (ψ_1) will be issued with certainty if $h = 1$, but it may also be issued if $h = 2$. Given a bad report, the equilibrium contract offers are $\mathbf{z}(\psi_1) = \big((0, \mathbf{e}), (k, \mathbf{c}_2^\dagger)\big)$, which yields the agent the same as if the audit technology had not been hired. However, given a good report, the offered contracts are $\mathbf{z}(\psi_2) = \big((k, \mathbf{c}_2^*), (k, \mathbf{c}_3^{\dagger\dagger})\big)$ and the agent is better off, whether he observes $h = 2$ or $h = 3$. The gain from the good report comes from the fact that the agent no longer has to assure the investors (through the contract he offers) that he does not have the worst signal ($h = 1$); that assurance has been provided by the audited report.

The impact of an audit technology is more complex if the sequential- (instead of CK-) stability criterion is employed. We illustrate the basic issues in the two-signal/two-outcome case depicted in figures 9–1 and 9–2.

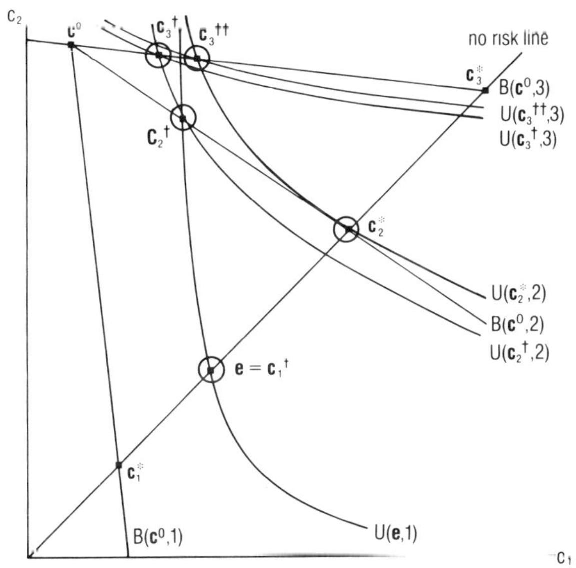

Figure 9–3. Impact of an Auditor on Separating Equilibria

Assume that there only are two possible reports, ψ_1 or ψ_2, and that the likelihood of the good report (ψ_2) given good news ($h = 2$) is equal to the likelihood of the bad report (ψ_1) given bad news ($h = 1$). That probability, denoted ρ, is a measure of *audit quality*. The investors' posterior beliefs are

$$p(h = 2 | \psi_2, \rho) \equiv \frac{\rho \cdot p(h = 2)}{(1 - \rho) \cdot p(h = 1) + \rho \cdot p(h = 2)}$$

$$p(h = 1 | \psi_1, \rho) \equiv \frac{\rho \cdot p(h = 1)}{\rho \cdot p(h = 1) + (1 - \rho) \cdot p(h = 2)}$$

As figures 9–1 and 9–2 illustrate, a sequentially stable equilibrium can be either a separating equilibrium or a pooling equilibrium. The determining factor is the investors' belief that they are dealing with an agent who has good news. Let $\hat{p}$ denote the dividing point in those beliefs—i.e., $U(\mathbf{c}_2^\dagger, 2)$ does not intersect $B(\mathbf{c}^0, H)$ if, and only if, $p(h = 2) < \hat{p}$. This dividing point plays a key role in determining whether an audit technology has positive expected value to the agent, as the following proposition demonstrates.

Proposition 9.6

If equilibria are sequentially stable in the two-signal/two-outcome case, then

(a) Hiring an audit technology has *positive* expected *value* for both $h = 1$ and $h = 2$ if

$$p(h = 2) < \hat{p} < p(h = 2 | \psi_2, \rho)$$

(b) Hiring an audit technology has *zero value* for both $h = 1$ and $h = 2$ if

$$p(h = 2) < p(h = 2 | \psi_2, \rho) < \hat{p}$$

(c) Hiring an audit technology can have *either positive or negative value* if

$$\hat{p} < p(h = 2) < p(h = 2 | \psi_2, \rho)$$

In cases (a) and (b), no report and the bad report both induce the separating equilibrium. The difference is in the impact of the good report. In case (b) the good report induces the separating equilibrium, and hence the audit technology has zero value. In case (a) the good report induces a pooling equilibrium which makes the agent better off, whether he has good news or bad news. In case (c), no report and the good report both induce pooling equilibria, with the latter being preferred to the former. The bad report may induce either a pooling or a separating equilibrium, but irrespective of his news the agent is worse off than in the no-report case. Whether the potential gains from the good report offset the potential losses from the bad report depends on the specifics of the problem.

Now consider the impact of increasing audit quality in the two-signal/ two-outcome case. Let $\bar{U}(h, \rho)$ denote the agent's expected utility if he has observed h and the audit technology reports ψ_h with probability ρ, for example,

$$\bar{U}(2, \rho) = \rho \cdot U\big(z_2(\psi_2), 2\big) + (1-\rho) \cdot U\big(z_2(\psi_1), 2\big)$$

The following proposition identifies the consequences of increasing ρ under the two equilibrium concepts.

Proposition 9.7

Consider a two-signal/two-outcome case and let $\frac{1}{2} < \rho' < \rho'' < 1$ denote two audit qualities:

(a) If the CK-stability criterion is employed, then

(i) $\bar{U}(h, \rho') = \bar{U}(h, \rho'') \qquad \text{all } h \in H$

(ii) $\lim_{\rho \to 1} \bar{U}(2, \rho) = U(\mathbf{c}_2^{\dagger}, 2) < \bar{U}(2, 1) = u(c_2^*)$ and

$$\bar{U}(1, \rho) = u(e) \qquad \text{all } \rho$$

(b) If the sequential stability criterion is employed, then

(i) $\bar{U}(2, \rho') < \bar{U}(2, \rho'') \qquad \text{if } \phi(h = 2 | \psi_2, \rho'') > \hat{\phi}$

(ii) $\lim_{\rho \to 1} \bar{U}(2, \rho) = \bar{U}(2, 1) = u(c_2^*)$

$$\lim_{\rho \to 1} \bar{U}(1, \rho) = \bar{U}(1, 1) = u(e)$$

Observe that if the CK-stability criterion is employed, an audit technology has zero value no matter how high its quality, unless it fully reveals the agent's private information. However, if the sequential-stability criterion is imposed, higher audit quality induces higher agent-expected utility if he has observed good news. Furthermore, in the limit, as audit quality approaches the provision of a fully revealing report, the agent's expected utility approaches the expected utility of a fully revealing report.

In the latter case, if the agent has bad news an increase in ρ increases $U(z_1(\psi_2), 1)$ if $p(h = 2 | \psi_2, \rho) > \hat{p}$, but it decreases the likelihood of reporting ψ_2. In the limit $U\big(z_1(\psi_2), 1\big)$ approaches $u(c^*_2)$, but $(1-\rho) \cdot U\big(z_1(\psi_2), 1\big)$ approaches zero and hence condition (b) holds.

Verified Ex Post Information

The preceding section considered the impact of a verified report that is produced before the agent selects his contract offer to investors. In this section we consider a report that is produced after the contract is offered, but before the agent's consumption is determined. In this case, the consumption contract is $c(x, \psi, q)$—i.e., consumption is a function of output x, ex post report ψ, and capital investment q.

The reporting system, denoted η, is part of the contract offered to investors. The agent can choose to either include η in his contract or exclude it, but he cannot influence the signal that will be generated by that system. Both the agent and the investors believe that output x and report ψ will be generated in accordance with the joint conditional-probability function $\phi(x, \psi | q, h, \eta)$. The set of possible reports is denoted $\Psi(q, \eta)$.

Reports that provide no additional information about the agent's private signal are clearly irrelevant. To ensure that we are considering reporting systems that are potentially valuable to the agent, we assume that it provides additional information about the signal.

Definition

Reporting system η is *H-informative* if for all $h_1 \neq h_2, h_1, h_2 \in H$, there exists some $x \in X(q)$ and $\psi \in \Psi(q, \eta)$ such that

$$\phi(\psi | x, q, h_1, \eta) \neq \phi(\psi | x, q, h_2, \eta)$$

If we impose the CK-stability criterion, then the separating-equilibrium contracts in the no-reporting case are again denoted $\mathbf{z}^\dagger$. The equilibrium contracts given the option to use η are denoted $\mathbf{z}^\dagger(\eta)$. The impact of the option to use η, given the CK-stability criterion, is stated in the following proposition.

Proposition 9.8

If reporting system η is H-informative and the CK-stability criterion is imposed, then reporting system η will be included in the contract offered to investors if, and only if, $h \in H^*$ and $h > 1$. Furthermore,

$$U(z_h^*, h) \geq U(z_h^\dagger(\eta), h) > U(z_h^\dagger, h) \qquad \text{if } h \in H^* \text{ and } h > 1$$

If the agent believes that his project is profitable and there are worse signals, then the agent seeks to assure investors that he does not have a worse signal. A reporting system that is H-informative has two benefits. First, it provides information that permits the agent with signal h to more efficiently provide assurances that he has not received a worse signal. Second, the increased expected utility for worse signals that would also use η relaxes the constraints associated with those signals. These benefits can never provide an expected utility greater than can be achieved with a system that perfectly reveals the agent's signal.

Observe that, given the CK-stability criterion, a reporting system could have zero value if the report is provided prior to contracting, but have positive value if the report is provided after contracting. That is, in this case, knowing later is better than knowing sooner if the information is imperfect! This is because an imperfect ex ante report will not change the risks an agent must bear to assure investors that he does not have a worse signal. However, by commiting to an ex post report (the report must not be known by the agent at the time of contracting), the agent can reduce the risks he must bear to provide those assurances.

As in the ex ante reporting case, the impact of an ex post reporting system is more complex if we impose the sequential- (instead of the CK-) stability criterion. We limit our discussion to the two-signal/two-outcome case and assume that $p(h = 2) > \hat{p}$ (i.e., the no reporting equilibrium is a pooling equilibrium). The equilibrium contracts when no reporting system is available are denoted $\mathbf{z}^{\ddagger}$ and the equilibrium contracts when reporting system η is available are denoted $\mathbf{z}^{\ddagger}(\eta)$.

If the agent has received good news, then he can improve his side-bet with investors by using η (or he can use commitment to an informative report to assure investors that he does not have bad news). If he has received bad news, then he must also use η unless he prefers to admit that he has bad news. Consequently, he may choose to use η even though it will make him worse off than if η was not available, that is, he must accept a worse side-bet if he wishes to disguise that he has bad news.

Proposition 9.9

If reporting system η is H-informative and the sequential-stability criterion is imposed, then the following results apply to the two-signal/two-outcome case in which $p(h = 2) > \hat{p}$:

(a) $U(z_2^{\ddagger}, 2) < U(z_2^{\ddagger}(\eta), 2) \leq U(z_2^{*}, 2)$
(b) $U(z_1^{\ddagger}, 1) > U(z_1^{\ddagger}(\eta), 1) \geq U(z_1^{*}, 1)$

Presignal Contracting

Thus far we have assumed that the agent acquires a private signal prior to offering a contract to investors (postsignal contracting). To some extent, the timing of the contract offer is controllable by the agent. In particular, he may be able to contract with investors prior to the acquisition of his private signal (presignal contracting). This section examines the optimal presignal contract and the value of the private signal.

The optimal presignal contract is denoted $\mathbf{z}^p = \{\mathbf{z}_1^p, \ldots, z_H^p)$, where $z_h^p = (q_h^p, \mathbf{c}_h^p)$ specifies the agent's capital investment and consumption as functions of the private signal he reports to investors. As before, $\mathbf{c}_h$ expresses consumption as a function of the reported output x and capital investment q. The agent reports his signal to investors and he could lie about what he observed. However, invoking the *revelation principal*, we restrict our attention to contracts that induce the agent to tell the truth. Since both the agent and the investors *commit* to the presignal contract, the investors require only that their expected return be non-negative when computed across all signals. It does not have to be non-negative on a signal-by-signal basis, which is effectively what is required in postsignal contracting. The optimal presignal contract is determined as follows:

$$\bar{U}(\mathbf{z}^p) = \underset{\mathbf{z}}{\text{maximize}} \quad \bar{U}(\mathbf{z}) \equiv \sum_{h \in H} U(z_h, h) \cdot p(h)$$

$$\text{subject to} \quad \bar{B}(\mathbf{z}) \equiv \sum_{h \in H} B(z_h, h) \cdot p(h) \geq 0$$

$$U(z_h, h) \geq U(z_l, h) \qquad \text{all } h, l \in H$$

The following proposition characterizes the optimal presignal contract and compares the agent's expected utility from this contract to that obtained from the postsignal contracts and that obtained if there is no private signal. Let $\mathbf{z}^\dagger$ denote the postsignal equilibrium contracts; it will depend on the type of stability criterion imposed, but the results in the following proposition are independent of those criteria. Let z^n denote the optimal no-signal contract.

Proposition 9.10

The optimal presignal contract has the following characteristics.

(a) $c_h^p(x, q_h^p) = \bar{c}^p = \sum_{h \in H^*} \sum_{x \in X(k)} (x - k) \cdot p(x|k, h) \cdot \phi(h) + e$

(b) $\bar{U}(\mathbf{z}^p) \geq \bar{U}(z^n)$, with strict inequality if, and only if, $H^* \neq H$ and $H^* \neq \phi$.

(c) $\bar{U}(\mathbf{z}^p) > \bar{U}(\mathbf{z}^\dagger)$.

Condition (a) states that the agent bears no risk, his consumption is equal to the expected output minus the expected capital investment plus his endowment. The expectation reflects the fact that $q_h = k$ if, and only if, the signal received is from the set of signals that indicate that the investment project is profitable (i.e., $h \in H^*$). Obtaining a private signal is obviously at least as good as obtaining no signal if there is presignal contracting (the agent can always offer a contract that is independent of the signal). However, to have strictly positive value the set of signals must be such that there are some signals that indicate the project is profitable and some that indicate it is unprofitable. Assuming that the private signals influence outcome beliefs, condition (c) states that the agent will be better off if he can contract prior to obtaining his private signal instead of contracting after he has obtained it. The basic reason for this is that obtaining the private signal prior to contracting implies that there are risks that the agent must bear. Ex ante, his expected consumption will be the same as in presignal contracting case, but, ex post, it will vary with the signal he receives.

These results are illustrated in figure 9–4. It is the same case as that presented in figure 9–1 except that different points are identified. Given postsignal contracting, the postsignal consumption contracts are again $\mathbf{e}$ and $\mathbf{c}_2^\dagger$. Hence, prior to obtaining his private signal, he faces two types of uncertainty about his consumption. First, ex post, the consumption contract will be either $\mathbf{e}$ or $\mathbf{c}_2^\dagger$, depending on which signal he receives. Second, given good news, his consumption will vary with the outcome that is reported. On the other hand, if the agent receives no signal, he implements the project (i.e., $q^n = k$ in this example) and bears no risk (his consumption is $\mathbf{c}^n$, which is the point of intersection between $B(\mathbf{c}^0, H)$ and the no-risk line). The agent also bears no risk if there is presignal contracting. His consumption in that case is denoted $\mathbf{c}^p$ and it is higher than $\mathbf{c}^n$ since the agent will not implement the project if he receives bad nesws, but will do so if he receives good news. The basic relationships are

$$\bar{c}^n \equiv c_1^* \cdot p(h = 1) + c_2^* \cdot p(h = 2) < \bar{c}^p \equiv e \cdot p(h = 1) + c_2^* \cdot p(h = 2)$$

$$c_2^* = \sum_{x \in X(k)} c_2^\dagger(x, k) \cdot \phi(x|k, 2)$$

Commitment is crucial in the above analysis. If the agent receives good news then he would like to renege on the contract and if he receives bad news

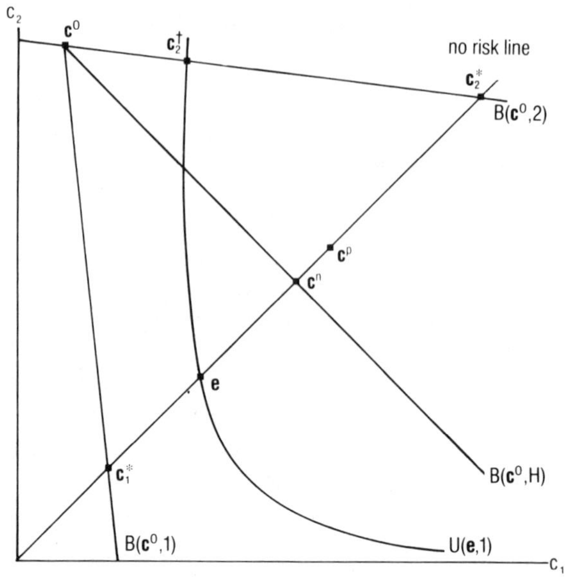

Figure 9–4. Pre-, Post-, and No-Signal Contracts

then the investors would like to renege. Observe that the agent only requires risk sharing and capital if he receives good news. Therefore, his contract could take the form of an agreement on the part of the investors to pay him a fixed amount $(\bar{c}^p - e)$ if he receives bad news and to provide the necessary investment capital $(k - e)$ in return for a specified share of the output $(x - \bar{c}^p)$ if he receives good news. An alternative form is for the agent to obtain $k - e$ units of capital at the time of contracting (i.e., when the securities are issued) and to invest k units in the project if he receives good news or in the market if he receives bad news.

The second approach is a practical means of implementing presignal contracting. Moreover, the funds held by the firm between contracting and project investment provides a possible explanation for the existence of financial slack (e.g., the holding of cash and liquid assets), and the alternative of investing in the market portfolio is consistent with diversified security holdings in other firms. Myers and Majluf [1984] provide an explanation for financial slack that also results from the acquisition of private information by the managers of firms; however, they focus on the conflict between old and new investors in on-going firms.

Observe that if securities are sold prior to the acquisition of private information there is no need for the agent to report that information, but there is no reason for him not to do so. If he does report his private information the price of the securities will increase if he reports good news and will decrease if he reports bad news.

Concluding Remarks

This paper has examined several aspects of signaling equilibria in a model of new issues markets. The basic signaling device is assuming to be a contingent contract that specifies the agent's consumption conditional on observed outcomes. Subsequent analysis considers the impact of pre- and postcontract audited reports. A crucial issue in each of these contexts is the nature of the signaling equilibria that occurs when the agent has good news and investors assign a high probability to him having good news. In that context there is no perfect sequential equilibrium and one must appeal to some other criterion to identify which contract will be offered and accepted. The Cho and Kreps (CK) stability criterion implies that the agent will select a separating contract that convinces investors that he has good news. The sequential-stability criterion, on the other hand, implies that the agent will select a pooling contract that is acceptable to investors even though they remain uncertain about whether the agent has good or bad news. The analysis demonstrates that the impact and value of audited reports, particularly precontract reports, depends critically on which criterion is employed. Under CK-stability, a precontract report can only have value if it *convinces* investors that the agent does not have bad news, whereas under sequential stability that report can have value if it merely induces investors to assign a *high probability* to the agent having good news. We have little or no evidence as to the predictive power of the two criteria. Our analysis suggests that empirical or experimental examination of this issue may be a fruitful area of future research.

Notes

1. See Milgrom [1981] for a discussion of this representation.

2. It is particularly important that the agent may not be able to undo the incentive effects of a contract by short-selling his firm's securities. See Hughes and Conroy [1986] for an analysis in which the agent is permitted to trade in the securities he issues.

3. More precisely, it is a *Bayesian* Nash equilibrium. See Harsanyi [1968].

4. Observe that in the consumption space depicted here, investor indifference curves closer to the origin imply greater expected utility, while the reverse is true for agents. In this and subsequent figures $U(\mathbf{c}, h)$ represents the set of consumption plans that provide the agent with the same expected utility as $\mathbf{c}$ if he has observed h and $B(\mathbf{c}, h)$ represents the set of consumption

plans that provide the investors with the same expected return as **c** if the agent has observed h and invested k.

5. This is a nonrestrictive assumption since the agent can always obtain **e** by offering a contract that is rejected.

6. Selten [1975] earlier introduced a similar equilibrium concept, which he termed a *perfect equilibrium*. In our context, both concepts generically produce the same results.

7. In Kreps and Wilson [1982] each player has a finite number of pure strategies. In our game the agent has an infinite number of contracts he can offer. We assume that the analysis extends to our context, noting that our game can be approximated by one in which there are a finite number of possible contracts. That is, we can make the number of possible contracts finite by assuming that there is an upper bound on the "feasible" consumption contracts and that consumption units are not infinitely divisible.

8. Assuming a finite approximation to the set of possible contracts, let $N+1$ equal the number of possible contracts. The consistency requirement can be satisfied by letting, for example,

$$\pi_{an}(z|1) = \frac{1}{N+n} \quad \text{and} \quad \pi_{an}(z|2) = \frac{1}{(N+n)^2} \qquad \text{for } z \neq z_2^{\dagger}.$$

9. We assume that if the agent is indifferent between two contracts, he chooses the contract that we designate. Alternatively, we could consider contracts that are arbitrarily close to $\mathbf{c}_2^{\dagger}$.

10. This criterion was originally proposed by Kreps [1984], but that paper has been incorporated into Cho and Kreps [1987]. They refer to it as an intuitive criterion since contracts that fail to satisfy this criterion are demonstrated to also fail to be stable equilibria as formally defined by Kohlberg and Mertens [1986].

11. The failure of $\mathbf{z}^2$ to satisfy the stability criterion can be seen by letting $z = (k, \mathbf{c}_2^{\dagger})$; hence, $H(z) = \{2\}$, $U(z, 2) > U(z_2, 2)$, and $B(z, 2) \geq 0$.

12. See appendix for proofs of all propositions.

13. See Amershi [1984] for an interesting analysis of the implications of the spanning condition for the moral hazard and adverse selection problems. He relates this condition to the demand for a sufficient statistic and obtains characterizations of optimal contracts similar to ours.

14. If we let z denote any contract in the shaded region, then $H(z) = \{1, 2\}$. Both $h = 1$ and $h = 2$ satisfy the first part of the criterion, but $h = 1$ does not satisfy the second. That is, the investors will reject z if they think that it is offered only by the agent when $h = 1$.

15. That is, the contract offered by the agent must maximize his expected utility given his signal and the investors' acceptance set, and the investors' acceptance set must include all contracts for which their posterior beliefs indicate they will receive a non-negative expected return.

16. $\mathbf{z}^{\ddagger}$ is the sequential equilibrium that provides the agent with the highest expected utility given $h = 2$. It is sequentially rational if, for example, the investors have consistent beliefs

$$P = [p(1|z) = 1, \text{ if } z \neq (k, \mathbf{c}^{\ddagger}), \quad \text{and} \quad p\big(1|(k, \mathbf{c}^{\ddagger})\big) = p(1)]$$

17. See lemma 9A.5 in the appendix. We consider multiple outcomes, but the proof would be more straightforward if we limited the number of outcomes to two. A similar result for the two-outcome insurance game is provided by lemma 4 of Wilson [1977].

18. That is, $\phi(x|k, h, \psi) = \phi(x|k, h)$. For an analysis in which the audited reports provide additional information about the outcome see Titman and Trueman [1986].

19. See Feltham and Hughes [1987] for another analysis of the impact of audited reports based on the use of the CK-stability criterion. That analysis differs from the one presented here in

that it assumes that agent preferences are represented by a negative exponential utility function, the return is normally distributed with a privately known mean, the set of possible private signals is a continuum, and only linear contracts can be offered. That more specific structure facilitates examination of the impact on audit technology value of variations in parameters representing audit quality, the type of signal the agent has received, the agent's aversion to risk, and the riskiness of his return.

APPENDIX 9

Let

$$\underline{U}(z) \equiv \Sigma_x u[c(x)] \cdot \underline{\phi}(x)$$

$$\bar{U}(z) \equiv \Sigma_x u[c(x)] \cdot \bar{\phi}(x)$$

$$\underline{B}(z) \equiv \Sigma_x [x - c(x) - e + q] \cdot \underline{\phi}(x)$$

$$\bar{B}(z) \equiv \Sigma_x [x - c(x) - e + q] \cdot \bar{\phi}(x)$$

Observe that

$$U(z, h) = w(h) \cdot \bar{U}(z) + [1 - w(h)] \cdot \underline{U}(z) \tag{9A.1}$$

and

$$B(z, h) = w(h) \cdot \bar{B}(z) + [1 - w(h)] \cdot \underline{B}(z)$$

Let

$$Z^0 \equiv \{z \in Z \mid \bar{B}(z) = 0 \quad \text{and} \quad \underline{B}(z) = 0, q = k\}$$

Lemma 9A.1

Given spanning (SC), the following conditions hold:

(a) For any signals $h_1 < l < h_2$ and any contract z,

$$U(z, l) = w \cdot U(z, h_2) + (1 - w) \cdot U(z, h_1) \tag{9A.2}$$

$$B(z, l) = w \cdot B(z, h_2) + (1 - w) \cdot B(z, h_1)$$

where $$w = \frac{w(l) - w(h_1)}{w(h_2) - w(h_1)}$$

(b) For any two contracts $z_1, z_2 \in Z$, either $U(z_1, h) = U(z_2, h)$ for all $h \in H$ or at most one $h \in H$.

(c) If for any two contracts $z_1, z_2 \in Z$ there exists a unique $w \in (0, 1)$ such that $w \cdot \bar{U}(z_1) + (1 - w) \cdot \underline{U}(z_1) = w \cdot \bar{U}(z_2) + (1 - w) \cdot \underline{U}(z_2)$, then either $U(z_1, l) < U(z_2, l)$ for all $w(l) > w$ and $U(z_1, l) > U(z_2, l)$ for all $w(l) < w$, or the reverse inequalities hold.

(d) Given MLRC, if z is such that $c(x)$ is increasing in x, then $U(z, h_1) < U(z, h_2)$ if, and only if, $h_1 < h_2$.

(e) For any two contracts $z_1, z_2 \in Z$, either $B(z_1, h) = B(z_2, h)$ for all $h \in H$ or at most one $h \in H$.

(f) If for any two contracts $z_1, z_2 \in Z$ there exists a unique $w \in (0, 1)$ such that $w \cdot \bar{B}(z_1) + (1 - w) \cdot \underline{B}(z_1) = w \cdot \bar{B}(z_2) + (1 - w) \cdot \underline{B}(z_2)$, then either $B(z_1, l) < B(z_2, l)$ for all $w(l) > w$ and $B(z_1, l) > B(z_2, l)$ for all $w(l) < w$, or the reverse inequalities hold.

Proof:

(a) Begin with equation (9A.2), substitute for $U(z, h_1)$ and $U(z, h_2)$ using (9A.1), and simplify using the definition of w. The result is $U(z, l) = w(l) \cdot \bar{U}(z) + [1 - w(l)] \cdot \underline{U}(z)$, which is consistent with (9A.1).

(b) If $\underline{U}(z_1) = \underline{U}(z_2)$ and $\bar{U}(z_1) = \bar{U}(z_2)$, then $U(z_1, h) = U(z_2, h)$ for all $h \in H$. If either $\underline{U}(z_1) \neq \underline{U}(z_2)$ and/or $\bar{U}(z_1) \neq \bar{U}(z_2)$, then

$$w \cdot \bar{U}(z_1) + (1 - w) \cdot \underline{U}(z_1) = w \cdot \bar{U}(z_2) + (1 - w) \cdot \underline{U}(z_2)$$

if, and only if,

$$w = \frac{\underline{U}(z_2) - \underline{U}(z_1)}{\bar{U}(z_1) - \underline{U}(z_1) - \bar{U}(z_2) + \underline{U}(z_2)}$$

and the denominator does not equal zero.

(c) A unique $w \in (0, 1)$ exists if either (i) $\bar{U}(z_1) - \underline{U}(z_1) - \bar{U}(z_2) + \underline{U}(z_2) < \underline{U}(z_2) - \underline{U}(z_1) \leq 0$ or (ii) both inequalities are reversed. In case (i), $U(z_1, l) < U(z_2, l)$ for all $w(l) > w$ and $U(z_1, l) > U(z_2, l)$ for all $w(l) < w$. The reverse inequalities hold in case (ii).

(d) MLRC implies that $\underline{U}(z) < \bar{U}(z)$, and the result then follows directly from SC.
(e) The proof is similar to (b).
(f) The proof is similar to (c). Q.E.D.

Lemma 9A.2

Any sequential equilibrium strategy **z** must be such that

1. If $l < h$, then either $\bar{U}(z_h) = \bar{U}(z_l)$ and $\underline{U}(z_l) = \underline{U}(z_h)$

   or $\bar{U}(z_h) > \bar{U}(z_l)$ and $\underline{U}(z_l) > \underline{U}(z_h)$

2. $\bar{B}(z_h) \geq 0$ for all $h \in H$.

Proof:

(a) Since $w(h) > w(l)$, if neither of the two conditions hold, then one or both of the following violations of the equilibrium must occur: l strictly prefers z_h to z_l or h strictly prefers z_l to z_h.
(b) The proof is by contradiction. Assume that there is some equilibrium contract z_y offered by all $h \in H_y \subseteq H$ (where H_y can be a single signal or a set) such that $\bar{B}(z_y) < 0$. Since the contract is accepted by investors there must be at least one signal $h \in H_y$ such that $B(z_y, h) \geq 0$ and $w(h) < 1$. (H_y cannot consist of only the best signal, $w(h) = 1$, since the investors would not accept that contract if $\bar{B}(z_y) < 0$.)

Observe that the investors will accept any contract $z \in Z^0$, since they break-even for all $h \in H$. We now prove that h strictly prefers some $z \in Z^0$ to z_y. Consider the following choice problem for h:

$$\begin{aligned} &\text{maximize} && U(z, h) \\ &\text{subject to} && B(z, h) \geq 0 \\ &&& \bar{B}(z) \leq 0 \end{aligned}$$

The feasible set includes both z_y and Z^0, and the latter consists of all the contracts z for which both constraints are binding. Therefore, the contradiction follows from the fact that both constraints are binding in the optimal solution and they are not binding for z_y. (If the first constraint is excluded, then the problem is unbounded, which violates the first constraint. If the second constraint is excluded, then the solution is the riskless contract that pays c_h^*, which violates the second constraint.) Q.E.D.

Algorithm 9A.1

This algorithm identifies a strategy $\mathbf{z}$ in which the agent offers a different contract for each signal $h \in H^*$.

1. Let $h = 1$ and

$$z_1 = \begin{cases} (0, e) & \text{if } \bar{x}(k, 1) \leq k \\ (k, c_1^*) & \text{if } \bar{x}(k, 1) > k \end{cases}$$

2. (a) Let $h = h + 1$.
   (b) If $\bar{x}(k, h) \leq k$, $z_h = (0, \mathbf{e})$.
   (c) If $\bar{x}(k, h) > k$, z_h solves the following problem:

$$\underset{z \in Z}{\text{maximize}} \quad U(z, h)$$

$$\text{subject to} \quad U(z, l) \leq U(z_l, l) \quad \text{all } l < h. \tag{9A.3}$$

$$B(z, h) \geq 0 \tag{9A.4}$$

   (d) If $h < H$, go to (a), otherwise stop.

The Lagrangian for step 2(c) is

$$U(z, h) - \sum_{l=1}^{h-1} \mu_l \cdot [U(z, l) - U(z_l, l)] + \lambda_h \cdot B(z, h) \tag{9A.5}$$

and differentiating with respect to $c(x)$ for each x provides first-order condition

$$u'(c_h(x)) = \lambda_h \cdot \left[1 - \sum_{l=1}^{h-1} \mu_l \cdot \frac{\phi(x|k, l)}{\phi(x|k, h)} \right]^{-1} \tag{9A.6}$$

Lemma 9A.3

The solution to step 2(c) of algorithm 9A.1 is such that for all $h \geq 2$ and $h \in H^*$,

(a) $B(z_h, h) = 0$ and $B(z_h, l) \leq 0$ if $l < h$.
(b) $U(z_h, h - 1) = U(z_{h-1}, h - 1)$ and $U(z_h, l) < U(z_l, l)$ if $l < h - 1$.

Proof

(a) $B(z_h, h) \neq 0$ implies that $\lambda = 0$, which in turn implies by condition (9A.6) that $c_h(x)$ must be such that $u'(\cdot) = 0$. The latter is impossible, given nonsatiation. Hence, constraint (9A.4) must be binding.

$$B(z_h, h) = w(h) \cdot \bar{B}(z_h) + [1 - w(h)] \cdot \underline{B}(z_h) = 0 \quad \text{and} \quad \bar{B}(z_h) \geq 0$$

(from lemma 9A.2(b)) imply that

$$B(z_h, l) = w(l) \cdot \bar{B}(z_h) + [1 - w(l)] \cdot \underline{B}(z_h) \leq 0 \quad \text{for } w(l) < w(h).$$

(b) Observe that if $\mu_l = 0$ for all $l < h$, then $c_h(x)$ must be a constant. However, a constant such that $B(z_h, h) = 0$ would be preferred to z_l by all $l < h$. Therefore, constraint (9A.3) must be binding for at least one $l < h$. This implies that $c_h(x)$ is increasing in x.

The remainder of the proof is by *induction*. If $h = 2$, then $U(z_2, 1) = U(z_1, 1)$ follows immediately. If $h > 2$ is the smallest signal in H^*, then the result follows from the fact that $U(z_l, l) = u(e)$ for all $l < h$, and $U(z_h, l)$ is strictly increasing in l (by lemma 9A.1(d)).

Now assume that (b) holds for all signals up to and including any arbitrary $h \in H^*, h > 2$, and prove that it holds for $h + 1$. Observe that (a) and lemma 9A.1(f) imply that $B(z_h, l) \geq 0$ for all $l > h$—i.e., z_h is a feasible contract for all better signals. This, plus the fact that z_h does not satisfy condition (9A.6) for $h + 1$, establishes that,

$$U(z_{h+1}, h + 1) > U(z_h, h + 1) \tag{9A.7}$$

The remainder of the proof is by *contradiction*.

Assume that $U(z_{h+1}, h) < U(z_h, h)$. Since by construction $U(z_h, l) \leq U(z_l, l)$ for all $l < h$ and there exists some $l < h$ such that $U(z_{h+1}, l) = U(z_l, l)$, it follows that

$$U(z_{h+1}, l) \geq U(z_h, l) \tag{9A.8}$$

From lemma 9A.1(a) there exists a w such that

$$U(z_{h+1}, h) = w \cdot U(z_{h+1}, h + 1) + (1 - w) \cdot U(z_{h+1}, l) \tag{9A.9}$$

$$U(z_h, h) = w \cdot U(z_h, h + 1) + (1 - w) \cdot U(z_h, l) \tag{9A.10}$$

However, (9A.7), (9A.8), (9A.9), and (9A.10) imply that

$$U(z_{h+1}, h) > U(z_h, h)$$

which contradicts our initial assumption.

Now *assume* that $U(z_{h+1}, h) = U(z_h, h)$ and $U(z_{h+1}, l) = U(z_l, l)$ for some $l < h$. By assumption, $U(z_h, h-1) = U(z_{h-1}, h-1)$. Hence, if $l = h-1$, then $U(z_{h+1}, h-1) = U(z_h, h-1)$, which contradicts lemma 9A.1(b), since z_h and z_{h+1} cannot be equivalent contracts and satisfy (9A.6). If l is the largest signal less than $h-1$ such that $U(z_{h+1}, l) = U(z_l, l)$, then by assumption

$$U(z_{h+1}, l) = U(z_{l+1}, l)$$

$$U(z_{h+1}, l+1) < U(z_{l+1}, l+1)$$

However, that would imply that $U(z_{h+1}, h+1) < U(z_{l+1}, h+1)$ by lemma 9A.1(c), which would contradict the optimality of z_{h+1}. Q.E.D.

Lemma 9A.4

If contract z is such that $U(z, h) > U(z_h, h)$ and $B(z, h) \geq 0$, then $B(z, l) < 0$ is a necessary condition for $U(z, l) > U(z_l, l)$ if $l < h$.

Proof: Proof is by contradiction. Let l denote the smallest signal less than h such that $U(z, l) > U(z_l, l)$ and $B(z, l) \geq 0$. Observed that z is a preferred, feasible solution to l's problem, which contradicts our assumption that z_l is the solution to his problem. Q.E.D.

Proof of Proposition 9.1

Consider the solution to algorithm 9A.1 as the proposed equilibrium. By construction, the agent never strictly prefers z_h to z_l if he has observed $l < h$. Lemma 9A.3(a) establishes that z_h is feasible if he has observed $l > h$, but it will not satisfy condition (9A.6), implying that z_l is strictly preferred to z_h for $l > h$. Hence, the agent will offer z_h if he observes h and the investors' acceptance set is

$$A = \{z | z = z_h, \text{ some } h \in H, \quad \text{or} \quad B(z, 1) \geq 0\}$$

Constraint (9A.4) ensures that the investors receive a non-negative expected return. If they hold the following beliefs,

$$P = [p(h | z_h) = 1, \text{ all } h \in H, \quad p(1 | z) = 1, \text{ all } z \neq z_h, \text{ all } h \in H]$$

then $\gamma = (P, \mathbf{z}, A)$ is a sequential equilibrium.

This equilibrium satisfies the CK-stability criterion. Any contract z that is preferred to z_h, if the agent observed h, must violate either (9A.3) or (9A.4). If z

violates (9A.4), then it directly violates condition (2) of the CK-stability criterion. If z violates constraint (9A.3) for some $l < h$, then lemma 9A.4 establishes that condition (2) of the stability criterion is violated by l.

No other separating equilibrium can satisfy the CK-stability criterion, since it would imply the existence of a contract z that is preferred to z_h for one, and only one, signal $h \in H^*$ and is acceptable to investors. Furthermore, no pooling equilibrium (i.e., one in which $z_h = z_l$ for some $h, l \in H^*$) can satisfy the CK-stability criterion. If $h > l$, then $B(z_h, h) > 0$ and there exists a contract z that is preferred to z_h, given signal h, but is less preferred for all other signals in the pool, and satisfies $B(z, h) \geq 0$.

Part (b) of proposition 9.1 follows from (9A.6) and lemma 9A.3(b).

Q.E.D.

Lemma 9A.5

All sequentially stable pools are convex.

Proof: From lemma 9A.2(a) we know that if $h_1 < l < h_2$ and $z_{h_1} = z_{h_2} = z_y$, then $\bar{U}(z_l) = \bar{U}(z_y)$ and $\underline{U}(z_l) = \underline{U}(z_y)$ i.e., z_l and z_y provide the same level of expected utility given any signal. Let H_l denote the pool of which l is a member. The investors will break-even in any sequentially stable pool since the investors will reject any contract for a pool in which they lose and the agents in a pool can always find an alternative feasible contract they all prefer if the investors are making a positive profit on their contract. However, if $B(z_y, H_y) = B(z_l, H_l) = 0$, then, given $\bar{B}(z_y) > 0$ and $\bar{B}(z_l) > 0$ from lemma 9A.2(b), either $B(z_y, H_y \cup H_l) > 0$ or $B(z_l, H_y \cup H_l) > 0$, which implies that the agents in pools H_y and H_l can find an alternative *common contract* they all prefer and that will be acceptable to investors. Q.E.D.

Algorithm 9A.2

This algorithm identifies a strategy $\mathbf{z}$ in which the agent may offer the same contract for more than one signal.

1. Let $h = 1$ and

$$z_{11} = \begin{cases} (0, \mathbf{e}) & \text{if } \bar{x}(k, 1) \leq k \\ (k, \mathbf{c}_1^*) & \text{if } \bar{x}(k, 1) > k \end{cases}$$

2. (a) Let $h = h + 1$.
   (b) If $\bar{x}(k, h) \leq k$, $z_{lh} = (0, \mathbf{e})$ for all $l \in \{1, \ldots, h\}$.
   (c) If $\bar{x}(k, h) > k$, let d denote the best type worse than h from which h separates himself if h is himself separated from all better types. For each $d = 0, 1, \ldots, h-1$, solve the following problem, where $H_{hd} = \{d+1, \ldots, h\}$:

$$U(z^*_{hd}, h, d) = \underset{z \in Z}{\text{maximize}} \qquad U(z, h)$$

$$\text{subject to} \qquad U(z, l) \leq U(z_{ld}, l) \qquad \text{all } l \leq d \tag{9A.11}$$

$$\sum_{l \in H_{hd}} B(z, l) \cdot p(l \mid H_{hd}) \geq 0 \tag{9A.12}$$

Note: For $d = 0$, there is no constraint (9A.11).
   (d) Let $d^*_h \in \operatorname{argmax} U(z^*_{hd}, h, d)$ and let

$$z_{lh} = \begin{cases} z^*_{hd} & \text{for } l \in \{d^*_h + 1, \ldots, h\} \\ z_{ld} & \text{for } l \in \{1, \ldots, d^*_h\} \end{cases}$$

   (e) If $h < H$, go to (a), otherwise let $z_h = z_{hH}$, all $h \in H$, and stop. The Lagrangian for the maximization problem in step 2(c) is

$$U(z, h) - \sum_{l=1}^{d} \mu_l \cdot [U(z, l) - U(z_{ld}, h)] + \lambda \cdot B(z, H_{hd})$$

and differentiating with respect to $c(x)$ for each x provides first-order condition

$$u'(c_{hd}(x)) = \lambda \cdot \frac{\phi(x \mid k, H_{hd})}{\phi(x \mid k, h)} \cdot \left[1 - \sum_{l=1}^{d} \mu_l \cdot \frac{\phi(x \mid k, l)}{\phi(x \mid k, h)}\right]^{-1}$$

Lemma 9A.6

The solution to step 2(c) in algorithm 9A.6 is such that for $h \geq 2$ and $h \in H^*$:

(a) Constraint (9A.12) is binding.
(b) Constraint (9A.11) is only binding for $l = d$, $d > 0$.
(c) The solution to step 2(d) is such that $B(z_{hh}, l)$ is monotone increasing in l, for $h > 1$, $h \in H^*$.

Proof: The proofs of (a) and (b) parallel the proof of lemma 9A.3 and are not repeated here. (c) holds if, and only if, $\underline{B}(z_{hh}) < \bar{B}(z_{hh})$. Assume to the contrary that $\underline{B}(z_{hh}) \geq \bar{B}(z_{hh})$, which with (9A.12) implies that $B(z_{hh}, 1) \geq 0$.

If $d_h^* = 0$, then $U(z_{hh}, 1) \geq U(z_{11}, 1)$ and Jensen's inequality imply that $B(z_{hh}, 1) < B(z_{11}, 1) = 0$, a contradiction.

If $d_h^* \geq 1$, then $U(z_{1h}, 1) \geq U(z_{hh}, 1)$ implies that $B(z_{hh}, 1) < 0$, a contradiction (otherwise, both constraints (9A.11) and (9A.12) could be relaxed by including $h = 1$ in the pool). Q.E.D.

Proof of Proposition 9.2

Given the convexity of the pools from lemma 9A.5, algorithm 9A.2 identifies the equilibrium pooling contracts. Observe that if h is separated from all $l > h$, then the algorithm identifies the "best" sequential equilibrium for h given the set $\{1, \ldots, h\}$. As in algorithm 9A.1, we begin at the worst signal and work up. At each stage we determine $z_{1h}, \ldots, z_{hh}$, where z_{lh} is the contract offered by the agent if he observes l and the set of possible signals is $\{1, \ldots, h\}$.

The algorithm ensures that, for all $l \in H_y$, the agent prefers z_y to the contracts for all "better" pools. Since, by lemma 9A.6(c), the contracts for "worse" pools are acceptable to investors if offered by h_y and the agent has chosen z_y, it follows that the agent prefers z_y to all other acceptable contracts if he has observed h_y. The algorithm does not directly ensure that other members of the pool prefer not to defect from it. Pooling constraints could be included to preclude defection. However, given lemma 9A.5(c), if the pooling constraint is binding for any $l \in H_y$, then that implies that h_y would not have chosen to include l in his pool—dropping l from the pool would relax both the pooling constraint and constraint (9A.11). Q.E.D.

Proof of Proposition 9.4

(a) *Separating Equilibria*: The equality for $h \in H \setminus H^*$ follows directly from propositions 9.1 and 9.3. For $h \in H^*$, the strict inequality follows from the fact that z_h^* maximizes $U(z, h)$ subject to $B(z, h) \geq 0$, whereas z_h satisfies the same constraint plus additional constraints (see (9A.3)) that are binding unless $h = 1$.

(b) *Pooling Equilibria*: If $h \in H \setminus H^*$ or $h = 1$, then $z_h^* = (0, \mathbf{e})$ or $(k, \mathbf{c}_1^*)$. The expected utility for these signals can be higher, but not lower, in a pooling equilibrium.

If $h = h_y$ and $h \in H^*$, then z_y satisfies the constraint $B(z, h) \geq 0$ but is subject to $B(z, H_y) \geq 0$, which is a more restrictive constraint unless $y = h$. z_y is also subject to other constraints (see (9A.11)) which are binding unless $h = 1 \in y$.

If $h \neq h_y$ we have two possibilities. Figure 9–2 illustrates a case where the bad-news agent is made worse off by perfect revelation of h—i.e., $U(\mathbf{c}^{\ddagger}, 1) > U(\mathbf{e}, 1)$. The case where $U(z_h, h) < U(z_h^*, h)$ can be illustrated by constructing an example in which $H = \{1, 2, 3\}$ and $Y = \{\{1\}, \{2, 3\}\}$. If $h = 2$, then costless verification eliminates the agent's gain from disguising that he has not observed $h = 3$, but provides a gain by assuring investors that he has not observed $h = 1$; the net gain to the agent can be positive. Q.E.D.

Proof of Proposition 9.5

Separating equilibria depend only on the support of the investors' beliefs (and not on the form of the distribution over that support). Hence, if $H(\psi) = H$ for all $\psi \in \Psi(h)$, then the separating equilibrium for each report is the same as without the report. Therefore, a necessary condition for the audit technology to have value is that some report ψ eliminates some signal $l < h$.

The sufficiency of eliminating some $l < h$ ($l \in H^*$ or l is the best signal in $H \setminus H^*$) follows from the algorithm in the proof of proposition 9.1. Lemma 9A.2(a) establishes that constraint (9A.1) is always binding for the adjacent signal. Therefore, eliminating l relaxes a binding constraint for step $l + 1$, resulting in a strict increase in $U(z_{l+1}, l + 1)$. This in turn relaxes a binding constraint for $l + 2$, with similar effects on up to H. Therefore, for any $h > l$, $U(z_h, h)$ is strictly increased. Q.E.D.

Proof of Proposition 9.7

(a) Under the CK-stability criterion, the equilibrium is the same for *all* values of ρ less than 1 (no matter how close to 1). For $\rho = 1$, the good report excludes the possibility of bad news and we have the perfect-report equilibrium.

(b) Under the sequential-stability criterion, pooling occurs if $p(h = 2|\psi_2, \rho) > \hat{p}$, which yields a higher expected utility than separation. If both ρ' and ρ'' result in pooling, then $\bar{U}(2, \rho') < \bar{U}(2, \rho'')$ follows from the fact that $B(z, H) \geq 0$ is a more restrictive binding constraint with investor beliefs $p(h = 2|\psi_2, \rho')$ than with $p(h = 2|\psi_2, \rho'')$.

For any $\varepsilon > 0$ there exists a $\delta > 0$ such that for all ρ satisfying $1 - \delta < \rho < 1$, $\|\mathbf{c}^\ddagger(\rho) - \mathbf{c}_2^*\| < \varepsilon$, where $\mathbf{c}^\ddagger(\rho)$ is the equilibrium pooling contract given ρ and a good report. Since $\mathbf{c}^\ddagger(\rho)$ converges uniformly to $\mathbf{c}_2^*$ as ρ goes to one, $U(\mathbf{c}^\ddagger(\rho), h)$ converges uniformly to $u(\mathbf{c}_2^*)$ for both $h = 1$ and $h = 2$. However, as ρ goes to one the probability of the good report approaches one if $h = 2$, but approaches zero if $h = 1$. Q.E.D.

Proof of Proposition 9.8

There are no benefits to using η if $h \in H \backslash H^*$ or $h = 1 \in H^*$ since, given separation, the contract $(0, \mathbf{e})$ or $(k, \mathbf{c}_1^*)$ cannot be improved upon in those cases. The agent's decision problem given the use of η and $h \in H^* (h > 1)$ is the same as in the proof of proposition 9.1 except that z now specifies whether η is used or not and, if η is used, consumption is expressed as a function of both x and ψ (instead of just x) and probability function $\phi(x, \psi|k, h, \eta)$ is used (instead of $\phi(x|k, h)$). The Lagrangian and first-order conditions given in the proof of proposition 9.1 are similarly changed, with the latter taking the form

$$u'(c_h(x, \psi)) = \lambda_h \cdot \left[1 - \sum_{l=1}^{h-1} \mu_l \cdot \frac{\phi(x, \psi|k, l, \eta)}{\phi(x, \psi|k, h, \eta)}\right]^{-1}$$

The agent's contract choice must always satisfy $B(z, h) \geq 0$ and z_h^* is the optimal contract given only that constraint. Consequently, $z_h^\dagger(\eta)$ cannot improve upon that contract.

If $h \in H^*$ $(h > 1)$ and η is H-informative, then for some $l < h$, $\mu_l \neq 0$ and there exists some x and ψ such that

$$\frac{\phi(x, \psi|k, l, \eta)}{\phi(x, \psi|k, h, \eta)} \neq \frac{\phi(x|k, l)}{\phi(x|k, h)}$$

Consequently, the first-order conditions establish that $c_h(x, \psi)$ depends non-trivially on ψ, which implies that $z_h^\dagger(\eta)$ strictly improves upon $z_h^\dagger$. Q.E.D.

Proof of Proposition 9.9

In the pooling equilibrium, the contract must satisfy $B(z, H) \geq 0$, which is more restrictive than $B(z, 2) \geq 0$. Consequently, $\mathbf{c}_2^\dagger(\eta)$ cannot provide the agent with any higher expected utility than c_2^*. The following demonstrates that the agent obtains strict improvement with $\mathbf{c}_2^\dagger(\eta)$ over $\mathbf{c}_2^\dagger$ if $h = 2$. (This is similar to the approach used by Holmstrom [1982] in a similar theorem in a moral hazard context.)

Given H-informativeness, there exists a set $\bar{\Psi} \subset \Psi$ (for each x) such that

$$D(x) \equiv \frac{\phi(x, \bar{\Psi}|k, 2, \eta)}{\phi(x, \bar{\Psi}|k, H, \eta)} - \frac{\phi(x, \bar{\Psi}^c|k, 2, \eta)}{\phi(x, \bar{\Psi}^c|k, H, \eta)} > 0$$

Let $\delta c(x, \psi)$ represent a variation in $c^\ddagger(x)$ such that it is positive and constant for all $\psi \in \bar{\Psi}$, negative and constant for all $\psi \in \bar{\Psi}^c$, and

$$\delta c(x, \bar{\Psi}) \cdot \phi(x, \bar{\Psi}|k, H, \eta) + \delta c(x, \bar{\Psi}^c) \cdot \phi(x, \bar{\Psi}^c|k, H, \eta) = 0$$

Therefore, $c(x, \psi) \equiv c^\ddagger(x) + \delta c(x, \psi)$ satisfies the constraint $B(z, H) \geq 0$ (which is the only constraint in this problem). For small variations, the change in the agent's expected utility given output x and signal $h = 2$ is

$$\begin{aligned}\delta U^\ddagger(x, 2) &= u'(c^\ddagger(x)) \cdot [\delta c(x, \bar{\Psi}) \cdot \phi(x, \bar{\Psi}|k, 2, \eta) + \delta c(x, \bar{\Psi}^c) \cdot \phi(x, \bar{\Psi}^c|k, 2, \eta)] \\ &= u'(c^\ddagger(x)) \cdot \delta c(x, \bar{\Psi}) \cdot \phi(x, \bar{\Psi}|k, H, \eta) \cdot D(x) > 0\end{aligned}$$

Consequently, if the agent has good news he can improve upon $U(\mathbf{c}^\ddagger, 2)$ if he has an H-informative system. Any such improvement must make him worse off if he has bad news since the constraint $B(z, H) \geq 0$ ensures that investors are no worse off. (For example, $\delta U^\ddagger(x, 1) < 0$ for the variation constructed above.) Of course, the agent can never do worse than consuming his endowment. Q.E.D.

References

Amershi, A.H. [1984]. "A Theory of Informativeness Under Asymmetric Information." Working Paper, University of British Columbia.

Berge, J.E., Dickhaut, J.W., and Senkow, D.W. [1986]. "Signalling Equilibria in Experimental Markets: Rothschild and Stiglitz vs. Wilson vs. Riley." Working Paper, University of Minnesota.

Cho, I.K., and Kreps, D.M. [1987]. "Signaling Games and Stable Equilibria." *Quarterly Journal of Economics* 102, 179–221.

Dasgupta, P., and Maskin, E. [1986]. "The Existence of Equilibrium in Discontinuous Economic Games, I: Theory and II: Applications." *Review of Economic Studies* 53, 1–41.

Feltham, G.A., and Hughes, J.S. [1987]. "The Role of Audits and Audit Quality in Valuing New Issues." Working Paper, University of British Columbia.

Grossman, S.J., and Hart, O.D. [1983]. "An Analysis of the Principal-Agent Problem." *Econometrica* 51, 7–45.

Grossman, S.J., and Perry, M. [1986]. "Perfect Sequential Equilibrium." *Journal of Economic Theory* 39, 97–119.

Hakansson, N.H., Kunkel, J.G., and Ohlson, J.A. [1982]. "Sufficient and Necessary Conditions for Information to Have Social Value in Pure Exchange." *Journal of Finance* 37, 1169–1181.

Harsanyi, J.C. [1967–1968]. "Games with Incomplete Information Played by 'Bayesian' Players: Parts I to III." *Management Science* 14, 159–182, 320–334, and 486–502.

Holmstrom, B. [1979]. "Moral Hazard and Observability." *Bell Journal of Economics* 10, 74–91.

Holmstrom, B. [1982]. "Moral Hazard in Teams." *Bell Journal of Economics* 13, 324–340.

Hughes, J.S., and Conroy, R. [1986]. "Risk Sharing Implications of Insider Trading in an Exchange Economy With Private Information." Working Paper, University of British Columbia.

Kohlberg, E., and Mertens, J.-F. [1986]. "On the Strategic Stability of Equilibria." *Econometrica* 54, 1003–1037.

Kreps, D.M. [1984]. "Signalling Games and Stable Equilibria." Working Paper, Stanford University.

Kreps, D.M., and Wilson, R. [1982]. "Sequential Equilibria." *Econometrica* 50, 863–894.

Kunkel, J.G. [1982]. "Sufficient Conditions for Public Information to Have Social Value in a Production and Exchange Economy." *Journal of Finance* 37, 1005–1013.

Leland, H.E., and Pyle, D.H. [1977]. "Informational Asymmetries, Financial Structure, and Financial Intermediation." *Journal of Finance* 32, 371–387.

Milgrom, P.R. [1981]. "Good News and Bad News: Representation Theorems and Applications." *Bell Journal of Economics* 12, 380–391.

Myers, S.C., and Majluf, N.S. [1984]. "Corporate Financing and Investment Decisions When Firms Have Information That Investors Do Not Have." *Journal of Financial Economics* 13, 187–221.

Ohlson, J.A., and Buckman, G. [1981]. "Toward a Theory of Financial Accounting: Welfare and Public Information." *Journal of Accounting Research* 19, 399–433.

Rothschild, M., and Stiglitz, J. [1976]. "Equilibrium in Competitive Insurance Markets: An Essay on the Economics of Imperfect Information." *Quarterly Journal of Economics* 90, 629–649.

Selten, R. [1975]. "A Reexamination of the Perfectness Concept for Equilibrium Points in Extensive Games." *International Journal of Game Theory* 4, 25–55.

Titman, S., and Trueman, B. [1986]. "Information Quality and the Valuation of New Issues." *Journal of Accounting and Economics* 8, 159–172.

Wilson, C.A. [1977]. "A Model of Insurance Markets with Incomplete Information." *Journal of Economic Theory*, 167–207.

10 MANAGERIAL COMPENSATION: *Linear-Sharing vs. Bonus-Incentive Plans Under Moral Hazard and Adverse Selection**

Masako N. Darrough
Neal M. Stoughton

In the fall of 1978, with the Chrysler Corporation perilously close to bankruptcy, Lee Iaccoca accepted the difficult job of running the corporation with an annual salary of \$360,000, options to buy 400,000 shares of Chrysler common stock at \$11 each, plus special payments amounting to more than a million dollars.[1] Next summer, he volunteered to reduce his base salary to \$1.00 for a period of one year.[2] Although this may not be a typical example, it is nonetheless illustrative of the nature of incentive compensation plans at the senior management level. "Successful" senior managers are extremely highly paid. Fox and Peck [1985] report the median total compensation of chief executive officers in large manufacturing firms to be \$442,000.[3,4] Although

* An earlier version of this paper was presented in seminars at UBC, UC-Berkeley, UCLA, Columbia, Davis, Minnesota, NYU, Northwestern and the 1984 summer meetings of the Econometric society. We are grateful for comments from the participants, in particular Michael Whinston. We would also like to thank Jerry Feltham for his numerous helpful suggestions. Stoughton's research is partially supported by Grant 410-83-0786 R 1 provided by the Social Sciences and Humanities Research Council of Canada.

the variation seems to be large, all the figures contained in this report are in the six-digit range. It is readily apparent that both level and composition of top executive compensation packages is different from that of workers in other occupations. Particularly notable is the recent trend toward paying a substantial portion of the total compensation in the form of incentive plans, such as annual bonus, long-term performance reward, stock options, and restricted stocks.[5] Most (92%) of the manufacturing firms in the Fox–Peck survey used annual bonus plans for their senior executives in 1984; 88% of these actually paid bonuses. A particular form of incentive plan such as deferred bonus might partly be motivated by tax considerations, but it appears that provision of proper incentive is the raison d'etre.[6]

In this paper, we investigate the issue of managerial compensation as incentive contracts with a special focus on two widely observed contractual forms: linear-sharing and bonus-salary plans. The linear-sharing contract is represented by $\phi(y) = w + sy$, where $\phi(y)$ is the pecuniary compensation, w is the fixed salary, s is the proportional share, and y is the output (profit). Special cases of interest are a pure salary contract ($s = 0$), a pure rental contract ($w < 0$, $s = 1$), and a pure piece-rate contract ($w = 0$, $s < 1$). The bonus-salary form is piecewise linear with a fixed salary up to some level and an additional share above—i.e. $\phi(y) = w$ if $y < b$ and $\phi(y) = w + s(y - b)$ if $y \geq b$ where b is the threshold level. Proportional bonuses and stock options (with exercise price of b) are obvious examples. Certain types of budget-based compensation may take this piecewise linear form: the process of participative budget (standard) setting is an example, where the threshold is the budget against which managerial performance is measured. Demski and Feltham [1978] have analyzed budget-based contracts with dichotomous reward levels and found that they may be preferable to linear-sharing contracts. We also show in this paper advantages of the budget-based contracts in promoting "self-selection", particularly when two-attribute private information exists.

The particular setting we have in mind for our analysis is that of a standard agency model with precontractual private information. A principal (representing shareholders) with a fixed amount of capital is interested in engaging an agent (manager) to carry out a project on her behalf. The agent is endowed with (precontractual) private information which is useful in assessing the profitability of the project. This information (sometimes referred to as signal or news) may concern the agent's innate general ability, project-specific ability, or may be related to the project profitability independent of his ability. The source or the means by which this private information accrues to the agent is exogenous to our model. We assume, however, that the information is private (to the agent) and is not available to the principal (i.e., information asymmetry). The outcome of the project depends upon the amount of inputs (capital and effort) employed and, in addition, on the stochastic state of nature. Both the principal and agent participate in negotiating for a mutually beneficial contract. Once the contract is agreed upon, the agent takes appropriate action by combining his effort with capital supplied by the principal. When the final outcome is realized, the two share the profit according to the sharing rule. We assume that the principal is risk-neutral, since she is able to diversify her portfolio, whereas the agent is both risk- and effort-averse, since he is heavily invested in human capital. Effort aversion implies that the agent is not willing to expend additional effort without commensurate compensation. In negotiating the contract, therefore, the principal pays particular attention to two considerations: moral hazard and adverse selection. Since it is costly to monitor effort and the outcome is stochastic, the reward scheme has to motivate the agent to take the optimal action. In addition, since the agent has private information which is unobservable to the principal, the scheme has to preclude any opportunity for "exploitation." In other words, the compensation mechanism the principal designs must be *incentive compatible.*[7]

By incorporating both moral hazard and adverse selection in an agency relationship, we investigate the nature of "equilibrium" contracts which the principal will offer to the agent. The contracts represent a Bayesian Nash equilibrium in the presence of moral hazard and asymmetric information. We assume, as usual, that the principal knows the agent's utility function and the support of the signal distribution, but not the signal itself. In general, the principal has the choice of (1) offering identical contracts regardless of the signal recieved (pooling contract); (2) offering a *menu* of contracts from which the agent chooses the most *desirable* one (separating contracts); or (3) a combination of pooling and separating. Our purpose is to solve for (fully) separating contracts, since we assume that the signal distribution is such that aiming for expected (average) values is strictly inferior to the principal.

The feasible contracts have to be good enough to lure the manager away from his (privately known) alternative opportunity. Of course, the menu will have to induce effort commensurate with expectation, as well. We explore in detail the incentive-compatible separating contracts which accomplish simultaneously "truth telling" and "incentive provision."[8]

Our model characterizes a situation with precontractual information asymmetry (adverse selection), moral hazard, and risk aversion. The approach taken has its genesis in the work of Guasch and Weiss [1980] and Bhattacharya [1980] who analyze the properties of dichotomous contingent contracts in terms of their ability to separate workers ex ante by productivity. Our model differs from recent contingent-contracting models in the employment literature (e.g., Hart [1983] and Shapiro and Stiglitz [1984]) in the following sense: (1) the managerial compensation can be made contingent on the state of nature; (2) the state of nature represented by a viable indicator of performance can be independently verified; and (3) controllability of the agent's action is limited by the lack of a one-to-one relationship between productive inputs and realized states.

In our model, as in much of the insurance literature, the focus is on the strategic behavior of the uninformed who makes the first move by proposing a menu. Unless the principal has other means of extracting information costlessly, she has no choice but to deal with the agent's private information as a part of the contracting process. If communication of the private information were to take place, the agent needs a way of communicating credibly (signaling) with an assurance of no exploitation. The principal might say to the agent "Tell me the truth because I will respect the private information you possess." This will not work unless the principal enters into a binding agreement as to how the information is to be used prior to the agent having revealed that information. Thus communication and contracting will take place simultaneously, since only this guarantees the principal's precommitment. The agent effectively signals his information by the choice he makes. It is shown later that the information is revealed fully in our specialized models.

In order to assess questions concerning the performance of the two contracting forms, we employ the assumptions of exponential utility and normal distributions. The combination of these two has long been known to provide desirable analytic properties in the context of information theory. For example, exponential utility admits a separation of income and incentive effects; normal distributions are "closed" under addition as well as conditioning on new information.

The organization of the paper is as follows. In the next section, a general problem of optimal incentive contracts with moral hazard and/or adverse selection is presented. Following this, we explore the case where the agent's private information represents his expected product for the project, and contracts take a simple linear form. The difficulties of combining moral hazard and adverse selection are illustrated with the aid of diagrams. A bonus-salary scheme is then analyzed under the assumption that both expected product and standard deviation are signals received. It is shown that these contracts lead not only to strictly second-best effort levels but also to fully revealing predictions as to the agent's information. The resulting solution is therefore a methodological contribution to the theory of multiattribute screening as well. The paper concludes with a discussion on welfare comparisons of the two contractual forms.

Statement of the General Problem

The agent receives private information (signal or news) ξ on the profitability of the project prior to the contract choice. The principal does not know the exact nature of this signal but is assumed to have a prior belief on the support of the ξ distribution, where ξ is a vector of real-valued parameters. In particular, in the next two sections we interpret ξ to be first a single parameter representing the average (marginal) productivity of effort in the linear sharing model and then two parameters representing average (marginal) productivity and standard deviation of output in the bonus-salary model. With a normal distribution assumed, these parameters order the "types" of private information in the sense of first- and second-order stochastic dominance. The first is consistent with Milgrom's [1981] concept of "more favorable" information. The value(s) of ξ are continuously distributed on a "cube" and we refer to the specific realization of ξ as the type of information (or agent's type). The sequence of events can be summarized as shown below.

t_0	t_1	t_2	t_3	t_4
Agent receives ξ	Principal offers a menu	Agent picks a contract	Agent commits effort	Output is realized and observed

We assume that the principal is risk-neutral while the agent is both risk- and effort-averse, and has a Von Neumann–Morgenstern utility function. The principal's problem, then, is to design a menu of contracts so as to maximize her expected profit:

$$\underset{\phi_\xi(y),\, \rho(\xi)}{\text{maximize}}\; E\pi\big(\phi_\xi(\tilde{y})\big) \tag{A}$$

subject to

$$\forall\xi:\; EU\big(\phi_\xi(\tilde{y}), \rho(\xi)|\xi\big) \geq \underline{U}(\xi) \tag{10.1}$$

$$\forall\xi:\; EU\big(\phi_\xi(\tilde{y}), \rho(\xi)|\xi\big) \geq EU\big(\phi_{\xi'}(\tilde{y}), \rho(\xi')|\xi\big) \quad \text{all } \xi' \tag{10.2}$$

$$\forall\xi:\; \rho(\xi) \in \underset{\hat{\rho}}{\text{argmax}}\, EU\big(\phi_\xi(\tilde{y}), \hat{\rho}|\xi\big) \tag{10.3}$$

where $\tilde{y}$ is the output, $\phi_\xi(y)$ is the menu of contracts, $E\pi$ is expected profit (over $\tilde{y}$, ξ), $\rho(\xi)$ is optimal effort, and EU is expected utility.

These three constraints are due to the following: (1) the agent must be at least as well off in this employment as elsewhere (individual rationality); (2) the agent does not misrepresent his type (self-selection); and (3) the agent's action is chosen after the contract is signed (moral hazard).

The principal's problem represented by (A) above, however, has a problem in interpretation. In a standard agency model with moral hazard but without adverse selection [i.e., (A) without (10.2)], a principal with strong bargaining power will compensate her agent such that his expected utility is just slightly above (or equal to) that of his alternate opportunity, $\underline{U}$ (Holmstrom [1979]). Thus the market-opportunity constraint is binding and the principal extracts all the surplus (if any). When the agent has private information which may be favorable or unfavorable (due to his innate ability or to acquisition of privileged information), however, it is more difficult for the principal to determine the agent's market opportunity. We thus endogenize the agent's market opportunity by considering the "dual" problem to (A). The principal's problem is then modified to that of maximizing the agent's utility subject to a minimum-profit constraint (i.e., the principal's market opportunity). In other words, the principal will be indifferent in equilibrium as to which agent type she hires. Thus we replace the agent's market-opportunity constraint by the following:[9]

$$\forall \xi: \ \underset{\phi_\xi(y),\, \rho(\xi)}{\text{maximize}} \ EU(\phi_\xi(\tilde{y}), \rho(\xi) | \xi) \tag{B}$$

subject to

$$\forall \xi: \ E\pi(\phi_\xi(\tilde{y})) = 0 \tag{10.1'}$$

$$\forall \xi: \ EU(\phi_\xi(\tilde{y}), \rho(\xi) | \xi) \geq EU(\phi_{\xi'}(\tilde{y}), \rho(\xi') | \xi) \quad \text{all } \xi' \tag{10.2}$$

$$\forall \xi: \ \rho(\xi) \in \underset{\hat{\rho}}{\text{argmax}} \, EU(\phi_\xi(\tilde{y}), \hat{\rho} | \xi) \tag{10.3}$$

Posing the problem from the agent's perspective is reasonable if the principal is a large number of investors operating in a competitive capital market and the agent has the opportunity to obtain capital from and share risks with the investors at the competitively determined cost of capital. The agent is then viewed as the price-taker of capital and expects to receive "rent" for better performance.

The equilibrium concept employed is that of Nash with the restriction that only separating contracts are considered. Pooling contracts are not considered (by virtue of the fact that expected profit is set to zero for each agent type). This can be justified by assuming that the principal's prior distribution over ξ, in problems (A) and (B), induces separation (see Riley [1985]). Notice that the restriction to separating contracts removes the conflict of objectives for agents with different values of ξ since it is proven (in the context here) that there is a Pareto optimal separating contract.

Holmstrom [1979] and Clarke and Darrough [1980], among others, have applied the Lagrange–Ljusternik theory (Ioffe and Tihomirov [1979]) to find necessary conditions for this type of problem. Although these necessary conditions have led to specific solutions in the exponentially distributed case, they have not been useful for other functional forms. We use a direct method instead by exploiting the assumed restrictions of exponential utility and normal distribution.

Linear Contracts

We now turn to the analysis of the linear-sharing contracts where the compensation of the agent is linear in output; $\phi(\tilde{y}) = w + s\tilde{y}$. The return from the agent's effort (such as accounting profit net of all other input costs), $\tilde{y}$, is assumed to be stochastic and normally distributed—i.e., $\tilde{y} = \mu\rho + \sigma\tilde{\varepsilon}$, where μ is the marginal (and average) productivity of effort, σ is the standard deviation of $\tilde{y}$, and $\tilde{\varepsilon}$ is normally distributed with zero mean and unit variance. The agent receives a signal, $\xi = \mu$. The assumption of exponential utility gives us

$$U = -\frac{1}{a}e^{-a\phi(y) + \frac{1}{2}\rho^2}$$

where a is the coefficient of absolute risk aversion.[10]

In deriving the solution to problem (B), we consider first the optimal effort constraint (10.3). We then characterize the self-selection constraint (10.2) and the objective function. Finally, we evaluate the zero-profit constraint (10.1′). The assumption of normality and contract linearity implies that expected utility satisfies the following equation (which may be derived using characteristic function techniques).

$$EU = -\frac{1}{a}e^{-aw - as\mu\rho + \frac{1}{2}a^2s^2\sigma^2 + \frac{1}{2}\rho^2} \tag{10.4}$$

Since the agent's productivity is known to him, the first order condition is obtained by setting the partial derivative of (10.4) (with respect to ρ) equal to zero. This yields

$$\rho = as\mu \tag{10.5}$$

which we refer to as the "second-best" effort level. Note that this level is independent of w (since utility is separable in w and ρ) and σ^2 (since effort increases output in the sense of first-order stochastic dominance).

To compare this with a first-best contract in which effort and productivity are observable, notice first that optimal risk sharing requires that the risk-averse agent be paid a fixed wage, $\phi(\tilde{y}) = w$. Then the competitive zero-profit wage level would be $w = \rho\mu$. Substituting these into equation (10.4) and differentiating yields $\rho = a\mu$, the *first-best-effort* expenditure. We see that the second-best level given by equation (10.5) is always less than the first-best level as long as $s < 1$, and in both cases optimal effort is proportional to productivity.

We now identify an agent's induced preferences over the contract space (s, w). To see his tradeoffs, we derive an indifference map in (s, w) by totally differentiating the expected utility function with respect to w and s and then setting $dEU = 0$. We obtain

$$-a\,dw - a\mu\rho\,ds + a^2 s\sigma^2\,ds = 0$$

or

$$\frac{dw}{ds} = (as\sigma^2 - \mu\rho) \tag{10.6}$$

Thus it is clear that the indifference map of an agent depends upon his productivity and the effort level expended. At each value of s, given agent type μ, the indifference curves are parallel to each other; this is a consequence of the exponential utility assumption. Substituting equation (10.5) into (10.6) then gives

$$\frac{dw}{ds} = -as(\mu^2 - \sigma^2) \tag{10.7}$$

Although vertically parallel, the convexity as well as the slope of the indifference curves depends upon whether or not $\mu \geq \sigma$. We shall focus on the case where the support of the distribution of μ lies above σ so that increasing the agent's share of output implies that he can be given a smaller wage.

We now determine the principal's payoff in the same (s, w) space. Since the principal's return is $\tilde{y} - \phi(\tilde{y})$, her expected return is

$$E(\tilde{y} - \phi(\tilde{y})) = \mu\rho - (w + s\mu\rho) = (1 - s)\mu\rho - w \tag{10.8}$$

from an agent of type μ. This identifies the isoprofit curves as $w = (1 - s)\mu\rho -$ constant. Once again, by substituting the optimal effort equation (10.5), we obtain the zero profit condition:

$$w = (1 - s)as\mu^2 \tag{10.9}$$

The zero-isoprofit curves converge at two points: the origin and at $w = 0$, $s = 1$. With moral hazard and linear contracts, we know that if $s = 0$, then

$\rho = 0$; thus resulting in zero expected output. If $s = 1$, then the agent receives 100% of the expected output in the form of a share, leaving nothing to be paid as a fixed salary.

We now introduce adverse selection.[11] An agent receives private information on his productivity. This agent can be of any type. Alternatively, we can envision that there are many agents (hereafter referred to as different agent types) with different productivities only one of which is to be hired. It is common knowledge that the support of μ is $[\underline{\mu}, \bar{\mu}] \subseteq R_+$, an interval on the positive real line. Furthermore, σ is the same for all agents and known to all.

The impact of the self-selection constraint on the feasible contract set is best illustrated by considering a case with two agent types: μ_L and μ_H with $\mu_L < \mu_H$. Figure 10–1 shows two zero-profit curves for these two agents, one indifference curve for agent μ_L and two indifference curves for agent μ_H. Agent μ_L has the highest EU if his contract consisted of the w and s combination represented by the point L. Similarly, agent μ_H would prefer contract H to any other point in the zero-profit curve. However, not knowing the type of either agent, if the principal offered L and H, both agents will select H and self-selection will not take place. In order to separate the two types, the principal has to offer a menu consisting of L and H', where H' is just outside of the indifference curve of agent μ_L. The welfare loss of the self-selection constraint in this example is entirely borne by agent μ_H and is represented by the expected utility difference of the two indifference curves.

Where there are a continuum of agent types on an interval, the set of equilibrium contracts yields a curve referred to as the *offer curve*. Geometrically, the offer curve is derived by the *inner envelope* of the indifference curves of agents with $\mu > \sigma$.[12] Analytically, we derive the solution as follows.

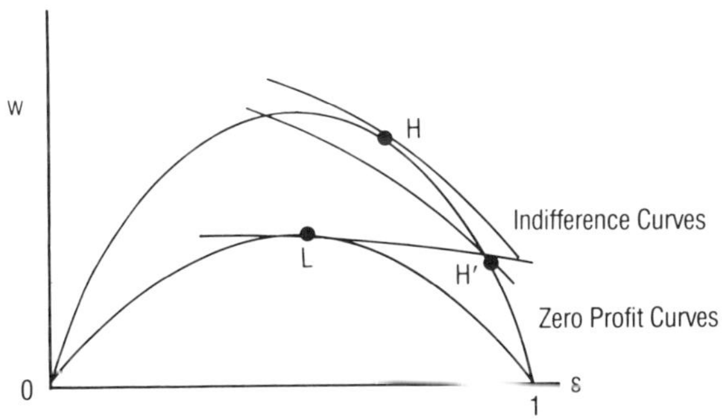

Figure 10–1. Linear Contract

First, solve for $as\mu^2$ from (10.9) and substitute into (10.7) to obtain a differential equation for the offer curve:[13]

$$\frac{dw}{ds} = \frac{w}{s-1} + as\sigma^2 \tag{10.10}$$

With an appropriate boundary condition, (10.10) will determine a unique offer curve. The solution to (10.10) is

$$w = a\sigma^2(s-1)\{s + \ln(1-s)\} + (1-s)M \tag{10.11}$$

where

$$M = \left\{\frac{w_R}{1-s_R} + a\sigma^2[s_R + \ln(1-s_R)]\right\} \tag{10.12}$$

determined by the boundary (or reference) condition (s_R, w_R). Equations (10.11) and (10.12) represent the three constraints of problem (B). Maximizing the expected utility of each type amounts to the selection of the appropriate reference individual. Choosing some agent arbitrarily as the reference individual, we can maximize his expected utility given the expected profit criterion. Thus this particular agent's indifference curve must be tangent to the zero-profit curve corresponding to his type. In the appendix we demonstrate infeasibility (i.e., zero-profit cannot be satisfied) if any individual other than the lowest type is chosen as the reference and that all agents' expected utilities are monotonically increasing in M. These two properties imply that for the left end point of the probability distribution $\underline{\mu}$, equation (10.7) must equal the derivative of (10.9) evaluated at $\underline{\mu}$. That is,

$$\underline{\mu}^2 - 2s_R\underline{\mu}^2 = s_R(\sigma^2 - \underline{\mu}^2)$$

and therefore

$$s_R = \frac{\underline{\mu}^2}{\sigma^2 + \underline{\mu}^2}$$

From (10.9),

$$w_R = (1-s_R)as_R\underline{\mu}^2$$

so that, using (10.12),

$$M = a\left(\underline{\mu}^2 + \sigma^2 \ln\frac{\sigma^2}{\sigma^2 + \underline{\mu}^2}\right) \tag{10.13}$$

Figure 10–2 portrays the equilibrium offer curve defined by (10.11) and (10.13). The offer curve is monotonically decreasing and concave as long as $\mu > \sigma$.[14] Observe that "better" agents are forced to undergo wage reductions and share increases. Notice also the strict second-best nature of the equilibrium offer schedule. Again we illustrate the welfare loss incurred by the

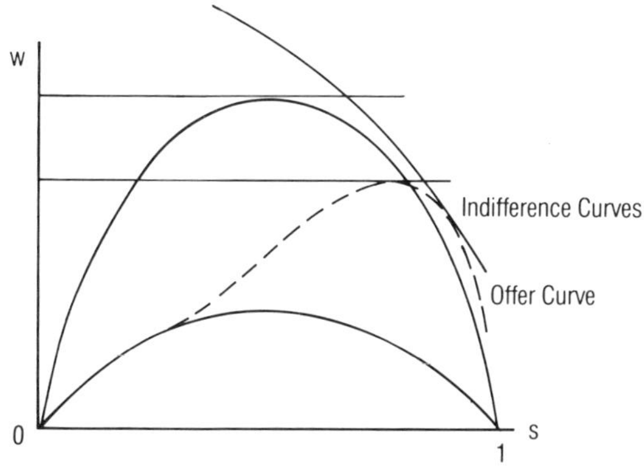

Figure 10–2. Bonus Salary Contract

agent with $\mu = \sigma$, in contrast with the perfect information case. Since his indifference curves are flat, his welfare is only affected by his wage.[15] The welfare loss (in certainty equivalent dollars) may be measured by comparing the maximum of the offer curve (achieved at some $s > 0.5$) to the top of the isoprofit curve, $a\mu^2/4$ $(= a\sigma^2/4)$.

Bonus-Salary Contracts

In this section, we extend our analysis to bonus contracts, defined as

$$\phi(\tilde{y}) = \begin{cases} w & \text{if } \tilde{y} < b \\ w + s(\tilde{y} - b) & \text{if } \tilde{y} \geq b. \end{cases} \tag{10.14}$$

That is, the agent receives a fixed salary unless output is above some predetermined "bonus point or budget," b, in which case he also receives a proportionate share of each incremental dollar.

The principal is faced with a continuum of agent types defined by (μ, σ). Although the support of the distribution of types is known to the principal, neither μ nor σ is observable by her. The principal wishes to design a menu of incentive-compatible contracts to maximize EU. A key aspect of the analysis is that the agent's private information now has two dimensions and the simple linear contract is inadequate for signaling. The bonus contract provides a second dimension to the agent's signal.[16]

The following assumptions are in effect:

$$U(\phi, \rho) = -\frac{1}{a} e^{-a\phi(\tilde{y}) + \frac{1}{2}\rho^2}$$

$$\tilde{y} = \mu\rho + \sigma\tilde{\varepsilon} \qquad \tilde{\varepsilon} \sim N(0, 1)$$

$$\mu \in [\underline{\mu}, \bar{\mu}] \qquad \sigma \in [\underline{\sigma}, \bar{\sigma}]$$

Given a menu of contracts, each agent will choose an $\{s, w, b\}$ triple from the feasible set so as to maximize his expected utility. Of course in the process, he will also choose an optimal level of effort to maximize his expected utility.

The assumptions of exponential utility and normal density functions are now invoked so that we can substitute constraints into the objective function directly. The contract structure can then be directly incorporated into the *EU* equation. This also allows the optimal-effort choice to be substituted. Necessary conditions for self-selection and equal profit are then combined to solve for a feasible menu.

In order to see the effort chosen by an agent of ability μ, given an arbitrary compensation schedule (w, s, b), we first calculate expected utility:

$$EU(\phi(\tilde{y}), \rho) = -\frac{1}{a}\{E[e^{-a(w + s(\tilde{y} - b)) + \frac{1}{2}\rho^2} | \tilde{y} > b] + E[e^{-aw + \frac{1}{2}\rho^2} | \tilde{y} < b]\} \tag{10.15}$$

Following techniques appearing in Mood et al. [1974, p. 164], these two conditional expectations may be evaluated using

$$\text{Prob}(\tilde{y} < b) = N\left[\frac{b - \mu\rho}{\sigma}\right]$$

and

$$E[e^{-as(\tilde{y} - b)} | y > b] = e^{-as(\mu\rho - b) + \frac{1}{2}a^2 s^2 \sigma^2} N\left[\frac{\mu\rho - b}{\sigma} - as\sigma\right]$$

where $N[z]$ denotes the cumulative distribution function of the standardized (zero mean, unit variance) normal density.

Substituting into equation (10.15) yields the following expression for expected utility:

$$EU = -\frac{1}{a} e^{-aw + \frac{1}{2}\rho^2} \{e^{-as(\mu\rho - b) + \frac{1}{2}a^2 s^2 \sigma^2} N[\delta] + N[-\Delta]\} \tag{10.16}$$

where

$$\Delta = \frac{\mu\rho - b}{\sigma} \qquad \text{and} \qquad \delta = \Delta - as\sigma$$

Equation (10.16) appears as a weighted average of two conditional expectations. The first term is the expected utility, conditional on receiving the bonus, times a risk-adjusted probability $N[\delta]$, while the second term is simply the conditional expectation times the actual probability of falling below the bonus level. At this point we make a further definition to clarify the distributional properties of the expected utility function. Define the function

$$L(z) \equiv \frac{N'[z]}{N[z]}$$

$L(z)$ is interpreted as a cumulative likelihood ratio.[17] It is decreasing, convex, asymptotic to $-z$ as $z \to -\infty$ and asymptotic to zero as $z \to \infty$ (see figure 10.3). With this definition, a simple algebraic exercise using the normal density and the definitions of δ and Δ yields the result that

$$EU = -\frac{1}{a} e^{-aw + \frac{1}{2}\rho^2} \left\{ \frac{L(-\Delta)}{L(\delta)} + 1 \right\} N[-\Delta] \tag{10.17}$$

Agent's Optimal-Effort Choice

The optimal choice of effort is derived by partially differentiating (10.17) with respect to ρ and setting the resulting expression equal to zero.[18]

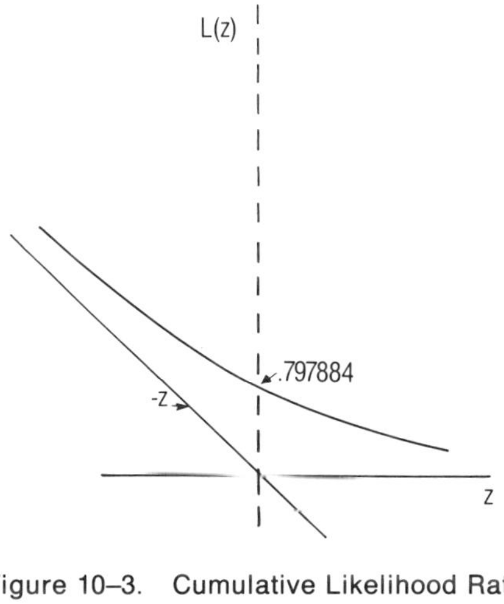

Figure 10–3. Cumulative Likelihood Ratio

$$-\rho\left\{\frac{L(-\Delta)}{L(\delta)}+1\right\}+\frac{\mu}{\sigma}\left\{\frac{L'(-\Delta)L(\delta)+L(-\Delta)L'(\delta)}{L(\delta)^2}\right\}$$

$$+\frac{\mu}{\sigma}\left\{\frac{L(-\Delta)}{L(\delta)}+1\right\}L(-\Delta)=0$$

Considerable simplification obtains when the last two terms are summed. This yields

$$-\rho\left\{\frac{L(-\Delta)}{L(\delta)}+1\right\}+as\mu\frac{L(-\Delta)}{L(\delta)}=0 \tag{10.18}$$

or

$$\rho^*=\frac{as\mu}{1+\dfrac{L(\delta)}{L(-\Delta)}} \tag{10.19}$$

Rewriting (10.19) as $\rho\{L(-\Delta)+L(\delta)\}=as\mu L(-\Delta)$, we can interpret the first-order conditions as a familiar marginal condition of equating marginal disutility of effort to marginal utility of effort due to an increase in the total pecuniary compensation. By expending one more unit of effort, the exponent of the utility function will change by ρ (from disutility) and by $as\mu$ (from benefit) *adjusted* appropriately by the probability terms. Since $L(\delta)/(L(-\Delta))>0$, effort is strictly second-best and always less than a *linear* contract with slope s.

In order to ensure that (10.19) represents a local maximum we check the second-order condition by partially differentiating (10.18) once more and evaluate it at the optimal effort level:

$$L(\delta)<\frac{\sigma(1+as\mu\rho-\rho^2)}{\mu\rho} \tag{10.20}$$

This is equivalent to the assumption that marginal cost increases faster than marginal benefit. Thus (10.17) imposes a (minimum) condition on the value for s (profit share), given a, μ, and ρ.

Agent's Self-Selection Constraint

We now turn to the self-selection constraint: the principal wishes to design a menu of contracts so that each agent will choose the *correct* one. This implies the agent will be worse off by selecting contracts not designed for him. In order to find out how this condition must be reflected in the incentive structure, we investigate the agent's choice of a contract from the menu. Totally differentiating the expected utility equation (10.15) with respect to

$\phi \equiv (w, s, b)$ gives the necessary condition for a critical point.[19] By the envelope theorem, the total differentiation is simplified as

$$\frac{dEU(\phi)}{d\phi} = \frac{\partial EU(\phi, \rho^*(\phi))}{\partial \rho} \frac{\partial \rho}{\partial \phi} + \frac{\partial EU(\phi, \rho^*)}{\partial \phi} = \frac{\partial EU(\phi, \rho^*)}{\partial \phi} = 0 \quad (10.21)$$

where $\rho^*(\phi)$ is the optimal effort by the agent, given ϕ.

Therefore—from equations (10.16) and (10.17)—

$$\left\{\frac{L(-\Delta)}{L(\delta)} + 1\right\} N[-\Delta]dw + \left\{\sigma\left[\left(\frac{\mu\rho - b}{\sigma}\right) - as\sigma\right]ds - sdb\right\} N[\delta]\frac{N'[-\Delta]}{N'[\delta]}$$
$$+ N'[-\Delta]\sigma ds = 0$$

Dividing by $N[-\Delta]$, employing the first-order condition (10.18) and the definition of δ, simplifies the previous expression to

$$as\mu\frac{L(-\Delta)}{L(\delta)}dw + \sigma\rho\delta\frac{L(-\Delta)}{L(\delta)}ds + \sigma\rho L(-\Delta)ds - s\rho\frac{L(-\Delta)}{L(\delta)}db = 0$$

or

$$as\mu dw + \sigma\rho\{\delta + L(\delta)\}ds - s\rho db = 0 \quad (10.22)$$

Equation (10.22) gives the relation along the offer "surface" that must hold to first-order, so that expected utility of an agent of ability (μ, σ) performing effort ρ, is stationary at the contract (w, s, b). The first term is obviously strictly positive, the third negative, and the middle term is also strictly positive since $L(\delta) > -\delta$ for δ negative. This is in accordance with one's intuition since holding ρ, s, and b constant and increasing the wage is an improvement, as is decreasing the bonus point, ceteris paribus. What is not so apparent, a priori, is whether increases in the share make the agent better or worse off. In the previous section, we saw that for linear contracts this sign depended on the marginal productivity. With the salary and bonus contract of this section, increasing the share is an unambiguous improvement, but the marginal benefit goes to zero as the risk-aversion effect ($as\sigma$) dominates the incentive effect ($(\mu\rho - b)/\sigma$).

Principal's Constraint

Given the contract structure (10.14), the expected profit of the principal can be calculated as a function of the agent's type (μ, σ). The resulting expression is[20]

$$E\pi = E[y - (y - b)s - w \mid y \geq b] + E[y - w \mid y < b]$$
$$= -w + \mu\rho - s(\mu\rho - b) - \sigma s\{L(-\Delta) - \Delta\} N[-\Delta]$$

If $E\pi = 0$, then

$$w = \mu\rho - s(\mu\rho - b) - \sigma s\{L(-\Delta) - \Delta\} N[-\Delta] \qquad (10.23)$$

Since $L(-\Delta) - \Delta > 0$, it is clear that expected profit is less than the expected value of the principal's share under a linear contract with an intercept of $w - sb$—i.e., $\mu\rho(1 - s) - w + sb$. This represents a loss to the principal from having a concave payoff pattern even though she is risk-neutral. As is also evident from (10.23), the variance of the agent has a negative impact on expected profit. The last term represents the value of the *call option* that the agent has on the firm's output.[21]

The constraints of the principal's problem are now specified; however, a general analytic solution is still difficult to obtain without further assumptions.

An Explicit Solution

We now develop one explicit solution to the problem of moral hazard cum adverse selection. As is clear, the necessary and sufficient conditions in the present form are still too general to provide a unique solution for the menu. These are the three constraints to be satisfied:

1. $$\rho = \frac{as\mu}{1 + \dfrac{L(\delta)}{L(-\Delta)}} \qquad \text{(effort-choice)} \qquad (10.19)$$

2. $$as\mu dw + \sigma\rho\{\delta + L(\delta)\} ds - s\rho db = 0 \qquad \text{(self-selection)} \qquad (10.22)$$

3. $$\begin{aligned} w &= \mu\rho - s\Delta\sigma - \sigma s\{L(-\Delta) - \Delta\} N(-\Delta) \\ &= \mu\rho - s\sigma\{N'[\Delta] + \Delta N[\Delta]\} \qquad \text{(zero-profit)} \qquad (10.23) \end{aligned}$$

Our plan of attack is as follows: Assume that the principal conjectures that the agent's choice of s reveals his true standard deviation, σ. Given this choice of s and the inferred σ, the parameter b uniquely determines the agent's marginal (and average) product μ. If the relation between offered contract pairs of (s, b) is chosen judiciously, each agent will have no incentive to deviate from these expectations. Just as before, the gradient along the contract surface then becomes a sufficient statistic for the agent's payoff-relevant attributes. The solution to the resulting differential equation defines the offer surface; and the optimization problem reduces to the selection of the appropriate boundary condition.

In order to proceed with the plan, we make the following simplifying assumptions.

1. Along the offer surface in the (w, s, b) space, the product of a, s, and σ is constant:
$$a s \sigma = G \tag{10.24}$$
where G is the constant.
2. Δ is also constant along the offer surface.
3. $L(\delta) = a s \sigma \qquad (10.25)$

With these assumptions, it can be shown that the following self-selection condition holds along the equilibrium contract schedule:[22]

$$dw = K^2 a s \mu^2 ds \tag{10.26}$$

where $K = 1/[1 + L(\delta)/L(-\Delta)]$, a constant between zero and one. Equation (10.26) defines the relation that must hold for self-selection on the contract curve as projected into the (w, s) space. Notice now that the zero-profit condition may be written as

$$w = K a s \mu^2 - \theta \tag{10.27}$$

where $\theta = s\sigma\{N'[\Delta] + \Delta N[\Delta]\}$ is a (positive) constant. Therefore the offer curve as projected into (w, s) space is characterized by

$$w = \frac{1}{K}\frac{dw}{ds} - \theta \qquad \text{or} \qquad \frac{dw}{ds} = Kw + K\theta$$

The solution to this differential equation is

$$w = Ae^{Ks} - \theta \tag{10.28}$$

where A is determined by the appropriate boundary condition. This solution reflects the three constraints of our problem.

Equation (10.28) yields a monotonic increasing and convex (projection) curve on the (w, s) plane. The solution, however, is not a curve but a surface (or a family of surfaces which depend upon the initial condition) in the (w, s, b) space. This is so since for any σ, s is uniquely determined, but b is monotonic increasing in μ. Thus the offer surface is convex, increasing on the (w, s) and (w, b) planes. It should be emphasized though that there is a one-to-one correspondence between an agent (or agents) of ability (σ, μ) and the contract of his choice (w, s, b) on the surface. Thus once a choice is made, the principal can always infer the agent's ability fully; where s reveals σ, and b reveals μ uniquely. By design, s and σ are inversely related, for $a s \sigma = G$, and b and μ are positively related, for $b = K a s \mu^2 - \Delta\sigma$, given σ.

The net result of making assumptions 1, 2, and 3 is that there is only one free contract parameter value that remains to specify a unique menu. In other words, the precise specification of a value for any *one* parameter among (δ, K, Δ, G) fixes the values of all the parameters. Hence, we may, without loss of generality, examine the principal's choice of δ to achieve a constrained Pareto optimum.

In order to see how the expected utility of a typical agent is affected by this choice, we differentiate EU with respect to δ. By the envelope theorem (applied due to the self-selection constraint), total differentiation of EU amounts to

$$\frac{\partial EU}{\partial \delta} = -\frac{1}{a} e^{-aw+\frac{1}{2}\rho^2} N[-\Delta] L(-\Delta) \{\Delta^2 - 1 + \Delta L(\delta)\} < 0$$

where $\Delta = \delta + L(\delta)$.

This is negative, since $N[-\Delta]$, $L(-\Delta)$ and $\{\Delta^2 - 1 + \Delta L(\delta)\}$ are strictly positive. This further implies that

$$\frac{\partial EU}{\partial as\sigma} > 0 \qquad \text{and} \qquad \frac{\partial EU}{\partial \Delta} < 0$$

The principal, therefore, achieves a *constrained Pareto optimum*, by choosing $as\sigma$ to be as large as possible.[23] As a result, the value of Δ is made lower. Recall that

$$\Delta = \frac{\mu\rho - b}{\sigma} \tag{10.29}$$

and that

$$\Delta = \delta + as\sigma = \delta + L(\delta) > 0 \qquad \forall \delta$$

This means that $N[\Delta] > \frac{1}{2}$, that is, the probability of receiving some bonus is always higher than 50%. On the other hand, as the value of $as\sigma = L(\delta)$ is made larger, the probability is reduced. Thus the agents have, in effect, traded off the probability of receiving a bonus for a larger "piece of the action" in the event they are entitled to receive it.

Rewriting (10.29) for b, we obtain

$$b = \mu\rho - \Delta\sigma = E(\tilde{y}) - \Delta\sigma = KG\frac{\mu^2}{\sigma} - \Delta\sigma$$

where Δ and G are fixed. We can see that the bonus points (forecasts or budgets) are positively related to μ and negatively related to σ. Moreover, they are strictly less than the expected profit by $\Delta\sigma$. An agent with a higher value of σ will select a lower b compared with another with the same μ but a lower σ.

Conclusion

In this paper, we have incorporated both moral hazard and adverse selection in an analysis of the market for managerial talent. We believe that an integrated treatment of these two issues is warranted at the higher levels where agents have significant discretionary decision-making power, possess skills and information that are neither easily observable nor quantifiable, and operate in stochastic environments. Two contract structures have been analyzed: a linear-sharing and a fixed-salary–proportional-bonus contract.

The linear contract serves the pedagogical purpose of illustrating the nature of our principal/agent problem with private information. The informational asymmetry and incentive problems impose substantial costs on the agent and principal in contrast to the first-best case. Of course, this result partially stems from the restricted form of contract structure as well as the absence of opportunity for recontracting ex post, even though our solutions exhibit a fully revealing property. It is of interest to note that the fixed component of the linear contract (the *intercept*) is not sufficient alone; the accompanying sharing rate is also necessary in order to discern the agent's signal. This result contrasts with the solution to models where moral hazard and adverse selection are treated as sequential or separate problems.

We further extended the analytical procedure in the case of the bonus-salary contract where a weaker information structure was assumed; the agent's private information consists of both mean and standard deviation of output. Screening and motivation are again accomplished. In this case, offered contracts are represented as a surface (rather than a curve) with the following three properties: (1) the mean is positively related to the bonus point, (2) the standard deviation is inversely proportional to the bonus share, and (3) the fixed salary is an exponentially increasing function of the bunus share.[24] Optimal effort under the bonus regime turns out to be strictly less than that under linear contracts at each share level. It is difficult to establish a complete welfare dominance of one contractual form over the other. An obvious advantage of the bonus-salary form is its ability to sort out agents by their types when the type index is two-dimensional. It can also be shown that for the case with a single attribute, the bonus-salary form provides higher expected utility for the very high-productivity agents. This is mainly due to the fact that the high-productivity agents are forced to take excessively high shares with low wage levels under the linear form.

In order to compare the two forms, we provide a simple numerical example of a problem when the mean is the only unknown attribute. The parameter values are $a = 1$, $\mu = 0.1$, $\sigma = 0.5$. For the bonus-salary contract, we set the share equal to one (since σ is known). The expected utility of agents of various types under the linear-sharing regime without adverse selection (EU), the linear-sharing regime with adverse selection (EU_L) and the bonus-salary regime (EU_{BS}) are shown in table 10–1.

Notice that expected utility is monotonically increasing in the type variable for all regimes and that adverse selection imposes welfare costs on each type for both contract forms above the minimum productivity level. The important feature of this illustration is that the bonus-salary contract provides better results than the linear contract for all types above $\mu = 0.5$ while the situation is reversed for low-productivity types.

While the structural assumptions or preferences and beliefs (as to the density function) are necessitated for reasons of analytic tractability, the graphical approach shows how one might proceed more generally in such problems. Nevertheless, our contracts do suffer from the following two considerations: (1) they are not necessarily optimal within a wider class of incentive mechanisms and (2) the local analysis employed herein does not always justify a global interpretation of the results.

Neglected in our analysis are alternative methods of acquiring relevant information. While intrafirm tournaments à la Lazear and Rosen [1981], Holmstrom [1982], or Bhattacharya [1983] may not be feasible (since the number of senior managers in each organization tends to be small), performance comparison with managers of firms with similar characteristics may provide better results. Multiperiod contracts, recontracting procedures, reputation, and learning behavior might also be important considerations.

Our analysis indicates that a Pareto improvement on the part of both principal and agents may be possible with more relevant information. For example, firms gather and require information on managers via resume and reference letters. Incentives for intermediation exist where economies of scale in information acquisition can be realized, as suggested by the existence of

Table 10–1. Numerical Example—Unknown Mean

μ	s	EU	EU_L	EU_{BS}
0.10	0.04	−0.999	−0.999	−1.085
0.33	0.50	−0.984	−0.994	−1.040
0.36	0.60	−0.978	−0.989	−1.020
0.42	0.70	−0.964	−0.979	−1.001
0.50	0.80	−0.938	−0.959	−0.968
0.62	0.90	−0.890	−0.912	−0.907
0.73	0.95	−0.934	−0.855	−0.846
0.95	0.99	−0.677	−0.716	−0.710

"head-hunters." Attempts by agents to signal by means outside of this model would also be expected. Whether such behavior takes the form of the cards they carry, the educational/professional degrees they acquire, or the company they keep, the importance of the joint and simultaneous problem of motivation and information is acknowledged by both firms and the managers they hire. Our model represents a formal look at an integration of these two objectives.

Notes

1. The latter was a payment to compensate for the loss of severance benefits, etc. from the former employer, Ford.

2. *Wall Street Journal*, April 4, 1979; June 24, 1980.

3. *Top Executive Compensation 1986 Edition* by Harland Fox and Charles A. Peck. This annual report analyzes compensation of the five highest paid executives of over 1000 companies in six types of business: manufacturing, gas and electric utilites, retail trade, commercial banks, insurance, and construction. There were 475 manufacturing firms surveyed, which include 42% of the manufacturers with $100 million or more in sales listed of the NYSE or the AMEX.

4. The CEO is usually (but not necessarily) the higest paid executive. Median total compensation of other executives as a percentage of the CEO's compensation varies from 58% (second highest) to 35% (fifth highest).

5. Incentive bonus plans are also becoming more common in nonmanufacturing sectors. For example, 81% of banks, 67% of insurance companies, 68% of the retailers, and 91% of construction companies had a plan as of May 1985. The size of the median bonus award as a percentage of base salary for chief executive officers ranges from 34% (banks) to 56% (manufacturing). These percentages are significantly higher than ten years ago. A large proportion of these firms include bonus awards in the earning base for calculating pensions (Fox and Peck [1985]).

6. Smith & Watts [1982] and Miller & Scholes [1982] discuss in detail various types of compensation plans used mainly in the U.S. They argue that, although tax implications are important in the choice of compensation plans, the objective of incentive plans is "to align the managers' incentives with firm value maximization."

7. Our problem is a special case of the generalized principal/agent problem of optimal coordination of Myerson [1982], which consists of agents reporting their type to a mediator and the principal directing their actions through the third party. Moreover the principal also respects the constraints imposed by the delegation of authority to the mediator.

8. Moral hazard and/or asymmetric information issues have been discussed extensively in the literature. A large portion is concerned with the design of optimal incentive mechanisms with moral hazard only (e.g., Holmstrom [1979], Shavell [1979], Grossman and Hart [1983] among others) or with asymmetric information alone (the insurance models of Rothschild and Stiglitz [1976] and Wilson [1977]; the models of monopoly pricing and regulation, Baron and Myerson [1982], Katz [1983], and Goldman, Leland and Sibley [1984]; and auctions: Riley and Samuelson [1981], and Myerson [1981]). Beginning with Mirrlees [1979], a handful but growing number of papers have been combining both moral hazard and asymmetric information within the same model. Christensen [1981] is perhaps the first to integrate postcontractual communication of private information with moral hazard in optimal contracting. Holmstrom

and Weiss [1985] also deal with this problem in the macroeconomic context of examining effects on aggregate investment fluctuations. Important papers dealing with the issue of moral hazard and adverse selection (i.e., where precontractual information asymmetry is present) are Sappington [1980]; Harris, Kriebel, and Raviv [1982]; and Antle and Eppen [1985], all of which consider a risk-neutral agent whose private information is distributed on a finite support.

9. The approach we have just outlined is formally equivalent to defining the dual of the (usual) agency problem and involves exchanging the constraint on the agent's for that of the principal. This approach appears to be commonly used in the insurance literature (e.g., Spence and Zeckhauser [1971]). The paper by Feltham and Hughes in this volume takes a similar approach in the context of an entrepreneur "going public." They assume that the informed agent moves first, and demonstrate that in that context only separating contracts satisfy the intuitive criterion proposed by Cho and Kreps [1987].

10. The utility function is multiplicatively separable in income and disutility of effort. Unfortunately, this method of representing disutility is not arbitrary since we will be constraining the contract structure.

11. Our assumptions represent an extension of the Leland–Pyle [1977] model which considers adverse selection with exponential utility and normal distributions but without moral hazard.

12. The offer curve is the *outer envelope* of indifference curves when $\mu < \sigma$.

13. Notice at this point the importance of the crucial assumption that the variance of all agents' output be equal and known by the principal. Otherwise, the slope of the offer curve, dw/ds, cannot be used to "infer" the agent's ability.

14. If $\mu < \sigma$, then the equilibrium offer curve is monotonically increasing up to $\mu = \sigma$, concave for $s < 0.5$ and convex for $s > 0.5$.

15. The return from additional effort in this case is exactly offset by the disutility of effort and risk, regardless of the value of s.

16. A paper that considers multidimensional signaling in the context of investment banking is that of Hughes [1986], albeit in which there is no moral hazard problem.

17: The function $L(\cdot)$ defined above is the left-tail version of Mill's ratio and is studied extensively in statistics. See Barlowe and Proshen [1965].

18. A useful formula for the derivative of the likelihood ratio is:

$$L'(z) = -L(z)\big(z + L(z)\big).$$

19. As before, the *total* derivative characterizes the self-selection constraint because the agent must account not only for the local effect of changes in contract parameters, but also the inferences made by the principal upon the selection of the contract. The agent *strictly* prefers one specific contract to all others among those of the menu offered by the principal.

20. This is accomplished by noting that

$$E[s(y-b) \mid y \geq b] = \frac{d}{d\zeta} E[e^{\zeta s(y-b)} \mid y \geq b]_{\zeta=0}$$

and employing the techniques of Mood et al. [1974] to show that

$$E[e^{\zeta s(y-b)} \mid y \geq b] = \exp[\zeta s(\mu\rho - b) + \tfrac{1}{2}\zeta^2 s^2 \sigma^2]\, N[\Delta + \zeta s\sigma]$$

Differentiating the previous equation and dividing by the exponential function yields

$$E[s(y-b) \mid y \geq b] = [s(\mu\rho - b) + \zeta s^2\sigma^2] N[\Delta + \zeta s\sigma] + N'[\Delta + \zeta s\sigma] s\sigma$$

The final step consists of setting $\zeta = 0$, taking account of the definition of Δ and remembering $N'[-z] = N'[z]$ and $N[-z] = 1 - N[z]$.

21. Brennan [1979] has derived this option-pricing formula which is analogous to the well-known Black–Scholes formula.

22. Along with assumption 1, equation (10.19) becomes

$$\rho = Kas\mu \tag{10.19*}$$

where K is another constant $(0 < K < 1)$. This is because assumptions 1 and 2 together imply that δ is also constant along the offer surface. Employing the definition of Δ, we have

$$\Delta = \frac{Kas\mu^2 - b}{\sigma} = \frac{a(Kas\mu^2 - b)s}{G}$$

which means that (along the offer curve)

$$d(\Delta G) = 0 \qquad \text{or} \qquad d(Kas^2\mu^2 - bs) = 0$$

This implies that

$$d(bs) = 2Kas\mu^2 ds$$

Inserting (10.19*) into the self-selection constraint (10.22) yields

$$\frac{1}{K}dw + \sigma\Delta ds + \sigma\{L(\delta) - as\sigma\}ds - sdb$$

$$= \frac{1}{K}dw + Kas\mu^2 ds - d(bs) + \sigma\{L(\delta) - as\sigma\}ds = 0$$

Finally, assumption 3 guarantees that the final term vanishes yielding (10.26).

23. One expects that there is an upper bound for the value of s such as $s \leq 1$.

24. These properties are *not inconsistent* with general findings made by Fox and Peck [1985] (and earlier editions). If we assume that "better" agents (higher μ and lower σ) tend to have positions at higher levels within both an organization and the industry (by sales), then we find that salary as well as bonus as a percentage of salary (hence bonus itself) are monotonic increasing in the "level." In addition, in 1984, 77% (construction) to 91% (banking) of the firms with bonus plans actually paid bonus, whereas the percentages varied from 67% (construction) to 93% (retail trade) in 1983 and 56% (gas and electric) to 90% (retail trade) in 1982. These again are *not inconsistent* with our result that $N[\Delta] > \frac{1}{2}$.

APPENDIX 10
The Choice of Initial Condition

Proposition 10A.1

Maximizing the expected utility of the reference agent is a Pareto improvement for all agents of ability above him.

Proof: Clearly the reference agent is best off if his indifference curve is just tangent to his isoprofit curve as well as the offer curve. Thus, we wish to show that other agents are also made better off. For any agent, his expected utility is

$$EU = -\frac{1}{a}e^{-aw-\frac{1}{2}a^2s^2(\mu^2-\sigma^2)}$$

Thus, maximizing EU is equivalent to maximizing

$$V = w + \tfrac{1}{2}as^2(\mu^2 - \sigma^2)$$

subject to $w = (1 - s)as\mu^2$ (isoprofit condition).

Substituting this constraint into V, we get

$$V = as\mu^2 - \tfrac{1}{2}as^2(\sigma^2 + \mu^2) \qquad (10A.1)$$

For any initial condition (w_R, s_R) for the agent of ability μ_R, the offer curve is

$$w = (s-1)a\sigma^2[s + \ln(1-s)] + (1-s)M$$

where

$$M = as_R\mu_R^2 + a\sigma^2[s_R + \ln(1-s_R)] \tag{10A.2}$$

The slope of this offer curve is

$$\frac{dw}{ds} = a\sigma^2\{2s + \ln(1-s)\} - M$$

Since the indifference curve of each agent is tangent to the offer curve, the above slope must be equal to the slope of the indifference curve, that is,

$$a\sigma^2\{2s + \ln(1-s)\} - M = as(\sigma^2 - \mu^2)$$

$$as(\sigma^2 + \mu^2) + a\sigma^2 \ln(1-s) = M \tag{10A.3}$$

The equation (10A.2) relates s to any agent's ability. From (10A.1), maximizing $V =$ maximizing $\{as\mu^2 - \frac{1}{2}as^2(\sigma^2 + \mu^2)\}$.

To see how V is related to the initial condition M, we evaluate

$$\frac{dV}{dM} = \frac{dV}{ds}\frac{ds}{dM} = a[\mu^2 - s(\sigma^2 + \mu^2)]\left[\frac{1-s}{a\{\mu^2 - s(\sigma^2 + \mu^2)\}}\right] = 1 - s > 0$$

So V is higher, the higher M is. Now, to maximize M by choosing the initial share, we set $dM/ds = 0$:

$$\frac{dM}{ds_R} = \frac{a\{\mu^2 - s(\sigma^2 + \mu^2)\}}{1-s} = 0$$

where

$$s = \frac{\mu^2}{\sigma^2 + \mu^2} \tag{10A.4}$$

And this is maximum, since

$$\frac{d^2M}{ds^2} = \frac{-a\sigma^2}{(1-s)^2} < 0$$

Equation (10A.4) is obtained when we set the reference agent's indifference curve to be tangent to his isoprofit curve, that is,

$$as(\sigma^2 - \mu^2) = a\mu^2 - 2as\mu^2$$

$$s = \frac{\mu^2}{\sigma^2 + \mu^2}$$

Q.E.D.

Proposition 10A.2

Any contract below the reference individual will not be offered.

Proof: This proposition basically says that when the initial condition is determined by maximizing the reference agent's expected utility, the offer curve will satisfy the isoprofit condition only for agents of higher and not lower ability.

From (10A.2), we have a relationship between the ability of agents and the accompanying constant M. Substituting $s = \mu^2/(\sigma^2 + \mu^2)$ and differentiating M with respect to μ yields:

$$\frac{dM}{d\mu} = 2a\mu\left(1 - \frac{\sigma^2}{\sigma^2 + \mu^2}\right) > 0$$

Thus the value of the constant increases with the ability of the reference agent. Since a particular value of M for a particular reference agent is the highest possible without violating the zero profit condition, when the reference point is moved to agents of higher ability, any agents below will no longer satisfy zero profit. Hence this portion of the offer curve will not be offered. Q.E.D.

References

Antle, R., and Eppen, G. [1985]. "Capital Rationing, Organizational Slack, and Project Auditing." *Management Science* 31, 163–174.

Barlowe, R.E., and Proschen, F. [1965]. *Mathematical Theory of Reliability*. New York: John Wiley.

Baron, D.P., and Myerson, R.B. [1982]. "Regulating a Monopolist with Unknown Costs." *Econometrica* 50, 911–930.

Bhattacharya, S. [1980]. "Nondissipative Signaling Structures and Dividend Policy." *Quarterly Journal of Economics* 95, 1–24.

Bhattacharya, S. [1983]. "Tournaments and Incentives: Heterogeneity and Essentiality." Working Paper, Stanford University.

Brennan, M.J. [1979]. "The Pricing of Contingent Claims in Discrete Time Models." *Journal of Finance* 34, 53–68.

Cho, I-K., and Kreps, D.M. [1987]. "Signaling Games and Stable Equilibria." *Quarterly Journal of Economics* 102, 179–221.

Christensen, J. [1981]. "Communication in Agencies." *Bell Journal of Economics* 12, 661–674.

Clarke, F.H., and Darrough, M.N. [1980]. "Optimal Incentive Schemes: Existence and Characterization." *Economics Letters* 5, 305–310.

Demski, J.S., and Feltham, G.A. [1978] "Economic Incentives in Budgetary Control Systems." *Accounting Review* 53, 336–359.

Fox, H., and Peck, C.A. [1985]. *Top Executive Compensation: 1986 Edition.* New York: The Conference Board.

Goldman, M.B., Leland, H., and Sibley, D. [1984]. "Optimal Nonuniform Prices." *Review of Economic Studies* 51, 305–319.

Grossman, S.J., and Hart, O.D. [1983]. "An Analysis of the Principal-Agent Problem." *Econometrica* 51, 7–45.

Guasch, L., and Weiss, A. [1980]. "Wages as Sorting Mechanisms in Competitive Markets with Asymmetric Information: A Theory of Testing." *Review of Economic Studies* 47, 653–664.

Harris, M., Kriebel, G., and Raviv, A. [1982]. "Asymmetric Information, Incentives, and Intrafirm Resource Allocation." *Management Science* 28, 604–620.

Hart, O.D. [1983]. "Optimal Labor Contracts Under Asymmetric Information: An Introduction." *Review of Economic Studies* 50, 3–35.

Holmstrom, B. [1979]. "Moral Hazard and Observability." *Bell Journal of Economics* 10, 74–91.

Holmstrom, B. [1982]. "Moral Hazard in Teams." *Bell Journal of Economics* 13, 324–340.

Holmstrom, B., and Weiss, L. [1982]. "Managerial Incentives, Investment and Aggregate Implications." Working Paper, Northwestern University.

Hughes, P.J. [1986]. "Signalling by Direct Disclosure under Asymmetric Information." *Journal of Accounting and Economics* 8, 119–142.

Ioffe, A.D., and Tihomirov, V.M. [1979]. *Theory of Extremal Problems.* Amsterdam: North Holland.

Katz, M.L. [1983]. "Non-Uniform Pricing, Output and Welfare Under Monopoly." *Review of Economic Studies* 50, 37–56.

Lazear, E., and Rosen, S. [1981]. "Rank-Order Tournaments as Optimum Labour Contracts." *Journal of Political Economy* 89, 841–864.

Leland, H., and Pyle, D. [1977]. "Informational Asymmetries, Financial Structure and Financial Intermediaries." *Journal of Finance* 32, 371–381.

Milgrom, P.R. [1981]. "Good News and Bad News: Representation Theorems and Applications." *Bell Journal of Economics* 12, 380–391.

Miller, M., and Scholes, M. [1982]. "Executive Compensation, Taxes, and Incentives." In *Financial Economics*, W.F. Sharpe and C. Cootner (eds.), Englewood Cliffs, NJ: Prentice-Hall.

Mirrlees, J. [1979]. "The Implications of Moral Hazard for Optimal Insurance." Working Paper, Nuffield College, Oxford.

Mood, A., Graybill, F., and Boes, D. [1974]. *Introduction to the Theory of Statistics* New York: McGraw-Hill.

Myerson, R.B. [1981]. "Optimal Auction Design." *Mathematics of Operations Research* 6, 58–73.

Myerson, R.B. [1982]. "Optimal Coordination Mechanisms in Generalized Principal-Agent Problems." *Journal of Mathematical Economics* 10, 67–81.

Riley, J.G. [1985]. "Competition with Hidden Knowledge." *Journal of Political Economy* 93, 958–976.

Riley, J.G., and Samuelson, W.F. [1981]. "Optimal Auctions." *American Economic Review* 71, 381–392.

Rothschild, M., and Stiglitz, J.E. [1976]. "Equilibrium in Competitive Insurance Markets: An Essay on the Economies of Imperfect Information." *Quarterly Journal of Economics* 90, 629–649.

Sappington, D. [1980]. "Precontractual Information Asymmetry Between Principal and Agent: The Continuous Case." *Economics Letters* 5, 371–75.

Shapiro, C., and Stiglitz, J. [1984]. "Equilibrium Unemployment as a Worker Discipline Device." *American Economic Review* 74, 433–444.

Shavell, S. [1979]. "Risk Sharing and Incentives in the Principal and Agent Relationship." *Bell Journal of Economics* 10, 55–73.

Smith, C.W., and Watts, R.L. [1982]. "Incentive and Tax Effects of Executive Compensation Plans." Working Paper, University of Rochester.

Spence, M., and Zeckhauser, R. [1971]. "Insurance, Information and Individual Action." *American Economic Review* 61, 380–389.

Wilson, C.A. [1977]. "A Model of Insurance Markets with Incomplete Information." *Journal of Economic Theory* 16, 167–207.

11 INTRAFIRM RESOURCE ALLOCATION AND DISCRETIONARY ACTIONS*

Ronald A. Dye

The purpose of this paper is to investigate some aspects of intrafirm resource allocation as accomplished through transfer pricing techniques. Existing theories of transfer prices have several deficiencies. In the traditional transfer pricing models, researchers have posited that central management possesses as much information about the production technologies of divisions as do the division managers themselves (see, e.g., Hirshleifer [1956], Gould [1964]). Given this assumption, central management, by specifying what quantities each division should produce, can achieve the same level of profits as can be achieved by taking the more circuitous, but equivalent, route of specifying the prices that will induce individual division managers to select these same quantities. Consequently, while traditional transfer pricing models identify the implicit prices of intrafirm transfers (which may have some intrinsic

* I would like to thank Joel Demski and Jerry Feltham for detailed comments and suggestions on a previous draft of this paper, and Stan Baiman for many illuminating discussions on transfer pricing.

interest), these transfer prices need serve no allocational role, and so the failure to implement a transfer pricing scheme has no impact on firm profits in such models.

More recently, Harris, Kriebel, and Raviv [1982] have identified a role for decentralization by means of the agency/asymmetric information route. Unfortunately, they too do not establish the desirability of transfer prices. Instead, they show how headquarter's assignments of particular divisional output levels (which are based on communication between headquarters and division managers) can be supported alternatively by means of a set of prices for the resources the managers use.

In spite of the literature's failure to distinguish between intrafirm allocations based on quantity or price assignments, we argue that a distinction between these allocation mechanisms does exist, and that a fundamental difference between them consists of whether division managers are given discretion over their production operations. If quantities of outputs are specified by headquarters, then manufacturing divisions are given freedom only in selecting inputs, whereas if the price of the manufacturing division's output is specified, then the division has discretion over both input and output levels. Thus, the relative desirability of prices or quantities is in fact a special case of the relative desirability of discretion or no discretion.

The "prices vs. quantities" question has been addressed in the economics literature from a social planner's viewpoint (see Weitzman [1977a], [1977b], Laffont [1977]). This literature has limited relevance to the question of intrafirm resource allocation for two reasons. First, the owners of a firm can specify the link between a division's profits and a division manager's compensation, so questions of intrafirm resource allocation cannot be addressed without explicit reference to such compensation schemes. Second, since the output of one division may be the input of another division, the "quantities" solution might appear to be superior to the "price" solution in terms of the ability of the quantities solution to coordinate interdivisional production operations. No counterparts to these issues exist in the "price vs. quantities" literature.

In the succeeding sections, a simple model of a multidivision firm is developed to analyze optimal intrafirm resource allocation. This model distinguishes between transfer pricing and other nondiscretionary (transfer quantity) schemes. This set-up allows for a relatively complete description of optimal contracts in a multiagent firm, and provides a basis for comparing alternative intrafirm allocation mechanisms.

Model

Any analytic model of transfer pricing is necessarily a multiagent model: There must be someone other than the principal to whom (and from whom) resources are transferred. Notwithstanding this fact, in this section we begin by introducing a variant of the standard one-principal–one-agent model, in order to present some preliminary notation and results.

The biggest difference between the model here and the canonical agency model consists of the production technology of the agent, $x = X(a, z, L)$. $\tilde{z}$ denotes a stochastic factor influencing output (with density $h(z)$), a denotes the effort (or plan) of the agent selected *before* z occurs, and L denotes an external input (e.g., labor) acquired at a price per unit P after the agent observes z. Schematically,

contract offered	action taken	z observed (only by agent)	L chosen	output (x) obtains; agent is compensated; external input (L) paid for

This technology permits the agent to apply additional factor inputs after uncertainty regarding production conditions has been resolved, and it allows for separate treatment of *planning* and *production* phases. We introduce this technology so that contracts that specify that the agent must produce a particular output can be honored (this is in contrast to the usual agency production function). x and L are publicly observable; a and z are privately observed by the agent.

To complete the specification of this model, we let $V(\cdot)$ denote the principal's preferences for consumption, $U(c) - g(a)$ denotes the agent's preferences for consumption c and effort a, and $\bar{U}$ denotes the opportunity cost to the agent of working for the principal (measured in utils). Both the agent and the principal are bound to the contract for the entire production period.

The following specialization of the production technology eases the analysis considerably: $x = X(z, L)$, $z \sim f(z|a)$, $a \in [\underline{a}, \bar{a}]$, X is twice-continuously differentiable with X_1, $X_2 > 0$ and $X_{22} < 0$ (subscripts denote partial derivatives). The consequences of this specialization, which is assumed throughout, will be noted below.

The optimal contract solves the following mathematical program ($E_a(\cdot)$ indicates that the expectation is to be taken conditional on the agent's action choice a).

Program 1

$$\underset{s,a}{\text{maximize}}\ E_a\{V[\tilde{x} - s(x, \tilde{L}) - P\tilde{L}]\}$$

$$\text{(i)}\quad \text{for all } (z, a), \qquad \tilde{L} = L(z, a) \in \arg\max_{L} U(s(X(z, L), L))$$

$$\text{(ii)}\quad a \in \arg\max_{\hat{a}} E_{\hat{a}}[U(s(X(z, \tilde{L}), \tilde{L}))] - g(\hat{a})$$

$$\text{(iii)}\quad E_a[U(s(X(z, \tilde{L}), \tilde{L}))] - g(a) \geq \bar{U}$$

$$\text{(iv)}\quad s(x, L) \geq -K \qquad \text{for all } x, L$$

The introduction of constraints (i) is the new feature of this model. Since the principal does not observe a or z, and the agent is delegated the task of choosing L, the agent will choose L to maximize his own utility. (Since there is no uncertainty after L is selected, utility and *not* expected utility is maximized). It is straightforward to show that, even though the principal and agent are asymmetrically informed with respect to the value of z, there is no value in having the agent communicate z to the principal. (For more general production technologies and for cases in which some uncertainty remains to be resolved when L is chosen, this result may not hold. See Baiman and Evans [1983], Christensen [1981], Dye [1983], Melumad and Reichelstein [1985] or Penno [1984] for additional results on the value of communication in traditional principal/agent contexts.) Constraints (ii), (iii), and (iv) are, respectively, constraints reflecting the agent's self-interested behavior in choosing his action, the lower bound on the utility the agent may receive by accepting employment from the principal, and the lower bound on the agent's payment s.

To write the solution to program 1, we need a bit more notation: let $z = z(x, L)$ be *the* value of z that corresponds to observing (x, L). (This is unique because $X_1 > 0$ and X, L are observable.) $H(z) \equiv \max_L X(z, L) - PL$. Then we have theorem 11.1 (proved in the appendix).

Theorem 11.1

If the agent's actions can be characterized by first-order conditions, then a solution to program 1 is given by $s(x, L)$, where

$$s(x, L) = \begin{cases} \hat{s}(z) & \text{if} \quad z = z(x, L) \quad \text{and} \quad x - PL = H(z) \\ -K & \text{otherwise} \end{cases}$$

where $\hat{s}(z)$ is defined by

$$\frac{V'[H(z) - \hat{s}(z)]}{U'(\hat{s}(z))} = \lambda + \mu \frac{f_a(z \mid a)}{f(z \mid a)} + \delta(z)$$

where λ, μ, and $\delta(z)$ are respectively, multipliers for constraints (ii), (iii), and (iv); and $\delta(z)$ is zero for all z with $\hat{s}(z) > -K$.

Theorem 11.1 demonstrates in this context that all ex ante optimal contracts involve ex post optimal utilization of L, that is, the agent always chooses the level of input which maximizes $X(z, L) - PL$ (which is the same input choice the principal would make). This result depends on the ability of the principal to infer z from observation of X and L. Also, theorem 11.1 establishes that, even if the principal has private information about the cost of the input (L) not held by the agent, the principal will have no incentive to distort the price of the input to alter the agent's incentives: the principal can only reduce his own income by writing the agent's contract in a way that incorrectly represents the principal's input costs. This result is generalized in the following corollary.

Corollary 11.1

The principal's utility can be increased (weakly) by disclosing to the agent any information that does not effect the agent's perception of the density $f(z \mid a)$.

As an example, suppose (contrary to fact) that the realization of $\tilde{z}$ is observed by the principal and not the agent. If the agent were delegated choice of L, the principal always would be better off (weakly) by disclosing z to the agent before the agent chose L. There also exist settings in which the principal is better off by providing the agent with information that does affect the agent's perception of $f(z \mid a)$ (e.g., information that would eliminate all uncertainty regarding the relation between the agent's action and z); but, in general, the situation involving communication of information about $f(z \mid a)$

is sensitive to model specification (see Christensen [1982], Demski and Sappington [1985]).

Finally, theorem 11.1 demonstrates that contracts yielding ex post optimal input choices need not be of the form $s(x, L) = s(x - PL)$ and therefore what might appear to be a logical alternative solution to the problem—viz., let the agent purchase the input and compensate him solely in terms of the output he produces—is in general inferior to the contract specified in theorem 11.1. Although the latter solution assigns property rights to the person consuming the resource (i.e., the agent), it is not generally desirable here because the information that is lost (knowledge of L) reduces the ability of the principal to infer z, the variable affected by the agent's action and upon which the contract should (optimally) depend. As with franchising operations, knowledge of outputs may provide more valuable information about the agent's action levels in conjunction with knowledge of input levels. This provides an example of the virtues of line-item reporting. Theorem 11.5 will identify conditions under which contracts of the form $s(x - PL)$ are optimal.

We now begin an analysis of the transfer pricing problem.

Due to the externalities one division may impose on another, contracts that maximize the profits a principal receives from any given division might not be of the same form as contracts that maximize the profits the principal receives from all divisions collectively. In particular, it might seem that, since greater coordination between divisions can be achieved when each division knows the inputs and outputs for other divisions, contracts that eliminate discretion over an individual division's inputs and outputs may improve overall firm efficiency (relative to contracts that provide such discretion). Contracts that specify the prices at which divisions can buy or sell inputs provide divisional discretion over the quantities supplied or demanded. Thus, the possible superiority of *prices over quantities* is actually a special case of the superiority of *discretion over no discretion.* Although this debate can be resolved only by analyzing a multidivision firm, we provide some preliminary results based on the single-division firm that will be supplemented below in the discussion of multidivision firms.

Definition 11.1

A contract s is a *quantity contract* provided that s is of the form

$$s(x, L) = \begin{cases} \tilde{s}(L) & x = x^0 \\ -K & x \neq x^0 \end{cases}$$

All other contracts are *discretionary contracts.*

Quantity contracts are typically not optimal in single-principal–single-agent environments. Theorem 11.2 provides one set of conditions that are sufficient to guarantee the strict suboptimality of quantity contracts.

Theorem 11.2

If $L(z)$ denotes the ex post optimal quantity of the labor input as a function of the realized value z of random state $\tilde{z}$, then a necessary and sufficient condition for quantity contracts to be optimal is

$$\frac{X_1(z, L(z))}{X_2(z, L(z))} = \frac{X_{12}(z, L(z))}{X_{22}(z, L(z))}$$

In particular, if z and L are weak complements in production for any set Z of z's having positive probability of occurrence, then quantity contracts are not optimal.

Proof: Since $L(z)$ is the ex post-optimal choice of labor input given state z, $L(z)$ satisfies

$$X_2(z, L(z)) = P \tag{11.1}$$

For quantity contracts to be optimal, there must exist some x^0 such that

$$X(z, L(z)) = x^0 \tag{11.2}$$

By totally differentiating (11.1), we get

$$L'(z) = \frac{-X_{12}(z, L(z))}{X_{22}(z, L(z))} \tag{11.3}$$

By totally differentiating (11.2), we get

$$L'(z) = \frac{-X_1(z, L(z))}{X_2(z, L(z))} \tag{11.4}$$

(11.3) and (11.4) must be identities in z. This proves the first claim. The second claim follows immediately, because X_1, X_2, and $-X_{22}$ are all positive and X_{12} is non-negative when z and L are weakly complementary.

In extending the model of the previous section to one in which transfer pricing can be discussed, we add a second agent while preserving as much symmetry between agents as possible. Call the agent previously discussed the *manufacturing division manager*, and the production technology he runs the *manufacturing division*. We now introduce a distribution (or retail) division and its manager, with production technology and preferences respectively represented by $r = R(a^R, w, x)$, $w \sim l(w)$, and $U^R(c) - g^r(a^r)$. The chronology of the previous section is retained:

contract offered	a^R taken	w observed (by distribution manager only)	x applied	retail distribution output (r) obtains

The output of the manufacturing division is an input to the retail division, so a potential role for transfer prices exists. In addition to specifying intra-divisional timing sequences, we must adopt some convention regarding interdivisional production sequences. Given the present context, it seems reasonable to postulate that the actions are chosen simultaneously by the division managers, that w and z are concurrently observed, and that the manufacturing division manager chooses L before x is applied by the retail division manager, since x is an input to R. Also, as before, we specialize R by postulating $r = R(w, x)$, $w \sim f(w|a^r)$, and $a^r \in [\underline{a}, \bar{a}]$, with R_1, $R_2 > 0$, $R_{22} < 0$.

Contracts between the division managers and the principal can depend upon all publicly observable variables x, L, and r. Also, since the manufacturing division's output is an input to the retail division, the appropriate level of x (and hence L) depends on the retail division's realization of w, as well as z. Given our technological assumptions, the value of w can be inferred ex post from publicly available information; but, unless the manufacturing division is informed by the retail division of w's realized value, only by accident will the manufacturing division select L consistent with overall maximum profits. Thus, in addition to having contracts depend upon x, L, and r, we shall assume that both managers' compensations depend upon the retail manager's announced value of w (announced values being denoted by $\hat{w}$). Note that there is no comparable incentive to have the manufacturing division manager announce z, since the retail manager's actions do not influence the manufacturing division's output.

With these preparatory comments completed, we proceed to specify the mathematical program that characterizes the pair of optimal contracts offered by the principal to these agents to maximize his expected utility. (As a mnenomic device, we index the manufacturing manager's contract and preferences by M. Also, $E_{a^R, a^M}[\cdot]$ indicates that the expectation is to be taken conditional on the manufacturing and retail division managers respectively choosing actions a^R and a^M.)

Program 2

$$\max_{s^R,\, s^M} E_{a^R,\, a^M}\{V[\tilde{r} - s^M(\tilde{r}, \tilde{x}, \tilde{L}, \hat{w}) - s^R(\tilde{r}, \tilde{x}, \tilde{L}, \tilde{w}) - P\tilde{L}]\}$$

subject to

$$\text{(i)} \quad \tilde{r} = R\big(w, X(z, \bar{L}(z, \hat{w}))\big)$$

$$\text{(ii)} \quad \tilde{x} = X(z, \bar{L}(z, \hat{w}))$$

$$\text{(iii)} \quad \tilde{L} = \bar{L}(z, \hat{w}) \in \arg\max_{L} s^M\big(R(\hat{w}, X(z, L)), X(z, L), L, \hat{w}\big)$$

$$\text{(iv)} \quad w = \hat{w}(w) \in \arg\max_{\bar{w}} E_{a^R,\, a^M}[U^R(s^R(\tilde{r}, \tilde{x}, \tilde{L}, \bar{w})) | w]$$

$$\text{(v)} \quad a^R \in \arg\max_{a} E_{a,\, a^M}[U^R(s^R(\tilde{r}, \tilde{x}, \tilde{L}, \hat{w}))] - g^R(a), \quad \text{given } a^M$$

$$\text{(vi)} \quad a^M \in \arg\max_{a} E_{a^R,\, a}[U(s^M(\tilde{r}, \tilde{x}, \tilde{L}, \hat{w}))] - g(a), \quad \text{given } a^R$$

$$\text{(vii)} \quad E_{a^R,\, a^M}[U^R(s^R(\tilde{r}, \tilde{x}, \tilde{L}, \hat{w}))] - g^R(a^R) \geq \bar{U}^R$$

$$\text{(viii)} \quad E_{a^R,\, a^M}[U(s^M(\tilde{r}, \tilde{x}, \tilde{L}, \hat{w}))] - g^M(a^M) \geq \bar{U}^M$$

$$\text{(ix)} \quad s^R(r, x, L, w) \geq -K, \quad \text{for all } r, x, L, w$$

$$\text{(x)} \quad s^M(r, x, L, w) \geq -K, \quad \text{for all } r, x, L, w$$

Constraints (i) and (ii) define $\tilde{r}$ and $\tilde{x}$. By constraint (iii), the production manager uses labor $\bar{L}(z, \hat{w})$ given his personal observation of z and the retail division manager's announcement $\hat{w}$. Note that the manufacturing division manager's compensation in (iii) depends on the actual revenues R of the retail division, which in turn depend on the actual value w of the retail division manager's private information, although the manufacturing manager (and the principal) can discern the actual (vs. announced) value of w only after the manufacturing division's manager has chosen L. Consequently, the manufacturing manager must make an inference about the actual value of w, based on its announced value $\hat{w}$, in order to select L. In constraint (iii), I have assumed that, conditional on the retail manager's announcement $\hat{w}$, the manufacturing manager evaluates $R(\cdot)$ at $(\hat{w}, x)$, that is, I have assumed that the manufacturing manager believes the retail manager's announcement is truthful. This presumption by the manufacturing manager is justified by constraint (iv), which requires that the retail manager's contract be constructed so as to give him no incentive to lie. (If this were not initialy the case, it is easy to show, by a "revelation principle" style argument, that the retail manager's contract can be redesigned to make truthtelling incentive-compatible, without adversely affecting either manager's real decisions or compensation (typically, the production manager's contract would have to be revised concurrently to obtain this result).) Thus, given realizations z and w of $\tilde{z}$ and $\tilde{w}$ and announcement $\hat{w}$ of $\tilde{w}$, the realizations of the production and retail division managers' outputs are respectively given in (ii) and (i). Constraints (v) and (vi) simply impose rationality on the managers: anticipating his subsequent announcement strategy and the effort level of the production manager, the retail manager chooses his effort level to maximize his expected utility, according to (v). Constraint (vi) is the counterpart to (v) for the production manager; (vii) and (viii) are constraints on the expected utilities the managers derive from employment; while (ix) and (x) define lower bounds on the payments made under the contracts.

Program 2 turns out to have a simple solution, as is indicated in theorem 11.3. (In the theorem's statement, $w = w(r, x)$ is *the* value of w consistent with (r, x).)

Theorem 11.3

If the principal is risk-neutral, and each agent's action $a^i > \underline{a}$ $(i = R, M)$ can be characterized by first-order conditions, then the solution to program 2 is given by a pair of contracts s^R, s^M of the following form:

$$s^R(r, x, L, \hat{w}) = \begin{cases} \hat{s}^R(w) & \text{if } w = w(r, x) = \hat{w} \\ -K, & \text{otherwise} \end{cases}$$

$$s^M(r, x, L, \hat{w}) = \begin{cases} \hat{s}^M(z) & \text{if } z = z(x, L),\ r - PL = H(z, \hat{w}) \\ -K, & \text{otherwise} \end{cases}$$

where

$$H(z, w) = \underset{L}{\text{maximize}}\, R(w, X(z, L)) - PL$$

and

$$\frac{1}{U^{R\prime}(\hat{s}^R(w))} = \lambda^R + \mu^R \frac{f_a(w \mid a^R)}{f(w \mid a^R)} + \delta^R(w)$$

$$\frac{1}{U^{M\prime}(\hat{s}^M(z))} = \lambda^M + \mu^M \frac{f_a(z \mid a^M)}{f(z \mid a^M)} + \delta^M(z)$$

for some positive constants λ^R, λ^M, μ^R, and μ^M; and $\delta^j(\cdot)$ is zero whenever $\hat{s}^j(\cdot) > -K, j = R, M$. (See the appendix for proof.)

Theorem 11.3 has the following implications. First, each division manager's compensation fundamentally depends on only those variables which are informative about his actions, since $\hat{s}^R$ depends only on w and $\hat{s}^M$ depends only on z.[1] Second, input choices are ex post optimal. Third, the managers' contracts are characterized essentially by the standard (Holmström) formulation. Fourth, the problems of multiple Nash equilibria, randomized strategies, etc. which render the problems of many agencies unsusceptible to analysis (see Antle [1982]), do not arise here when the principal is risk-neutral.

In this two-agent case, the counterpart to a quantity contract is a contract that specifies that the manufacturing division is to produce, and the retail division is to consume, a constant level of the manufacturing division's output, regardless of the realized values of z and w. This is a narrow definition of a quantity contract; it does not allow the quantity elicited by the principal to vary with the agents' claims regarding their production environments. The reason for defining quantity contracts in this way is discussed further under "Conclusions."

As noted above, because of potential problems of coordination between divisions, it might seem that the circumstances under which quantity contracts are optimal might be broader in multiple- than single-division settings. However, under almost exactly the same circumstances as above, quantity contracts are strictly suboptimal. More precisely, we have theorem 11.4.

Theorem 11.4

A necessary condition for quantity contracts to be optimal is that $R(w, x)$ be separable in w and x. In particular, if w and x are strictly complementary ($R_{12} > 0$) on a set of positive probability, then quantity contracts are not optimal.

Proof: Since this proof is similar in style to the proof of theorem 11.2, the argument is abbreviated. If there exists x^0 such that the optimal choice, $L(z, w)$, of L involves $X(z, L(z, w)) = x^0$, then $L_2(z, w) = 0$. But, $L(z, w)$ must maximize $R(w, X(z, L)) - PL$ and therefore satisfy the first-order condition:

$$R_2\big(w, X(z, L(z, w))\big)X_2(z, L(z, w)) = P \qquad (11.5)$$

Differentiating this first-order condition with respect to w, we get

$$L_2(z, w) = -R_{21}X_2/(R_{22}X_2^2 + R_2X_{22}) \qquad (11.6)$$

(the arguments of these functions have been omitted to conserve space) which is zero for all (z, w) only if R_{21} is identically zero, that is, only if R is separable in w and x. The second claim in the statement of the theorem follows immediately.

Theorem 11.4. establishes that quantity and discretionary contracts are not equivalent. The reason for the nonequivalence here is that there is residual uncertainty regarding production conditions at the time the contract is specified.

Aggregation Issues

In the preceding model, transfer prices do not appear explicitly. In this section, we consider a model in which the performance of a division manager is evaluated in terms of his division's accounting profits, which depend on what transfer prices prevail. We proceed to identify conditions in which transfer prices can perform the task of creating appropriate incentives for division managers. Specifically, when can a firm's owners achieve maximum expected profits by compensating division managers only on the basis of accounting profits constructed upon a system of transfer prices? This is both a problem in transfer pricing and a problem in information aggregation. This section first analyzes this problem in a single-principal–single-agent context. The question in that context reduces to: when can the division manager's compensation $s(x, L)$ (as described earlier) be written solely as a function of his division's (i.e., the firm's) profits $x - PL$? Theorem 11.5 provides one answer.

Theorem 11.5

If the optimal contract can be characterized by first-order conditions, then a sufficient condition for the solution $s(x, L)$ to program 1 to be a function of $x - PL$ is that

$$\frac{\partial}{\partial z}\frac{f_a(z|a)}{f(z|a)} > 0 \qquad \text{and} \qquad X_1(z, L) > 0$$

Proof: If

$$\frac{\partial}{\partial z}\frac{f_a(z|a)}{f(z|a)} > 0 \qquad \text{and} \qquad X_1(z, L) > 0$$

it follows that $\hat{s}(z)$ (defined in theorem 11.1) is increasing and $H(z) \equiv \max_L X(z, L) - PL$ is strictly increasing. Consequently $z(H)$, the inverse of $H(z)$, is strictly increasing and $r(x - PL) \equiv \hat{s}[z(x - PL)]$ is increasing.

If the manager is compensated with r and $\tilde{z} = z$ occurs, the manager's utility-maximizing choice of L maximizes $X(z, L) - PL$ since r is increasing. (We assume here that if the manager is indifferent among several choices of L, he still maximizes $X - PL$.) Therefore, the manager's compensation under both r and s is the same for each realization of z. Therefore, he takes the same action under both contracts, and the owner is indifferent between these contracts as well.

Notice that the optimal contract in theorem 11.5 is a function of only the firm's profits in spite of the fact that, for arbitrary choices of L, the profits $X(z, L) - PL$ contain less information about z and hence about the manager's action a than does the pair (X, L). The reason for the optimality of this contract is that given z, the choice of L by the manager is not arbitrary, and so, given the manager's utility maximizing selection of L, $X(z, L) - PL$ reveals z just as the pair (X, L) does. Alternatively put, though $X - PL$ is not sufficient for (X, L) with respect to z, $\operatorname{Sup}_L X(z, L) - PL$ is sufficient for (X, L) with respect to z. Thus, whether a function of a vector of variables is sufficient for the vector with respect to some unknown parameter depends upon whether this function is defined before or after the manager's optimal actions are taken. This ambiguity in the notion of sufficiency does not arise in classical statistics, because the random variables to which the notion is classically applied are described by nonmanipulable, exogenously given distributions. (See also Amershi [1984] for a rigorous development of the relation between the classical statistical notion of sufficiency and sufficiency in contractual contexts.)

In the case of a two-division firm, the result corresponding to theorem 11.5 involves establishing conditions under which each division manager's compensation optimally depends on only the intermediate input's transfer price and the divisions' accounting profits. In general, we should expect some welfare loss from such compensation schemes relative to schemes that depend on all of R, X, L. But, if we borrow an approach from the literature on rational expectations (see, e.g., Lucas [1972]) and are content with describing the allocations and utilities achievable through compensation schemes that depend upon divisional profits and the first-best transfer prices without concern for the mechanism used to calculate these prices,[2] then it is possible to obtain a conclusion for the two division firm quite similar to theorem 11.5. In theorem 11.6 below, we assume that there is some unspecified mechanism capable of computing the first-best transfer price $p_t(w, z)$ conditional on $(\tilde{w}, \tilde{z}) = (w, z)$, and that each division manager's compensation can depend only on this transfer price and the accounting profits (based on this transfer price) of *both* divisions. The example following theorem 11.6 illustrates a case where each manager's compensation depends on the transfer price and (only) *his* division's accounting profits.

Theorem 11.6

Suppose $X(z, L)$ and $R(w, x)$ are twice continuously differentiable, with $X_1, X_2, R_1, R_2 > 0$; $X_{22}, R_{22} < 0$; $X_{12}, R_{12} > 0$, and the first-best level of the input L is positive for all realizations of z and w. Further suppose that

$$\frac{\partial}{\partial z}\frac{f_a(z|a^M)}{f(z|a^M)} \quad \text{and} \quad \frac{\partial}{\partial w}\frac{f_a(w|a^R)}{f(w|a^R)}$$

are increasing in z and w respectively for each a^M and a^R.[3] Then, a solution to program 2 exists, with each division manager's compensation being a function of both divisions' accounting profits $p_t x - PL$ and $r - p_t x$, and p_t, where $p_t = p_t(z, w)$ is the first-best transfer price conditional on (z, w).

Example:

If $X = z\sqrt{L}$ and $R = w \log x$, the lower bounds $\underline{w}$ and $\underline{z}$ of the supports of $\tilde{w}$ and $\tilde{z}$ satisfy $\underline{z}^2 \underline{w} \geq 2Pe$ (e is the base of the natural logarithm),

$$\frac{f_a(w|a^M)}{f(w|a^M)} \quad \text{and} \quad \frac{f_a(z|a^R)}{f(z|a^R)}$$

are both increasing in their first arguments, and optimal contracts are characterized by first-order conditions, then a solution to program 2 (specialized to this example) exists, with each division manager's compensation a function of only his own division's accounting profits and $p_t(w, z)$, the first-best transfer price corresponding to (w, z).

We close this section with two comments. First, the assumption that some unspecified mechanism exists which is capable of calculating the first-best transfer price for each realization of (w, z) implicitly requires the existence of some measurement mechanism: it can be shown, under the hypotheses of theorem 11.6, that if the transfer price is $p_t(\hat{w}, \hat{z})$, where $\hat{z}$ (resp. $\hat{w}$) is the manufacturing (resp. retail) manager's announcement of z (resp. w), and $p_t(\cdot)$ is the first-best transfer pricing schedule, then each manager has an incentive to overstate the value of the realization of his private information, assuming the other manager reports his information truthfully and assuming that contracts take the form described in the proof of theorem 11.6. Thus, knowledge of the first-best $p_t(w, z)$ must be obtained by some monitor and cannot simply be elicited from the managers without distortion, unless the compensation schedules deviate from the optima described in theorem 11.6.

Remark: It may be of interest to note here that neither manager has an incentive to understate the value of his private information, if he believes the other manager tells the truth, when the principal bases each manager's compensation on the inferred values of (w, z) from observation only of the transfer price p_t and corporate-wide profits, as in the proof of theorem 11.6. (The informational set-up here is this: subsequent to observing $\tilde{w}$, the retail manager announces (possibly falsely) that the realized value of $\tilde{w}$ is $\hat{w}$ to some black box (the principal does *not* hear this announcement); similarly, the manufacturing manager announces $\tilde{z}$ to the black box. The black box produces the first-best transfer price $p_t(\hat{w}, \hat{z})$ consistent with these announcements—and this transfer (as well as the divisional profits based on this transfer price) is made public to everyone. Refer to figure 11–1.

In figure 11–1, the line labeled p_t^0 is the set $\{(w, z) | p_t(w, z) = p_t^0\}$; the line π^0 is the set $\{(w, z) | R(w, X(z, L(z, w))) - PL(z, w) = \pi^0\}$. Suppose w_0, z_0

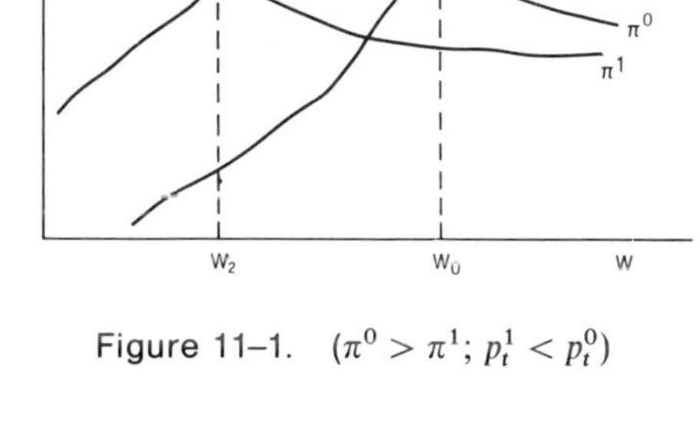

Figure 11–1. $(\pi^0 > \pi^1;\ p_t^1 < p_t^0)$

is such that $p_t(w_0, z_0) = p_t^0$ and $R(w_0, X(z_0, L(z_0, w_0))) - PL(z_0, w_0) = \pi^0$. Accordingly, if the principal observed the transfer price p_t^0 and corporate-wide profits π^0, he would infer that (w_0, z_0) is the realization of $(\tilde{w}, \tilde{z})$.

Suppose the retail manager decided to report $w_1 < w_0$ when $\tilde{w} = w_0$ and $\tilde{z} = z_0$. Since $p_t(w, z)$ increases with w (see the proof of theorem 11.6), it follows that the principal would infer (incorrectly) that (w, z) belongs to the line labeled p_t^1 (i.e., the set $\{(w, z) | p_t(z, w) = p_t^1\}$ where $p_t^1 = p_t(w_1, z)$. Moreover, the firm's corporate-wide profits will drop to $\pi^1 \equiv R(w_0, X(z_0, L(z_0, w_1))) - PL(z_0, w_1)$ (since, if the manufacturing manager maximizes his division's accounting profits, taking the transfer price p_t^1 as given, he will produce $L(z_0, w_1)$ – the amount that would have maximized corporate-wide profits if $(\tilde{w}, \tilde{z}) = (w_1, z_0)$). This will lead the principal to infer (incorrectly) that the realized (w, z) belongs to the line labeled π^1—i.e., the set $\{(w, z) | R(w, X(z, L(z, w))) - PL(z, w) = \pi^1\}$). The intersection of the lines π^1 and p_t^1 occurs at some point, say (w_2, z_2). Thus, (w_2, z_2) will be the principal's inference of the realization of $(\tilde{w}, \tilde{z})$ if the retail manager announces to the black box that $\tilde{w} = w_1$. Notice that w_2 is strictly less than w_0, the true realization of $\tilde{w}$, so if the retail manager's compensation in increasing in the principal's inference of $\tilde{w}$ (from observation of p_t and corporate-wide profits), the retail manager will never underreport the realization of $\tilde{w}$ for the purpose of affecting which transfer price is chosen.

A similar argument applies for the manufacturing manager. It is somewhat more complicated to demonstrate that each manager obtains strict gains by over-reporting (assuming the other manager is truthful). This argument is not presented here.

Our second concluding comment is that, as the proofs of theorem 11.6 and the example reveal, the division managers' contracts depend upon the prevailing transfer price. This is a general result: transfer prices cannot be specified independently of the compensation of the division managers.

Conclusions

Three conclusions emerge from this essay. First, transfer prices yield allocations which differ from those associated with transfer "quantities." More generally, intrafirm resource allocation mechanisms that provide divisional managers with discretion yield allocations different from those that do not, when production uncertainties have not been resolved at the time the transfer prices (or quantities, or the extent of discretion) must be decided upon. If we allowed the "quantity contracts" in the preceding discussion to vary depending upon the realized values of the productivity parameters z and w, then the distinction between contracts that give division managers' discretion in their action choices and contracts that do not vanishes. To repeat, the existence of uncertainty which is not yet resolved is central to distinguishing the performance of transfer pricing mechanisms from other intrafirm resource-allocation schemes. Second, transfer pricing schemes and other allocation mechanisms cannot be analyzed independently of the compensation of the people responsible for production operations; such mechanisms are defined only in reference to management's compensation. Third, the loss of information for contracting purposes arising from aggregation cannot be evaluated by appealing to arguments based on classical sufficient statistics.

Notes

1. Some accountants might interpret this result as being consistent with responsibility accounting, restating the result as: "the manager's compensation depends only on what he controls." Caution is required in applying this latter interpretation, however, since each manager's compensation also depends on random variables beyond his control.

2. Just as in the theory of rational expectations, one does not ask what mechanism generates the expectations.

3. This last condition is referred to as the monotone likelihood ratio property or MLRP. See Lehmann [1959].

APPENDIX 11

Proof of Theorem 11.1

Let $r(x, L)$ be *any* contract offered to the agent. Let $L^r(z)$ be the input the agent selects when he observes z and is compensated with r. Let $L(z)$ attain $\max_L X(z, L) - PL$. We first claim that, for $r(x, L)$ to be optimal, $L^r(z) = L(z)$. Suppose not Define $s(x, L)$ as follows:

$$s(x, L) = \begin{cases} -r(X(z, L^r(z)), L^r(z)) & \text{where } z = z(x, L) \\ & \quad\; x = X(z, L(z)) \\ & \quad\; L = L(z) \\ -K & \text{otherwise} \end{cases}$$

$s(x, L)$ compensates the agent with the same amount as does $r(x, L)$ for all realizations of z, provided that the agent employs the ex post optimal input level. Hence, $s(x, L)$ induces the same action a as does $r(x, L)$. Clearly, since $L^r(z) \neq L(z)$ (by assumption), $s(x, L)$ is preferred by the principal to $r(x, L)$.

In other words, we have just shown that any solution to program 1 must be ex post optimal. Moreover, by defining $\bar{s}(z)$ by $\bar{s}(z) = r\big(X(z, L^r(z)), L^r(z)\big)$, it is clear that any optimal contract can be written in the form

$$s(x, L) = \begin{cases} \bar{s}(z) & \text{when } z = z(x, L) \\ & \qquad x = X(z, L(z)) \\ & \qquad L = L(z) \\ -K & \text{otherwise} \end{cases}$$

for some contract $\bar{s}(z)$. To search for the optimal contract among those of this form (if K is sufficiently large), we require the solution to the following program (which is equivalent to program 1):

$$\underset{s}{\text{maximize}}\, E[V\big(H(z) - \hat{s}(z)\big)]$$

subject to

$$a \in \arg\max E[U(\hat{s}(z))] - g(a)$$

and

$$E[U(\hat{s}(z))] - g(a) \geq \bar{U}$$

(since the agent will not deviate from the ex post optimal choice of inputs, if K is sufficiently large). This is, of course, the standard principal/agent problem, necessary conditions for which are written in the statement of theorem 11.1, provided that the agent's actions are characterized by first-order conditions.

Proof of Theorem 11.3

Since observation of x, L, and r permit inference of z and w, it is easy to induce truthful reporting of w by the retail division manager as well as the ex post optimal input selection $L = L(z, w)$ by the manufacturing division manager (see proof of theorem 11.1); these two properties will be features of any solution to program 2.

Now, consider two sets of observables (x, L, r) and (x', L', r') such that the inferred random variables are (z, w) and (z, w'). Any contract to the manufacturing manager that does not pay the manager the same amount when (x, L, r, w) and (x', L', r', w') are observed cannot be optimal. To see this, construct a new contract which pays the certainty equivalent of the original contract, that is, define $\hat{s}^R(z)$ by

$$U^R(\hat{s}^R(z)) = E[U\big(s^R(z, w)\big)|z]$$

Because of risk-aversion, $E[\hat{s}^R(z)] < E[s^R(w, z)]$ (unless $s^R(z, w)$ varies with w on a set of no measure), and $\hat{s}^R(z)$ induces the same action as does $s^R(z, w)$. Therefore $s^R(z, w)$ cannot be optimal unless it is almost surely independent of w.

This demonstrates that the manufacturing division manager's compensation is almost surely independent of the distribution manager's actions. Hence, problems of subgame-dominated equilibria and randomized equilibrium strategies which plague many multiagent models do not arise here. Therefore, the solution to the principal's problem is as stated in theorem 11.3. (Similar comments apply with respect to the distribution division's manager.)

Proof of Theorem 11.6

The first-best transfer pricing rule, $p_t(w, z)$, is determined from the first-order conditions of the global maximization problem:

$$\max_L R(w, X(z, L)) - PL$$

which is achieved by, say, $L(z, w)$. It is given by either of the following equivalent expressions:

$$p_t(w, z) = P/X_2(z, L(z, w)) \tag{11A.1}$$

$$p_t(w, z) = R_2(w, X(z, L(z, w))) \tag{11A.2}$$

As stated above, we assume here that some unspecified mechanism exists which computes the transfer price $p_t(w, z)$ according to these formulas for each realized (w, z).

We shall show next that knowledge of each division's profits (computed with $p_t(\cdot)$) together with knowledge of the transfer price completely determines the realization (w, z) if each division manager's compensation is weakly increasing in his division's profits and corporate-wide profits. To see this, first note that—by this last assumption—given p_t, w, and z, the retail manager maximizes his compensation by selecting that x which attains

$$\max_x R(w, x) - p_t x \tag{11A.3}$$

if $p_t = p_t(w, z)$, since this choice of x will simultaneously maximize both his division's profits and corporate-wide profits if the manufacturing manager chooses that L attaining

$$\max_L p_t X(z, L) - PL \tag{11A.4}$$

This follows directly from the definition of $p_t(w, z)$. Similarly, the manufacturing manager has an incentive to choose the L attaining (11A.4) if the retail manager chooses that x attaining (11A.3).

Consequently, for fixed (w, z), the choices of x, L attaining (11A.3) and (11A.4) constitute Nash equilibrium choices for these managers.

Now note that differentiation of (11A.1) with respect to w shows that $p_t(w, z)$ strictly increases in w (because the hypotheses of the theorem are sufficient to guarantee $L_2 > 0$), and differentiation of (11A.2) with respect to z shows that $p_t(w, z)$ is strictly decreasing in z (because the hypotheses also guarantee that $dp_t/dz = R_{22}(X_1 + X_2 L_1) < 0$).

Therefore, the isotransfer-price contours in (w, z) space—e.g., $\{(w, z) | p_t(w, z) = K\}$—are upward-sloping.

Furthermore, by the envelope theorem,

$$\frac{d}{dw} R(w, X(z, L(z, w))) - PL(z, w) = R_1(w, X(z, L(z, w))) > 0$$

$$\frac{d}{dz} R(w, X(z, L(z, w))) - PL(z, w) = R_2(w, X(z, L(z, w)))X_1(z, L(z, w)) > 0.$$

so, the corporate isoprofit contours in (w, z) space—e.g., $\{(w, z)| R(w, X(z, L(z, w))) - PL(z, w) = K\}$—are downward-sloping. Note, by our preceding remarks that, given $p_t(w, z)$ as specified by (11A.1) or (11A.2), each division-manager's Nash-equilibrium action choice corresponding to a fixed (w, z) will result in the sum of the divisions' accounting profits equaling the firm's corporate-wide maximum profits. Consequently, knowledge of each division's accounting profits, in conjunction with the transfer pricing rule used to calculate those profits, completely determines which (w, z) occurred (by computing the intersection of the pertinent isotransfer and isoprofit contours), as was claimed (see figure 11–2).

If Π^s denotes the sum of the divisional profits Π^R and Π^M, and $w^{-1}(\Pi^s, p_t)$, $z^{-1}(\Pi^s, p_t)$ denote *the* (w, z) pair consistent with (Π^s, p_t), we can write the following contracts:

$$s^M(\Pi^R, \Pi^M, p_t) = \hat{s}^M(z^{-1}(\Pi^R + \Pi^M, p_t)) \qquad (11A.5)$$

$$s^R(\Pi^r, \Pi^M, p_t) = \hat{s}^R(w^{-1}(\Pi^R + \Pi^M, p_t)) \qquad (11A.6)$$

Notice that if a division manager decided to adopt an action that did *not* maximize his division's accounting profits, the sum of the division's accounting profits would drop, and the values of $z^{-1}(\Pi^R + \Pi^M, p_t)$, $w^{-1}(\Pi^R + \Pi^M, p_t)$ would drop as well (see figure 11–2). Therefore, since $\hat{s}^i(\cdot)$ is increasing by MLRP ($i = R, M$), the division manager's compensation

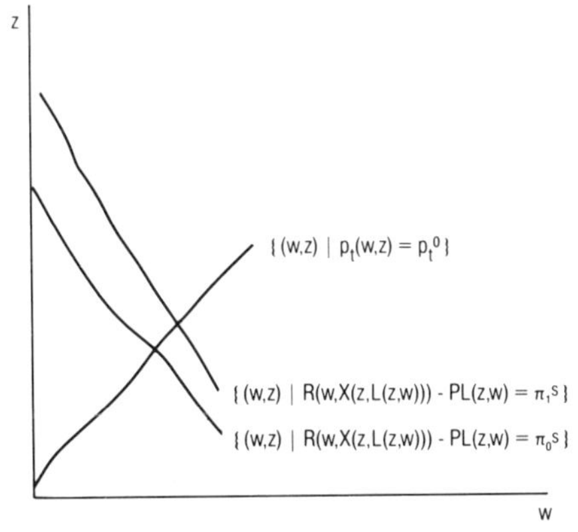

Figure 11–2. $(\pi_0^s < \pi_1^s)$

would drop also—i.e., each manager's compensation is increasing in his own divisions and corporate-wide accounting profits, given the assignments (11A.5) and (11A.6), so each manager has an incentive to choose actions in accordance with (11A.3) and (11A.4).

With the specifications made in (11A.5) and (11A.6), each manager is encouraged to take exactly the same actions he would have taken had he been compensated on the basis of x, L, and r (and is paid the same amount), so both the principal and the managers have no incentive to observe any of these variables, provided the transfer price p_t and the divisional profits $r - p_t x$, $p_t x - L$ computed on the basis of this transfer price, are known. This completes the proof.

Proof of Example

To verify the claims made in the statement of the example, note that for any fixed (w, z), the globally optimal choice of L is $w/2P$, and therefore, the first-best transfer price is $p_t(w, z) = \sqrt{2Pw}/z$ (this is calculated by determining that p_t for which $\max_L p_t X(z, L) - PL$ is achieved at $L = w/2P$). It follows that, for fixed (w, z), the manufacturing division's maximal divisional profits are $w/2$, so its isoprofit contours $\{(w, z) | \max_L p_t(w, z) X(z, L) \quad PL = K\}$ arc vertical in (w, z) space and increasing to the right. Since $p_t(w, z)$ is clearly increasing in w and decreasing in z, it follows that observation of the manufacturing division's accounting profits and $p_t(w, z)$ reveals both w and z.

A similar argument shows that observaton of the retail division's accounting profits and p_t also reveals w and z. The rest of the claims made in the statement of the example are verified by the arguments used to prove theorem 11.6.

References

Amershi, A. [1984]. "A Theory of Informativeness under Asymmetric Information." Working Paper, University of British Columbia.

Antle, R. [1982]. "The Auditor as an Economic Agent." *Journal of Accounting Research* 20, 503–527.

Baiman, S., and Evans, H. [1983]. "Pre-decision Information and Participative Management Control Systems." *Journal of Accounting Research* 21, 371–395.

Christensen, J. [1981]. "Communication in Agencies." *Bell Journal of Economics* 12, 661–674.

Christensen, J. [1982]. "The Determination of Performance Standards and Participation." *Journal of Accounting Research* 20, 589–603.

Demski, J., and Sappington, D. [1985]. "Delegated Expertise." Working Paper, Yale University.

Dye, R. [1983]. "Communication and Post-Decision Information." *Journal of Accounting Research* 21, 514–533.

Gould, J.R. [1964]. "Internal Pricing in Firms When There Are Costs of Using An Outside Market." *Journal of Business* 37, 61–67.

Harris, M., Kriebel, C., and Raviv, A. [1982]. "Asymmetric Information, Incentives, and Intrafirm Resource Allocation." *Management Science* 28, 604–620.

Hirshleifer, J. [1956]. "On the Economics of Transfer Pricing." *Journal of Business* 29, 172–184.

Laffont, J. [1977]. "More on Prices vs. Quantities." *Review of Economic Studies* 44, 177–182.

Lehman, E. [1959]. *Testing Statistical Hypotheses.* New York: Wiley.

Lucas, R. [1972]. "Expectations and the Neutrality of Money." *Journal of Economic Theory* 4, 103–124.

Melumad, N., and Reichelstein, S. [1985]. "Centralization versus Delegation and the Value of Communication." Working Paper, Stanford University.

Penno, M. [1984]. "Asymmetry of Pre-decision Information and Management Accounting." *Journal of Accounting Research* 22, 177–191.

Weitzmann, M. [1977a]. "Prices vs. Quantities." *Review of Economic Studies* 44, 477–491.

Weitzmann, M. [1977b]. "Is the Price System or Rationing More Effective in Getting a Commodity to Those Who Need It Most." *Bell Journal of Economics* 8, 517–524.

12 ACCOUNTANTS' LOSS FUNCTIONS AND INDUCED PREFERENCES FOR CONSERVATISM*

Rick Antle
Richard A. Lambert

The purpose of this paper is to analyze the properties of optimal incentive schemes, and their implications, for accountants in a simple model of the accountant's role in the production of information for a user. We find that a key property of the optimal incentive scheme for the accountant is its asymmetry: typically, the accountant will be penalized differently for different types of errors. This asymmetry has implications for the structure of auditors' legal liability and for accountants' preferences for conservative accounting practices.

The concept of conservatism was once commonly expressed in the admonition to "anticipate no profits but anticipate all losses." Recently, this conception of conservatism has come under attack. For example, in the Statement of

* Helpful comments by Sidney Davidson, Joel Demski, Nicholas Dopuch, Jerry Feltham, Froystein Gjesdal, and workshop participants at the University of Chicago, Cornell University, and New York University are gratefully acknowledged, as is the financial support of the Institute of Professional Accounting at the University of Chicago (Antle) and the Accounting Research Center of the Kellogg Graduate School of Management at Northwestern University (Lambert).

Financial Accounting Concepts No. 2, the FASB writes that under this definition, the concept of conservatism

> tends to conflict with significant qualitative characteristics, such as representational faithfulness, neutrality, and comparability (including consistency). . . . The Board emphasizes that any attempt to understate results consistently is likely to raise questions about the reliability and integrity of information about those results and will probably be self-defeating in the long run. . . . The best way to avoid the injury to investors that imprudent reporting creates is to try to ensure that what is reported represents what it purports to represent. . . . Conservatism in financial reporting should no longer connote deliberate, consistent understatement of net assets and profits. (paragraphs 92–97)

Nevertheless the FASB states "there is a place for a convention such as conservatism—meaning prudence—in financial accounting and reporting, because business and economic activities are surrounded by uncertainty, but it needs to be applied with care" (paragraph 92). We feel that the major problem with this statement is that the reference to prudence is too vague to constitute a meaningful definition of conservatism. In this paper, we develop a precise definition of conservatism, albeit at the expense of adopting a limited universe of discourse. Our definition has the virtue that it focuses on the direction of accountants' and auditors' efforts, and it is consistent with the notions of unbiased and truthful reporting.[1] We examine whether (and under what conditions) a demand for conservatism arises *endogenously* in the simple economic setting we examine.

Moreover, discussions of the motivations for conservatism have traditionally focused on the consequences to the *user* of the financial statements. For example, Devine [1963] explored the following rationales for conservatism:

1. Accountants are compensating for the biases of management.
2. Accountants are compensating for the fact that users of financial statements are more prone to optimism than pessimism.
3. Accountants are reacting to the asymmetry of users' loss functions, so that losses are felt by users more deeply than gains.

In contrast, our analysis examines the consequences of adopting conservative practices to both the user *and* the accountant. We formulate an agency model (e.g., Harris and Raviv [1979], Holmstrom [1979]) in which a user hires an accountant to produce information that is of value to the user. The user must motivate the accountant to incur private costs in the production of information, and to truthfully report the findings of the information production activities. Thus we model the accountant as an economic agent, and study the optimal incentive scheme used to motivate him (see Antle [1982]). As mentioned earlier, asymmetry is a key property of the optimal incentive scheme, and this asymmetry can give rise to the accountant's preference for conservative practices.

Aside from the issues involving auditors' legal liability and accountants' conservatism, our model can also be used to study some components of the cost of implementing various information production alternatives. We use the model to capture the cost of paying an accountant to supply labor input into an information production function, and ask how the expected payments to the accountant change as the characteristics of the information production function change. In particular, we show that the expected payments to the accountant are decreasing in the fineness of the information system being implemented.

The remainder of this paper is organized as follows. We first present the user's primary decision problem, the information production technology, and the user's contracting problem with the accountant. Then we document several properties of the optimal incentive scheme for the accountant. Next, we define conservative accounting practices and show that accountants have private incentives to adopt conservative practices. An analysis of the costs of moving to finer information systems follows. The final section concludes and summarizes the paper.

Model

In this section we formulate the problem of a decision maker (also referred to as a user) who must make a decision, d, in the face of uncertainty. The set of decisions available to the risk-neutral user is denoted D. For simplicity, we assume there are two possible states of nature, w_1 and w_2. Let p denote the prior probability of w_2. If the user chooses decision d and state w occurs, the user realizes the consequence $x = x(d, w)$.

In order to improve the decision, the user can hire an accountant to produce additional information about the probabilities of the states. (The details of the information production process are introduced later.) The information systems we consider generate one of two signals: y_1 or y_2. Let r_{ij} be the probability that signal y_i is received given the state is w_j. We assume r_{11} and r_{22} are (strictly) between 0.5 and 1.0. This implies that y_1 corresponds with w_1 and y_2 corresponds with w_2. f_{ij} is the joint probability of receiving signal y_i and realizing state w_j, and Φ_{ij} is the probability of state w_j occurring conditional on signal y_i being received. Initially, we assume the information system is fixed, that is, the parameters r_{11} and r_{22} are exogenous. Later, we will discuss issues involving the choice of an information system.

For much of our analysis, no further specification of the user's decision set, D, or the outcome function, $x(\cdot, \cdot)$, is required. However, it will be useful to couch the analysis in terms of a specific model. For concreteness, the user can decide to continue to operate a firm which, if w_2 is realized, remains a "going concern" and if w_1 is realized, goes bankrupt. If the user continues to operate the firm and it remains a going concern, the user will receive x_h, but if he continues to operate a firm that goes bankrupt, he receives $x_l < x_h$. If the user discontinues operations, he will receive x_o. To avoid a trivial solution, we assume $x_l < x_o < x_h$. Note that w_1 represents "unfavorable" circumstances and w_2 represents "favorable" circumstances. Also, in many cases the a priori probability of w_2 will be high, so we assume $p > 0.5$.

The accountant can issue one of two possible reports: a qualified opinion (signal y_1) or an unqualified opinion (signal y_2). The user's decision can be made conditional on the accountant's report, which is suggestive of a potential investor who uses an auditor's opinion as information in his investment decision problem. We refer to the user's problem in the absence of incentive problems with the accountant as the user's *primary-decision problem.*

A necessary condition for the accountant's report to be valuable to the user is that the user's operating decision depends on the report issued. This implies that the posterior probabilities of the states must satisfy:

$$\Phi_{11}x_l + (1 - \Phi_{11})x_h < x_o \tag{12.1a}$$

$$(1 - \Phi_{22})x_l + \Phi_{22}x_h > x_o \tag{12.1b}$$

The first condition states that when the accountant issues a qualified opinion, the user is better off shutting down the firm. The second condition states that when the accountant issues an unqualified opinion, it is optimal for the user to continue to operate the firm. For example, if the losses incurred by the user for making the (ex post) wrong decision are identical, that is, $x_h - x_o = x_o - x_l$, (12.1a, b) imply that the posterior probability of state 1 exceeds 0.5 after signal 1 is reported, and the posterior probability of state 2 exceeds 0.5 after signal 2 is reported.

Assuming the user finds it cost-effective to acquire the information, his expected payoff (before payment to the accountant) is

$$[(1 - p)r_{11} + p(1 - r_{22})]x_o + (1 - p)(1 - r_{11})x_l + pr_{22}x_h \tag{12.2}$$

This expression is used in the subsequent analysis.

We now discuss the information production mechanism in more detail.[2] Specifically, we assume that the user hires an accountant, who produces information under conditions of two types of moral hazard. First, the accountant privately decides whether to expend effort, $a \in \{0, 1\}$ with 0 representing no expenditure of effort. Second, the accountant privately observes the results of these information production activities, and the user relies on the accountant's report as to the information produced. That is, the information system that produces y_1 and y_2 with the probabilities specified above is invoked only if the accountant supplies an effort $a = 1$. Further, only the accountant directly observes y_i. If the accountant does not work (supplies $a = 0$), no information is produced. We model this as the receipt of a signal from an uninformative system, which is one that generates y_2 with probability p, regardless of the true state.

After receiving y_i, the accountant reports a purported y_i, say $\mathbf{y_i}$, to the user. The user offers a contract to the accountant which specifies the payments to the accountant in all circumstances that both can observe, ex post. We assume both the accountant and the user observe the state ex post, therefore, the contract can be based on four contingencies, which are simply all possible combinations of accountant's reports and states:[3]

(i) Accountant reports $\mathbf{y_1}$ and state is w_1.
(ii) Accountant reports $\mathbf{y_1}$ and state is w_2.
(iii) Accountant reports $\mathbf{y_2}$ and state is w_1.
(iv) Accountant reports $\mathbf{y_2}$ and state is w_2.

Observe that (i) and (iv) involve ex post correct reports for the accountant, and that (ii) and (iii) involve ex post erroneous reports. We will see later that it is important to distinguish among the various types of errors and reports. Reporting $\mathbf{y_2}$ (conditions appear favorable) when w_1 is realized (conditions are unfavorable) will have different consequences to the accountant than reporting $\mathbf{y_1}$ when w_2 is realized.

Since the state is observed ex post the contract will not depend on either the decision made by the user on the basis of the accountant's report or the outcome (x) of that decision.[4] Note also that even though the state is observable ex post, the first-best (full information) solution will not generally be obtainable, as it would in the standard agency model. This is because the randomness in the accountant's information system (measurement error) is not captured in the specification of w_1 and w_2.

The accountant's utility function is assumed to be additively separable into an income (s) component and effort (a) component as follows:

$$H(s, a) = U(s) - V(a)$$

with $U' > 0$ and $U'' < 0$. We set $V(0) = 0$ and $V(1) = V$. Let s_{ij} be the payment to the accountant if he reports $\mathbf{y_i}$ and the state turns out to be w_j. Let $U_{ij} = U(s_{ij})$ be the utility of the payments. When the accountant is offered the contract $\{U_{ij}\}_{i,j=1,2}$, his expected utility as a function of his strategy is

$$EH(a = 1, \text{report truth}) = \sum_{i,j} U_{ij} f_{ij} - V \tag{12.3a}$$

$$EH(a = 0, \text{always report } \mathbf{y_1}) = U_{11}(1-p) + U_{12}p \tag{12.3b}$$

$$EH(a = 0, \text{always report } \mathbf{y_2}) = U_{21}(1-p) + U_{22}p \tag{12.3c}$$

$$EH(a = 1, \text{always lie}) = U_{21}f_{11} + U_{22}f_{12} + U_{11}f_{21} + U_{12}f_{22} - V \tag{12.3d}$$

It is easy to show that all other strategies of the accountant are dominated by those listed above.

As in Grossman and Hart [1983], the user's presumed risk neutrality allows us to separate the costs of implementing a given information system from the benefits that arise from obtaining the information. In particular, the problem of determining the least-cost method of implementing a given information system can be analyzed independently of the structure of the user's primary decision problem. If the user chooses to motivate the accountant to supply no effort ($a = 0$), the optimal contract is obviously to pay the accountant a constant wage.

The only interesting case, therefore, involves motivating the accountant to work ($a = 1$). By applying the "revelation principle" (see Myerson [1979], Harris and Townsend [1981], and Antle [1982]), we can show that the user's expected cost is no higher if he confines himself to those contracts that induce the accountant to truthfully report the state. Certainly, the benefits to the user in his primary-decision problem are at least as high if the accountant truthfully reports, therefore, we will only examine contracts with this property. The user's problem, then, is to choose the least costly contract that motivates the accountant to work and tell the truth. If $W = U^{-1}$, we have $s_{ij} = W(U_{ij})$, and the user's problem is[5]

$$\underset{\{U_{ij}\}}{\text{minimize}} \quad \sum_{i,j} W(U_{ij}) f_{ij} \tag{12.4}$$

subject to

$$\sum_{i,j} U_{ij} f_{ij} - V \geq U_{11}(1-p) + U_{12}p \tag{12.4a}$$

$$\sum_{i,j} U_{ij} f_{ij} - V \geq U_{21}(1-p) + U_{22}p \tag{12.4b}$$

$$\sum_{i,j} U_{ij}f_{ij} - V \geq U_{21}f_{11} + U_{22}f_{12} + U_{11}f_{21} + U_{12}f_{22} - V \qquad (12.4c)$$

$$\sum_{i,j} U_{ij}f_{ij} - V \geq \theta \qquad (12.4d)$$

Constraints (12.4a)–(12.4c) ensure that working and telling the truth is as good a strategy as any for the accountant. (12.4d) implies that the accountant's expected utility is at least θ, which we interpret as the opportunity cost (measured in units of expected utility) to the accountant of accepting the user's offer.

In the next section, we document several properties of the optimal (i.e., least-expected-cost) contract which is acceptable to the accountant and motivates him to work and truthfully report the signal he observes.

Properties of the Optimal Compensation Scheme That Implements a Given Information System

The purpose of this section is to document several properties of the optimal method of compensating the accountant for a fixed information system—i.e., for constant r_{11} and r_{22}. We first prove a series of lemmas about the solution to the user's contracting problem with the accountant, and use these lemmas to prove two propositions. (Proof of the lemmas is given in the appendix.) The first proposition records the intuitive fact that for any given report, the accountant will be paid more if the report is correct than if it is incorrect, as well as the fact that for any given state, the accountant is paid more for correctly identifying it than for being incorrect. The second proposition shows that the accountant's compensation scheme is asymmetric in a way that is precisely specified below. The asymmetry of the compensation scheme will play a major role in our analysis of moving to more conservative information systems in the next section.

To analyze the solution to the user's contracting problem with the accountant, it is convenient to adopt a Lagrange multiplier approach. Let μ_i be the Lagrange multiplier on the ith constraint, $i = 1, 2, 3$. Let λ be the multiplier on the minimum-utility constraint. The Lagrange multipliers must all be non-negative; however, as lemma 12.1 records, not all of the multipliers are strictly positive.

Lemma 12.1

Constraint (12.4c) [EH(work, tell the truth) $\geq EH$(work, always lie)] is not binding, that is, $\mu_3 = 0$.

Because the user's problem is a concave mathematical program, lemma 12.1 justifies dropping constraint (12.4c). This enables us to characterize the optimal compensation scheme as in lemma 12.2, provided that we assume an interior solution for the U_{ij}.

Lemma 12.2

The optimal contract satisfies

$$[U'(s_{11})]^{-1} = \lambda + \mu_2 - \mu_1((1 - r_{11})/r_{11})$$

$$[U'(s_{12}')]^{-1} = \lambda + \mu_2 - \mu_1(r_{22}/(1 - r_{22}))$$

$$[U'(s_{21})]^{-1} = \lambda + \mu_1 - \mu_2(r_{11}/(1 - r_{11}))$$

$$[U'(s_{22})]^{-1} = \lambda + \mu_1 - \mu_2((1 - r_{22})/r_{22})$$

Lemma 12.2 can be used to show that constraints (12.4a) and (12.4b) are binding. This is recorded in lemma 12.3.

Lemma 12.3

Constraints (12.4a) and (12.4b) are binding, that is, $\mu_1 > 0$ and $\mu_2 > 0$.

Lemmas 12.2 and 12.3 imply our first proposition.

Proposition 12.1

The optimal contract satisfies: $U_{11} > U_{12}$, $U_{22} > U_{21}$, $U_{11} > U_{21}$, and $U_{22} > U_{12}$.

Intuitively, this proposition means that whatever the accountant reports, he is paid more if the report is correct than if it is incorrect. Similarly, whatever the true state, the accountant is paid more if the report is correct than if it is incorrect. These results are comforting, but not surprising. They are consistent with casual observation of the properties of the compensation schemes of accountants and auditors; if they failed in our model, the model's validity would be suspect.

Lemmas 12.1, 12.2, and 12.3 can be used to discover less-obvious properties of the optimal compensation scheme for the accountant. As we mentioned earlier, the accountant's contract will typically be asymmetric. Since the contract is a function of two variables, the report and the state, the definition of asymmetry deserves attention. Two candidates for the definition of a symmetric contract are specified, and an asymmetric contract is defined to be one that is not symmetric.

Definition 12.1

The accountant's contract is strongly symmetric if $U_{11} = U_{22}$ and $U_{12} = U_{21}$.

Definition 12.2

The accountant's contract is weakly symmetric if $U_{11} - U_{21} = U_{22} - U_{12}$.

Definition 12.1 restricts the accountant's payment to depend only on whether the report was correct. The accountant is paid one amount if the report is correct, but whether he correctly identifies w_1 or w_2 is irrelevant when the accountant's contract is strongly symmetric. Similarly, the accountant is paid another amount if the report is incorrect, but the type of error is irrelevant.

Definition 12.2 is weaker than definition 12.1 in the sense that strong symmetry implies weak symmetry. Definition 12.2 allows the accountant to be paid a different amount if he correctly identifies w_1 than if he correctly identifies w_2. The payment received for incorrectly identifying w_1 can also be different than the payment for incorrectly identifying w_2. However, the penalty for incorrectly identifying a state relative to correctly identifying it must be the same for each state.

Proposition 12.2 provides necessary and sufficient conditions for the contract to be weakly or strongly symmetric.

Proposition 12.2

The optimal contract satisfies

$$U_{11} - U_{21} = (p/(1-p))(U_{22} - U_{12}) \tag{12.5}$$

and therefore is weakly symmetric if and only if $p = 0.5$. The optimal contract is strongly symmetric if and only if $p = 0.5$ and $r_{11} = r_{22}$.

With $p > 0.5$, the accountant is penalized relatively more for incorrectly identifying w_1 than for incorrectly identifying w_2. That is, the accountant is penalized relatively more when he reports that conditions are favorable and is wrong than when he reports that conditions are unfavorable and is wrong. This property corresponds to the likely consequences to an auditor of making various types of errors. For example, the results of issuing an erroneous unqualified opinion can be litigation, loss of reputation, and even criminal prosecution. The results of issuing an erroneous qualified opinion might include loss of the client, but are probably less severe than those associated with issuing an erroneous unqualified opinion.

The asymmetric loss function occurs due to the asymmetric a priori probabilities of the states, and a little thinking reveals the intuition for this. If the probability of w_2 is high, the accountant can be correct most of the time by adopting the strategy of not working and always reporting $\mathbf{y}_2$. Therefore, the penalty imposed on the accountant if w_1 occurs after the accountant has issued $\mathbf{y}_2$ must be high in order to prevent the accountant from adopting this strategy. On the other hand, the high a priori probability of w_2 means that the penalty for w_2 occurring after $\mathbf{y}_1$ need not be very high in order to prevent the accountant from not working and always reporting $\mathbf{y}_1$. As p approaches 0.5, the penalties for the two errors become closer; however, even if $p = 0.5$, the accountant's loss function is not strongly symmetric unless $r_{11} = r_{22}$.

In the case of auditors' legal liability, this reason for imposing an asymmetric loss function on the auditor contrasts sharply with the traditional explanations. For example, one reason given as to why auditors are penalized more severely for issuing erroneous unqualified opinions than for issuing erroneous qualified opinions involves the difficulty of measuring the losses incurred by those who relied on an erroneous qualified opinion. It is claimed that measurement difficulties impede the imposition on auditors of the opportunity losses of those who could have invested but, relying on a qualified audit report, did not. However, critics of this reasoning point out that sellers of the firm's securities constitute a group whose loss is no harder to measure than that incurred by buyers who relied on an erroneous unqualified report.

Our analysis reveals a different connection between the practice of severely penalizing auditors for issuing erroneous unqualified opinions and optimal contracting with the auditor. Such penalties are efficient when the a priori probability that conditions are favorable (i.e., financial statements are materially correct) is high, because they inhibit the auditor from doing no work and issuing an unqualified opinion. Inflicting severe penalties for issuing erroneous qualified opinions is not efficient from a contracting perspective. Even mild penalties are effective because, given the high probability of favorable conditions, the auditor would not issue a qualified opinion without having performed some work which caused him to revise that probability downward. It is important to note that if the priors were reversed, so that the probability of unfavorable conditions was high, these results would reverse and it would be efficient to penalize auditors heavily for issuing erroneous qualified opinions.

The following example illustrates the asymmetry of the accountant's loss function. Let $p = 0.75$, and $r_{11} = r_{22} = 0.875$. Assume that the accountant has a square-root utility function for money (i.e., $U(s) = s^{1/2}$), $V = 1$, and $\theta = 4.0$. The optimal contract is

$$U_{11} = 5.666666 \qquad U_{12} = 3.444444$$
$$U_{21} = 0.333333 \qquad U_{22} = 5.222222.$$

Note that the penalty for incorrectly identifying w_1 relative to correctly identifying it is three times as large as the corresponding penalty for w_2. Also note that the accountant's payment is smallest if w_1 occurs after he reports $\mathbf{y}_2$.

The asymmetry of the accountant's loss function does not depend on the structure of the user's primary-decision problem (this contrasts with the approach taken in Scott [1975], and is consistent with that recommended in Magee [1975]), other than through the assumption that the user wishes to motivate the accountant to work at the lowest expected cost.

For the cases of the user's primary-decision problem discussed earlier, note that even if the user has a weakly symmetric loss function (i.e., $x_h - x_o = x_o - x_l$), the user structures the accountant's loss function to be asymmetric. Moreover, if the user's loss function is asymmetric such that $x_h - x_o > x_o - x_l$ (so that the user's loss is greater for incorrectly identifying state 2), the user structures the accountant's loss function to be asymmetric in the opposite direction. The accountant's loss function is asymmetric because it is an efficient way to motivate him to incur private costs (e.g., expend effort) in the production of information and to report truthfully to the user.

In the next section, we discuss the implications of the asymmetric loss function on the accountant's preferences over information systems.

Accountant's Preference for Conservative Systems

Since the accountant is heavily penalized if w_1 occurs after he reports $\mathbf{y}_2$, he may find it desirable to take steps to lessen the probability that this occurs. One possibility is to adjust investigation procedures to reduce the probability that the information system reports y_2 when w_1 is the true state. If the user ignores the accountant's ability to alter his investigation strategy, we will show that the accountant would like to adopt such "conservative" practices.

The first step is to define what constitute "more conservative practices." The traditional definition of a conservative accounting procedure is one that calls for quick recognition of losses and slow recognition of gains. Thus, the timing of income recognition is a crucial element in the traditional definition, and the definition focuses exclusively on the numbers reported and not on the information contained in those numbers. While we cannot capture a time element in our single-period model, we believe that we can capture at least some of the spirit of the notion of conservatism by following Devine [1963]. Devine rejected the traditional definition of conservative accounting practices as being too narrow. He proposed that conservatism "may be identified with reporting 'favorable' indications with some reluctance and reporting unfavorable indications promptly and with unmistaken emphasis" (p. 129).

While we generally agree with Devine, formulating an operational definition of a conservative accounting practice is a subtle exercise. Observe that, in light of the revelation principle, the reference to "reporting" in Devine's definition should not be taken to refer to the accountant's strategy of truthfully reporting the results of his efforts. The revelation principle implies that there can be no social gains to deviating from this truthful strategy, and the accountant's loss function generated by the user's problem as specified in (12.4), (12.4a–4d) guarantees that there are no private gains either. Therefore, in our model it is not fruitful to define conservatism in terms of issuing biased reports, where bias is defined in terms of the accountant's private information.

We will define a more conservative accounting practice in terms of the probabilistic structure of the accountant's (and, because of the accountant's truthful reporting, the user's) underlying information system. Our reasoning is that a more conservative practice is one that has a higher likelihood of identifying unfavorable conditions, given that unfavorable conditions exist. Therefore, we will define conservatism as a property of the information system that generates the accountant's signals, and we will analyze the preference for conservative systems by analyzing the choice among alternative information systems.

In order for an analysis of the choice among information systems to be meaningful, some constraints must be placed on the set of allowable information systems. For example, if the accountant could (at no additional cost) select an information system with $r_{11} = r_{22} = 1.0$, he would be guaranteed of never making an error. Obviously, the user would also prefer the accountant to select this information system, since it would be optimal for the user in both his primary-decision problem and in his contracting problem with the accountant.

In the absence of a complete model of the costs to the user and accountant of alternative information systems, the specification of the set of allowable information systems is arbitrary. Our approach is to construct the set of allowable information systems based on their value in the user's primary-decision problem. In the absence of incentive problems with the accountant, the user would be indifferent over the information systems in that set.

For the user's decision problem described earlier, the user's expected payoff from employing an information system is (from equation (12.2))

$$[(1-p)r_{11}+p(1-r_{22})]x_o+(1-p)(1-r_{11})x_l+pr_{22}x_h$$

Rearranging this yields:

$$px_o+(1-p)x_l+(1-p)r_{11}(x_o-x_l)+pr_{22}(x_h-x_o) \qquad (12.6)$$

The overall probability of correctness of the information system is $C=(1-p)r_{11}+pr_{22}$. Substituting this into equation (12.6) reveals that the user's expected payoff in the primary decision problem is

$$\begin{aligned} &px_o+(1-p)x_l+(1-p)r_{11}(x_o-x_l)+(C-(1-p)r_{11})(x_h-x_o)\\ &=px_o+(1-p)x_l+C(x_h-x_o)+(1-p)r_{11}[(x_o-x_l)-(x_h-x_o)] \qquad (12.7)\end{aligned}$$

If the user's loss function is weakly symmetric (i.e., $x_h-x_o=x_o-x_l$), then the user is indifferent (in his primary-decision problem) over all information systems with the same probability of correctness.[6] We therefore restrict our attention to information systems with the same overall correctness probability.

Formally, we characterize an information system by its conditional probabilities of signals given states, r_{11} and r_{22}. The following definition defines the equivalence class of information systems that have correctness parameter C.

Definition 12.3

$\eta(C)$ is the equivalence class of information systems defined by

$$\eta(C)=\{(r_{11},r_{22})\,|\,(1-p)r_{11}+pr_{22}=C;\ 0.5<r_{11}<1;\ 0.5<r_{22}<1\}$$

We now define a measure of conservatism of information systems within $\eta(C)$ as follows:

Definition 12.4

Let η^1 and η^2 denote information systems in $\eta(C)$, and let the conditional probabilities of signals given states be r_{11}^1 and r_{22}^1 for η^1 and r_{11}^2 and r_{22}^2 for η^2. Then η^1 is more conservative than η^2 if $r_{11}^1 > r_{11}^2$.

Holding the overall correctness of the information system constant (i.e., remaining in $\eta(C)$), as r_{11} increases, Φ_{22} increases; that is, as r_{11} increases, if the system reports that circumstances are favorable, the probability that they actually are favorable increases. Increasing r_{11} therefore means that the information system is more likely to identify unfavorable circumstances as such. Finally, as r_{11} increases, the probability that the system reports that circumstances are favorable decreases; that is, the probability that y_2 is reported decreases. This seems to correspond well to the idea that a conservative system is one that does not falsely emit favorable signals.

A crucial difference between our definition of a more conservative practice and the traditional definition is that in our model the accountant does not bias the report or say that conditions appear unfavorable when his information is that conditions are favorable. In our model the accountant is always motivated to work and to tell the truth. Conservatism refers to the choice of investigation procedures/information gathering activities that lead to the probabilities r_{11} and r_{22}. A more conservative practice (one with a higher r_{11}) can be obtained only by increasing the probability of making an error in the other direction (r_{22} is lower) if both the more and the less conservative systems are members of the same $\eta(C)$.

In this section we assume that the accountant's choice of an information system within $\eta(C)$ is not observable by the user.[7] The following proposition demonstrates that if the user solves his contracting problem with the accountant ignoring the ability of the accountant to select an information system within $\eta(C)$, the accountant will select the most conservative system in $\eta(C)$. That is, let $\{\mathbf{U_{ij}}\}$ be the optimal contract generated by (12.4) and (12.4a–d) when the accountant's information system is $(\mathbf{r_{11}}, \mathbf{r_{22}})$, with $\mathbf{C} = (1-p)\mathbf{r_{11}} + p\mathbf{r_{22}}$. Consider the set of all information systems in $\eta(\mathbf{C})$. Given the contract $\{\mathbf{U_{ij}}\}$, suppose the accountant is permitted to privately choose any information system in $\eta(\mathbf{C})$.

Proposition 12.3

When $p > 0.5$, the accountant's expected utility is an increasing function of r_{11}.

So we see that the accountant, if given a choice among several information systems with the same overall correctness, would choose the most conservative system. This preference is induced by the accountant's compensation scheme and, as we discuss later, can be overcome by redesigning the accountant's contract. Of course, Proposition 12.3 implies that inducing the accountant to prefer a system other than the most conservative is costly for the user, in the sense that the expected payment to the accountant will rise.

It is interesting to note that the accountant's preference for conservative systems is driven by the fact that the prior probability that conditions are favorable is high (i.e., greater than 0.5). This induces the asymmetry of the accountant's loss function, which is the driving force behind this result. As we discussed in the preceding section, changing the prior probabilities so that the probability of unfavorable circumstances is high would reverse the asymmetry of the loss function. This would give the accountant incentives to be "liberal." Thus we again see the crucial role of the prior probabilities in determining the efficient structure of the accountant's compensation, and, therefore, his preferences.

If the owner anticipates the accountant's ability to choose among information systems in a given $\eta(C)$ and wishes the accountant to choose any information system in $\eta(C)$ other than the most conservative one, the owner must alter his contracting problem with the accountant to insure the incentive compatibility of the accountant's information system choice. To simplify the formulation of the appropriate incentive-compatibility constraints, assume that the accountant has the ability to choose one of two information systems with the same correctness parameter. The two information systems are identified by their likelihood probabilities, $\eta^1 = (r^1_{11}, r^1_{22})$ and $\eta^2 = (r^2_{11}, r^2_{22})$, with corresponding joint probabilities f^1_{ij}, f^2_{ij}, etc. If the accountant chooses η^1, his utilities for various strategies of effort supply and reporting are given in (12.3a–d), with f^1_{ij} replacing f_{ij}. Similarly, if he chooses η^2, his utilities for various strategies are given by replacing f_{ij} with f^2_{ij} in (12.3a–d). If the user wishes the accountant to choose η^1, his contracting problem with the accountant becomes

$$\underset{\{U_{ij}\}}{\text{minimize}} \quad \sum_{i,j} W(U_{ij}) f^1_{ij} \tag{12.8}$$

subject to

$$\sum_{i,j} U_{ij} f^1_{ij} - V \geq U_{11}(1-p) + U_{12} p \tag{12.8a}$$

$$\sum_{i,j} U_{ij} f^1_{ij} - V \geq U_{21}(1-p) + U_{22} p \tag{12.8b}$$

$$\sum_{i,j} U_{ij} f_{ij}^1 - V \geq U_{21} f_{11}^1 + U_{22} f_{12}^1 + U_{11} f_{21}^1 + U_{12} f_{22}^1 - V \quad (12.8c)$$

$$\sum_{i,j} U_{ij} f_{ij}^1 - V \geq \sum_{i,j} U_{ij} f_{ij}^2 - V \quad (12.8d)$$

$$\sum_{i,j} U_{ij} f_{ij}^1 - V \geq U_{21} f_{11}^2 + U_{22} f_{12}^2 + U_{11} f_{21}^2 + U_{12} f_{22}^2 - V \quad (12.8e)$$

$$\sum_{i,j} U_{ij} f_{ij}^1 - V \geq \theta \quad (12.8f)$$

We begin analysis of this problem by obtaining a lemma analogous to lemma 12.1.

Lemma 12.4

Constraints (12.8c) and (12.8e) are not binding.

The following proposition records the fact that the remaining additional incentive-compatibility constraint, (12.8d), is equivalent to imposing a condition related to the weak symmetry of the accountant's loss function.

Proposition 12.4

Constraint (12.8d) is equivalent to $U_{11} - U_{21} \leq U_{22} - U_{12}$ if η^1 is less conservative than η^2, and (12.8d) is equivalent to $U_{11} - U_{21} \geq U_{22} - U_{12}$ if η^1 is more conservative than η^2. Assume that $p > 0.5$. Then if η^1 is more conservative that η^2, this constraint is not binding. If η^1 is less conservative than η^2, this constraint is binding, and the accountant's loss function is weakly symmetric, that is, $U_{11} - U_{21} = U_{22} - U_{12}$.

It can now be seen that our restriction of the set of information systems available to the accountant to two was merely a convenience. If weak symmetry is imposed on the accountant's loss function, the accountant becomes indifferent over all information systems in $\eta(C)$. Therefore, if the user wishes the accountant to implement any system in $\eta(C)$ other than the most conservative (which might be the case if a risk neutral user faced an asymmetric loss in his primary-decision problem), the user must impose the constraint insuring weak symmetry of the accountant's loss function, and must endure the attendant increase in expected payment to the accountant.

Again, note that the accountant's loss function is not constructed to mimic the user's loss function.

We conclude this section by analyzing one final issue. Suppose the user can observe the accountant's choice of information system, and therefore can contract with the accountant in such a way as to eliminate the costs arising from moral hazard on this choice. When would the user and accountant contract to implement the most conservative information system in $\eta(C)$?

Given that the gross benefits to the user in his primary decision problem are the same for all information systems in $\eta(C)$, the user will prefer to contract for a more conservative system when it lowers the expected payment to the accountant. The conditions under which these expected payments fall with the degree of conservatism of the accounting system appear to be very complicated. The sequence of examples in table 12–1 demonstrates that local moves to more conservative systems do not always result in lower expected payments to the accountant. As seen in these examples, whether there is social value to moves to more conservative systems depends on the joint probabilities of the signals and states and the accountant's utility function. While we have not fully characterized the conditions under which such local moves are socially optimal, we have shown that they are optimal when the accountant has a square-root utility function and we start with a system that has equal likelihoods.

Table 12–1. Numerical Examples of the Impact of More Conservative Systems*

p	c	r_{11}	r_{22}	$U(s)$	U_{11}	U_{12}	U_{21}	U_{22}	$\sum_{i,j} W(U_{ij})f_{ij}$
0.51	0.8	0.591838	0.999999	$s^{1/2}$	27.22	13.06	16.88	23.00	541.67
0.51	0.8	0.682540	0.912853	$s^{1/2}$	26.26	13.98	15.98	23.86	544.19
0.51	0.8	0.909297	0.694990	$s^{1/2}$	23.92	16.23	13.79	25.97	543.39
0.51	0.8	0.999999	0.607844	$s^{1/2}$	23.00	17.12	12.93	26.80	540.39
0.51	0.8	0.591838	0.999999	$\ln(s)$	25.34	14.87	14.99	24.81	.59662E + 11
0.51	0.8	0.682540	0.912853	$\ln(s)$	25.19	15.02	14.90	24.90	.59251E + 11
0.51	0.8	0.909297	0.694990	$\ln(s)$	24.83	15.36	14.70	25.10	.55099E + 11
0.51	0.8	0.999999	0.607844	$\ln(s)$	24.68	15.50	14.61	25.18	.52370E + 11
0.8	0.9	0.500004	0.999999	$s^{1/2}$	38.00	15.50	8.00	23.00	574.00
0.8	0.9	0.611114	0.972222	$s^{1/2}$	33.00	16.75	7.29	23.18	561.32
0.8	0.9	0.888889	0.902778	$s^{1/2}$	25.11	18.72	6.16	23.46	537.67
0.8	0.9	0.999999	0.875000	$s^{1/2}$	23.00	19.25	5.86	23.54	530.61

* In all cases $\theta = 20$ and $V = 3$.

Proposition 12.5

Assume $r_{11} = r_{22}$ and $U(s) = 2s^{1/2}$. Then the expected payment to the accountant falls when a marginally more conservative information system is implemented.

It is important to note that proposition 12.5 concerns the optimality of small moves toward conservatism. We have not addressed the question of whether it is always optimal to adopt the most conservative system. In the examples in table 12–1, the most conservative system is always associated with the lowest expected payment. Table 12–2 presents examples in which the most conservative system is not the least costly to motivate (among systems of equal levels of overall correctness). The examples are somewhat pathological in that the overall correctness of the information systems is lower than the a priori probability of w_2, therefore the user would not expend resources to purchase any of these systems.

We do not know if it is optimal to adopt the most conservative system in all reasonable cases, but we offer the following intuition. Notice that as the accounting system gets more conservative, the payment to the accountant when he reports that conditions are favorable but conditions are in fact unfavorable gets very low. Bounds on this payment might imply that it is optimal to stop short of adopting the most conservative system.

We can also offer some intuition as to why local moves to more conservative systems are not optimal in some cases. Suppose that the prior probability that conditions are favorable is very close to 0.5. Also suppose that the information system currently in place is one that very precisely identifies favorable conditions (i.e., r_{22} is close to 1), provided that the accountant works. Then compensation schemes that heavily penalize the accountant for reporting that conditions are unfavorable when they are favorable are likely to be very efficient (i.e., close to first-best). If the

Table 12–2. Numerical Examples in which the Most Conservative System is not Optimal*

p	c	r_{11}	r_{22}	$U(s)$	U_{11}	U_{12}	U_{21}	U_{22}	$\sum_{i,j} W(U_{ij})f_{ij}$
0.7	0.6	0.500001	0.642857	$s^{1/2}$	70.00	0.00	0.00	30.00	1140.00
0.7	0.6	0.529628	0.501588	$s^{1/2}$	320.32	0.00	0.00	137.28	22919.45
0.7	0.6	0.533331	0.500001	$s^{1/2}$	300.00	0.00	0.00	128.57	20185.72

* In all cases $\theta = 20$ and $V = 3$.

accountant works, he can achieve many of the gains of correctly identifying both states while almost surely avoiding the severe penalty associated with issuing an erroneous favorable report. If we make the information system more conservative while maintaining the same overall level of correctness, r_{22} must come down. This means that the information system will make more "mistakes" when conditions are favorable. This will reduce the efficiency of a scheme which motivates the accountant by inflicting severe penalties for issuing erroneous favorable reports.

In the next section, we change the focus from the costs of implementing systems in a given $\eta(C)$, and ask how expected payments to the accountant change as we move across correctness categories. In fact, we will be slightly more general and ask what happens to the expected payments to the accountant as we implement finer information systems. We show that this component of the cost of the information system (i.e., the expected payment to the accountant) is decreasing in the fineness of the system being implemented.

Expected Costs of Implementing a More Informative System

Suppose the user has the opportunity to choose the parameters of the information system (i.e., r_{11} and r_{22}) that the accountant implements. This choice might entail the purchase of, for example, computer hardware or software packages, or the installation of an auditing system to improve the quality of the source documents fed into the accounting system. This section addresses the relation between the level of expected payments to the accountant and the user's selection of the information system parameters. The following notational definition is convenient for addressing this issue.

Definition 12.5

For a given $\eta = (r_{11}, r_{22})$, $K(\eta)$ is the value of the objective function, (12.4) at the optimal solution to the user's problem (12.4), (12.4a–d) when the information system in the user's problem is η.

Given our specification of the user's problem, a natural issue to examine is the relation between the $K(\eta)$ and $K(\eta')$ when η and η' have different levels of the correctness parameter. After all, the user would find a more correct system more valuable in his primary-decision problem, and it would be interesting to know whether the expected payments to the accountant reinforce or offset the benefits of the improvement in the quality of the user's primary decision.

It turns out that the answer to this question can be obtained as a corollary from a more general proposition. Following Marschak and Miyasawa ([1968], condition (B), p. 150), we make the following definition.

Definition 12.6

η is more informative than η' if there exists a matrix $B = \{\beta_{ij}\}_{i,j=1,2}$ with $\beta_{ij} \geq 0$ for all i, j and $\Sigma_{j=1,2}\, \beta_{ij} = 1$ for all i, such that

$$\begin{bmatrix} r_{11} & 1 - r_{11} \\ 1 - r_{22} & r_{22} \end{bmatrix} \begin{bmatrix} \beta_{11} & \beta_{12} \\ \beta_{21} & \beta_{22} \end{bmatrix} = \begin{bmatrix} r'_{11} & 1 - r'_{11} \\ 1 - r'_{22} & r'_{22} \end{bmatrix}$$

It is well-known that in the absence of structure on the user's primary-decision problem, the user will find a more-informative system as valuable as a less-informative system in his primary-decision problem. The following proposition provides the relation between the informativeness of the information system and the expected payments to the accountant.

Proposition 12.6

If η is more informative than η', then $K(\eta) < K(\eta')$.

Now consider an information system, say η', that has correctness parameter C'. If $C > C'$ there will exist an information system in $\eta(C)$ that is more informative than η'. The following corollary is then immediate.

Corollary 12.1

If $\eta' \in \eta(C')$ and $C > C'$, then $\exists\, \eta \in \eta(C)$ such that $K(\eta) < K(\eta')$.

Proposition 12.6 states that one component of the cost of an information system, the expected payment to the accountant, falls as the informativeness of the system grows. This calls into question the common practice of assuming, in analyses in which the implementation of information-production activities is not modelled, that information costs are increasing in the informativeness of the information system. This assumption may be reasonable for the components of information system cost arising from the installation of the basic technology (computer system, etc.), but, to the extent that our model of the input of an accountant into the information production function captures the essence of the activity,[8] this assumption is not reasonable for the components of information system cost arising from the purchase of the required labor inputs to the system.

Conclusion

We have examined optimal incentive schemes for accountants and applied the results to three areas: auditors' legal liability, accountants' preferences for conservative accounting practices, and the cost of paying accountants as the information systems they implement become more informative. The key to much of our analysis is the asymmetry of optimal-incentive schemes for the accountant.

Asymmetry has direct implications for auditors' legal liability. If there is a high a priori probability that the financial statements are materially correct, optimal incentive schemes for the auditor penalize the auditor more for issuing an erroneous unqualified opinion than for issuing an erroneous qualified opinion. This matches casual empirical observation of the legal liability of auditors, and is driven by economically intuitive forces. Given the high probability of materially correct financial statements, the auditor could be correct most of the time by doing no auditing and issuing an unqualified opinion. To avoid inducing the auditor to take this shirking strategy, optimal-incentive schemes penalize him heavily for issuing an erroneous unqualified opinion. The high a priori probability of materially correct statements also implies that no such problem exists with respect to the issuance of qualified opinions; the auditor would not issue a qualified opinion without having done some work which indicates that it is in order.

The asymmetry of the optimal incentive scheme also has implications for accountants' preference for conservative accounting practices. Left free to choose any information system within a given correctness class, the accountant would choose the most conservative one unless the user actively designs the accountant's incentive scheme to discourage it. To prevent the accountant from prefering the most conservative system, the user must impose symmetry on the accountant's loss function.

If the user could choose the degree of conservatism of the accounting system, it is not clear when he would choose the most conservative system. We showed that there are circumstances in which a move to a marginally more conservative accounting system would reduce the user's expected payment to the accountant. There are also situations in which such a move would result in increased expected payments to the accountant. The exact conditions that determine whether the expected payment is decreased must involve the joint probabilities of signals and states and properties of the accountant's utility function. The question of whether the expected payment to the accountant is always lowest at the most conservative system was left open, although all of our reasonable examples had this property.

Up to this point, all our comparisons involved systems of equal overall correctness. Given our specification of the user's primary-decision problem, information systems that issue the correct signal with the same probability have equal value to the user. If there are additional costs to generating the accountant's information system, we have assumed that they are constant across systems that are equally correct.

Finally, we turned away from studying systems of equal correctness and asked how the expected payments to the accountant changed as the system in which he worked became more informative. We showed that more informative systems are cheaper to implement, at least in terms of the expected payment to the accountant. Therefore, this component of the cost of the infomation system reinforces the increased benefits of finer information in the user's primary-decision problem.

Of course, our model was extremely simple and omitted almost all institutional details. We assumed that the user contracted directly with the accountant instead of modeling the complex structure of third parties, lawyers, judges, etc. The model had only one period and two states. The restriction to two states was especially convenient because it simplified the task of defining conservative accounting practices. We defined conservatism in terms of the information system's conditional probability of indicating unfavorable conditions when they exist. Extending this definition to a model that allows several states would probably involve partitioning the states into favorable and unfavorable subsets.

Notes

1. By our definition we mean, e.g., accounting and auditing techniques that are designed to detect unrecorded liabilities or phantom assets instead of phantom liabilities and unrecorded assets. In a sense, then, this paper is much more about conservative accounting and auditing practices than conservative reporting.

2. Our model of the accountant's role in information production follows Antle [1982] and Balachandran and Ramakrishnan [1982].

3. The assumption that both the accountant and the user observe the state ex post no matter what action is selected may be rather strong in some contexts. However, this assumption is required to ensure that there are two different errors in the model, i.e., report y_1 and state is w_2,

and report y_2 and state is w_1. Since our objective here is to analyse the consequences to the accountant of different types of errors, it is obviously necessary that the model include more than one type of error.

4. This depends critically on the assumption that the user is risk-neutral.

5. Because U is strictly concave, W is strictly convex. The objective function, then, is a strictly convex function of the U_{ij}. Since the constraints are linear functions of the U_{ij}, assuming the U_{ij} are bounded will guarantee the existence of a solution to problem (12.4).

6. As specified earlier, we must also have $\Phi_{11} > 0.5$ and $\Phi_{22} > 0.5$ in order for the user's decision to depend on the report generated.

7. This amounts to assuming that the accountant has some latitude in deciding where to apply effort, as well as the effort level to supply. The crucial difference in these two types of decisions is that the effort decision entails a direct disutility whereas the choice of η does not.

8. An important implicit assumption underlying proposition 12.6 is that the accountant's disutility for supplying any action level is the same whether that action is supplied under η or η'. If working in a more informative system increased the disutility of supplying high effort, then our result may not go through. On the other hand, if working in a more informative system is "easier", then this effect would reinforce the effects in the theorem and the result would still hold.

APPENDIX 12
Proofs

Proof of Lemma 12.1

Suppose the constraint is binding. Then

$$\begin{aligned}
U_{11} r_{11}(1-p) + U_{12}(1-r_{22})p + U_{21}(1-r_{11})(1-p) + U_{22}r_{22}p - V \\
= U_{21}r_{11}(1-p) + U_{22}(1-r_{22})p + U_{11}(1-r_{11})(1-p) \\
+ U_{12}r_{22}p - V \\
\Rightarrow (U_{21} - U_{11})(2r_{11} - 1)(1-p) = (U_{22} - U_{12})(2r_{22} - 1)p
\end{aligned}$$

By assumption $r_{11} > 0.5$ and $r_{22} > 0.5$, therefore $2r_{11} - 1 > 0$ and $2r_{22} - 1 > 0$, which implies $\text{sign}[U_{21} - U_{11}] = \text{sign}[U_{22} - U_{12}]$.

Case 1

$U_{22} - U_{12} = 0$. This implies $U_{21} - U_{11} = 0$. Let $U_{22} = U_{12} = U_2$ and $U_{21} = U_{11} = U_1$. We have

$$EH[\text{work, tell the truth}] = U_1(1-p) + U_2 p - V$$
$$< U_1(1-p) + U_2 p = EH[\text{not work, always report state 1}]$$

which violates (12.4a).

Case 2

$U_{22} - U_{12} > 0$, which implies $U_{21} - U_{11} > 0$. We have

$$\begin{aligned} &EH[\text{work, tell the truth}] \\ &\quad = U_{11}r_{11}(1-p) + U_{12}(1-r_{22})p + U_{21}(1-r_{11})(1-p) \\ &\qquad + U_{22}r_{22}p - V \\ &\quad < U_{21}r_{11}(1-p) + U_{22}(1-r_{22})p + U_{21}(1-r_{11})(1-p) \\ &\qquad + U_{22}r_{22}p - V \\ &\quad = U_{21}(1-p) + U_{22}p - V \\ &\quad < U_{21}(1-p) + U_{22}p = EH[\text{not work, always report state 2}] \end{aligned}$$

But this violates (12.4b).

Case 3

$U_{22} - U_{12} < 0$, which implies $U_{21} - U_{11} < 0$. Using the same technique as in case 2, this assumption implies (12.4a) is violated. Q.E.D.

Proof of Lemma 12.2

Problem (12.4) can be written as

$$\begin{aligned} \underset{\{U_{ij}\}}{\text{maximize}} &- \Sigma\, W(U_{ij})f_{ij} + \lambda\{\Sigma\, U_{ij}f_{ij} - V - \theta\} \\ &+ \mu_1\{U_{11}(r_{11}-1)(1-p) + U_{12}(-r_{22})p \\ &+ U_{21}(1-r_{11})(1-p) + U_{22}r_{22}p - V\} \\ &+ \mu_2\{U_{11}r_{11}(1-p) + U_{12}(1-r_{22})p + U_{21}(-r_{11})(1-p) \\ &+ U_{22}(r_{22}-1)p - V\} \end{aligned}$$

The first-order condition on U_{11} is

$$-W'(U_{11})r_{11}(1-p)+\lambda r_{11}(1-p)+\mu_1(r_{11}-1)(1-p)+\mu_2 r_{11}(1-p)=0$$
$$\Rightarrow W'(U_{11})=\lambda+\mu_2+\mu_1[(r_{11}-1)/r_{11}]$$

Since $W'(U_{11})=1/U'(s_{11})$, the characterization of s_{11} follows. The other cases are similar. Q.E.D.

Proof of Lemma 12.3

From the Kuhn–Tucker conditions, we have $\mu_1 \geq 0$ and $\mu_2 \geq 0$.

Case 1

$\mu_1=\mu_2=0$. Using the conditions derived in lemma 12.2, we have $1/U'(s_{ij}) = \lambda$ for all i, j. This implies $s_{ij}=k$ for all i, j. Since the accountant is then paid a constant, he prefers not to work, violating (12.4a) and (12.4b).

Case 2

$\mu_1=0$ and $\mu_2>0$. The optimal sharing rule satisfies

$$1/U'(s_{11})=1/U'(s_{12})=\lambda+\mu_2>\lambda$$
$$1/U'(s_{21})=\lambda-\mu_2[r_{11}/(1-r_{11})]<\lambda$$
$$1/U'(s_{22})=\lambda-\mu_2[(1-r_{22})/r_{22}]<\lambda$$

This implies $s_{11}=s_{12}=s_1$, $s_1>s_{21}$, and $s_1>s_{22}$. It is then easy to show that (12.4a) is violated.

Case 3

$\mu_1>0$ and $\mu_2=0$. Using the same technique as in case 2, this implies (12.4b) is violated. Q.E.D.

Proof of Proposition 12.1

Since r_{11} and r_{22} are greater than 0.5, $[r_{22}/(1-r_{22})]>[(1-r_{11})/r_{11}]$. Multiplying both sides of this inequality by $-\mu_1$, which by lemma 12.3 is strictly negative, and adding $\lambda + \mu_2$ to both sides gives

$$\lambda + \mu_2 - \mu_1[r_{22}/(1-r_{22})] < \lambda + \mu_2 - \mu_1[(1-r_{11})/r_{11}]$$

$$\Rightarrow 1/U'(s_{12}) < 1/U'(s_{11}) \quad \text{by lemma 12.2}$$

$$\Rightarrow U_{11} > U_{12} \quad \text{since } U(\cdot) \text{ is concave}$$

The proof that $U_{22} > U_{21}$ is similar.

To prove $U_{11} > U_{21}$, it is convenient to define κ to be the accountant's expected utility at optimum, that is,

$$\kappa = U_{11}r_{11}(1-p) + U_{12}(1-r_{22})p + U_{21}(1-r_{11})(1-p) + U_{22}r_{22}p - V \tag{12A.1}$$

By lemma 12.3, $\mu_1 > 0$ and $\mu_2 > 0$, which imply (12.4a and b) hold as equalities, therefore

$$\kappa = U_{11}(1-p) + U_{12}p$$

$$\Rightarrow U_{12} = (\kappa/p) - U_{11}[(1-p)/p] \tag{12A.2}$$

and

$$\kappa = U_{21}(1-p) + U_{22}p$$

$$\Rightarrow U_{22} = (\kappa/p) - U_{21}[(1-p)/p] \tag{12A.3}$$

Substituting (12A.2) and (12A.3) into (12A.1) gives

$$U_{11}(1-p)r_{11} + \{(\kappa/p) - U_{11}[(1-p)/p]\}p(1-r_{22}) + U_{21}(1-p)(1-r_{11})$$
$$+ \{(\kappa/p) - U_{21}[(1-p)/p]\}pr_{22} = \kappa + V$$

Rearranging terms yields $U_{11} - U_{21} = V/[(r_{11} + r_{22} - 1)(1-p)] > 0$, since r_{11} and r_{22} are each greater than 0.5. Hence, $U_{11} > U_{21}$.

To prove $U_{22} > U_{12}$, subtract (12A.2) from (12A.3) to get $U_{22} - U_{12} = (U_{11} - U_{21})[(1-p)/p] > 0$. Q.E.D.

Proof of Proposition 12.2

The equation $U_{22} - U_{12} = [(1-p)/p]\,(U_{11} - U_{21})$ was proven in the proof of proposition 12.1. The fact that the optimal contract is weakly symmetric—i.e., $U_{22} - U_{12} = U_{11} - U_{21}$—if and only if $p = 0.5$ is easily seen from this expression.

It remains to be shown that the contract is strongly symmetric if and only if $p = 0.5$ and $r_{11} = r_{22}$. If $p \neq 0.5$, the contract is not weakly symmetric, so it cannot be strongly symmetric. Therefore, we need to show that if $p = 0.5$, the contract is strongly symmetric if and only if $r_{11} = r_{22}$.

When $p = 0.5$, the expressions derived in the proof of proposition 12.1 imply that $U_{12} = 2\kappa - U_{11}$; $U_{22} = 2\kappa + z - U_{11}$; and, $U_{21} = U_{11} - z$, where κ is the accountant's expected utility from the optimal contract (as in the proof of proposition 12.1) and $z = V/[(r_{11} + r_{22} - 1)(1 - p)]$. These equalities allow us to reduce the user's problem to choosing the optimal level of U_{11}. In particular, the user's problem is

$$\max_{U_{11}} \sum f_{ij} W[U_{ij}(U_{11})]$$

The first-order condition on U_{11} is

$$\sum f_{ij} W'[U_{ij}(U_{11})][\partial U_{ij}/\partial U_{11}] = 0$$

Using the expressions for $U_{ij}(U_{11})$ derived above, the first-order condition on U_{11} becomes

$$0.5[r_{11} W'(U_{11}) + (1 - r_{11}) W'(U_{21}) - (1 - r_{22}) W'(U_{12}) - r_{22} W'(U_{22})] = 0$$

which implies

$$r_{11} W'(U_{11}) + (1 - r_{11}) W'(U_{21}) = (1 - r_{22}) W'(U_{12}) + r_{22} W'(U_{22})$$

Substituting $U_{21} = U_{11} - z$ and $U_{12} = U_{22} - z$, we obtain

$$r_{11} W'(U_{11}) + (1 - r_{11}) W'(U_{11} - z) = (1 - r_{22}) W'(U_{22} - z) + r_{22} W'(U_{22})$$

which implies $U_{11} = U_{22}$ when $r_{11} = r_{22}$, $U_{11} < U_{22}$ when $r_{11} > r_{22}$ and $U_{11} > U_{22}$ when $r_{11} < r_{22}$. Therefore, $U_{11} = U_{22}$ if and only if $r_{11} = r_{22}$. Q.E.D.

Proof of Proposition 12.3

Suppose the accountant can select an information system with probabilities $(r_{11}, r_{22}) \in \eta(C)$. Given the contract $\{\mathbf{U_{ij}}\}$, the accountant's expected utility if he works and truthfully reports is

$$\begin{aligned} &\mathbf{U_{11}} r_{11}(1 - p) + \mathbf{U_{12}}(1 - r_{22})p + \mathbf{U_{21}}(1 - r_{11})(1 - p) + \mathbf{U_{22}} r_{22} p - V \\ &\quad = (\mathbf{U_{11}} - \mathbf{U_{21}}) r_{11}(1 - p) + (\mathbf{U_{22}} - \mathbf{U_{12}}) r_{22} p + \mathbf{U_{21}}(1 - p) + \mathbf{U_{12}} p - V \end{aligned}$$

Substituting $C = r_{11}(1 - p) + r_{22} p$ into the above, we have

$$\begin{aligned} &= [\mathbf{U_{11}} - \mathbf{U_{21}} - (\mathbf{U_{22}} - \mathbf{U_{12}})] r_{11}(1 - p) + (\mathbf{U_{22}} - \mathbf{U_{12}}) C \\ &\quad + \mathbf{U_{21}}(1 - p) + \mathbf{U_{12}} p - V \end{aligned}$$

Proposition 12.2 states that

$$\mathbf{U}_{11} - \mathbf{U}_{21} = [p/(1-p)](\mathbf{U}_{22} - \mathbf{U}_{12}) \Rightarrow \mathbf{U}_{11} - \mathbf{U}_{21} - (\mathbf{U}_{22} - \mathbf{U}_{12}) > 0$$

when $p > 0.5$. Therefore, the accountant's expected utility if he works and truthfully reports is an increasing function of r_{11}, under the restriction that the variation of r_{11} is done so as to hold the overall correctness of the information system at C. Further, since the accountant's expected utility does not depend on r_{11} if he does not work, the strategy (work, truthfully report) is still optimal for the accountant after an allowable increase in r_{11}. Q.E.D.

Proof of Lemma 12.4

Lemma 12.1 implies that (12.8c) is not binding. Writing out (12.8e), we have

$$\begin{aligned}
&U_{11}r_{11}^1(1-p) + U_{12}(1-r_{22}^1)p + U_{21}(1-r_{11}^1)(1-p) + U_{22}r_{22}^1 p - V \\
&\qquad \geq U_{21}r_{11}^2(1-p) + U_{22}(1-r_{22}^2)p \\
&\qquad\quad + U_{11}(1-r_{11}^2)(1-p) + U_{12}r_{22}^2 p - V, \\
&\qquad \Leftrightarrow U_{11}[(1-p)(r_{11}^1 - 1 + r_{11}^2)] + U_{12}[p(1-r_{22}^1 - r_{22}^2)] \\
&\qquad\quad + U_{21}[(1-p)(1-r_{11}^1 - r_{11}^2)] \\
&\qquad\quad + U_{22}[p(r_{22}^1 - 1 + r_{22}^2)] \geq 0, \\
&\qquad \Leftrightarrow (U_{11} - U_{21})[(1-p)(r_{11}^1 - 1 + r_{11}^2)] \\
&\qquad\quad + (U_{12} - U_{22})[p(1-r_{22}^1 - r_{22}^2)] \geq 0
\end{aligned}$$

If (12.8e) is binding so that equality holds, $\text{sign}[U_{21} - U_{11}] = \text{sign}[U_{22} - U_{12}]$, since $r_{11}^1, r_{11}^2, r_{22}^1$, and r_{22}^2 are all greater than or equal to 0.5. Now apply the analysis of the three possible cases in the proof of lemma 12.1 to show that (12.8e) can not be binding. Q.E.D.

Proof of Proposition 12.4

Writing out (12.8d), we have

$$\begin{aligned}
&U_{11}r_{11}^1(1-p) + U_{12}(1-r_{22}^1)p + U_{21}(1-r_{11}^1)(1-p) + U_{22}r_{22}^1 p - V \\
&\qquad \geq U_{11}r_{11}^2(1-p) + U_{12}(1-r_{22}^2)p + U_{21}(1-r_{11}^2)(1-p) \\
&\qquad\quad + U_{22}r_{22}^2 p - V
\end{aligned}$$

$$\Leftrightarrow U_{11}(r_{11}^1 - r_{11}^2)(1-p) + U_{12}[(1-r_{22}^1) - (1-r_{22}^2)]p + U_{21}[(1-r_{11}^1) - (1-r_{11}^2)](1-p) + U_{22}(r_{22}^1 - r_{22}^2)p \geq 0$$

$$\Leftrightarrow U_{11}(r_{11}^1 - r_{11}^2)(1-p) + U_{12}(r_{22}^2 - r_{22}^1)p + U_{21}(r_{11}^2 - r_{11}^1)(1-p) + U_{22}(r_{22}^1 - r_{22}^2)p \geq 0$$

Since $\eta^1 \in \eta(C)$ and $\eta^2 \in \eta(C)$,

$$C = r_{11}^1(1-p) + r_{22}^1 p = r_{11}^2(1-p) + r_{22}^2 p$$

therefore, $(r_{11}^1 - r_{11}^2)(1-p) = (r_{22}^2 - r_{22}^1)p \equiv \delta$. Using this notation, (12.8d) is equivalent to $U_{11}\delta + U_{12}\delta - U_{21}\delta - U_{22}\delta \geq 0$. This holds if and only if $\delta(U_{11} - U_{21}) \geq \delta(U_{22} - U_{12})$. If $\delta > 0$, as is the case when η^1 is more conservative than η^2, this is equivalent to $U_{11} - U_{21} \geq U_{22} - U_{12}$, and if $\delta < 0$, it is equivalent to $U_{11} - U_{21} \leq U_{22} - U_{12}$.

The statements about when (12.8d) is binding follow from the implication of proposition 12.3 that, when the constraint is omitted, the accountant will choose the most conservative system in $\eta(C)$. Q.E.D.

Proof of Proposition 12.5

Because the user can observe the accountant's choice of an information system, the user's problem as specified in (12.4), (12.4a–b) is a sufficient object of analysis. Also, since $U = 2s^{0.5}$, $s_{ij} = (U_{ij})^2$. Using lemma 12.2, the expected payment to the accountant is

$$\begin{aligned}\Sigma s_{ij} f_{ij} &= \Sigma (U_{ij})^2 f_{ij} \\ &= \left[\lambda + \mu_2 - \mu_1\left(\frac{1-r_{11}}{r_{11}}\right)\right]^2 r_{11}(1-p) \\ &\quad + \left[\lambda + \mu_2 - \mu_1\left(\frac{r_{22}}{1-r_{22}}\right)\right]^2 (1-r_{22})p \\ &\quad + \left[\lambda + \mu_1 - \mu_2\left(\frac{r_{11}}{1-r_{11}}\right)\right]^2 (1-r_{11})(1-p) \\ &\quad + \left[\lambda + \mu_1 - \mu_2\left(\frac{1-r_{22}}{r_{22}}\right)\right]^2 r_{22}p \\ &= \lambda^2 - 2\mu_1\mu_2 + \mu_1^2 m_1 + \mu_2^2 m_2 \end{aligned} \tag{12A.4}$$

where

$$m_1 = (1-p)\left(\frac{1-r_{11}}{r_{11}}\right) + p\left(\frac{r_{22}}{1-r_{22}}\right) \quad \text{and}$$

$$m_2 = (1-p)\left(\frac{r_{11}}{1-r_{11}}\right) + p\left(\frac{1-r_{22}}{r_{22}}\right)$$

Since μ_1 and μ_2 are strictly positive (lemma 12.3), we know that (12.4a) and (12.4b) hold as equalities, and further that the right-hand side of (12.4a) is equal to the right-hand side of (12.4b). Substituting the characterizations of the U_{ij} given in lemma 12.2 into these three equations allows us to solve for μ_1, μ_2, and λ:

$$\lambda = [\theta + V]/2 \tag{12A.5}$$

$$\mu_1 = 0.5[(m_2+1)/(m_1m_2-1)]V \tag{12A.6}$$

$$\mu_2 = 0.5[(m_1+1)/(m_1m_2-1)]V \tag{12A.7}$$

Note that m_1+1 and m_2+1 are positive, therefore $\mu_1 > 0$ and $\mu_2 > 0$ imply $m_1m_2 - 1 > 0$.

Substituting (12A.5), (12A.6) and (12A.7) into (12A.4) yields

$$\Sigma s_{ij}f_{ij} = \lambda^2 - 0.5\left[\left(\frac{m_2+1}{m_1m_2-1}\right)\left(\frac{m_1+1}{m_1m_2-1}\right)\right]V^2$$

$$+ 0.25\left(\frac{m_2+1}{m_1m_2-1}\right)^2 V^2 m_1 + 0.25\left(\frac{m_1+1}{m_1m_2-1}\right)^2 V^2 m_2$$

$$= \left(\frac{[\theta+V]}{2}\right)^2 + 0.25V^2\left(\frac{m_1+m_2+2}{m_1m_2-1}\right) \tag{12A.8}$$

Holding the overall probability of correctness at $C = (1-p)r_{11} + pr_{22}$, we wish to compute $d\Sigma s_{ij}f_{ij}/dr_{11}$. Note that $r_{22} = (C/p) - [(1-p)/p]r_{11}$, so $dr_{22}/dr_{11} = -[(1-p)/p]$. Using (12A.8), we have

$$\frac{d\Sigma s_{ij}f_{ij}}{dr_{11}} = 0.25V^2\left[\frac{d\left(\dfrac{m_1+m_2+2}{m_1m_2-1}\right)}{dr_{11}}\right]$$

$$= \left[\frac{0.25V^2}{(m_1m_2-1)^2}\right]\left\{(m_1+1)^2\left(\frac{dm_2}{dr_{11}}\right) + (m_2+1)^2\left(\frac{dm_1}{dr_{11}}\right)\right\}$$

$$= \left[\frac{0.25V^2}{(m_1m_2-1)^2}\right]\{-(m_1+1)^2[(1-r_{11})^{-2} + r_{22}^{-2}]$$

$$+ (m_2+1)^2[r_{11}^{-2} + (1-r_{22})^{-2}]\}$$

where the last equality follows by substituting for dm_1/dr_{11} and dm_2/dr_{22}:

$$dm_1/dr_{11} = -(1-p)[r_{11}^{-2} + (1-r_{22})^{-2}]$$

$$dm_2/dr_{11} = (1-p)[(1-r_{11})^{-2} + r_{22}^{-2}]$$

Evaluating this derivative at $r_{11} = r_{22} = r$,

$$d\Sigma s_{ij} f_{ij}/dr_{11} = \{0.25V^2(1-p)[m_1 m_2 - 1]^{-2}\} \times [(1-r_{11})^{-2} + r_{22}^{-2}][-(m_1+1)^2 + (m_2+1)^2]$$

therefore $\text{sign}[d\Sigma s_{ij} f_{ij}/dr_{11}] = \text{sign}[-(m_1+1)^2 + (m_2+1)^2]$. But with $r_{11} = r_{22} = r$, we have

$$m_1 = (1-p)[(1-r)/r] + p[r/(1-r)]$$

$$m_2 = (1-p)[r/(1-r)] + p[(1-r)/r]$$

Since $r > 0.5$, $r/(1-r) > (1-r)/r$, and with $p > 0.5$, this implies $m_1 > m_2$

$$\Rightarrow (m_1+1)^2 > (m_2+1)^2$$

$$\Rightarrow -(m_1+1)^2 + (m_2+1)^2 < 0$$

$$\Rightarrow d\Sigma s_{ij} f_{ij}/dr_{11} < 0$$

Q.E.D.

Proof of Proposition 12.6

By assumption, there exists a matrix $B = \{\beta_{ij}\}_{i,j=1,2}$ with $\beta_{ij} \geq 0$ for all i, j and $\Sigma_{j=1,2}\, \beta_{ij} = 1$ for all i, such that

$$\begin{bmatrix} r_{11} & 1-r_{11} \\ 1-r_{22} & r_{22} \end{bmatrix} \begin{bmatrix} \beta_{11} & \beta_{12} \\ \beta_{21} & \beta_{22} \end{bmatrix} = \begin{bmatrix} r'_{11} & 1-r'_{11} \\ 1-r'_{22} & r'_{22} \end{bmatrix}$$

Let $\{U'_{11}, U'_{12}, U'_{21}, U'_{22}\}$ be the optimal contract under η'. It will be convenient to let κ be the accountant's expected utility if he works and truthfully reports with this contract, that is,

$$\kappa = U'_{11} r'_{11}(1-p) + U'_{12}(1-r'_{22})p + U'_{21}(1-r'_{11})(1-p) + U'_{22} r'_{22} p - V$$

Define $\{U_{11}, U_{12}, U_{21}, U_{22}\}$ as follows:

$$U_{11} = \beta_{11} U'_{11} + \beta_{12} U'_{21}$$

$$U_{12} = \beta_{11} U'_{12} + \beta_{12} U'_{22}$$

$$U_{21} = \beta_{21} U'_{11} + \beta_{22} U'_{21}$$

$$U_{22} = \beta_{21} U'_{12} + \beta_{22} U'_{22}$$

If the accountant works and truthfully reports, his expected utility under $\{U_{11}, U_{12}, U_{21}, U_{22}\}$ and η is

$$
\begin{aligned}
&U_{11}r_{11}(1-p) + U_{12}(1-r_{22})p + U_{21}(1-r_{11})(1-p) + U_{22}r_{22}p - V \\
&\quad = r_{11}(1-p)[\beta_{11}U'_{11} + \beta_{12}U'_{21}] + (1-r_{22})p[\beta_{11}U'_{12} + \beta_{12}U'_{22}] \\
&\qquad + (1-r_{11})(1-p)[\beta_{21}U'_{11} + \beta_{22}U'_{21}] \\
&\qquad + r_{22}p[\beta_{21}U'_{12} + \beta_{22}U'_{22}] - V \\
&\quad = (1-p)[\beta_{11}r_{11} + \beta_{21}(1-r_{11})]U'_{11} + p[\beta_{11}(1-r_{22}) + \beta_{21}r_{22}]U'_{12} \\
&\qquad + (1-p)[\beta_{12}r_{11} + \beta_{22}(1-r_{11})]U'_{21} + p[\beta_{12}(1-r_{22}) \\
&\qquad + \beta_{22}r_{22}]U'_{22} - V \\
&\quad = \kappa \geq \theta \quad \text{by feasibility of } \{U'_{11}, U'_{12}, U'_{21}, U'_{22}\} \text{ under } \eta'
\end{aligned}
$$

Also by feasibility of $\{U'_{11}, U'_{12}, U'_{21}, U'_{22}\}$ under η',

$$\kappa \geq \max\{(1-p)U'_{11} + pU'_{12}, (1-p)U'_{21} + pU'_{22}\}.$$

Therefore,

$$
\begin{aligned}
\kappa &\geq \beta_{11}[(1-p)U'_{11} + pU'_{12}] + \beta_{12}[(1-p)U'_{21} + pU'_{22}] \\
&= (1-p)[\beta_{11}U'_{11} + \beta_{12}U'_{21}] + p[\beta_{11}U'_{12} + \beta_{12}U'_{22}] \\
&= (1-p)U_{11} + pU_{12}
\end{aligned}
$$

and,

$$
\begin{aligned}
\kappa &\geq \beta_{21}[(1-p)U'_{11} + pU'_{12}] + \beta_{22}[(1-p)U'_{21} + pU'_{22}] \\
&= (1-p)[\beta_{21}U'_{11} + \beta_{22}U'_{21}] + p[\beta_{21}U'_{12} + \beta_{22}U'_{22}] \\
&= (1-p)U_{21} + pU_{22}
\end{aligned}
$$

Therefore, working and truthfully reporting is the optimal strategy for the accountant under $\{U_{11}, U_{12}, U_{21}, U_{22}\}$ and η.

Since $\{U'_{11}, U'_{12}, U'_{21}, U'_{22}\}$ is an optimal contract, proposition 12.1 implies that $U'_{11} \neq U'_{21}$ and $U'_{12} \neq U'_{22}$. Convexity of $W(\cdot)$ and Jensen's inequality yield

$$
\begin{aligned}
W(U_{11}) &= W(\beta_{11}U'_{11} + \beta_{12}U'_{21}) < \beta_{11}W(U'_{11}) + \beta_{12}W(U'_{21}) \\
W(U_{12}) &= W(\beta_{11}U'_{12} + \beta_{12}U'_{22}) < \beta_{11}W(U'_{12}) + \beta_{12}W(U'_{22}) \\
W(U_{21}) &= W(\beta_{21}U'_{11} + \beta_{22}U'_{21}) < \beta_{21}W(U'_{11}) + \beta_{22}W(U'_{21}) \\
W(U_{22}) &= W(\beta_{21}U'_{12} + \beta_{22}U'_{22}) < \beta_{21}W(U'_{12}) + \beta_{22}W(U'_{22})
\end{aligned}
$$

Therefore,

$$\begin{aligned}
K(\eta) &= W(U_{11})r_{11}(1-p) + W(U_{12})(1-r_{22})p + W(U_{21})(1-r_{11})(1-p) \\
&\quad + W(U_{22})r_{22}p \\
&< r_{11}(1-p)[\beta_{11}W(U'_{11}) + \beta_{12}W(U'_{21})] + (1-r_{22})p[\beta_{11}W(U'_{12}) \\
&\quad + \beta_{12}W(U'_{22})] + (1-r_{11})(1-p)[\beta_{21}W(U'_{11}) + \beta_{22}W(U'_{21})] \\
&\quad + r_{22}p[\beta_{21}W(U'_{12}) + \beta_{22}W(U'_{22})] \\
&= (1-p)[\beta_{11}r_{11} + \beta_{21}(1-r_{11})]W(U'_{11}) + p[\beta_{11}(1-r_{22}) \\
&\quad + \beta_{21}r_{22}]W(U'_{12}) + (1-p)[\beta_{12}r_{11} + \beta_{22}(1-r_{11})]W(U'_{21}) \\
&\quad + p[\beta_{12}(1-r_{22}) + \beta_{22}r_{22}]W(U'_{22}) \\
&= (1-p)r'_{11}W(U'_{11}) + p(1-r'_{22})W(U'_{12}) \\
&\quad + (1-p)(1-r'_{11})W(U'_{21}) + pr'_{22}W(U'_{22}) \\
&= K(\eta') \qquad \text{Q.E.D.}
\end{aligned}$$

References

Antle, R. [1982]. "The Auditor as an Economic Agent." *Journal of Accounting Research* 20, 503–527.

Balachandran, B., and Ramakrishnan, R. [1982]. "A Theory of Large Audit Partnerships: Audit Firm Size and Fees." Working Paper, Northwestern University.

Devine, C. [1963]. "The Rule of Conservatism Reexamined." *Journal of Accounting Research* 1, 127–138.

Grossman, S., and Hart, O. [1983]. "An Analysis of the Principal-Agent Problem." *Econometrica* 51, 7–45.

Harris, M., and Raviv, A. [1979]. "Optimal Incentive Contracts with Imperfect Information." *Journal of Economic Theory* 20, 231–259.

Harris, M., and Townsend, R. [1981]. "Resource Allocation under Asymmetric Information." *Econometrica* 49, 33–64.

Holmstrom, B. [1979]. "Moral Hazard and Observability." *Bell Journal of Economics* 10, 74–91.

Magee, R. [1975]. "Discussion of Auditor's Loss Functions Implicit in Consumption-Investment Models." *Journal of Accounting Research Supplement* 13, 121–123.

Marschak, J., and Miyasawa, K. [1968]. "Economic Comparability of Information Systems." *International Economic Review* 9, 137–174.

Myerson, R. [1979]. "Incentive Compatibility and the Bargaining Problem." *Econometrica* 47, 61–73.

Scott, W. [1975]. "Auditor's Loss Functions Implicit in Consumption-Investment Models." *Journal of Accounting Research Supplement* 13, 91–117.

Subject Index

Author Index